THE PRINCETON REVIEW

Cracking the CLEP

THE PRINCETON REVIEW

Cracking the CLEP

BY TOM MELTZER AND PAUL FOGLINO

1999 EDITION

RANDOM HOUSE, INC.
NEW YORK
www.randomhouse.com

Princeton Review Publishing, L.L.C.
2315 Broadway, Second Floor
New York, NY   10024
E-mail: info@review.com

Excerpts from "Mending Wall" and "Stopping by Woods on a Snowy Evening" from The Poetry of Robert Frost, edited by Edward Connery Lathem. Copyright © 1951 by Robert Frost. Copyright 1923 © 1969 by Henry Holt and Co., Inc. Reprinted by permission of Henry Holt Co., Inc.

Excerpt from "Sonny's Blues" © 1957 by James Baldwin. Copyright renewed. Collected in Going to Meet the Man. Published by Vintage Books. Reprinted by permission of the James Baldwin Estate. "Sonny's Blues" was originally published in Partisan Review.

Excerpt from "The Second Coming" reprinted by permission of Simon & Schuster from The Poems of W.B. Yeats: A New Edition, edited by Richard J. Finneran. Copyright © 1924 by Macmillan Publishing Company, Renewed 1952 by Bertha Georgie Yeats.

"Loveliest of trees, the cherry now" from The Collected Poems of A.E. Houseman published by Henry Holt and Company, Inc.

ISBN 0-375-75212-9

Editor: Lesly Atlas
Production Editor: Kristen Azzara
Designer: Illeny Maaza
Production Coordinator: Robert McCormack
Illustrations by: The Production Department of The Princeton Review

Manufactured in the United States of America on partially recycled paper.

9 8 7 6 5 4 3 2 1

1999 Edition

ACKNOWLEDGMENTS

We'd like to thank John Katzman for entrusting us with this project, and our editor, Celeste Sollod, for all her guidance and hard work. We'd also like to thank all the teachers and writers at Princeton Review from whom we've learned so much about how to convey difficult and, at times, boring material in an interesting way. Thanks to all our family and friends, particularly Libby O'Connor and Lisa Vingleman, for putting up with us. Tom thanks his mother for being such a stickler about grammar when he was young.

We'd also like to thank The Princeton Review's editing and production crew: John Bergdahl, Amy Bryant, Greta Englert, Kristin Fayne-Mulroy, Effie Hadjiioannou, Julian Heath, Peter Jung, Sara Kane, Meher Khambata, Illeny Maaza, Robert McCormack, Brendan Milburn, Russell Murray, John Pak, Glen Pannell, Dinica Quesada, Matthew Reilly, and Lisa Ruyter.

And thanks to the public library systems: if you don't use the library regularly, you're missing out on a lot! The Milwaukee library, in which Tom did a lot of his research, is particularly and surprisingly good. Finally, thanks to Columbia University for its core curriculum. Columbia students always complain that the core doesn't serve any purpose, but we're living proof that the core prepares you well for at least one thing in life: writing a book about the CLEP.

CONTENTS

PART I

Orientation

1

What is the CLEP?

WHAT ARE THE CLEP EXAMS AND WHY SHOULD YOU TAKE THEM?

The CLEP exams are college placement tests, as are the better-known AP (Advanced Placement) exams. CLEP exams, however, are generally easier than AP exams. If your prospective school accepts both exams, you are almost always better off taking the CLEP. The acronym CLEP stands for "College-Level Examination Program."

There are thirty-four different CLEP exams. The five covered in detail in this book are the most popular, which are the General Exams: English Composition, College Mathematics, Humanities, Social Sciences, and Natural Sciences. Colleges and universities frequently use these exams to place students out of, and award students credit for *distribution requirements*. (Distribution requirements usually mandate that you take a number of courses in a certain discipline but do not require any *specific* course.) For instance, a passing grade on the Humanities exam may earn you one or two course credits (three to eight course-hour credits, if your future school awards credit according to how many hours a week a course meets) and exempt you from your humanities requirement (quite a boon if, for example, you are a humanities-hating biology major). The General Exams are designed to correspond to survey courses freshmen are required to take.

The twenty-nine exams discussed in the final chapter of this book (in very general terms only) are the subject exams. Schools often use these to award credit for *specific courses* offered at the school. For example, a passing grade on the General Biology exam could earn you one or two course credits (three to eight course-hour credits) and exempt you from any obligation to take introductory biology courses.

Were you to pass the CLEP biology exam, it would be as if you had walked into that biology class on the last day of the semester and passed the final exam without ever having attended classes or labs. The CLEP, however, is likely to be much easier than any final exam written by a college professor.

Most CLEP exams are multiple-choice. They are easier than the AP tests, and, accordingly, some schools that award AP credit do not award CLEP credit. Almost all community colleges and state schools maintain generous CLEP policies. One Princeton Review employee passed enough CLEP exams to earn one year's worth of credits at the University of Texas. Private colleges and universities vary in their CLEP policies. Some award credit for all thirty-four exams; others award credit for only a few select subject exams; others still use the CLEP to place students out of lower-level classes (e.g., foreign languages) but will not award college credit for passing grades.

CLEP exams are graded on a scale of 200 to 800, as are the SAT and many other ETS exams. Every school sets its own threshold at which it awards credit for CLEP scores. Call your prospective school(s) for information about its (their) CLEP policy.

Call your potential schools, and ask them about their CLEP policy. Will they give you credit for a good grade? Will a good grade place you out of a class? The admissions or dean's office should know the answer.

HOW AND WHEN TO TAKE CLEP EXAMS

CLEP exams are offered at over 1,000 schools and test sites nationwide. Many of these schools offer the exams on set dates only, three or four times a year. Some schools offer the exam only to students currently enrolled at the school. Other schools, however, administer the test to anyone at anytime. Call or write the College Board for a list of test sites, then call each site to learn its policy. The College Board has a number of regional offices; its main office is in New York at: 45 Columbus Avenue, New York, NY 10023-6992. The phone number is (212) 713-8000. Or you can write to: CLEP, P.O. Box 6601, Princeton, NJ 08541-6601, and ask for a copy of the publications *CLEP Colleges* and *Information for Candidates and Registration Form.*

Some tests—those with free response (non-multiple choice) sections—can only be taken at a specific time each year, even at schools that otherwise offer testing at your convenience. If you wish to take a free-response exam—and we recommend you do for the English Composition test—you must call your test center and ask the date on which it will be offered.

Taking a CLEP exam is similar to taking the pencil-and-paper version (as opposed to the computer version) of the SAT. You sit in a room with a bunch of other test-takers and a proctor and fill in bubbles on an answer sheet with your #2 pencil. The CLEP, however, is more straightforward than the SAT; whereas the SAT often tries to trick you into picking answers that "look good" but don't hold up under closer inspection, the CLEP is designed to steer clear of areas of ambiguity. This is because the CLEP is an *achievement* test (one that tests what you have learned) rather than an *aptitude* test (one that tries to figure out how smart you are). That, and the fact that the CLEP is less than half as long (90 minutes versus three hours plus), should make taking the CLEP a much less stressful experience than was taking the SAT.

> If your future college gives the same credit for the CLEP and the AP, take the CLEP: it's much easier!

ABOUT THIS BOOK

We've assumed that most people buying this book are only planning on taking one or two of the five general exams. We realize that you might skip right to the chapter about the test(s) you are taking, passing over any introductory chapters such as this one. **Don't do it!**

Chapter 2, "Basic Test-taking Techniques," offers strategies that will be key to improving your score on all of the CLEP tests. These strategies may vary slightly from test to test, in which case we will mention that in the section devoted to that particular test, but they are generally the same. Learn and know the basic test-taking techniques. Some of them may contradict common assumptions, but they really work! Practice our techniques on our sample tests. Practicing them on our tests will enable you to use them with confidence on test day.

Then you can turn to the section(s) that covers the test(s) you plan to take. In addition to the techniques in chapter 2, each section of the book offers test-taking strategies and tips, review material, and a diagnostic test followed by a long section explaining the correct and incorrect answers.

If you read the chapters on all five exams, you will find that some material is repeated, in somewhat altered form. Do not skip over this information, as it does differ slightly from chapter to chapter. You should also read this information because it concerns good test-taking skills, which you should review as often as you can stand to.

You will find fairly thorough reviews in the English Grammar and College Mathematics sections; there is not enough room in this book for thorough reviews of the other three subjects (each of which would require a small textbook), so instead we tell you what you will need to learn and where you can go to learn it.

After reading a chapter and taking the diagnostic test, make sure to read through the explanations to all the answers, even those accompanying questions you answered correctly. These explanations contain important review material.

2

Basic Test-Taking Techniques

MAXIMIZING YOUR EFFECTIVENESS ON THE CLEP

Always take the path of least resistance on multiple-choice tests. Do not answer the questions that give you trouble until you have answered ALL the questions you can answer easily.

When taking the CLEP, you should try to maximize your ability to answer as many questions correctly as possible.

This means that you should go into the exam knowing your strengths and weaknesses, and tailor your approach so as to maximize your strengths and minimize your weaknesses. Seek out those questions testing your field of expertise and answer them first. Save those questions in your areas of weakness for last; that way, if you never get to them, you will have minimized your losses.

For example, in College Mathematics, if you find that you are relatively good at questions involving probabilities and statistics but weak on questions about sets, then you should skip all of the latter until you have answered all of the former. In English Composition, if you find that you are good at "Improving Sentences" questions, but weak on "Revising a Work in Progress," then you should skip all of the latter (questions 26 to 43 on Part I) until you have answered all of the former (questions 16 to 25 AND questions 44 to 55). Remember:

- **You do not have to do the questions in the order they appear.** In fact, you may answer the questions in whatever order you like, provided you work on Section I for only the first 45 minutes and Section II for only the second 45 minutes. If you want to start Section I with the final question and work backwards, you may do so: there is no ETS regulation preventing it.

YOUR SCORE

The CLEP exams are graded on a scale from 200 to 800. Look familiar? Yes, it's the same scale used for the SAT. Just what grades you will need to earn credit for your work on CLEP exams is determined by your prospective school (contact the admissions office before taking the exams). Some schools don't accept the tests at all, while others use them as placement exams (you won't get out of any courses, but will end up in a more advanced section or course if you get a good score).

The rest of the nation's colleges and universities establish their own cut-off grades, above which a satisfactory performance on the CLEP will earn you valuable college credits AND exempt you from a long and difficult class. The cut-off varies depending on the test. For the College Mathematics exam, at many schools, it's usually between a 450 and a 500, meaning you will have to score somewhere around the sixty-fifth percentile. On the English Composition exam, the cut-off is also often between a 450 and a 500, but that means you'd have to score around the sixtieth percentile. The chapters devoted to the specific CLEP exams discuss scores in more detail.

To receive what many schools regard as an acceptable score, you will have to earn about half the raw score points available to you on the exam. You can do this by answering exactly half the questions and getting them all right, or by answering more than half and making a few mistakes. Chances are you will have time to answer more than half the questions on the test. Since you do not need to finish this exam in order to get a passing grade, however, you should not rush to finish it. Rushing will only cause you to make mistakes.

TIME MANAGEMENT

DON'T RUSH

There are two common reasons people choose incorrect answers on this test. The first is that they simply do not know the answer to a question, and they make an incorrect guess. You will need to review the material tested in order to minimize the number of these mistakes (review sections are included in the sections on College Mathematics and English Composition exams; recommendations for further reading are included for the rest).

The second, and by far the easier one to remedy, is carelessness. Test takers in a hurry to finish the exam misread questions, misread answer choices, and needlessly pressure themselves into taking "educated guesses" before they have fully considered all the answer choices. If you slow down just a little, you will find that you make many fewer mistakes of this type.

> Don't forget to bring a watch with you to the exam.

BUT DON'T WASTE TIME, EITHER

This does not mean, however, that you should take the test at a snail's pace. On the contrary, your goal is to move efficiently through the test. Every question is worth exactly the same number of points toward your final grade—this is not like the television game show *Jeopardy*, in which questions get more difficult as the dollar values get higher. All questions are worth the same amount, and the more questions you answer correctly, the higher your score will be. So:

◆ **Never spend an inordinate amount of time on any one question.** Your goal is to find those questions that you are most likely to answer correctly, answer them, taking the time to minimize the possibility of careless mistakes, and then move on to the next question, repeating the process up to ninety-nine times throughout the exam.

Suppose it doesn't take you 45 minutes to answer all the questions you know the answers to on a section. Should you fold your hands and let the rest of your time pass unused? Hmm, how to put this in the least subtle way? NO! NO NO NO! ABSOLUTELY NOT!! You want to spend whatever time remains taking your best guesses on as many questions as possible. To prove this, read on about the so-called "guessing penalty" on the CLEP exams.

PROCESS OF ELIMINATION (POE) AND THE "GUESSING PENALTY"

ETS instructions and purported test experts often mention a "guessing penalty," implying that test takers somehow lose points by guessing. This is rarely true on any multiple-choice test, and it certainly isn't true on the CLEP exams.

Each question on the English Composition, Humanities, Social Sciences, and Natural Sciences exams has five answer choices: one correct and four incorrect. In terms of your raw score, the penalty for answering a question incorrectly is −1/4 point; a correct answer is worth one point. Therefore, if you guessed randomly on five questions, probabilities say you would get one right (for +1 point) and four wrong ($4 \times -1/4 = -1$ point). You would end up with 0 points for the five questions—the same score you would get for leaving all five questions blank!

On the College Mathematics exam, each question has four answer choices, one correct and three incorrect. In terms of your raw score, the penalty for answering a question incorrectly is −1/3 point; a correct answer is worth one point. Therefore, if you guessed randomly on four questions, probabilities say you would get one right (for +1 point) and three wrong ($3 -1/3 = -1$ point). You would end up with 0 points for the five questions—the same score you would get for leaving all four questions blank!

Therefore:

- ◆ **There is no guessing penalty on the CLEP exams. Random guesses are neither rewarded nor penalized.**

This point is important, so it bears repeating. To put the scoring in easy-to-understand monetary terms, it is as if you receive four dollars for every correct answer and lose one dollar for every incorrect answer. Guess randomly on five questions and you will most likely get one correct, netting four bucks, and four wrong, costing you four bucks. You would break even.

What would have happened if you had been able to eliminate one wrong answer on each of those questions? Now the chances are much improved that you will get two right and three wrong, in which case, you would wind up five dollars ahead on five nearly random guesses.

On the math test, it is as if you receive three dollars for every correct answer and lose one dollar for every incorrect answer. Guess randomly on four questions, and you will most likely get one correct, netting three bucks, and three wrong, costing you three bucks. In other words, you would break even. What would have happened if you had been able to eliminate one wrong answer on each of those questions? Now the chances are good that you will get two right and two wrong, in which case, you would wind up four dollars ahead on four nearly random guesses.

> Be aggressive when you take multiple-choice exams. ETS exams are designed to reward aggressive guessing. If you can eliminate at least one answer choice, make a guess.

Therefore:

◆ **Guess if you can eliminate even one answer choice.** These tests (all standardized tests, really) present you with two distinct scenarios: 1) you know the answer to the question, and 2) you don't know the answer to the question. Scenario 1 is easy to deal with: you choose the correct answer and move on. Scenario 2, fortunately, is not hopeless; the beauty of a multiple-choice test is that you don't always need to know the correct answer in order to answer a question correctly. Knowing that one answer is definitely wrong, as we saw above, yields a reward if you guess one of the remaining answer choices. Eliminate two or three answer choices, and your chances increase even more (on the College Mathematics exam, you're done). Eliminate four answer choices on the other exams, and voilà, you have found the right answer!

TRANSFER YOUR ANSWERS TO THE ANSWER SHEET IN GROUPS

This minimizes the risk that you will misnumber and fill in your answer sheet incorrectly. Believe it or not, a Princeton Review study showed that this method also saves time.

1. Answer all the questions on a page that you intend to answer.

2. Circle your answers in the test booklet.

3. Mark those questions you are skipping (so you can find them easily if you decide to come back to them).

4. Then transfer your answers to your answer sheet.

BE PREPARED

Bring a handful of sharpened #2 pencils and a watch to the exam. The watch is important. You shouldn't have to depend on the proctor for updates on how much time you have left.

If you're taking more than one exam, bring a snack to have between tests. It will help replenish your energy.

SUMMARY

The College Board publishes a book called *The Official Guide to the CLEP*. It is the only source for questions that have appeared on actual CLEP tests. Buy it, or better still, look it over at the public library.

1. You do not have to do the questions in the order they appear.

2. Don't rush.

3. Never spend an inordinate amount of time on any one question.

4. There is no guessing penalty on the CLEP exams. Random guesses are neither rewarded nor penalized.

5. Guess if you can eliminate even one answer choice.

6. Transfer your answers to the answer sheet in groups.

These are basic test-taking techniques that can be applied to all the general CLEP tests; we'll cover techniques specific to each test in the appropriate section.

PART II

How to Crack the CLEP General Examination in English Composition

3

Overview of the English Composition Exam

WHY TAKE IT?

The English Composition Exam of the CLEP may help you evade your college's freshman composition class, one of the most dreaded of all college courses. For that reason alone, you should seriously consider taking this exam.

Just what grade you will need to earn credit for your work on this exam is determined by your prospective school (contact the admissions office before you take the test). Some schools don't accept the test at all (some of these schools accept the English AP; others still simply won't let you place out of freshman composition); while others use it as a placement exam (you won't get out of any courses, but will end up in a more advanced section if you get a good score).

The rest of the nation's colleges and universities establish their own cut-off grade, above which a satisfactory performance on the CLEP will earn you valuable college credits AND exempt you from a long, boring writing class. At many schools, that cut-off is between a 450 and a 500, meaning you will have to score somewhere around the sixtieth percentile.

WHAT'S ON THE TEST?

There are two versions of the CLEP English Composition exam: with an essay and without. Both versions are divided into two parts; you will have 45 minutes for each part. You should take the test with the essay. The essay test looks like this:

Part I

The English Composition Exam with Essay is offered in January, April, June, and October. Sign up early!

Question Type	Questions
Identifying Sentence Errors	1–15
Improving Sentences	16–25
Revising a Work in Progress	26–43
Improving Sentences	44–55

Part II

One essay question

The test without the essay looks like this:

Part I

Question Type	Questions
Identifying Sentence Errors	1–15
Improving Sentences	16–25
Revising a Work in Progress	26–43
Improving Sentences	44–55

Part II

Question Type	Questions
Revising a Work in Progress	56–64
Restructuring Sentences	65–74
Analyzing Writing	75–92
Identifying Errors	93–100

SHOULD YOU TAKE THE ENGLISH COMPOSITION TEST WITH THE ESSAY OR WITHOUT THE ESSAY?

With the essay!!! Unless you are the worst writer in the world (in which case you should probably skip this exam and take the freshman composition class at your college), the essay test is much easier. The English Composition without Essay test contains some very tricky question types—restructuring sentences and analyzing writing—that do not appear on the test with the essay. That is why you should take the test with the essay. This point cannot be made strongly enough. That is why we keep repeating it.

Furthermore, a summary of good essay techniques at the end of this chapter will show you how to write an essay the ETS graders will like. Once again: it is much easier to master the skills ETS looks for in grading essays than to master the skills necessary to answer the questions on part II of the English Composition without Essay test.

The only reason to take the English Composition without Essay test is if you need to take the exam before the next administration of the English Composition with Essay. The essay test is only given a few times each year; the test without the essay can be taken at any time. Call ETS or the College Board, get the dates when a local school is offering the English Composition with Essay, and sign up for it so you don't get stuck taking the more difficult exam.

WHAT TYPE OF QUESTIONS APPEAR ON THE TEST?

Questions on both formats of the exam are designed to test either your knowledge of basic grammar (identifying errors, improving sentences, revising a work in progress) or your ability to write coherently (the essay) and identify coherent writing (revising a work in progress, restructuring sentences, analyzing writing). According to ETS, grammar questions comprise between 55 and 60 percent of each test format, with the remainder of the exam made up of writing questions.

The more you practice taking the exam, the more confident you will be on test day. Do the drills in the chapters that follow, take our diagnostic test, and do all the English questions in the College Board book, *The Official Guide to the CLEP.* Your local library should have a copy.

The CLEP tests grammar with three different types of questions: Identifying Sentence Errors, Improving Sentences, and Revising a Work in Progress. Another question type—Restructuring Sentences—also requires you to apply grammatical principles: this type of question only appears on the English Composition without Essay test. If you take the English Composition with Essay test, your use of grammar will, of course, be taken into account by whoever grades your essay.

HOW WE'LL HELP YOU GET A HIGHER SCORE

Our techniques and study guide will help you improve your score. As you're taking the test, keep in mind the general test-taking techniques we described in chapter 2.

- ◆ Don't rush.
- ◆ Don't spend too much time on any one question.
- ◆ Use POE.
- ◆ You don't have to do the questions in the order they appear.
- ◆ Transfer your answers to the answer sheet in groups.

And of course, you will be less likely to make careless errors if you really know the material.

Because grammar questions make up over half the multiple choice questions you will see, let's review grammar first.

Call your potential schools and ask them about their CLEP policy. Will they give you credit for a good grade? Will a good grade place you out of a class? The admissions or dean's office should know the answer.

4

Grammar Review

CLEP grammar exams are not as daunting as you might first guess. We all know—it's an old cliché—that English is a *very difficult* language, full of strange rules and lots of annoying exceptions to those rules. If you had to learn all these rules and exceptions in order to do well on the CLEP, you'd very likely be in big trouble. So, however, would everyone else in the English-speaking world, with the possible exceptions of William Safire and Cecil Adams (he knows *everything*, you know).

Fortunately, CLEP grammar questions focus on a narrow scope of grammatical errors. The test writers are not so much curious as to whether you have mastered English grammar—they assume that you, like most everyone else, have not—as they are interested in finding out whether you can identify a few certain errors that create *ambiguity*.

Ambiguity is the CLEP's big bugaboo, and grammar questions on the CLEP test this concept almost exclusively. Furthermore, the test writers are obsessed with a certain few common errors that create ambiguity, so they test those few again and again. That is good news for you, because if you can learn to spot and correct these few errors, you will be able to answer nearly all of the CLEP's grammar questions.

Those errors fall under the following categories:

> Misplaced modifiers
> Pronouns
> Subject-verb agreement
> Verb tense
> Parallel construction
> Faulty comparison
> Redundancy
> Idiom

What follows is a review of each of these types of errors, with tips on how to spot and correct each one. First, however, we need to review a few basic grammatical terms.

GRAMMATICAL TERMS

PARTS OF SPEECH

noun—a person, place, or thing.
> The *grocer* sold me an *apple*.

pronoun—a word that can take the place of a noun, such as *he*, *she*, or *it*.
> The grocer sold *me* an apple, and *it* was very good.

verb—an action or a state of being.
> The grocer *sold* me an apple.
> The apple *was* green and delicious.

CLEP grammar questions are generally easier than CLEP reading and editing questions. Master the grammar, and you will be able to miss more of the tougher questions and still get a good score.

adjective—a word that describes a noun.

> The grocer sold me a *green*, *delicious* apple.

adverb— a word that describes a verb, an adjective, or another adverb.

> The grocer *cheerfully* sold me a *very* delicious apple.

preposition—a word that expresses the relationship between a noun or pronoun and something else (usually another noun), such as *in, around, behind, to,* and *from.*

> The grocer sold me an apple *from* Vermont.

conjunction—a word that connects different parts of a sentence, such words as *and, but,* and *or.*

> The grocer sold me an apple, *and* after I thanked him, I went on my
> way.

PARTS OF A SENTENCE

clause—a group of words containing both a subject and a verb. There are two types of clauses: dependent and independent.

dependent clause—a dependent clause, as its name suggests, cannot stand alone. Dependent clauses do not form complete sentences, because they are introduced either by a conjunction or a relative pronoun (*that, which, whom*).

> *That I love to eat.*
> *Because the apple is green.*

independent clause—independent clauses can stand alone. They are simpler than dependent clauses.

> *I love to eat.*
> *The apple is green.*

Independent clause: Santa
Dependent clause: Santa, Jr.

phrase—a group of words that cannot stand independently, because it lacks either a subject or a verb, but which, as a group, can function in the sentence as a part of speech. Below, the phrase "eating an apple" serves as the subject of the sentence.

> *Eating an apple* is something that I love to do.

prepositional phrase—a phrase (big surprise!) that begins with a preposition (bigger surprise still!). Sorry, there's just no other way to define a prepositional phase.

> The grocer sold me an apple *from the beautiful state of Vermont.*

There, that wasn't too bad, was it? Mark these definitions—with a bookmark or folded-down corner of the page—so you can find them easily as you read through the next few pages. While it isn't necessary to memorize them, it certainly wouldn't hurt. Plus, you'll gain some new erudition with which you can impress your friends. Regardless, you will probably learn them in the course of studying the grammar review, which begins . . . now!

THE EIGHT DEADLY SINS (OF GRAMMAR)

MISPLACED MODIFIERS

A modifier is a group of words that serves the same purpose as an adjective: it describes a noun. A modifying phrase is misplaced when it is impossible to figure out what the phrase is describing, or worse, when it is so placed that it describes the wrong noun. For example:

> Revolving around the sun at a furious rate, astronomers have discovered a body they believe to be the tenth planet in our solar system.

In this sentence, the modifying phrase "Revolving around the sun at a furious rate" is meant to describe the "body." However, the way the sentence is constructed, it is actually describing the "astronomers," because a modifier describes the noun closest to it. Misplaced modifiers can be easy to spot because they often give the sentences in which they appear comical meaning, as in the example above.

The sentence should be rewritten in one of the following ways:

> Revolving around the sun at a furious rate, a body believed to be the tenth planet in our solar system has been recently discovered by astronomers.

> or

> Astronomers believe that a body revolving around the sun at a furious rate is the tenth planet in our solar system.

Whenever you see a sentence that begins with a descriptive phrase, or when you see a descriptive phrase anywhere in the sentence, watch out for misplaced modifiers.

Which of the following sentences has/have a misplaced modifier? In the space provided, rewrite those that do.

Misplaced Modifier Drill

1. Under suspicion for a murder he did not commit, the fugitive eluded the police until he could find the actual killer.

   _____

   _____

2. Injected into cattle to increase their milk output, many consumers worry that bovine growth hormone is unsafe.

   _____

   _____

Many questions testing misplaced modifiers begin with a modifying clause, followed by a comma.

3. Like those calling for an end to all legal abortion, the conservative press labels those who call for abortion on demand "extremists."

   _____

   _____

4. Pete preferred watching the movie to reading the 500-page book for his report, which had the benefit of taking much less time to accomplish.

   _____

   _____

Check your answers on page 423.

PRONOUN ERRORS

Pronouns take the place of nouns. They are quite useful; without them, you would have to repeat a noun every time you wanted to use it. For example, the last sentence, without pronouns, would read: "Pronouns are quite useful; without pronouns, [your name here] would have to repeat the noun every time [your name here] wanted to use the noun." This would quickly get tedious.

Pronouns, however, when improperly used, allow for ambiguity, which the CLEP writers hate. For example:

Arnie and Bill flipped a coin, and he won.

"Who is 'he'?" you may ask. Good question. This is an obvious example of a pronoun with no clear antecedent. Here's one that's a little more subtle:

The law firm warned the company to settle its long-term outstanding debts, or it would have to file for bankruptcy.

Does the "it" refer to the law firm, or to the company? Perhaps the company has many debts coming due, and if it doesn't pay them off, it will be forced into bankruptcy. Or, perhaps the company's biggest debt is to the law firm, and the law firm must get paid or it will be forced into bankruptcy. The rule of thumb in CLEP land is: when a pronoun lacks a clear antecedent, use the noun, not the pronoun.

Pronouns must also agree with their antecedents in number and gender. It is incorrect to write:

Pronouns must agree with its antecedents.

because the antecedent, "pronouns," is plural, while the pronoun "its" is singular. The CLEP will make this trickier by using collective nouns, such as:

the team
the family
the company
everyone
everybody

Any time you see a pronoun in a grammar question, check to make sure that it is clear in both number and case.

In all of the above cases, the collective noun is singular, and takes a singular pronoun. Not surprisingly, these are words that most of us refer to, erroneously, with plural pronouns. The CLEP asks you about these precisely because most people get them wrong.

Whenever you see pronouns in a sentence, watch for pronoun errors. Make sure that each pronoun in question has a clear antecedent and that it agrees with that antecedent.

Pronoun Drill

Look at the following sentences. In which are the pronouns without clear antecedents? In which does the pronoun not agree with the antecedent? Circle erroneous pronouns and, in the margin or on a separate piece of paper, write the correct pronoun.

1. A teacher may try to win a class over with friendliness, but they must be careful not to be too friendly, or they will lose their authority.

   _____

   _____

2. The publishing company decided to postpone their October releases until November, when they could take advantage of Christmas shopping.

   _____

   _____

3. Everybody is entitled to his own opinion.

   _____

   _____

4. When a ship is moored at a wooden dock for too long a time, it may rot.

   _____

   _____

Check your answers on page 423.

SUBJECT-VERB AGREEMENT

Subjects and verbs, like pronouns and their antecedents, must agree in number. Again, the CLEP will try to trip you up by using collective nouns as subjects. Which of the following is correct?

The family (want/wants) to be together for the holiday.

The correct answer is "wants." "Family" is singular, and it takes a singular verb.

"Any fool can make a rule And every fool will mind it."
—Henry David Thoreau, on grammar

On all types of agreement questions—pronoun and subject-verb—watch for the CLEP writers to try to confuse you with long sentences. The test will put many words between subject and verb (or pronoun and antecedent) in an effort to make you forget to check for agreement. For example:

> The Secretary General of the United Nations, whose responsibilities range from presiding over the meetings of the General Assembly to traveling to the sites of international emergencies to brokering deals between hostile and distrustful nations, need to take a vacation every now and then.

This example is extreme, but you get the point: by the time you reach the verb ("need") you may very well have forgotten the subject ("Secretary General"), in which case you will miss the agreement error.

Always check to make sure that the subject and verb agree.

Subject-Verb Agreement Drill

Look over the following sentences, circling those verbs that do not agree with their subjects and, in the space provided below those sentences, writing your correction.

1. Among the largest casinos of Atlantic City sit one of the oldest churches in the United States.

   _____

   _____

2. The union negotiator, fearful that a hard-line approach could result in the closing of the factory and the firing of all employees, are offering to accept some layoffs.

   _____

   _____

3. The United States is still idealized by many outsiders because they have a functional democracy and a constitutional commitment to fundamental individual rights.

   _____

   _____

4. The ability of athletes to recuperate from long-term injuries are determined primarily by their physical condition before their injuries were sustained.

   _____

   _____

Check your answers on page 423.

Did you skip chapter 2? If you did, go back and read it! It is crammed with important test-taking tips!

VERB TENSE

The English language has six basic verb tenses. They are:

Present: I succeed   Present Perfect: I have succeeded

Past: I succeeded   Past Perfect: I had succeeded

Future: I will succeed   Future Perfect: I will have succeeded

There are six more verb tenses based on the six above, but with the verb "to be" added, that are called the **continuous** form of these tenses (e.g., continuous present: I am succeeding; continuous past perfect: I had been succeeding).

No, you do not need to know the names of these tenses to answer any CLEP questions; we review them here because it makes it easier to discuss the subject.

Of these tenses, three—the past, present, and future—are pretty straightforward. The future perfect rarely gives anyone any trouble, and, not surprisingly, is rarely found in CLEP questions. Most confusion stems over when and how to use the past perfect and the present perfect.

The **present perfect** is used to describe actions that began in the past but cannot be ascribed to a definite time. The present perfect is sometimes referred to in layman's terms as the indefinite past; it tells you that something happened (and sometimes is still happening), but does not ascribe a precise time to it. For example:

> Bill has enjoyed the fine wines of France's Bordeaux region.

This sentence neither tells us when Bill enjoyed these wines, nor that he has stopped enjoying them; only that at some time in the indefinite past, he has enjoyed them. <u>Never</u> use the present perfect for an action that took place at a precise time.

The **past perfect** is used <u>only in tandem</u> with the past tense. The past perfect is used when you want to describe two actions that took place in the past, and need to indicate that one happened prior to the other. Usually, there is a causal link between the two. For example:

> After Ron had eaten spoiled meat, he went to the hospital to be
> treated for food poisoning.

Because eating spoiled meat preceded Ron's trip to the hospital, and because the two have a causal link (eating bad meat caused Ron's hospital visit), the past perfect is appropriate. This bears repeating: *never* use the past perfect in a sentence unless you also use the past somewhere else in the sentence.

Always use the simplest form of the verb that makes sense. Be particularly careful whenever you see the past perfect in a grammar question: it is often used incorrectly on the CLEP.

Remember: the past perfect tense cannot appear in a sentence in which the past tense does not also appear.

Verb Tense Drill

Read the sentences below. Which have verbs in the incorrect tense? In the space below each incorrect sentence, write the correct form of the verb.

1. Guidance counselors suggest that students consider as many potential colleges as possible because doing so increased their chances of finding the perfect school for them.

   _____

   _____

2. Because the bridge had fallen, we took another, longer route to grandmother's house.

   _____

   _____

3. After the two nations had signed the treaty, they had disarmed the weapons amassed at each other's borders.

   _____

   _____

4. We arrived home to find that Marvin had ate the bean dip.

   _____

   _____

Check your answers on page 424.

PARALLEL CONSTRUCTION

The most basic sentence has just a subject and a verb. For example:

> Cole sits.

Sometimes, however, we want to express more complex ideas.

> Cole sits, watches television, and eats salted snack foods.

In the above sentence, the subject ("Cole") has three verbs. In order for the sentence to be correct, those three verbs must be parallel (as they are in the sentence above). If the sentence read "sits, watches television, and he is eating," it would be incorrect: the clause "he is eating" is not parallel to "sits" and "watches."

The rule of parallel construction should be followed when a sentence lists anything: verbs, nouns, adjectives, phrases, or clauses. For example:

> Our city has been burdened with *bad weather*, *a sagging economy*, and *a major power outage* this year.

ETS writes the test golf pros must take for certification. Sample question: The distance from the center line of a shaft hole to the farthest front portion of the face is the: (A) hostel offset (B) loft (C) lie (D) face progression (E) length. The correct answer is (D).

The governor promises to *increase* tax revenues, *lower* the deficit, and *offer* a tax break to incoming businesses.

Note that in the above sentence, you could also write "to increase...to lower...to offer;" however, you could **not** write "to increase...lower...to offer," because "lower" is not parallel to "to increase" and "to offer."

Parallel construction must also be maintained when you use one of the following:

> not only...but also
> either...or
> neither...nor
> both...and
> whether...or

For example:

> The football coach hopes **not only** *to record a winning season* **but also** *to gain a spot* in the playoffs.

Whenever you see lists in a sentence, keep your eyes peeled for parallel construction errors.

Parallel Construction Drill

Read the sentences below. Which contain parallel structure errors? In the space provided below each sentence, correct those that are incorrect.

1. Working longer hours is one way to earn more money, and to get a raise is another.

   _____

   _____

2. Stores that sell outdoor gear must offer products that are both pleasing to the eye and durable.

   _____

   _____

3. All but the most masochistic athletes prefer the thrill of victory to agonizing over defeat.

   _____

   _____

4. The general was convinced that he had secured the armory by massing his defensive forces at the only vulnerable spots, arming those forces, and by barricading the entryway so that only a few enemy forces could get through at a time.

_____

_____

Check your answers on page 424.

FAULTY COMPARISON

There's an old saying: you can't compare apples and oranges. Translated into grammatical terms, that means: whenever you make comparisons in a sentence, the things being compared have to be in the same part of speech and must agree in number. In other words, when you compare things, make sure they are comparable. What's wrong with the following sentence?

> The new conductor's style is less flamboyant than the old conductor.

This sentence incorrectly compares the new conductor's *style* with the old *conductor*. You cannot properly compare a style to a person, they are two entirely different things. The sentence should read:

> The new conductor's style is less flamboyant than the old conductor's style.

Try this one:

> Elephants eat more peanuts than monkeys.

In this sentence, the author is trying to compare an action—eating—as performed by two animals. But because the verb is not included in the second half of the sentence, it sounds as though elephants eat both peanuts *and* monkeys (although apparently they prefer peanuts). The sentence should read:

> Elephants eat more peanuts than monkeys eat. (Or, "than monkeys do.")

Whenever you see a comparison drawn on the CLEP, watch out for "apples and oranges" errors. Compare nouns to nouns and verbs to verbs, and make sure the two agree in form and are comparable.

ETS doesn't only write tests for academic institutions. The company also writes tests for the National Board of Podiatry Examiners, the American Society of Plumbing Engineers, the Institute for Nuclear Power Operations, and the International Council for Shopping Centers.

Faulty Comparison Drill

Look at the sentences below. Identify those with apples and oranges errors and, in the space provided below each sentence, correct those that are incorrect:

1. Cecily enjoys watching tennis more than the opera.

   _____

   _____

2. Unlike hollow-body electric guitars, Joe prefers solid-body guitars for their increased sustain.

   _____

   _____

3. The tone of political discourse in this country is more rancorous than it has been at any time since the days before the Civil War.

   _____

   _____

4. The cooks of western China use many more hot spices than other cooks.

   _____

   _____

Check your answers on page 424.

REDUNDANCY

The CLEP Subject Exam for Freshman College Composition is very similar to the General Exam in English Composition. If your school gives separate credit for both, take both!

Sometimes repeating oneself is useful. Perhaps you are speaking to someone who is hard of hearing. Or perhaps you need to remind a friend of an unpleasant obligation that your friend keeps trying to forget. Or you want to emphasize a point, such as that your readers should take the English Composition Exam with Essay. Maybe you just enjoy annoying people. Repetition is a very effective tool in that regard.

However, in written English, repetition is considered bad form. On the CLEP, the redundant phrase that appears most often is:

> *The reason* I want to go to the baseball game *is because* my favorite player will be starting for the home team.

"The reason" and "because" give the same information, and so the two are redundant. Eliminate one, so that the sentence reads either:

> *The reason* I want to go to the baseball game *is that* my favorite player will be starting for the home team.

or

> I want to go to the baseball game *because* my favorite player will be starting for the home team.

Redundancy Drill

Which of the following sentences contains redundancy errors? Identify the incorrect sentences and correct them in the space provided below:

1. Bill prefers his sports car better than his RV.

   _____

   _____

2. It is possible that the surprise party might happen.

   _____

   _____

3. The reason that I am running for office is not because I am seeking any personal gain, but because I wish to serve the public interest.

   _____

   _____

4. The doctor recommends that I should get plenty of bed rest.

   _____

   _____

Check your answers on page 424.

IDIOM

Idiom covers a wide range of persnickety rules. When the CLEP tests idioms, it mostly focuses on prepositions—which ones follow which verbs. For example, we say "I am happy *for* you," but we also say "I am happy *with* these results." Different usages have different meanings, and all you can do is memorize as many as you can and hope the CLEP asks you about ones you know. Here's a list of some of the most common idioms that appear on the CLEP:

The professor is regarded *as* the foremost expert in his field.

The professor is considered *to be* the foremost expert in her field.

Many great insights are attributed *to* her.

We are forbidden *to* smoke in this restaurant.

The restaurateur forbids smoking. (No preposition at all.)

The restaurateur prohibits his clients *from* smoking.

This restaurant has a prohibition *against* smoking.

The rule prevents us *from* smoking.

Shirley was delighted *with* the results of her CLEP exams.

She had been concerned *about* the test results before they arrived.

According to the *American Heritage Dictionary*, an idiom is "a speech form or an expression of a given language that is peculiar to itself grammatically or cannot be understood from the individual meanings of its elements."

Remember that all the basic grammar terminology you need is on page 20.

She grew more impatient *with* the mailman every day until her scores came.

She should have been more confident *about* her ability to score well.

I had confidence *in* her (especially since she had The Princeton Review's *Cracking the CLEP*.)

I bought *not only* the title to the Brooklyn Bridge *but also* the real estate beneath it!

When I told my friends, they told me that I was *neither* smart *nor* clever.

In fact, one said I was *not so much* foolish *as* I was addlebrained.

Of all the vices, I enjoy *both* avarice *and* sloth.

My actions are determined *as much by* avarice *as by* sloth.

However, I am *more likely* to be swayed by gluttony *than* by either avarice or sloth.

Tony's friends worried about *his* excessive studying. (Not *him*; -ing words serving as nouns—called gerunds—take the possessive.)

English is the course *in which* I will excel. (Not *where*)

You should try *to* do your best on the CLEP. (**Not** "try *and* do. . .")

SUMMARY

"Like everything metaphysical, the harmony between thought and reality is to be found in the grammar of the language."
—Ludwig Wittgenstein

1. Remember: the CLEP tests a limited number of grammatical errors over and over again. Learn to look for these first.

2. Look for anything that might create ambiguity in a sentence, and, if possible, eliminate it.

3. Pronouns, verbs, and modifying phrases are frequently the source of grammatical errors.

4. Review the grammar in this chapter frequently.

5

Question Types

GRAMMAR QUESTIONS

Because we just reviewed grammar, we'll start with grammar questions. The CLEP tests grammar with three different types of questions: Identifying Sentence Errors, Improving Sentences, and Revising a Work in Progress. Another question type, Restructuring Sentences, also requires you to apply grammatical principles: this type of question only appears on the English Composition without Essay test. If you take the English Composition with Essay test, your use of grammar will, of course, be taken into account by whoever grades your essay.

IDENTIFYING SENTENCE ERRORS

Identifying Sentence Errors questions are sentences that contain either one error or none. You have to choose which underlined part of the sentence is an error, or if none is.

Below is an easy example of an Identifying Sentence Errors question:

The members <u>of the chess</u> club <u>is</u> coming over <u>to watch</u> the
          A   B   C

<u>world chess championship</u> on television. <u>No error</u>
       D   E

Here's how to crack it

If the sentence has no errors, choose answer choice (E): No error. If the sentence contains an error, choose the letter corresponding to the error, which will be underlined. In the sentence above, the correct answer is (B); the verb "is" is singular, while its subject, "members," is plural.

Here are a few things to remember while doing Identifying Sentence Errors questions:

- **Parts of the sentence that are not underlined are correct.** Only underlined phrases are fair game in your hunt for grammatical errors. Also, as you search for errors, start with the core of the sentence, the subject-verb-direct object. Eliminate from view all prepositional phrases, modifiers, etc. until you've nailed down the basic structure and meaning of the sentence. THEN go back and make sure all the bells and whistles are in their proper places.

- **One-fifth of the sentences will be correct as written. Do not be afraid to pick (E) if that's what you think the answer is.**

- **Again, if you can eliminate even one answer, you must guess.** This means that you should answer ALL Identifying Sentence Errors problems, since you should always be able to eliminate at least one answer choice. They are the easiest questions on the test, so do them first to guarantee that you don't run out of time.

IMPROVING SENTENCES

Improving Sentences is another type of grammar question in which you have to look at a sentence and decide whether it is correctly written. Here is an example:

Given its proximity to subway and bus lines, <u>one wonders why more people aren't attracted to stadium events</u>.

(A) one wonders why more people aren't attracted to stadium events
(B) one might wonder why stadium events don't attract more people
(C) it is a wonder that more people don't attend events at the stadium
(D) the stadium should attract more people than it does
(E) the stadium should have attracted more people that it had

Here's how to crack it

The correct answer to this question is (D); answer choices (A), (B), and (C) all use misplaced modifiers, and answer choice (E) needlessly complicates the sentence with unnecessary shifts in verb tense.

When attacking Improving Sentences questions, remember:

◆ **One-fifth of the sentences will be correct as written. Don't be afraid to pick (A) if you think (B), (C), (D), and (E) are all wrong. (A) is always the same as the underlined phrase.**

◆ **As you look at an Improving Sentences question, remember the Eight Deadly Sins of Grammar discussed in chapter 4.** Nearly all the errors will fall into one of those eight categories. As you read the sentence:

◆ **Identify any error you see, then go to the answer choices and eliminate those that repeat that error.** Repeat this process until you are left with one answer choice: the correct one. If you cannot get it down to one answer choice but have eliminated at least one incorrect answer, guess from among the remaining answer choices and move on.

◆ **Watch out for -ing words, and always eliminate answer choices with the word "being" in them.** Words that end in -ing can be problematic because they can serve several functions. The word "swimming" can be a noun ("Swimming is my favorite sport."), a verb ("I am swimming in a sea of happiness."), or an adjective ("The swimming boy zipped past the floating fat man and splashed him."). Because of this versatility, -ing words can create ambiguity, which, as previously mentioned, ETS hates. Don't eliminate all answer choices with -ing

> If you're taking more than one exam, bring a snack to have between tests. It will help replenish your energy.

words in them, but be suspicious of them all and check other answer choices for less ambiguous wording. Always eliminate answers with the word "being" in them; ETS knows that everybody uses this word incorrectly and wants to punish YOU for everybody else's sins. Don't fall into the trap; just say "no" to "being."

REVISING A WORK IN PROGRESS

Revising a Work in Progress questions test a number of skills. They are meant to test your ability to spot errors in a first draft, some of which will be grammatical. For Revising a Work in Progress questions, there will be a reading passage, usually thirteen to sixteen sentences long, and then a series of questions about how the passage might be improved. The grammar questions will be exactly like Improving Sentences questions; they will show you a sentence from the passage and provide four alternatives to its current wording. On such questions, use the same approach described above for Improving Sentences questions.

See below for an example of a Revising a Work in Progress question.

WRITING SKILLS QUESTIONS

Three types of CLEP multiple-choice questions test writing skills: Revising a Work in Progress, Restructuring Sentences, and Analyzing Writing. Of these, only Revising a Work in Progress appears on the English Composition with Essay test; the other two appear in Part II of the multiple-choice test instead of an essay question.

Some of these questions will ask about poorly worded or awkwardly constructed sentences, or about the sequencing and overall organization of the passage. Sometimes you will be asked to combine two sentences into a single sentence. Occasionally, you will be asked a diction question: that is, you will be asked to decide whether the word the author has chosen is correctly used.

Here's a shortened version of what you will see on the test:

(1) *My neighbor's two-year-old loves to watch Hecky, the plaid dinosaur.* (2) *Because the show educates her parents believe they don't mind.* (3) *Some children aren't allowed to listen to the radio.*

Which of the following is the best way to revise sentence 2?

(A) (as it is now)
(B) Because the show is educational her parents believe they don't mind.
(C) Because her parents believe in the show as educating they don't mind.
(D) Her parents don't mind because they believe the show is educational.
(E) Her parents don't mind what they believe, and the show is educational.

> Always take the path of least resistance on multiple-choice tests. Do not answer the questions that give you trouble until you have answered ALL questions you can answer easily.

Which of the following is the best critique of sentence 3?

(A) It needs to end with a question mark.
(B) It changes the subject of the passage too abruptly.
(C) It should read "for the radio" instead of "to the radio."
(D) It is redundant.
(E) It is too long.

Correct answers: (D), (B)

Remember:

◆ **The CLEP hates ambiguity.** The CLEP's writing questions test your ability to clarify sloppy, misleading, and/or confusing passages. Some questions, such as the first sample question above, are extremely similar to Improving Sentences questions: part or all of a sentence will be presented with four alternatives, and you will be asked to choose the best alternative. Other questions, such as the second sample question above, ask about the organization of the passage.

A third type of question asks you to combine two sentences into one. Here's another sample mini-passage:

(1) *My neighbor's two-year-old loves to watch Hecky, the plaid dinosaur.* (2) *Her parents don't mind because they believe the show is educational.* (3) *But I'm not so sure.* (4) *The real dinosaurs weren't plaid.*

Which of the following is the best way to revise sentences 3 and 4 (reproduced below) so that they are combined into a single sentence?

But I'm not so sure. The real dinosaurs weren't plaid.

(A) But I'm not so sure real dinosaurs weren't plaid.
(B) I'm not so sure, but weren't there no real plaid dinosaurs?
(C) I, however, am not so sure; after all, real dinosaurs weren't plaid.
(D) Because real dinosaurs weren't plaid; I'm not so sure about it.
(E) Real dinosaurs weren't plaid: I'm not so sure.

Correct answer: (C)

Note that the correct answer uses transitions (*however*, *after all*) and punctuation (a semi-colon) to combine the two sentences. This is typical of such questions:

◆ **Questions that ask you to combine sentences focus on transitions and punctuation.**

Don't get caught up in the subject matter of a reading passage. Read for pleasure at home; on the CLEP, read to find the correct answer and move on.

You need to know the function of the following punctuation marks:

- comma—used to separate elements of a list and to connect two or more phrases that are separated by a conjunction.
  Example: Hecky is a plaid dinosaur, and I find him annoying.

- semi-colon—used to link two independent clauses that are connected in thought (i.e. talk about the same idea).
  Example: Hecky's songs are terrible; however, they are also impossible to get out of your head once you've heard them.

- colon—used to express the thought "as follows."
  Example: My neighbor's two-year-old wants only one thing for her birthday: a Hecky doll.

Know also the following conjunctions. These continue the flow of the sentence:
and
because
furthermore
not only . . . but also
luckily

These reverse the flow of the sentence:
but
however
nevertheless
nonetheless
unfortunately

A few final notes: save Revising a Work in Progress for last on Part I of the test with the essay. Skip over it and do all the Improving Sentences questions at the end of the section—they are easier and can be done more quickly— before returning to the Revising a Work in Progress questions. If you take the test without the essay, you will have both Revising a Work in Progress and Analyzing Writing on Part II of the exam. Save Revising a Work in Progress for second-to-last and do it before you do the Analyzing Writing questions.

Make sure you read the passages closely enough to get the main idea but no more closely: the more time you spend on reading, the less time you will have to answer questions. As with all parts of this test, never spend too long on any one question. Since all questions have an equal value on your final score, no one question is worth more than two minutes of your time.

On Part I of the test, don't answer the Revising Works in Progress questions (questions 26-43) until you have answered the second set of Improving Sentences questions (questions 44-55). The Improving Sentences questions are easier.

RESTRUCTURING SENTENCES

On Restructuring Sentences questions, you will be presented with a sentence and directions on how to alter the sentence. You will then have to choose from among the answer choices the word or phrase that appears in your new sentence.

This is what a Restructuring Sentences question looks like:

> **Sentence:** A gifted and charismatic performer, Elvis Presley had millions of devoted fans.
>
> **Directions:** Begin with <u>Millions of devoted fans</u>.
>
>   (A) because
>   (B) even though
>   (C) however
>   (D) also
>   (E) where

Restructuring Sentences questions can be tough. They don't appear on the English Composition with Essay test.

The correct answer to this question is (A). Your restructured sentence should have gone something like this:

Millions of devoted fans loved Elvis Presley because he was a gifted and charismatic performer.

These questions are tough because only a part of the correct answer—that is, the correctly restructured sentence—appears among the answer choices. The rest will exist only in your head. There's only one technique for these problems:

1. Read the sentence.

2. Read the directions.

3. Do not look at the answer choices.

4. Restructure the sentence in your head.

5. Look for the answer choice that reflects your restructured sentence.

These questions do not appear on the essay version of the test. Our advice: take the essay test and avoid these nasty questions entirely.

ANALYZING WRITING

Analyzing Writing questions are not unlike Reading Comprehension questions on the SAT, except that they are much more difficult. An Analyzing Writing passage is a finished piece of work (as opposed to Revising a Work in Progress passages, which are rough drafts). It may be a piece of fiction, a piece of nonfiction (a biographical sketch, a science article), a philosophical tract, or just about anything that could fall under the category of creative writing.

These are the trickiest questions on the test. Save them for last. Better still, take the essay version of the English Composition exam, because Analyzing Writing does not appear on that test.

If you must take the non-essay version of the test, remember the following:

◆ **Don't try to read between the lines. The correct answer will not call for you to draw far-reaching inferences, nor will it depend on your drawing an erudite inference.** You will be asked to decipher the author's intent; you may be asked to interpret the mood of the piece or to decide what a certain image symbolizes. Don't get fancy with these questions: the answers will be somewhere in the passage. Forget about your opinions for the test. You should only care about what the author thinks.

Analyzing Writing questions are the hardest on the exam. They don't appear on the English Composition with Essay test.

- **Don't eliminate an answer choice if you don't understand it.** The most difficult questions on this section are often those that ask confusing questions. Often, the correct answers will be worded in a confusing way. Eliminate answers when you know they are wrong, but not when their syntax frustrates you. Writing correct answers in confusing ways is one way in which ETS makes it harder for you to find the correct answer, and it works very well: most people will eliminate an answer if they don't understand it. Don't fall into that trap.

- **Don't get bogged down on any one question.** If a question stumps or confuses you, skip it. You can always come back to it later if you have time. Better still, take the exam with the essay and avoid Analyzing Writing altogether (Have we suggested this before? It bears repeating).

AN IMPORTANT FINAL WORD OF CAUTION

When attempting ANY question on the English Composition exam, remember:

- It is easier to identify incorrect answers than it is to identify correct ones.

The English Composition Exam with Essay is offered in January, April, June, and October. Sign up early!

- On all but the easiest questions, you should be trying to eliminate the four wrong answers rather than find the correct one.

This is because incorrect answers are incorrect for specific and identifiable reasons. Many questions have more than one correct answer, which is why trying to find the correct answer can be treacherous. If you go looking for the correct answer, you may end up choosing an incorrect answer which is closer to your version of the correct response but which contains some other mistake, a mistake you might have spotted had you taken the more critical approach we recommend.

SUMMARY

1. Don't do questions that require you to read a long passage until you've done ALL the shorter questions.

2. Avoid the tricky "Restructuring Sentences" and "Analyzing Writing" questions, which appear only on the English Composition without Essay exam, by taking the English Composition with Essay exam.

3. Be on the alert for ambiguity; it is the most frequent reason that an answer is incorrect.

4. On questions that require reading a passage, do not read between the lines.

5. Correct answers will not require you to draw subtle inferences.

6. Use POE to eliminate wrong answers, and guess if you can eliminate even one answer choice.

7. Don't get hung up on any one question.

6

The Essay Question

WHAT IS THE ESSAY QUESTION?

CLEP essay questions ask you to express an opinion about an issue (e.g. gun control, traditional versus experimental education, etc.) or, sometimes, an old cliché ("Birds of a feather flock together"). It does not matter what your opinion is, so long as you can back it up with a well-reasoned and well-organized argument.

HOW IS THE ESSAY GRADED?

After you take the test, your and everybody else's essays are shipped to a cafeteria full of teachers, two of whom grade your essay. They will have only a minute or two to read your essay and give it a grade between 2 (very bad) and 8 (very good). The grading supervisor will also look at your essay if: 1) the two graders differ in their assessment of your work by more than 2 points, 2) if you left your essay sheet blank, or 3) if your essay is not about the assigned topic. Only the supervisor may assign a grade of 0, which is the grade for no essay at all or an essay that is not about the subject. Essays on the wrong topic are given a 0 in order to dissuade unscrupulous test takers from writing essays before the test and somehow reproducing them in their test booklets (either by memorizing the entire essay—UGH!—or by somehow cribbing the essay and copying it during the test. This is both extremely risky and, given the likelihood that such an essay will earn a 0, not at all profitable). So long as you don't cheat or draw a total blank, the chances of your getting a 0 are pretty much nil, so don't even worry about it.

ETS claims that essays are graded "holistically." This means that graders are supposed to judge the overall impact of your essays, rather than checking them against a "shopping list" of fine points, details, and predetermined "talking points." Graders are also instructed to take the 45-minute time limit for preparing and writing your essay into account, and to look for what you have done well rather than focus on what you have done poorly.

All of this is good news for you. Graders are looking for signs that you have something reasonably intelligent to say and that you know how to say it in an organized manner. As previously mentioned, they are not given much time to, so their reading will be a superficial one. If you follow the instructions on the next few pages, you should be able to write an essay that satisfies the graders. And you will almost certainly get a better grade from them than you would get on Part II of the English Composition without Essay test.

> Essay graders only have a few minutes to read your essay and grade it. They look for general indicators of thought, coherence, and organization. Don't try to be too subtle or too fancy. As Joe Friday says, "Just the facts, ma'am."

A GOOD ESSAY

Let's start with a sample essay topic:

> Proponents of recent term-limit legislation, which limits the amount of time elected officials can serve, argue that such laws make politicians less beholden to lobbyists and donors and mandate an influx of fresh ideas to the political process. Opponents, however, argue that, by increasing the number of inexperienced legislators, such laws will actually give more power to lobbyists, fund-raisers, and long-term unelected government bureaucrats.

Write an argument in which you discuss whose argument, the proponents of term limits or its opponents, you find more persuasive. Explain your position using reasons and/or examples taken from your own experiences, philosophy, or reading.

- **The first thing you need to do is pick a position.** Go with your gut; there's no sense trying to guess what position will please the person grading your essay, because 1) it's impossible, and 2) the grader doesn't care what your opinion is, only whether you've written about it well.

- **The next thing you want to do is take two to three minutes to "brainstorm."** In your test booklet (but not on the form provided for you to write your essay on!), write down all the ideas that come to mind about the subject. Arguments for your position, hypothetical situations and/or examples from the news that support your position, flaws in the potential arguments of those on the other side of the issue...in short, anything you can think of that might be of help in your essay.

- **Next you want to organize your ideas in outline form.** Make each heading in your outline the subject of a paragraph, and try to outline a five-paragraph essay. The first paragraph will be your opening statement, in which you should state which side of the argument you are taking. The final paragraph should be your conclusion, in which you eloquently restate why you are on the right side of the argument. In the remaining three paragraphs, you should pursue one of the following strategies:

- **Three Good Points**—This is the simplest, most effective strategy. Look at the results of your brainstorming session and pick the three best points supporting your position. Make each of these points the subject of one paragraph. Make the weakest of the three points the subject of paragraph 2, and save the strongest point for paragraph 4. If your three points are interrelated and there is a natural sequence to arguing them, then by all means use that sequence, but again try to save your strongest point for last. Begin each paragraph by stating one of your three points, and then spend the rest of the paragraph supporting it. Use specific examples whenever possible to support your argument.

Don't be afraid to write in your test booklet. Take notes for your essay and cross out and circle multiple choice answers in the booklet. You're the only one who's ever going to use it!

- **The Historical Argument**—This strategy is very much like the "Three Good Points" strategy, except that your three points are replaced by three historical examples supporting your position. If your knowledge of history is strong, this is a good approach, because you will earn brownie points. Brownie points, incidentally, are awarded for any information you didn't learn from watching television. Replace the historical examples with literary examples and voilà, you have the "Literary Argument."

- **The "Straw Dog" Argument**—Pick a couple of arguments that someone taking the position opposite yours would take. State their arguments, then tear them down. Remember that proving that your opposition is wrong doesn't mean that you have proved you are correct; that is why you should choose only a few opposing arguments to refute. Summarize your opponent's arguments in paragraph two, dismiss them in paragraph three, and use paragraph four to make the argument for your side. Or, use one paragraph to summarize and dismiss each of your opponent's arguments, and then make the case for your side in your concluding paragraph.

A SAMPLE OUTLINE

Let's return now to our sample question. We'll take the position against term limits, since that's my position. Again, the grader won't care in the slightest what your position is (unless it's truly offensive), but we need a position in order to come up with a sample outline, and since I'm writing it, we'll take my position.

My brainstorm session might yield the following:

1. New office holders are more beholden to staff, lobbyists.

2. Permanent bureaucracy might wield more power than elected officials.

3. Voters can get rid of officials any time they want by voting them out.

4. 1994 Congressional elections proved that voters can get rid of incumbents.

5. New officials do not necessarily mean we get new ideas; logical flaw in argument for term limits.

6. Term limits are not mentioned in the Constitution.

7. Elections will still be expensive, and legislators will still be beholden to those who help fund their elections. Term limits don't solve the problem.

8. Real problem is big money and power overly influence the process. Those who argue for term limits miss the point. Right problem, wrong solution.

> In your essay, keep your ideas simple and state them clearly. Don't overdo it.

Now I have to figure out what I can use and where. My brainstorming session shows that I have a number of ideas about why supporters of term limits are wrong, so I should probably use the Straw Dog strategy. Points 1, 5, and 7 speak to my opponents' arguments, so I am going to devote a paragraph to presenting and refuting each of these arguments. Point 4 is a good example of point 3, so I want to keep them together. The other good points belong in the last paragraph, in which I will explain why we don't need term limits. Point 6 is relatively weak; I wrote it down because I was brainstorming, but now I've decided to throw it out, because my other points are better, and I already have enough for a good essay.

Next I'm going to put together an outline.

I. I am against term limits.

II. Too hard to get rid of incumbents? 1994 Congressional election.

III. New legislators will bring in new ideas? Not necessarily so. Nor is it impossible for old legislators to have new ideas.

IV. Will make legislators less beholden to lobbyists, fund raisers? Opposite is true!

V. Why term limits are bad: inexperienced legislators, campaigns will still be expensive, and candidates will still be beholden to those who finance campaigns. The real answer is campaign finance reform.

> "A good essay must have this permanent quality about it; it must draw its curtain round us, but it must be a curtain that shuts us in, not out."
> —Virginia Woolf
> (1882–1941)

Before I start to write, I should take a deep breath and understand what I am going to try to accomplish. Paragraph 1 could be short, maybe just a sentence or two, making a general statement of my position. However, if I can think of a clever device to introduce the subject, I will use it. Paragraphs 2, 3, and 4 will present arguments for term limits and my rebuttals to those arguments. In paragraph 5, I will show that term limits will have a negative effect. I will then try to show that my opponents' objectives—to make it easier for Congressmen to become independent of special interest groups and to make it easier for incumbents to be defeated—can be achieved through my solution, campaign finance reform.

WRITING THE ESSAY

As you write, keep the following pointers in mind.

- **Stick to your outline.** Make one major point per paragraph.

- **Whenever possible, back up your points with examples**.

- **Keep sentences as simple as possible.** Long sentences get convoluted very quickly and will give your grader a headache, putting him or her in a bad mood.

- **Use transition words to show where you are going.** When continuing an idea, use words such as "furthermore," "also," and "in addition." If you are making a number of related points, number them ("First. . . . Second. . . . And lastly....). When changing the flow of thought, use words such as "however," "on the other hand," and "and yet."

- **Throw in a few big words.** Don't use too many, and NEVER use a word if you are unsure of its meaning or proper usage.

- **An overly short essay will hurt you more than one that is overly long.** Try to fill the essay form.

SAMPLE ESSAYS—THE GOOD, THE BAD, AND THE UGLY

Now it's time to look at a few sample essays on the topic above. Below are a very good essay, an average essay, and a bad essay.

EXCELLENT ESSAY

There will always be people who think that today's problems are the worst problems anyone has ever faced. Those same people argue, inevitably, that radical changes are necessary if we, as a nation, are to avoid complete collapse. In the past, their causes have run the political gamut, from strict immigration quotas to nationalized industry. Today, their pet cause is term limits. Term-limit advocates seem to think that never has the government been so unresponsive to the desires of the people, so corrupted by special interests, so intractable as it is now. Laws that require us to replace these officials, they cry, is the only solution.

But let's look at the arguments these doomsayers put forward. Most point to the tremendous advantage incumbents have historically had—vast majorities of them were reelected, not infrequently without opposition, they note. The conclusion we are meant to draw is that it is simply too difficult to unseat an incumbent, and that we must therefore force incumbents out. However, we can force them out, and do, as evidenced by the 1994 Congressional elections, in which Republicans regained control of both houses in a stunning defeat of Democratic incumbency. The message of that election is clear: even without term limits, America has both the means and the ability to oust elected officials.

Term-limit supporters also argue that the stagnation in Congressional turnover results in a lack of fresh ideas. New legislators would bring in new ideas, they argue. This point, however, vanishes almost immediately upon inspection. There is no necessary correlation between newness to an office and innovative thinking. In fact, if anything, one would expect a new elected official to be more conservative than bold, as most people are when starting a new job. Nor is it necessarily true that old legislators are incapable of new ideas. The history of public service in this country is full of stories of midterm conversions to different viewpoints. And let us not forget that politicians are by nature poll watchers—their opinions and ideas change almost exactly as often as ours do.

"You expect far too much of a first sentence. Think of it as analogous to a good country breakfast: what we want is something simple, but nourishing to the imagination. Hold the philosophy, hold the adjectives, just give us a plain subject and verb and perhaps a wholesome, nonfattening adverb or two."
—Larry McMurtry, American author

Finally there is the argument that the current system provides too much influence to those special interests and fund raisers on whom candidates depend. The candidates move to Washington, the argument goes, lose touch with their home states and fall under the evil influence of "special interests." It is hard to see, however, how term limits would change any of this. Elections will still be expensive, and candidates will still need to raise money. In fact, with so many unknowns running for office, one can only assume that elections will become more expensive as candidates advertise in an effort to make themselves familiar to voters. This will make them more, not less, dependent on today's power brokers. Once in Washington, all these newcomers would create the danger that the more experienced among them—staff members, unelected bureaucrats, and special interest groups—would have the opportunity to wield more power. In whose hands do we want this power, those of our elected officials or those of unelected Washington lifers?

On the down side, term limits would give us inexperienced legislators. Their work would often be too slow and at other times too fast, executed without the foresight that experience provides. Nor would we have solved any of those problems caused by a stagnant government. Rather, stagnation would move from the surface, where we can see it and remove it when we wish to, and sink below the surface, manifested in those unelected government functionaries and hangers-on who make Washington their home. A much more sensible way to level the playing field, and to hobble influence peddling, would be to overhaul campaign finance laws in such a way as to deny wealthy candidates the electoral advantage they currently enjoy. For it is money, to paraphrase an old saying, that is the root of this particular evil.

ABOVE AVERAGE ESSAY

Supporters of term limits say that such laws will make politicians less dependent on lobbyists and donors, and that new candidates will bring fresh ideas to the political process. I do not think this is true.

It is true that things are not perfect in Washington D.C. Members of Congress lose touch with their homes, politics gets in the way of things actually getting done, special interest groups have too much power, and it is hard to unseat an incumbent. But let's face it, things are never perfect anywhere. And just because things aren't exactly right doesn't mean that term limits will solve all the problems.

Take the argument that term limits will result in new ideas in Washington D.C. It's true that if we bring new people to Washington, some of them may have new ideas. Of course, some of them may not. Maybe all of them will not. If we want to bring people with new ideas to Washington, the answer isn't just to throw the old politicians out. It is to vote for people with new ideas, which we are free to do right now without term limits.

When these new members of Congress all arrive together in Washington, with nobody around who knows how to get things done, who will they turn to for leadership? Each other? The voters? More likely, they will turn to the folks who know how Washington works. Those people are Federal employees, lobbyists, and party officials and fund-raisers. Many of these are good people, but their agendas are different from the Congresspeople's supporters back home. And some of them are not good people, they are the very people who term limit laws are supposed to be taking power away from.

The Congressional election of 1994 showed that when people want new representatives, they vote for them. They don't care who the incumbent is or who his powerful friends are. We have a way to get rid of members of Congress that we don't like without term limits: it's called the ballot box. That way was established in the Constitution, which, last time I checked, didn't say anything about term limits.

In short, term limits are a bad idea. By increasing the number of inexperienced legislators, term limits will give more power, not less, to lobbyists, fundraisers, and government bureaucrats.

AVERAGE ESSAY

I believe that term limits increase the amount of power that lobbyists, fundraisers, and bureaucrats will hold over our elected officials. Given a choice between one or the other, I prefer that the elected officials keep more power. At least they have to run for reelection. Then, they are held accountable for their actions. Unelected officials are not.

The system isn't perfect. Incumbents have great advantages over challengers. Everybody already knows them; they have political connections; they get more powerful the longer they stay in Congress, and can use that power to get reelected; and, it's easier for them to get the money they need to run. Term limits might "level the playing field," but they might not. Term limits are a roundabout way to get at the big problem - money - and they are a fundamental change to our way of government. I think we should be more careful when we change our government from the way it is in the Constitution.

People who argue for term limits say that they will bring "fresh ideas" to Congress. But what good are new ideas if you can't pass laws? All these new Congressmen won't know how the system works, and remember, politics is not easy; it takes know-how to pass legislation. By the time they learn how the system works, the term limits law will throw them out, and we'll start all over again with a new set of beginners. And how can we be sure that these new Congressmen will have fresh ideas? If that's what we want, maybe we should pass a law requiring Congressmen to come up with one fresh idea per week! That would be more to the point.

Anyway, the 1994 elections showed that, when people want new representatives, they can get rid of them without any term limits.

I think term limits is the wrong solution to a difficult problem. Campaign finance reform might be a better place to start, if we really want to change the way things are done in Washington D.C. But let's not take the power away from our elected representatives and give it to a bunch of people we didn't vote for. That would be a step in the wrong direction.

When you take the English Composition with Essay exam, you avoid two difficult question types that appear on the "without Essay" exam only: "Analyzing Writing" and "Restructuring Sentences." The English Composition with Essay exam is offered in January, April, June, and October. Sign up early!

POOR ESSAY

I find the argument of people who oppose term limits more persuasive. Term limits are bad because they deny us as Americans the right to vote for who we want to.

Let's say I like Congressman X. He represents me exactly the way I want to be represented. I want to vote for him, but term limits say I can't. This means the democratic process is no longer working. Why shouldn't I be able to vote for him if he's my choice?

If people want new ideas, they can vote for them. They don't need term limits to do that. As far as term limits getting rid of corruption in Washington, don't make me laugh. I'm not even going to get into that.

PRACTICE ESSAY QUESTIONS

1. There is an old French saying: "The more things change, the more they stay the same." Do you agree or disagree with this assertion? Do you think it is true in some instances, but not in others? Using specific examples, write an essay explaining your position, drawing on your personal experience, observations, or books you have read for support.

2. Senator Daniel Patrick Moynihan pointed out in an essay for *The New York Times* that there are currently more guns in circulation in the United States than there are citizens. He concluded that it is therefore too late to stem the U.S. "gun problem," and suggests that the U.S. should concentrate instead on regulating ammunition, of which there is a much less bounteous supply. His suggestions include heavy taxes on bullets and/or requiring that one have a federal license to buy ammunition. Write an essay in which you agree or disagree with Senator Moynihan's suggestions concerning federal regulation of ammunition. Support your position with relevant reasons and/or examples drawn from your own experience, observations, or reading.

SUMMARY

1. Read the essay question carefully, then decide on a position before you start writing.

2. Brainstorm, decide what your strongest arguments are, then 'rough out' an outline.

3. Organize your essay using one of the methods described on page 45.

4. Write clearly. Focus on one main point per paragraph.

5. Don't use words you don't know. Toss in a couple of 'big' words that you are comfortable with.

6. Indicate the direction your essay is taking with transition words.

7. Don't pad your essay, but don't write something that is much shorter than the essay form provided by ETS. A very short essay will probably get a low grade.

7

The Princeton Review
Sample English
Composition Exam

PART I

Time—45 minutes

55 questions

Directions: The following sentences test your knowledge of grammar, diction (choice of words), and idiom.

Some sentences are correct.

No sentence contains more than one error.

You will find that the error, if there is one, is underlined and lettered. Assume that elements of the sentence that are not underlined are correct and cannot be changed. In choosing answers, follow the requirements of standard written English.

If there is an error, select the <u>one underlined part</u> that must be changed to make the sentence correct and fill in the corresponding oval on your answer sheet.

If there is no error, select answer (E).

Example:

<u>The other</u> delegates and <u>him</u> immediately <u>accepted</u> the resolution <u>drafted</u> by the neutral states.
  A   B   C   D

<u>No error</u>
  E

Ⓐ ● Ⓒ Ⓓ Ⓔ

1. After <u>she attends</u> a session of the general
           A

   assembly, Patricia decided <u>that</u> she
                         B

   <u>wanted to learn</u> more about <u>the history of</u> the
        C   D

   United Nations. <u>No error</u>
                  E

2. Everyone <u>who went to</u> the conference,
             A

   <u>which attracted</u> eight hundred participants,
       B

   expressed <u>their</u> satisfaction <u>with the event</u>
            C   D

   during the exit survey. <u>No error</u>
                  E

3. The author James Joyce <u>used</u> a "stream-of-
                 A

   consciousness" <u>technique</u> <u>to simulate</u> the
             B   C

   muddled, rambling manner <u>in</u> which human
                     D

   beings think. <u>No error</u>
            E

4. Laws <u>requiring states to</u> notify communities
           A

   of the presence <u>of sex offenders</u> <u>violates</u> the
                 B   C

   constitutional guarantee against double

   jeopardy, according <u>to some</u> civil libertarians.
                     D

   <u>No error</u>
     E

5. The reason Patty wants <u>to buy</u> a new car
                  A

   <u>is because</u> the cost <u>of</u> repairing her used car
       B   C

   would be <u>greater than</u> its current value.
              D

   <u>No error</u>
     E

GO ON TO THE NEXT PAGE.

6. The prime minister agreed that <u>his cabinet</u>
                                            A

   members and <u>him</u> should be <u>subject to</u> the
                B   C

   same laws <u>that govern</u> all citizens. <u>No error</u>
                 D   E

7. Distillation, the process of <u>separating</u>
                                    A

   different components of a liquid <u>by heating</u>
                                         B

   the liquid, <u>that utilizes</u> the principle that
                C

   <u>different molecules</u> become agitated at
             D

   different temperatures. <u>No error</u>
                          E

8. The shop owner set out <u>to accomplish</u> three
                                A

   budgetary goals: to <u>reduce</u> inventory, to lower
                      B

   <u>worker-related</u> expenses, and <u>eliminating</u>
        C   D

   unnecessary advertising expenditures.

   <u>No error</u>
    E

9. <u>Faced with</u> declining revenues, the city
    A

   council had <u>to decide</u> between the
                B

   <u>equally unpleasant</u> options <u>of cutting</u> the
           C   D

   education budget and raising taxes. <u>No error</u>
                                       E

10. Cesar is an <u>inconsistent student</u>: he performs
                    A

    better in <u>classes</u> he enjoys, <u>such as</u> history,
                 B   C

    than <u>those</u> he doesn't like. <u>No error</u>
         D   E

11. The principal's decision <u>to cancel</u> the
                           A

    assembly <u>was influenced</u> as much <u>by</u> the
              B   C

    students' lack of interest <u>than</u> by the absence
                              D

    of the main scheduled speaker. <u>No error</u>
                                   E

12. <u>Because</u> our roof <u>was not designed</u> to bear a
     A

    great deal of weight, we were afraid it would

    <u>cave in</u> the day after two feet of <u>snow fell</u>.
       C   D
    <u>No error</u>

13. Although antibiotics appear to provide the

    remedy <u>to many</u> an infection, <u>its</u> overuse
             A   B

    <u>have led</u> to the rapid evolution of <u>hardier</u>, drug-
       C   D

    resistant strains of numerous diseases. <u>No error</u>
                                        E

14. The Celsius scale is <u>named after</u> the Swedish
                       A

    astronomer Anders Celsius, <u>who was</u> the first
                               B

    <u>describing</u> the <u>properties of</u> the centigrade
       C   D

    thermometer. <u>No error</u>
                 E

15. The professor and class <u>decided to</u> reschedule
                           A

    the discussion group for a different night,

    <u>the reason being</u> it was originally scheduled
      B

    during a religious holiday, which <u>would have</u>
                                    C

    prevented some <u>from attending</u>. <u>No error</u>
                      D   E

GO ON TO THE NEXT PAGE.

Directions: The following sentences test correctness and effectiveness of expression. In choosing answers, follow the requirements of standard written English: that is, pay attention to grammar, diction (choice of words), sentence construction, and punctuation.

In each of the following sentences, part of the sentence or the entire sentence is underlined. Beneath each sentence you will find five versions of the underlined part. Choice A repeats the original; the other four are different.

Choose the answer that best expresses the meaning of the original sentence. If you think the original is better than any of the alternatives, choose it; otherwise choose one of the others. Your choice should produce the most effective sentence—one that is clear and precise, without awkwardness or ambiguity.

Example:

Laura Ingalls Wilder published her first book <u>and she was sixty-five years old then</u>.

(A) and she was sixty-five years old then
(B) when she was sixty-five
(C) being age sixty-five years old
(D) upon the reaching of sixty-five years
(E) at the time when she was sixty-five

16. "Everlasting" is the name given to a group of plants whose leaves, while not truly eternal, maintain their original color and form <u>for a long time after it has fallen from its plant</u>.

   (A) for a long time after it has fallen from its plant
   (B) for a long time after they had fallen off the plant
   (C) for a long time after it fell
   (D) long after they have fallen
   (E) long after it had fallen

17. <u>Carnival is the period preceding Lent in the Christian calendar, it</u> is marked by feasting and often mischievous acts of merriment.

   (A) Carnival is the period preceding Lent in the Christian calendar, it
   (B) Carnival is the period which, preceding Lent in the Christian calendar, and it
   (C) Carnival, the period preceding Lent in the Christian calendar,
   (D) The period which is preceding Lent in the Christian calendar being Carnival,
   (E) Preceding Lent in the Christian calendar is a period called Carnival,

18. Although not as well-remembered as some of his contemporaries, <u>the body of work of Countee Cullen establish</u> him as one of the great poets of the Harlem Renaissance.

   (A) the body of work of Countee Cullen establish
   (B) the body of work created by Countee Cullen establishes
   (C) the body of work Countee Cullen created established
   (D) Countee Cullen created a body of work that establishes
   (E) Countee Cullen's body of work would establish

19. Cú Chulainn, a central figure in medieval Irish mythology, was said to be favored by the gods, <u>who gifted him with seven fingers on each hand, seven</u> toes on each foot, and seven pupils in each eye.

   (A) who gifted him with seven fingers on each hand, seven
   (B) who gifted him with seven fingers on each hand, with seven
   (C) who gifted him with seven of each of the following: fingers on each hand,
   (D) whose gifts to him included each hand having seven fingers, seven
   (E) whose gifts included two hands, seven-fingered, seven

GO ON TO THE NEXT PAGE.

20. Doctors who design weight-loss programs for patients would rather develop programs emphasizing exercise and sensible eating <u>as opposed to</u> those relying exclusively on a drastic reduction in caloric intake.

    (A) as opposed to
    (B) than
    (C) in contrast with
    (D) and not
    (E) versus

21. Even though information reaches people from more sources than ever before, surveys <u>are consistently demonstrating that people today misconceive more than people of</u> the four previous decades.

    (A) are consistently demonstrating that people today misconceive more than people of
    (B) make it demonstrable that people today hold more misconceptions, being less informed than
    (C) make a consistent demonstration of people today misconceiving, more so than those from
    (D) demonstrate with consistency that today's people hold more misconceptions than do people of
    (E) consistently demonstrate that people today hold more misconceptions than did people during any of

22. Dancers are more likely to develop chronic foot problems <u>than other professions</u>.

    (A) than other professions
    (B) than are people in other professions
    (C) as opposed to people whose professions are different
    (D) in contrast to professions of others
    (E) compared against other professions

23. More than any other individual, <u>the ascendancy of alternating current is Nikolai Tesla's responsibility</u>.

    (A) the ascendancy of alternating current is Nikolai Tesla's responsibility
    (B) the ascendancy of alternating current was caused by Nikolai Tesla
    (C) it was Nikolai Tesla who caused the ascendancy of alternating current
    (D) Nikolai Tesla's responsibility was the ascendancy of alternating current
    (E) Nikolai Tesla was responsible for the ascendancy of alternating current

24. Because the debate had not been resolved at the scheduled time, the council voted to <u>continue on with</u> the discussion indefinitely.

    (A) continue on with
    (B) continue on
    (C) continue
    (D) keep on continuing
    (E) keep continuing

25. Bilingual education has mixed results: studies show that students in such programs <u>learn more quickly but</u> enter mainstream society much more slowly.

    (A) learn more quickly but
    (B) are quicker to learn, however
    (C) although learning quicker,
    (D) both learn more quickly as well as
    (E) are learning more quickly at the same time they

GO ON TO THE NEXT PAGE.

Directions: Each of the following selections is an early draft of a student essay in which the sentences have been numbered for easy reference. Some parts of the selections need to be changed.

Read each selection and then answer the questions that follow. Some questions are about particular sentences or parts of sentences and ask you to improve sentence structure and diction (word choice). In making these decisions, follow the conventions of standard written English. Other questions refer to the entire essay or parts of the essay and ask you to consider organization, development, and effectiveness of language in relation to purpose and audience. After you choose each answer, fill in the corresponding oval on your answer sheet.

Questions 26 - 34 are based on the following draft of an essay:

(1) *We think of any cartoon drawing that appears on the funny page of a newspaper as a comic strip.* (2) *However, a true comic strip must have a number of panels—usually four, except on Sundays, when there are usually more.* (3) *While most comic strips are indeed funny, some are not comic at all.* (4) *"Mary Worth" and "Prince Valiant," to name two, are strips with ongoing dramatic or adventure-based story lines.*

(5) *Single-panel cartoons, such as "Dennis the Menace" and "Family Circus," are not truly comic strips.* (6) *The first comic strips appeared in newspapers just before the beginning of the twentieth century.* (7) *"The Katzenjammer Kids" was one of the first.* (8) *Other strips from the same time were "Mutt and Jeff" and "Buster Brown," all three of which remain familiar names.* (9) *Within a few decades, the movies were popular and cartoonists were creating films of popular comic-strip characters.* (10) *Many popular comic strips were animated by Hollywood.* (11) *Perhaps the most popular was "Popeye."* (12) *The strip lent itself perfectly to sound film, because of its many action sequences and reliance on verbal humor.* (13) *Comic strips also spawned another industry: comic books.* (14) *Dramatic strips were collected particularly and printed in book form, with an entire adventure or story line making up one book.*

26. Which of the following is the best way to revise the underlined portion of sentence 2 (reproduced below)?

    However, a true comic strip must have a number of panels—usually four, except on Sundays, when there are usually more.

    (A) four is the usual number, but on Sunday there's more
    (B) while there are usually four, there are usually more on Sunday
    (C) usually four, although Sunday strips usually have more
    (D) the number on all days but Sunday is four, with more then, usually
    (E) numbering four usually, with more on Sunday

27. The author could improve sentence 4 by replacing the word "with" with the phrase

    (A) that present
    (B) which are using
    (C) being composed by
    (D) whose intent is
    (E) possessed of

28. Sentence 5 should be moved so that it appears between sentences

    (A) 2 and 3
    (B) 3 and 4
    (C) 7 and 8
    (D) 10 and 11
    (E) 12 and 13

GO ON TO THE NEXT PAGE.

29. Which of the following is the best way to revise and combine sentences 7 and 8 (reproduced below)?

"The Katzenjammer Kids" was one of the first. Other strips from the same time were "Mutt and Jeff" and "Buster Brown," all three of which remain familiar names.

(A) "The Katzenjammer Kids," "Mutt and Jeff," and "Buster Brown" remain familiar names, despite the fact that they were early comic strips.
(B) First "The Katzenjammer Kids," then "Mutt and Jeff" and "Buster Brown" were early comic strips, they remain familiar today.
(C) Familiar today even though they were early are "The Katzenjammer Kids," "Mutt and Jeff," and "Buster Brown," all comic strips.
(D) Among those early comic strips, familiarity remains with "The Katzenjammer Kids," "Mutt and Jeff," and "Buster Brown."
(E) Among those early strips are some that remain familiar today, such as "The Katzenjammer Kids," "Mutt and Jeff," and "Buster Brown."

30. A third paragraph would best begin with sentence

(A) 7
(B) 8
(C) 9
(D) 11
(E) 14

31. The writer could best improve the passage by making which of the following changes to sentence 10?

(A) Change "by Hollywood" to "in Hollywood."
(B) Change "were" to "have been."
(C) Move the sentence so that it appears between sentences 8 and 9.
(D) Move the sentence so that it appears between sentences 11 and 12.
(E) Delete the sentence from the passage.

32. Which of the following describes the author's main goal in the first paragraph of the passage?

(A) Defining the term "comic strip"
(B) Presenting a complete history of the comic strip
(C) Distinguishing between comic strips and comic books
(D) Placing comic strips in a historical context with other graphic arts
(E) Resolving the debate over which comic strip was truly the first published in a newspaper

33. Which of the following words would most appropriately replace the word "spawned" in sentence 13?

(A) imagined
(B) generated
(C) manipulated
(D) opposed
(E) proposed

34. Which of the following is the best version of the underlined portion of sentence 14 (reproduced below)?

Dramatic strips were collected particularly and printed in book form, with an entire adventure or story line making up one book.

(A) (as it is now)
(B) would have been collected particularly
(C) were in particular collections
(D) in particular were collected
(E) are particularly collected

Questions 35 - 43 are based on the following draft of a student essay:

(1) *Ever since I can remember, my love for animals was always there.* (2) *Our house was a veritable menagerie, growing up.* (3) *We had house pets, three cats and two dogs, and a rabbit, in a small cage in the backyard.*

(4) *I finally got to go to the zoo for the first time for my fifth birthday party.* (5) *I was so excited that I couldn't sleep the night before.* (6) *When it came time to leave that morning, I ran out the front door to the car.* (7) *I wasn't disappointed.* (8) *I imagined the zoo would be the most wonderful place in the world that was full of strange, exotic animals I never saw before.* (9) *The first thing I saw were penguins.* (10) *My family, my friends, and me were lucky enough to arrive at feeding time.* (11) *The penguins were walking right up to their handlers and eating fish right out of their hands.* (12) *A fish would sometimes be thrown in the water, and a penguin would dive in after it, and eat it.* (13) *After that, a penguin would return to the land and strut about, as if proud.* (14) *We saw many other animals that day; my favorite is the hippopotamus.* (15) *Is it any wonder why now, a teenager, I work as a volunteer at that same zoo.*

35. Which of the following is the best way to revise the underlined portion of sentence 1 (reproduced below)?

    Ever since I can remember, <u>my love for animals was always there</u>.

    (A) my love for animals has always been there
    (B) my love was always for animals
    (C) I always love animals
    (D) I have always loved animals
    (E) what I love is animals, always

36. Which of the following revisions of sentence 3 (reproduced below) is both logical and grammatically correct?

    We had house pets, three cats and two dogs, and a rabbit, in a small cage in the backyard.

    (A) There were three cats and two dogs, house pets, and a rabbit, in a small cage, in the backyard.
    (B) In our backyard, we had a rabbit in a small cage, and five house pets, three cats and two dogs.
    (C) Of house pets, we had three cats and two dogs; in a small cage in the back yard, a rabbit.
    (D) In the backyard was a small cage, with a rabbit, in our house, three cats and two dogs.
    (E) Our family kept three cats and two dogs as house pets, and we also had a rabbit, which we kept in a small cage in the backyard.

37. Which of the following sentences, if added before sentence 4, would provide the best transition from the first to the second paragraph?

    (A) I loved all of my pets, although I loved my cocker spaniel, Snoops, best of all.
    (B) My birthday is on June 15.
    (C) As you might well imagine, from the time I could talk I was forever asking my parents to take me to see a zoo.
    (D) It was possible for us to keep all these animals because we lived in a rural area, where they had plenty of room to roam free when they needed to.
    (E) When I was a child, my parents usually took me and my friends to a baseball game on my birthday.

38. Sentence 7 would better fit the narrative flow of the passage if it appeared

    (A) before sentence 6
    (B) after sentence 8
    (C) before sentence 12
    (D) before sentence 16
    (E) after sentence 16

GO ON TO THE NEXT PAGE.

39. Which of the following is the best version of the underlined portion of sentence 8 (reproduced below)?

I imagined the zoo would be the most wonderful place in the <u>world that was full of strange, exotic animals I never saw before</u>.

(A) (as it is now)
(B) world, full of strange, exotic animals I had never seen before
(C) world, and that it was full of strange and exotic animals I have never before seen
(D) world, with strange, exotic animals never seen by me before to fill it
(E) world which is full of strange and exotic animals, and that I've never seen before

40. Which of the following words in sentence 10 needs to be changed in order for sentence 10 to be grammatically correct?

(A) me
(B) were
(C) enough
(D) to
(E) at

41. Which of the following is the best way to revise and combine sentences 12 and 13 (reproduced below)?

A fish would sometimes be thrown in the water, and a penguin would dive in after it, and eat it. After that, a penguin would return to the land and strut about, like it was proud.

(A) Occasionally a handler would throw a fish in the water, and a penguin would dive in after it, eat it, and, returning to the land, proudly strut about.
(B) Sometimes the handlers would throw fish into the water, and they would dive in after it and eat it, and then they would return to the land and strut about, as if proud.
(C) When a handler would throw a fish into the water, and a penguin would dive in after it and eat it, and afterwards return to the land and strut about like it was proud.
(D) A fish was sometimes being thrown into the water, and after it went a penguin, diving, eating, and then returning to the land and strutting about in pride.
(E) There were times where a handler would throw a fish into the water; that would cause a penguin to dive and eat it, then return to the land and, with pride, strut about.

42. The word "is" in sentence 14 should be replaced with the word

(A) are
(B) were
(C) was
(D) have been
(E) had been

GO ON TO THE NEXT PAGE.

43. Which of the following is the best way to revise sentence 15 (reproduced below)?

    Is it any wonder why now, a teenager, I work as a volunteer at that same zoo.

    (A) Is it any wonder why now I, a teenager, do volunteer work at the same zoo?
    (B) Do you wonder why I am now doing volunteer work as a teenager at that same zoo?
    (C) In case you are wondering, I work at that same zoo as a volunteer, now, as a teenager.
    (D) It should come as no surprise that, now that I am a teenager, I work as a volunteer at that same zoo.
    (E) Is it any wonder how I came to be a volunteering teenager working for the same zoo?

GO ON TO THE NEXT PAGE.

1 1 1 1 1 1 1 1 1 1 1 1 1

Directions: The following sentences test correctness and effectiveness of expression. In choosing answers, follow the requirements of standard written English: that is, pay attention to grammar, diction (choice of words), sentence construction, and punctuation.

In each of the following sentences, part of the sentence or the entire sentence is underlined. Beneath each sentence you will find five versions of the underlined part. Choice A repeats the original; the other four are different.

Choose the answer that best expresses the meaning of the original sentence. If you think the original is better than any of the alternatives, choose it; otherwise choose one of the others. Your choice should produce the most effective sentence—one that is clear and precise, without awkwardness or ambiguity.

Example:

Laura Ingalls Wilder published her first book <u>and she was sixty-five years old then</u>.

(A) and she was sixty-five years old then
(B) when she was sixty-five
(C) being age sixty-five years old
(D) upon the reaching of sixty-five years
(E) at the time when she was sixty-five

44. <u>Cataracts are spots on an eye's lens causing blurring, and it</u> can lead to blindness.

(A) Cataracts are spots on an eye's lens causing blurring, and it
(B) Cataracts are the spots on the lens of the eye that causes blurring, which
(C) Cataracts, spots on an eye's lens that cause blurring,
(D) On the lens of the eye may occur cataracts that cause blurring and it
(E) The blurring of the eye's lens are called cataracts, and it

45. The company must decide <u>whether they are going to have a lengthening of</u> employee's workweeks or hire more employees, but it must do one to increase productivity.

(A) whether they are going to have a lengthening of
(B) whether it will lengthen
(C) whether or not to have a lengthening of
(D) if they will be lengthening
(E) if they either lengthen the

46. <u>A tax decrease being wanted by the state's voters,</u> the bill's sponsor found the tax-break bill she sponsored passing through the legislature easily.

(A) A tax decrease being wanted by the state's voters,
(B) Being that state voters wanted a tax reduction,
(C) State voters have wanted a tax reduction, and then
(D) Because the state's voters wanted a tax reduction,
(E) When a reduction for taxes was wanted by the voters of the state,

47. A fossilized beaked bird found in China appears to have lived 147 million years ago, <u>predating the previously oldest known toothless bird</u> by almost 80 million years.

(A) predating the previously oldest known toothless bird
(B) predating the oldest bird previously thought to have no teeth
(C) making it older, regarding the toothless bird once thought oldest,
(D) and that puts it before the oldest known toothless bird, previously,
(E) and compared to the toothless bird previously though oldest it is older

GO ON TO THE NEXT PAGE.

48. Movie producers often spend <u>as much or more on advertising</u> a film as they spend on its shooting and production.

(A) as much or more on advertising
(B) as much as or more for advertising
(C) at least as much for the advertisement for
(D) at least as much on advertising
(E) at least as much, or more, on the advertising

49. The origin of much Appalachian folk music <u>had been</u> the ballad tradition of England and Scotland.

(A) had been
(B) is
(C) comes from
(D) originated with
(E) started at

50. Those who devised U.S. military policy in Vietnam wanted it <u>to defend South Vietnamese independence</u>, and also as a deterrent to future Communist military action.

(A) to defend South Vietnamese independence,
(B) to defend the independence of South Vietnam,
(C) defending the independence of South Vietnam
(D) to be defensive of South Vietnam and its independence
(E) to serve as a defense of South Vietnamese independence

51. The loss of the use of two fingers on his left hand did not <u>prevent Django Reinhardt to master</u> the art of jazz guitar.

(A) prevent Django Reinhardt to master
(B) prevent Django Reinhardt the mastering of
(C) prevent Django Reinhardt from mastering
(D) stop Django Reinhardt to master
(E) stop Django Reinhardt's mastery by

52. According to the political scientist Harrison Johnson, modern political discourse <u>is both more divisive and is less substantial than it was</u> at any time during this century.

(A) is both more divisive and is less substantial than it was
(B) is both more divisive and less substantial than it has been
(C) are both more divisive and less substantial than they were
(D) both has been more divisive and less substantive than it has been
(E) was both more divisive and less substantive than it was

53. William Carlos Williams, who was posthumously recognized as one of America's great twentieth-century poets, <u>lived like a relatively obscure</u> country doctor.

(A) lived like a relatively obscure
(B) lived his life in relative obscurity as a
(C) lived as though he were a relatively obscure
(D) was relatively obscure when he was a
(E) was relatively obscure, as a

54. Vampires seem to have been characters in our literary tradition <u>forever, their first literary appearance not occurring</u> until the Romantic period.

(A) forever, their first literary appearance not occurring
(B) forever, yet they literally appeared first not
(C) forever, even though the first appearance is not
(D) forever; however, their first appearances in literature did not occur
(E) forever; they will not appear in literature

GO ON TO THE NEXT PAGE.

55. Jesters and minstrels were to their time <u>what stand-up comedians and singer-songwriters are to</u> ours: entertainers whose work occasionally borders on social commentary.

(A) what stand-up comedians and singer-songwriters are to

(B) just like stand-up comedians and singer-songwriters are in

(C) similar to the stand-up comedian and singer-songwriter of

(D) just like a stand-up comedian and singer-songwriter is to

(E) what the stand-up comedian or singer-songwriter might be in

GO ON TO THE NEXT PAGE.

PART II

Time—45 minutes

45 questions

For English Composition without Essay Test

Directions: Each of the following selections is an early draft of a student essay in which the sentences have been numbered for easy reference. Some parts of the selections need to be changed.

Read each selection and then answer the questions that follow. Some questions are about particular sentences or parts of sentences and ask you to improve sentence structure and diction (word choice). In making these decisions, follow the conventions of standard written English. Other questions refer to the entire essay or parts of the essay and ask you to consider organization, development, and effectiveness of language in relation to purpose and audience. After you choose each answer, fill in the corresponding oval on your answer sheet.

Questions 56 - 64 are based on the following excerpt from a first draft of a magazine article:

(1) *Most people do not know this, but there are a number of mechanisms by which different types of bathroom scales measure weight.* (2) *In fact, there are four commonly used.* (3) *The most popular is the spring lever.* (4) *Should you step on a spring-lever scale, the springs expand and stretch the lever, which pulls the numbered dial to the correct reading.* (5) *Another you might know is the balance beam.* (6) *It is like the one used in a doctor's office.* (7) *To operate it, you slide weights across a beam until the beam is balanced.* (8) *The beam is balanced when the weights are so placed as to counterbalance what's on the scale.*

(9) *Most electronic scales use a strain-gauge mechanism.* (10) *Stretched beneath the platform is a small steel beam.* (11) *When weight is exerted on the platform, the small steel beam bends and stretches a wire, changing its resistance.* (12) *A computer calculates the resistance and translates it into a weight, which it displays in the read-out window.* (13) *Another type of electronic scale uses hydraulic pressure.* (14) *Instead of a steel beam, such a scale use two flexible containers, one full of liquid, the other empty.* (15) *A computer monitors the flow of fluid from one container to the other.* (16) *Cold tile floors and excessive humidity from hot showers can affect the accuracy of a scale.*

56. Which of the following is the best way to revise the underlined portion of sentence 1 (reproduced below)?

Most people do not know this, but there are a number of mechanisms by which different types of bathroom scales measure weight.

(A) There are
(B) This is not known to many people, the fact that there is
(C) Unknown by many, there are
(D) What many people do not know is that there are
(E) Many people would not know this; however, there is

57. Which of the following is the best way to revise and combine the underlined portion of sentences 2 and 3 (reproduced below)?

In fact, there are four commonly used. The most popular is the spring lever.

(A) In fact, there are four, which are used commonly, and most popular
(B) The fact is that four are common in use, most popularly
(C) The most popular of all in common usage, of which there are four,
(D) Four are used in common, and the one that is most popular
(E) There are four in common usage, the most popular of which

GO ON TO THE NEXT PAGE.

58. Which of the following would best replace "Should" at the beginning of sentence 4?

    (A) Whether
    (B) However
    (C) When
    (D) Because
    (E) Until

59. Which of the following is the best way to revise and combine sentences 5 and 6 (reproduced below)?

    Another you might know is the balance beam. It is like the one used in a doctor's office.

    (A) The balance beam is another one you might know, if you've ever been to a doctor's office.
    (B) Another common mechanism, often used for scales in doctors' offices, is the balance beam.
    (C) When you go to the doctor's office, you might see a balance beam, another popular scale mechanism.
    (D) Do you know about the balance beam, such as is found in a doctor's office?
    (E) As you may know, a doctor's office often has a balance beam scale.

60. The use of the word "what's" in sentence 8 is inappropriate because the word is

    (A) incorrectly contracted
    (B) impersonal, when a personal pronoun is required
    (C) not followed by a question mark, as it should be
    (D) too colloquial
    (E) too specific

61. Which of the following is the best version of sentence 10 (reproduced below)?

    Stretched beneath the platform is a small steel beam.

    (A) (As it is now)
    (B) A small steel beam stretches beneath the platform of a strain-gauge scale.
    (C) The mechanism stretches a small steel beam, beneath the platform.
    (D) This is the kind of scale where a small steel beam is stretched under the platform.
    (E) When a small steel beam is stretched beneath a platform, it is a strain-gauge mechanism.

62. Which of the following statements correctly identifies a grammatical error common to sentences 11 and 12?

    (A) Both are run-on sentences.
    (B) Both are sentence fragments.
    (C) Each contains at least one ambiguous pronoun.
    (D) Each shifts randomly from singular to plural verbs.
    (E) In each, the author shifts from the active to the passive voice.

63. Which of the following is the best way to revise the underlined portion of sentence 14 (reproduced below)?

    Instead of a steel beam, such a scale use two flexible containers, one full of liquid, the other empty.

    (A) Rather than a steel beam, this scale used two flexible containers
    (B) Two flexible containers being used instead of a steel beam
    (C) With a hydraulic scale, there is no steel beam, just two containers that are flexible
    (D) Hydraulic scales use two flexible containers
    (E) It is in the place of a steel beam, the use of two flexible containers

64. The relationship between sentence 16 and the rest of the passage would be strengthened if the author

    (A) used the sentence to start a new paragraph, and then continued with more information on the subject the sentence introduces
    (B) also mentioned, in sentence 16, how temperature and humidity affect each of the four types of scales discussed in the passage
    (C) moved the sentence to the beginning of the passage
    (D) stated which, cold tile floors or excessive humidity, more greatly distorts a scale's accuracy
    (E) deleted the phrase "from hot showers"

GO ON TO THE NEXT PAGE.

Directions: Effective revision requires choosing among the many options available to a writer. The following questions test your ability to use these options effectively.

Revise each of the sentences below according to the directions that follow it. Some directions require you to change only part of the original sentence; others require you to change the entire sentence. You may need to omit or add certain words in constructing an acceptable revision, but you should keep the meaning of your revised sentence as close to the meaning of the original sentence as the directions permit. Your new sentence should follow the conventions of standard written English and should be clear and concise.

Look through answer choices A-E under each question for the exact word or phrase that is included in your revised sentence and fill in the corresponding space on your answer sheet. If you have thought of a revision that does not include any of the words or phrases listed, try to revise the sentence again so that it does include the wording in one of the answer choices.

You may make notes in your test book, but be sure to mark your answers on the separate answer sheet.

Example:

Sentence: Owing to her political skills, Ms. French had many supporters.

Directions: *Begin with Many people supported*

    (A) so
    (B) while
    (C) although
    (D) because
    (E) and

Your rephrased sentence will probably read: "Many people supported Ms. French because she was politically skillful." This new sentence contains the correct answer: (D) because. None of the other choices will fit into an effective, grammatically correct sentence that retains the original meaning.

65. Although the guitar is now a mainstay of popular music, only a century ago it was used almost exclusively in flamenco music and obscure classical pieces.

    Begin with Only a century ago the guitar.
    (A) unlike
    (B) but now
    (C) even though
    (D) accordingly
    (E) therefore

66. We wondered why it was the quarterback, and not the halfback who scored four touchdowns, who received the award for the game's most valuable player.

    Change who received to received.
    (A) why was the quarterback
    (B) why did the quarterback
    (C) why would the quarterback
    (D) why the quarterback
    (E) why, if the quarterback

67. Many of the principles found in Enlightenment philosophy were embraced by the framers of the Constitution.

    Begin with Enlightenment philosophers.
    (A) with the framers of the Constitution embracing
    (B) caused the framers of the Constitution to embrace
    (C) and the framers of the Constitution embraced
    (D) of whom the framers of the Constitution embraced
    (E) which the framers of the Constitution embraced

GO ON TO THE NEXT PAGE.

68. The police did not have the manpower necessary to implement a thorough dragnet, and so the two fugitives managed to escape.

    Begin with <u>The two fugitives</u>.

    (A) because they
    (B) resulting from
    (C) as a result of which
    (D) because the police
    (E) since they

69. Even though Ralph Ellison completed only one novel during his lifetime, he is nonetheless counted among the great writers of the twentieth century by many.

    Begin with <u>Counted</u>.

    (A) many, even though
    (B) many, Ralph Ellison
    (C) many despite
    (D) many, nonetheless
    (E) many and completing

70. The professor announced that final grades would be based strongly on class participation, and only minimally on test results.

    Replace <u>based strongly</u> with <u>based less</u>.

    (A) as
    (B) and
    (C) opposed to
    (D) but
    (E) than

71. Of the three candidates we are currently considering for the job, Bill is certainly the most ambitious but least qualified.

    Change <u>three</u> to <u>two</u>.

    (A) most ambitious but less qualified
    (B) more ambitious and least qualified
    (C) most ambitious, least qualified
    (D) more ambitious, least qualified
    (E) more ambitious but less qualified

72. Major-league baseball teams are allowed to have twenty-five players on their rosters until the first of September, at which time they may expand their rosters to forty players.

    Begin with <u>On the first of September</u>.

    (A) players; before that date,
    (B) players when they may expand
    (C) players, until then
    (D) players, before September first
    (E) players; twenty-five

73. State law requires candidates to submit petitions with one thousand signatures from residents of each county to qualify for a ballot slot in a statewide election.

    Begin with <u>Candidates must</u>.

    (A) state law requires
    (B) it is required by state law
    (C) according to state law
    (D) state law requirements
    (E) are required by state law

74. The professor's book contained a detailed explanation of each of his three important economic theories.

    Change <u>explanation</u> to <u>explained</u>.

    (A) of each in detail
    (B) about each detailed
    (C) in detail of each
    (D) in detail each
    (E) of each detailed

GO ON TO THE NEXT PAGE.

Directions: Each of the following passages consists of numbered sentences. Because the passages are part of longer writing samples, they do not necessarily constitute a complete discussion of the issues presented.

Read each passage carefully and answer the questions that follow it. The questions test your awareness of a writer's purpose and of characteristics of prose that are important to good writing.

Question 75 - 83 refer to the following passage:

(1) *All I know about music is that not many people ever really hear it.* (2) *And even then, on the rare occasions when something opens within, and the music enters, what we mainly hear, or hear corroborated, are personal, private, vanishing evocations.* (3) *But the man who creates the music is hearing something else, is dealing with the roar rising from the void and imposing order on it as it hits the air.* (4) *What is evoked in him, then, is of another order, more terrible because it has no words, and triumphant, too, for that same reason.* (5) *And his triumph, when he triumphs, is ours.* (6) *I just watched Sonny's face.* (7) *His face was troubled, he was working hard, but he wasn't with it.* (8) *And I had the feeling that, in a way, everyone on the bandstand was waiting for him, both waiting for him and pushing him along.* (9) *But as I began to watch Creole, I realized that it was Creole who held them all back.* (10) *He had them on a short rein.* (11) *He was listening to Sonny.* (12) *He was having a dialogue with Sonny.* (13) *He wanted Sonny to leave the shoreline and strike out for deep water.* (14) *He was Sonny's witness that deep water and drowning were not the same thing—he had been there, he knew.*

75. It can be inferred that the narrator is

   (A) listening to a record
   (B) the doorman at a night club
   (C) a clarinetist attending a rehearsal
   (D) an audience member at a concert
   (E) a retired musician dictating his memoir

76. The author's assertions in sentences 1 and 2 are best characterized by which of the following?

   (A) It is useless to play music for an audience, because audiences do not appreciate music.
   (B) Audiences enjoy music not so much for its own sake as for something mysterious and personal it evokes in them.
   (C) People could be just as entertained contemplating their private thoughts as they are by a concert.
   (D) Audiences do not pay attention to the music when they go to see jazz played in a night club.
   (E) Music is to be valued solely for its therapeutic properties.

77. Which of the following best describes the relationship between the first two sentences and sentence 3?

   (A) The first two sentences present an assertion that sentence 3 refutes.
   (B) The first two sentences describe an event, and sentence 3 describes the author's reaction to that event.
   (C) Sentence 3 illustrates a point made in the first two sentences.
   (D) Sentence 3 draws a generalization based on specific points made in the first two sentences.
   (E) Sentence 3 contrasts the experiences of one group with the experiences of another described in the first two sentences.

GO ON TO THE NEXT PAGE.

78. Which of the following is closest to the meaning of the word "terrible" as it is used in sentence 4?

    (A) frightening
    (B) disgusting
    (C) distasteful
    (D) euphoric
    (E) of poor quality

79. Sonny and Creole are

    (A) actors
    (B) critics
    (C) musicians
    (D) ushers
    (E) bartenders

80. Which of the following best summarizes the event described in sentence 8?

    (A) Sonny finds a solution, which had previously eluded him, to what is troubling him.
    (B) Creole and Sonny enter into a dialogue.
    (C) The band takes a break and leaves the stage.
    (D) The narrator notes an observation that he later decides is incorrect.
    (E) Sonny abandons his work in despair.

81. The author uses which of the following for effect in sentences 10, 11, and 12?

    (A) florid descriptive terms
    (B) repetition and clipped cadence
    (C) surreal imagery
    (D) hyperbole
    (E) images of the ocean

82. In sentences 9 through 14, the author speculates that Creole is

    (A) angry with Sonny for not trying his hardest
    (B) cajoling Sonny into taking greater chances
    (C) using previous experiences as a swimmer to help Sonny
    (D) intentionally subverting Sonny's performance
    (E) waiting for Sonny to show up so the concert can begin

83. In sentences 13 and 14, the mentions of "shoreline" and "deep water" are

    (A) ironic
    (B) contradictory
    (C) metaphoric
    (D) primarily intended as visual imagery
    (E) meant to be interpreted literally

GO ON TO THE NEXT PAGE.

Questions 84 - 92 refer to the following passage:

(1) *The heavens seem to attract people who do not look at them very seriously.* (2) *In 1950, Immanuel Velikovsky, a psychoanalyst, wrote a book titled* Worlds in Collision. (3) *In it, he contended that at the time of the Exodus of the Israelites from Egypt in 1500 B.C., an encounter with a giant comet caused the earth either to slow down suddenly or to stop spinning altogether.* (4) *Among the consequences were floods, hurricanes, dust storms, fires, boiling seas, rivers the color of blood, the parting of the Red Sea, and the deposition of the manna that sustained the Israelites for forty years.* (5) *After fifty-two years the comet returned, causing among other things, the fall of the walls of Jericho.* (6) *In certain respects a very learned man, Velikovsky found evidence for these events not only in the Old Testament but also in the literature of other ancient cultures.*

(7) *Velikovsky was convinced that the giant comet sprang out of the planet Jupiter, had its two encounters with the earth, had an encounter with Mars, and then went on to become what is now the planet Venus.* (8) *Such a sequence of events, quite apart from what Velikovsky believed, were the consequences, calls for the abandonment of an entire edifice of observation and theory that physicists and astronomers have built since Galileo.* (9) *One can almost admire Velikovsky's imperturbable disregard of it.*

84. Which of the following describes the relationship of sentence 1 to the rest of the paragraph?

(A) It introduces one of the two contrasting groups that the rest of the passage describes.

(B) It establishes the author's credentials as an expert on the main subject of the passage.

(C) It explains how the argument that follows is organized.

(D) It presents an anecdote illustrative of a greater principle discussed later in the passage.

(E) It presents a generalization of which the rest of the passage is a single example.

85. The purpose of sentence 3 is to

(A) conclude a point introduced in sentence 2

(B) establish Velikovsky's credibility in order to later validate his research

(C) demonstrate that Velikovsky was a biblical scholar

(D) initiate a summary of the contents of Velikovsky's book

(E) suggest that Velikovsky's was the first effort to explain these phenomena scientifically

86. Which of the following best describes the function of sentence 4?

(A) It describes the effects of an incident that purportedly accounts for an episode of the Bible.

(B) It details the manner by which the comet described in sentence 3 caused the biblical events in question.

(C) It provides examples of occurrences typically synchronous with a comet's passing the Earth.

(D) It reconciles discrepancies between a biblical account and the geological record of the biblical era.

(E) It contradicts an argument previously made in the passage.

87. In sentence 6, the effect of using the phrase, "In certain respects a very learned man," is to

(A) imply that learning is not well evidenced in his astronomical speculations

(B) establish Velikovsky's credentials as an astronomer and theorist

(C) indicate the author's ambiguity regarding the validity of Velikovsky's theories

(D) disparage the profession of psychoanalysis

(E) clarify a previously mentioned dispute concerning Velikovsky's qualifications

GO ON TO THE NEXT PAGE.

88. Which of the following best describes the main purpose of sentence 6?

(A) to establish that Velikovsky did not rely exclusively on the Bible, but used numerous other sources

(B) both to describe Velikovsky's sources and to imply that his reliance on them represents a weakness in his methodology

(C) to contradict the assertion put forward in sentence 1

(D) to assert that Velikovsky was not trying to prove a religious point but was rather simply participating in a fundamental scientific inquiry

(E) to further demonstrate the possibility that rivers, under certain conditions, could turn the color of blood

89. The purpose of sentence 8 is to

(A) commend Velikovsky for his bravery and brinkmanship

(B) reflect on those theories of the origin of Venus that preceded Velikovsky's

(C) call into question the validity of the Old Testament as an historical source

(D) argue that great scientific advances often require one to break with precedent

(E) indicate a fundamental weakness in Velikovsky's theory

90. In sentence 8, the effect of the phrase, "quite apart from what Velikovsky believed were the consequences," is to

(A) indicate that the author feels unqualified to comment on the likelihood of such consequences

(B) argue that, regardless of those consequences, Velikovsky's work represents a hallmark advance in the field of astronomy

(C) remind the reader that those consequences are reported in the Old Testament

(D) summarily dismiss those consequences as also scientifically implausible

(E) assert that the sequence of events and their consequences must be considered separately

91. The author's tone throughout the passage is best described as one of

(A) reverence

(B) reportorial objectivity

(C) mean-spirited retaliation

(D) unbiased curiosity

(E) mild irony

92. Which sentences most clearly indicate the author's attitude toward Velikovsky's work?

(A) 1, 2, and 3

(B) 1, 2, and 7

(C) 1, 8, and 9

(D) 2, 4, and 5

(E) 3, 4, and 5

GO ON TO THE NEXT PAGE.

Directions: The following sentences test you knowledge of grammar, diction (choice of words), and idiom.

Some sentences are correct.

No sentence contains more than one error.

You will find that the error, if there is one, is underlined and lettered. Assume that elements of the sentence that are not underlined are correct and cannot be changed. In choosing answers, follow the requirements of standard written English.

If there is an error, select the one underlined part that must be changed to make the sentence correct and fill in the corresponding oval on your answer sheet.

If there is no error, select answer (E).

Example:

The other delegates and him immediately accepted the resolution drafted by the neutral states.
  A   B   C   D

No error
E

Ⓐ ● Ⓒ Ⓓ Ⓔ

93. Like many of the nation's great heroes,

Thomas Jefferson's life has been
           A

so thoroughly mythologized that it is difficult
      B   C

to separate biographical fact from fiction.
                        D

No error
E

94. During yesterday's game, the quarterback
    A   B

had sustained a crushing blow to the knees,
     C

rendering him immobile for several minutes.
           D

No error
E

95. Accepting her fate with all the inner strength
    A   B

she could muster, the martyr endured her
            C   D

execution in tranquil repose. No error
                     E

96. The teacher, by both constantly cajoling the
                  A

students to work harder and gradually
       B

increasing the level of difficulty of their

assignments, somehow manage to achieve the
              C

best improvements in the school system

year after year. No error
     D   E

97. The doctor recommended that the patient

should cut down her consumption of salty
  A   B

foods, because the patient was beginning
                    C

to show warning signs of hypertension.
  D

No error
E

GO ON TO THE NEXT PAGE.

98. The need for a traffic light at <u>the corner of</u>
                                          A

    Elm and Third <u>was amply demonstrated</u> by
                           B

    the two collisions that <u>occurred</u>
                              C

    <u>at that intersection</u> last night. <u>No error</u>
             D   E

99. <u>The necessity of</u> lowering <u>the crime rate</u> in
           A   B

    our neighborhood <u>is a task</u> too great to be
                          C

    handled <u>by a group of</u> resident volunteers
                    D

    alone. <u>No error</u>
                  E

100. It is <u>better</u> to keep your mouth shut
              A

     <u>and make people</u> wonder whether
              B

     <u>you are ignorant</u> than <u>opening</u> it and
              C   D

     removing all doubt. <u>No error</u>
                                E

STOP

IF YOU FINISH BEFORE TIME IS CALLED, YOU MAY CHECK YOUR WORK ON THIS SECTION ONLY.
DO NOT WORK ON ANY OTHER SECTION IN THE TEST.

SCORING YOUR TEST

This test is a facsimile of the ETS-written CLEP general exam in English Composition. Care has been taken to make sure that this test closely resembles the actual exam both in content and format. In other words, when you take the real CLEP, it should look a lot like the test you've just taken.

ETS has never released its scoring methods for the CLEP. ETS states in its literature that, if you get half the raw score points available to you on the test, you should score the national medium–usually between 480 and 500–on a given test.

Your raw score is determined by subtracting 1/4 the number of questions you answer incorrectly from the number of questions you answer correctly. Questions you leave blank are worth 0 points.

Typically, you need about 2/3 of the raw score points available on a test to score in the mid-600s on an ETS test, but, again, this is only speculation regarding the CLEP.

8

Answers and Explanations to the English Composition Exam

SECTION 1

QUESTIONS	EXPLANATIONS

Read this entire section, even the explanations for the questions you answered correctly. The material covered in these explanations add up to a pretty thorough review of the material tested on the CLEP. Plus, many explanations contain helpful test-taking tips.

1. After <u>she attends</u> a session of the general
                A

   assembly, Patricia decided <u>that</u> she
                          B

   <u>wanted to learn</u> more about <u>the history of</u> the
       C   D

   United Nations. <u>No error</u>
                  E

1. **(A)** is the correct answer. The word "decided" is the tip-off that this sentence is in the past tense. Answer choice (A) is in the present tense; it should read "she attended."

2. Everyone <u>who went to</u> the conference,
                A

   <u>which attracted</u> eight hundred participants,
     B

   expressed <u>their</u> satisfaction <u>with the event</u>
              C   D

   during the exit survey. <u>No error</u>
                     E

2. **(C)** is the correct answer. The collective noun "everyone" is singular and must take a singular pronoun. Because "their" is plural, it is incorrect. In its place should be "he," "she," or the awkward but neutral "s/he."

3. The author James Joyce <u>used</u> a "stream-of-
                      A

   consciousness" <u>technique</u> <u>to simulate</u> the
                B   C

   muddled, rambling manner <u>in</u> which human
                        D

   beings think. <u>No error</u>
             E

3. **(E)** is the correct answer. No problem here. Remember, about one in five of these will be correct as written; do not feel compelled to find an error in every single sentence.

4. Laws <u>requiring states to</u> notify communities
            A

   of the presence <u>of sex offenders</u> <u>violates</u> the
                  B   C

   constitutional guarantee against double

   jeopardy, according <u>to some</u> civil libertarians.
                      D

   <u>No error</u>
     E

4. **(C)** is the correct answer. The verb, "violates," does not agree with its subject, "Laws." Because you can't change the subject, you have to change the verb.

SECTION 1

QUESTIONS	EXPLANATIONS

5. The reason Patty wants <u>to buy</u> a new car
                          A

<u>is because</u> the cost <u>of</u> repairing her used car
   B   C

would be <u>greater than</u> its current value.
            D

<u>No error</u>
  E

5. **(B)** is the correct answer. "The reason . . . is because" is unidiomatic and redundant. "The reason . . . is that" would be better in this instance.

6. The prime minister agreed that <u>his cabinet</u>
                        A

members and <u>him</u> should be <u>subject to</u> the
        B   C

same laws <u>that govern</u> all citizens. <u>No error</u>
      D   E

6. **(B)** is the correct answer. In this situation, rewrite the sentence in your head, deleting the phrase "his cabinet members and." Now you have "The prime minister agreed that him should be subject. . ." It should be obvious now that "him" is incorrect.

7. Distillation, the process of <u>separating</u>
                       A

different components of a liquid <u>by heating</u>
                              B

the liquid, <u>that utilizes</u> the principle that
        C

<u>different molecules</u> become agitated at
      D

different temperatures. <u>No error</u>
              E

7. **(C)** is the correct answer. Here the test writers separate the subject and the verb and hope that you forget to reconnect them. Eliminate the appositive (a descriptive phrase between commas, in this case describing "Distillation") and you have "Distillation that utilizes the principle that different molecules become agitated at different temperatures." That is a sentence fragment. When you change "that utilizes" to "utilizes," the sentence makes sense.

8. The shop owner set out <u>to accomplish</u> three
                      A

budgetary goals: to <u>reduce</u> inventory, to
              B

lower <u>worker-related</u> expenses, and
        C

<u>eliminating</u> unnecessary advertising
    D

expenditures. <u>No error</u>
        E

8. **(D)** is the correct answer. (D) violates the rule of parallel construction. "The shop owner set out to accomplish" three things; those three things must be parallel in the sentence. Properly, those three things would be "to reduce," "to lower," and "<u>to eliminate</u>."

SECTION 1

9. <u>Faced with</u> declining revenues, the city
   A

   council had <u>to decide</u> between the
   B

   <u>equally unpleasant</u> options <u>of cutting</u> the
   C D

   education budget and raising taxes. <u>No error</u>
   E

9. **(E)** is the correct answer. No errors here; sorry. Note that words and phrases that are perfectly well constructed start to look like they might be wrong just because they are underlined. Don't fall into that trap; try to ignore the underlines while reading the sentence through.

10. Cesar is an <u>inconsistent student</u>: he performs
    A

    better in <u>classes</u> he enjoys, <u>such as</u> history,
    B C

    than <u>those</u> he doesn't like. <u>No error</u>
    D E

10. **(D)** is the correct answer. This is a tough one. As written, this sentence violates the "apples and oranges" rule. Properly the sentence should read that "Cesar performs better in classes he enjoys . . . than <u>in those</u> he doesn't like." Otherwise, the sentence says something nonsensical: that Cesar does better in classes he enjoys than <u>the classes he doesn't like</u> do in classes he enjoys. Yes, it makes no sense, but in written English you have to obey the rules, even when your intended meaning is obvious.

11. The principal's decision <u>to cancel</u> the
    A

    assembly <u>was influenced</u> as much <u>by</u> the
    B C

    students' lack of interest <u>than</u> by the absence
    D

    of the main scheduled speaker. <u>No error</u>
    E

11. **(D)** is the correct answer. This is an idiom question. Note that "as much" is not underlined, so you're stuck with it. You must complete the phrase "as much by . . ." with the phrase "as by . . ." somewhere further along in the sentence.

12. <u>Because</u> our roof <u>was not designed</u> to bear a
    A B

    great deal of weight, we were afraid it would

    <u>cave in</u> the day after two feet of <u>snow fell</u>.
    C D

    <u>No error</u>
    E

12. **(E)** is the correct answer. If you got this wrong, you probably picked (A) or (D). If you picked (A), it was because somewhere a long time ago someone erroneously taught you that it was impossible to begin a sentence with the word "because." While (D) sounds funny, it is perfectly correct; the snow fell in the past, and the verb is in the past tense.

SECTION 1

13. Although antibiotics appear to provide the

    remedy <u>to many</u> an infection, <u>its</u> overuse
    A B

    <u>have led</u> to the rapid evolution of <u>hardier</u>,
    C D

    drug-resistant strains of numerous diseases.

    <u>No error</u>
    E

13. **(B)** is the correct answer. Pronoun error. "Its" (singular) should agree with "antibiotics" (plural). If you chose (C), you recognized that there was an agreement error—but you chose to correct the wrong one. Unfortunately, you do not receive partial credit for this insight.

14. The Celsius scale is <u>named after</u> the Swedish
    A

    astronomer Anders Celsius, <u>who was</u> the first
    B

    <u>describing</u> the <u>properties of</u> the centigrade
    C D

    thermometer. <u>No error</u>
    E

14. **(C)** is the correct answer. Another tough one. This should read "to describe," not "describing." Remember that "-ing" words are often in the incorrect answers in the error identification and sentence correction sections of the test, because words ending in "-ing" can be adjectives (participles), nouns (gerunds), or verbs. They are, therefore, ambiguous. When in doubt, avoid ambiguity by using a word that does not end in "-ing."

15. The professor and class <u>decided to</u> reschedule
    A

    the discussion group for a different night,

    <u>the reason being</u> it was originally scheduled
    B

    during a religious holiday, which <u>would have</u>
    C

    prevented some <u>from attending</u>. <u>No error</u>
    D E

15. **(B)** is the correct answer. "The reason being" is an awkward construction. Remember the "being" rule; answer choices with the word "being" in them are wrong 90 percent of the time. You will be right much more often than you'll be wrong if you always assume that the word "being" is used incorrectly on the CLEP exam.

QUESTIONS	EXPLANATIONS

16. "Everlasting" is the name given to a group of plants whose leaves, while not truly eternal, maintain their original color and form <u>for a long time after it has fallen from its plant</u>.

   (A) for a long time after it has fallen from its plant

   (B) for a long time after they had fallen off the plant

   (C) for a long time after it fell

   (D) long after they have fallen

   (E) long after it had fallen

16. **(D)** is the correct answer. In (A), (C), and (E) "it" does not agree with its antecedent, "leaves." In (B), the verb tense is wrong. Remember, you cannot use the past perfect tense in a sentence unless you have also used the simple past tense.

17. <u>Carnival is the period preceding Lent in the Christian calendar, it</u> is marked by feasting and often mischievous acts of merriment.

   (A) Carnival is the period preceding Lent in the Christian calendar, it

   (B) Carnival is the period which, preceding Lent in the Christian calendar, and it

   (C) Carnival, the period preceding Lent in the Christian calendar,

   (D) The period which is preceding Lent in the Christian calendar being Carnival,

   (E) Preceding Lent in the Christian calendar is a period called Carnival,

17. **(C)** is the correct answer. In (A), you are presented with two independent clauses; they need a conjunction to connect them, or you can't join them in one sentence. (B) has the conjunction but, alas, a dependent clause up front; simplified, it reads "Carnival is a period which and it . . ." That makes no sense. (D) breaks the "being" rule. (E) has the unidiomatic "period called Carnival."

18. Although not as well-remembered as some of his contemporaries, <u>the body of work of Countee Cullen establish</u> him as one of the great poets of the Harlem Renaissance.

   (A) the body of work of Countee Cullen establish

   (B) the body of work created by Countee Cullen establishes

   (C) the body of work Countee Cullen created established

   (D) Countee Cullen created a body of work that establishes

   (E) Countee Cullen's body or work would establish

18. **(D)** is the correct answer. All the wrong answers have a misplaced modifier error. The clause "Although not as well-remembered as some of his contemporaries" describes Countee Cullen; therefore, Countee Cullen (not his body of work) must immediately follow the comma.

SECTION 1

QUESTIONS	EXPLANATIONS

19. Cú Chulainn, a central figure in medieval Irish mythology, was said to be favored by the gods, <u>who gifted him with seven fingers on each hand, seven</u> toes on each foot, and seven pupils in each eye.

   (A) who gifted him with seven fingers on each hand, seven
   (B) who gifted him with seven fingers on each hand, with seven
   (C) who gifted him with seven of each of the following: fingers on each hand,
   (D) whose gifts to him included each hand having seven fingers, seven
   (E) whose gifts included two hands, seven-fingered, seven

19. **(A)** is the correct answer. None of the incorrect answers maintains parallel construction.

20. Doctors who design weight-loss programs for patients would rather develop programs emphasizing exercise and sensible eating <u>as opposed to</u> those relying exclusively on a drastic reduction in caloric intake.

   (A) as opposed to
   (B) than
   (C) in contrast with
   (D) and not
   (E) versus

20. **(B)** is the correct answer. This is an idiom problem. "Doctors would rather . . ." The key is the word "rather," which needs the word "than" to correctly complete the comparison, as in "I would rather do well on the CLEP than do poorly; that's why I am reading this helpful book!"

21. Even though information reaches people from more sources than ever before, surveys <u>are consistently demonstrating that people today misconceive more than people of</u> the four previous decades.

   (A) are consistently demonstrating that people today misconceive more than people of
   (B) make it demonstrable that people today hold more misconceptions, being less informed than
   (C) make a consistent demonstration of people today misconceiving, more so than those from
   (D) demonstrate with consistency that today's people hold more misconceptions than do people of
   (E) consistently demonstrate that people today hold more misconceptions than did people during any of

21. **(E)** is the correct answer. (A) contains a needlessly complex verb structure ("are constantly demonstrating" instead of "demonstrate"), an apples and oranges error (it should read "more than <u>did</u> people"), and an idiom error ("people of the previous four decades"). (B) has a similar verb problem and a similar idiom problem. (C) is closer but still has an unnecessarily complicated verb and an idiom problem: those people aren't <u>from</u> the previous four decades in the way that someone is from, say, Florida. What we want is to indicate that we're talking about people who lived during the previous four decades. (E) makes that correction. (D) is wrong primarily because of a faulty verb tense ("do" is wrong; the sentence calls for the past tense, "did" here) and a misuse of the word "consistency," which makes the surveys sound like they have a measurable consistency, as do motor oil and cookie batter.

SECTION 1

QUESTIONS	EXPLANATIONS

22. Dancers are more likely to develop chronic foot problems <u>than other professions</u>.

   (A) than other professions
   (B) than are people in other professions
   (C) as opposed to people whose professions are different
   (D) in contrast to professions of others
   (E) compared against other professions

22. **(B)** is the correct answer. (A) contains a parallelism error, as the verb must be completed on both sides of the comparison, as it is in (B). (C), (D), and (E) are all idiomatically incorrect: the phrase "more likely" must be completed with the word "than."

23. More than any other individual, <u>the ascendancy of alternating current is Nikolai Tesla's responsibility</u>.

   (A) the ascendancy of alternating current is Nikolai Tesla's responsibility
   (B) the ascendancy of alternating current was caused by Nikolai Tesla
   (C) it was Nikolai Tesla who caused the ascendancy of alternating current
   (D) Nikolai Tesla's responsibility was the ascendancy of alternating current
   (E) Nikolai Tesla was responsible for the ascendancy of alternating current

23. **(E)** is the correct answer. All the incorrect answers contain misplaced modifier errors. The introductory modifying phrase "More than any other individual," describes Nikolai Tesla; the only way to make that clear is to follow the comma immediately with Tesla's name, as (E) does.

24. Because the debate had not been resolved at the scheduled time, the council voted to <u>continue on with</u> the discussion indefinitely.

   (A) continue on with
   (B) continue on
   (C) continue
   (D) keep on continuing
   (E) keep continuing

24. **(C)** is the correct answer. All the incorrect answer choices are unidiomatic. "Continue on" and "keep on continuing" are also redundant.

25. Bilingual education has mixed results: studies show that students in such programs <u>learn more quickly but</u> enter mainstream society much more slowly.

   (A) learn more quickly but
   (B) are quicker to learn, however
   (C) although learning quicker,
   (D) both learn more quickly as well as
   (E) are learning more quickly at the same time they

25. **(A)** is the correct answer. Remember, don't eliminate answer choice (A) on a sentence correction problem just because it "sounds funny." Parallelism must be maintained in this sentence, which is why "students . . . learn more quickly but enter . . . more slowly" is correct. (D) contains an idiom error; "both" in this case needs to be followed by "and," as in "I enjoy both chocolate and vanilla ice cream."

SECTION 1

QUESTIONS	EXPLANATIONS

Questions 26 - 34 are based on the following draft of an essay:

(1) *We think of any cartoon drawing that appears on the funny page of a newspaper as a comic strip.* (2) *However, a true comic strip must have a number of panels - usually four, except on Sundays, when there are usually more.* (3) *While most comic strips are indeed funny, some are not comic at all.* (4) *"Mary Worth" and "Prince Valiant," to name two, are strips with ongoing dramatic or adventure-based story lines.*

(5) *Single-panel cartoons, such as "Dennis the Menace" and "Family Circus," are not truly comic strips.* (6) *The first comic strips appeared in newspapers just before the beginning of the twentieth century.* (7) *"The Katzenjammer Kids" was one of the first.* (8) *Other strips from the same time were "Mutt and Jeff" and "Buster Brown," all three of which remain familiar names.* (9) *Within a few decades, the movies were popular and cartoonists were creating films of popular comic strip characters.* (10) *Many popular comic-strips were animated by Hollywood.* (11) *Perhaps the most popular was "Popeye."* (12) *The strip lent itself perfectly to sound film, because of its many action sequences and reliance on verbal humor.* (13) *Comic strips also spawned another industry: comic books.* (14) *Dramatic strips were collected particularly and printed in book form, with an entire adventure or story line making up one book.*

26. Which of the following is the best way to revise the underlined portion of sentence 2 (reproduced below)?

    However, a true comic strip must have a number of panels—usually four, except on Sundays, when there are usually more.

    (A) four is the usual number, but on Sunday there's more
    (B) while there are usually four, there are usually more on Sunday
    (C) usually four, although Sunday strips usually have more
    (D) the number on all days but Sunday is four, with more then, usually
    (E) numbering four usually, with more on Sunday

26. **(C)** is the correct answer. In (A), "there's" is singular when the plural is called for, and too colloquial. (B) has the vague and unnecessary "there are"; this can be said much more concisely, and is, in answer choice (C). (D), containing the phrase "with more then, usually," is vague and certainly not as concise as (C). (E) incorrectly uses the verb "numbering"; in this context, it means that the "number of panels is numbering . . . ," which is obviously redundant.

SECTION 1

QUESTIONS	EXPLANATIONS

27. The author could improve sentence 4 by replacing the word "with" with the phrase

    (A) that present
    (B) which are using
    (C) being composed by
    (D) whose intent is
    (E) possessed of

27. **(A)** is the correct answer. The word "with" in the original sentence means that the strips have, or present, ongoing dramatic plots. (B) is in the wrong tense, (C) violates the "being" rule, (D) posits a single intent for both strips, incorrectly stating that the two are singular in purpose (E) is just an unidiomatic use of the word "possessed."

28. Sentence 5 should be moved so that it appears between sentences

    (A) 2 and 3
    (B) 3 and 4
    (C) 7 and 8
    (D) 10 and 11
    (E) 12 and 13

28. **(A)** is the correct answer. Sentence 5 serves to define a comic strip and thus belongs in the first paragraph, in which the author sets out to accomplish that exact task. Thus, the answer must be (A) or (B). Because (4) continues a line of thought begun by (3), inserting (5) between them would unnecessarily interrupt the flow. (5) follows (2) very well, continuing its focus on the number of panels. Hence, (A) is the correct answer.

29. Which of the following is the best way to revise and combine sentences 7 and 8 (reproduced below)?

"The Katzenjammer Kids" was one of the first. Other strips from the same time were "Mutt and Jeff" and "Buster Brown," all three of which remain familiar names.

    (A) "The Katzenjammer Kids," "Mutt and Jeff," and "Buster Brown" remain familiar names, despite the fact that they were early comic strips.
    (B) First "The Katzenjammer Kids," then "Mutt and Jeff" and "Buster Brown" were early comic strips, they remain familiar today.
    (C) Familiar today even though they were early are "The Katzenjammer Kids," "Mutt and Jeff," and "Buster Brown," all comic strips.
    (D) Among those early comic strips, familiarity remains with "The Katzenjammer Kids," "Mutt and Jeff," and "Buster Brown."
    (E) Among those early strips are some that remain familiar today, such as "The Katzenjammer Kids," "Mutt and Jeff," and "Buster Brown."

29. **(E)** is the correct answer. (A) wrongly emphasizes that the strips listed "remain familiar names," when "remain familiar" would be more concise and less confusing. (B) is not a proper sentence: two independent clauses with no conjunction to tie them together. (C) is a garbled mess, with unnecessarily complicated verb structure ("they were early are") and the unidiomatic tag "all comic strips." You should know that there <u>has</u> to be a better way to construct this sentence. (D) has the odd, vague "familiarity remains with." Why not say that the strips remain familiar, instead? Answer choice (E) does, and so is the correct answer.

SECTION 1

QUESTIONS	EXPLANATIONS

30. A third paragraph would best begin with sentence

(A) 7
(B) 8
(C) 9
(D) 11
(E) 14

30. **(C)** is the correct answer. Sentence 9 introduces a new concept: how the comic strips influenced other media (first the movies, then comic books).

31. The writer could best improve the passage by making which of the following changes to sentence 10?

(A) Change "by Hollywood" to "in Hollywood."
(B) Change "were" to "have been."
(C) Move the sentence so that it appears between sentences 8 and 9.
(D) Move the sentence so that it appears between sentences 11 and 12.
(E) Delete the sentence from the passage.

31. **(E)** is the correct answer. Sentence 10 adds no information not already in sentence 9, so it can, and should, be deleted.

32. Which of the following describes the author's main goal in the first paragraph of the passage?

(A) defining the term "comic strip"
(B) presenting a complete history of the comic strip
(C) distinguishing between comic strips and comic books
(D) placing comic strips in a historical context with other graphic arts
(E) resolving the debate over which comic strip was truly the first published in a newspaper

32. **(A)** is the correct answer. Answer choice (B) is too broad; no one could present a complete history of anything in one paragraph. (C) addresses a subject not picked up by the passage until much later. Other graphic arts are not mentioned at all in the passage, so (D) is wrong, and because no debate such as the one mentioned in answer choice (E) is ever discussed, (E) is also wrong.

33. Which of the following words would most appropriately replace the word "spawned" in sentence 13?

(A) imagined
(B) generated
(C) manipulated
(D) opposed
(E) proposed

33. **(B)** is the correct answer. "To spawn" is "to produce"; "generate" is closest in meaning to "spawn." Substitute any of the other answers for "spawned" and reread the sentence. It should be apparent that the sentence makes no sense with any of the other four answer choices.

SECTION 1

34. Which of the following is the best version of the underlined portion of sentence 14 (reproduced below)?

    Dramatic strips were collected particularly and printed in book form, with an entire adventure or story line making up one book.

    (A) (as it is now)
    (B) would have been collected particularly
    (C) were in particular collections
    (D) in particular were collected
    (E) are particularly collected

34. **(D)** is the correct answer. Because "particularly" is an adverb, its usage in the original sentence is incorrect. The author wants to tell us that "dramatic strips in particular" were collected, not that they were "collected particularly." Answer choices (B) and (E) fail for the same reason. If you chose (C), you probably didn't see the word "collections." Go back and read the whole sentence, substituting answer choice (C) for the underlined portion, and you'll see that (C) makes no sense in context.

SECTION 1

Questions 35 - 43 are based on the following draft of a student essay:

(1) *Ever since I can remember, my love for animals was always there.* (2) *Our house was a veritable menagerie, growing up.* (3) *We had house pets, three cats and two dogs, and a rabbit, in a small cage in the backyard.*

(4) *I finally got to go to the zoo for the first time for my fifth birthday party.* (5) *I was so excited that I couldn't sleep the night before.* (6) *When it came time to leave that morning, I ran out the front door to the car.* (7) *I wasn't disappointed.* (8) *I imagined the zoo would be the most wonderful place in the world that was full of strange, exotic animals I never saw before.* (9) *The first thing I saw were penguins.* (10) *My family, my friends, and me were lucky enough to arrive at feeding time.* (11) *The penguins were walking right up to their handlers and eating fish right out of their hands.* (12) *A fish would sometimes be thrown in the water, and a penguin would dive in after it, and eat it.* (13) *After that, a penguin would return to the land and strut about, as if proud.* (14) *We saw many other animals that day; my favorite is the hippopotamus.* (15) *Is it any wonder why now, a teenager, I work as a volunteer at that same zoo.*

35. Which of the following is the best way to revise the underlined portion of sentence 1 (reproduced below)?

    Ever since I can remember, my love for animals was always there.

    (A) my love for animals has always been there
    (B) my love was always for animals
    (C) I always love animals
    (D) I have always loved animals
    (E) what I love is animals, always

35. **(D)** is the correct answer. Answer choice (A), while close, states "my love . . . has always been there" without telling us where "there" is. (C) and (E) are incorrectly in the present, and not the past, tense. (B) is unidiomatic and implies that the author loved <u>only</u> animals; lacking any other evidence, let's give the author the benefit of the doubt and assume s/he loved his/her family, too. Answer choice (D) leaves open that possibility.

SECTION 1

36. Which of the following revisions of sentence 3 (reproduced below) is both logical and grammatically correct?

    We had house pets, three cats and two dogs, and a rabbit, in a small cage in the backyard.

    (A) There were three cats and two dogs, house pets, and a rabbit, in a small cage, in the backyard.
    (B) In our backyard, we had a rabbit in a small cage, and five house pets, three cats and two dogs.
    (C) Of house pets, we had three cats and two dogs; in a small cage in the back yard, a rabbit.
    (D) In the backyard was a small cage, with a rabbit, in our house, three cats and two dogs.
    (E) Our family kept three cats and two dogs as house pets, and we also had a rabbit, which we kept in a small cage in the backyard.

36. **(E)** is the correct answer. Answer choices (A) and (B) leave it unclear as to whether the house pets were kept in one small cage with a rabbit, in the backyard, or in the house. Of the remaining choices, (E) is clearest on this issue, and also correctly emphasizes the main point, which is that the family kept animals. (D), on the other hand, emphasizes the animals' housing, while (C) reads like an inventory and states in the passive voice an idea that could be as well expressed in the active voice.

37. Which of the following sentences, if added before sentence 4, would provide the best transition from the first to the second paragraph?

    (A) I loved all of my pets, although I loved my cocker spaniel, Snoops, best of all.
    (B) My birthday is on June 15.
    (C) As you might well imagine, from the time I could talk I was forever asking my parents to take me to see a zoo.
    (D) It was possible for us to keep all these animals because we lived in a rural area, where they had plenty of room to roam free when they needed to.
    (E) When I was a child, my parents usually took me and my friends to a baseball game on my birthday.

37. **(C)** is the correct answer. The transition between paragraphs, in the original draft, is abrupt because it jumps from the subject of house pets to the subject of a visit to the zoo with no transitional sentence. Answer choice (C) provides that transition, connecting the author's love for animals with his/her desire to visit the zoo. None of the other answer choices incorporates both of these subjects.

SECTION 1

QUESTIONS	EXPLANATIONS

38. Sentence 7 would better fit the narrative flow of the passage if it appeared

    (A) before sentence 6
    (B) after sentence 8
    (C) before sentence 12
    (D) before sentence 16
    (E) after sentence 16

38. **(B)** is the correct answer. In its current location, sentence 7 states that the author "wasn't disappointed" by running out to the car. Given the overall subject of the passage, it would make more sense that the author was describing his/her feelings about the visit to the zoo. Hence, it should follow sentence 8, in which the author discusses his/her anxious anticipation of the visit to the zoo.

39. Which of the following is the best version of the underlined portion of sentence 8 (reproduced below)?

I imagined the zoo would be the most wonderful place in the world that was full of strange, exotic animals I never saw before.

    (A) (as it is now)
    (B) world, full of strange, exotic animals I had never seen before
    (C) world, and that it was full of strange and exotic animals I have never before seen
    (D) world, with strange, exotic animals never seen by me before to fill it
    (E) world which is full of strange and exotic animals, and that I've never seen before

39. **(B)** is the correct answer. Answer choice (A) uses the simple past ("saw") when the past perfect ("had seen") would be more appropriate because the sentence describes something that happened before something else in the past. Answer choice (C) incorrectly uses the present perfect ("I have never before seen"), as does (E). Answer choice (D) has lots of syntax errors, the worst of which is the way "to fill it" is separated from "strange, exotic animals," leaving in doubt whether "to fill it" accompanies "animals" or the "me."

40. Which of the following words in sentence 10 needs to be changed in order for sentence 10 to be grammatically correct?

    (A) me
    (B) were
    (C) enough
    (D) to
    (E) at

40. **(A)** is the correct answer. Reread the sentence eliminating "My family, my friends, and." The sentence would read "I was lucky," not "Me was lucky."

SECTION 1

QUESTIONS	EXPLANATIONS

41. Which of the following is the best way to revise and combine sentences 12 and 13 (reproduced below)?

A fish would sometimes be thrown in the water, and a penguin would dive in after it, and eat it. After that, a penguin would return to the land and strut about, like it was proud.

(A) Occasionally a handler would throw a fish in the water, and a penguin would dive in after it, eat it, and, returning to the land, proudly strut about.

(B) Sometimes the handlers would throw fish into the water, and they would dive in after it and eat it, and then they would return to the land and strut about, as if proud.

(C) When a handler would throw a fish into the water, and a penguin would dive in after it and eat it, and afterwards return to the land and strut about like it was proud.

(D) A fish was sometimes being thrown into the water, and after it went a penguin, diving, eating, and then returning to the land and strutting about in pride.

(E) There were times where a handler would throw a fish into the water; that would cause a penguin to dive and eat it, then return to the land and, with pride, strut about.

41. **(A)** is the correct answer. Answer choice (B) has a vague pronoun: does "they" refer to the penguins or the handlers? (C) is not a complete sentence, because the dependent clause "When a handler would throw a fish into the water" is never completed. (D) violates the "being" rule, and, like (C), is not a complete sentence. (E) joins two independent clauses but fails to use a conjunction; this choice would be better (although still worse than answer choice (A)) if the word "and" were inserted prior to the phrase "that would cause a penguin . . ."

42. The word "is" in sentence 14 should be replaced with the word

(A) are
(B) were
(C) was
(D) have been
(E) had been

42. **(C)** is the correct answer. The simple past is the appropriate tense here, as the author is recounting the events of his/her fifth birthday party.

SECTION 1

QUESTIONS	EXPLANATIONS

43. Which of the following is the best way to revise sentence 15 (reproduced below)?

Is it any wonder why now, a teenager, I work as a volunteer at that same zoo.

(A) Is it any wonder why now I, a teenager, do volunteer work at the same zoo?

(B) Do you wonder why I am now doing volunteer work as a teenager at that same zoo?

(C) In case you are wondering, I work at that same zoo as a volunteer, now, as a teenager.

(D) It should come as no surprise that, now that I am a teenager, I work as a volunteer at that same zoo.

(E) Is it any wonder how I came to be a volunteering teenager working for the same zoo?

43. **(D)** is the correct answer. Answer choices (B) and (C) state, oddly, that the author's job at the zoo is to be a teenager. Of the remaining answer choices, (D) is the clearest articulation of the idea presented.

44. <u>Cataracts are spots on an eye's lens causing blurring, and it</u> can lead to blindness.

(A) Cataracts are spots on an eye's lens causing blurring, and it

(B) Cataracts are the spots on the lens of the eye that causes blurring, which

(C) Cataracts, spots on an eye's lens that cause blurring,

(D) On the lens of the eye may occur cataracts that cause blurring and it

(E) The blurring of the eye's lens are called cataracts, and it

44. **(C)** is the correct answer. Answer choice (A) contains a pronoun agreement error, because "it" is singular and "cataracts" is plural. Answer choices (B), (D), and (E) incorrectly state that it is the blurring, and not the cataracts, that result in blindness.

45. The company must decide <u>whether they are going to have a lengthening of</u> employee's work-weeks or hire more employees, but it must do one to increase productivity.

(A) whether they are going to have a lengthening of

(B) whether it will lengthen

(C) whether or not to have a lengthening of

(D) if they will be lengthening

(E) if they either lengthen the

45. **(B)** is the correct answer. Answer choices (A), (D), and (E) contain a pronoun agreement error, because "company" is singular and "they" is plural. In (C), the phrase, "to have a lengthening of" is both needlessly verbose and idiomatically incorrect.

SECTION 1

QUESTIONS	EXPLANATIONS

46. <u>A tax decrease being wanted by the state's voters</u>, the bill's sponsor found the tax break bill she sponsored passing through the legislature easily.

   (A) A tax decrease being wanted by the state's voters,

   (B) Being that state voters wanted a tax reduction,

   (C) State voters have wanted a tax reduction, and then

   (D) Because the state's voters wanted a tax reduction,

   (E) When a reduction for taxes was wanted by the voters of the state,

46. **(D)** is the correct answer. Answer choices (A) and (B) violate the "being" rule. Of the remaining choices, (D) most succinctly expresses the causal relationship: <u>Because</u> the voters wanted the decrease, the sponsor found her bill passing easily.

47. A fossilized beaked bird found in China appears to have lived 147 million years ago, <u>predating the previously oldest known toothless bird</u> by almost 80 million years.

   (A) predating the previously oldest known toothless bird

   (B) predating the oldest bird previously thought to have no teeth

   (C) making it older, regarding the toothless bird once thought oldest,

   (D) and that puts it before the oldest known toothless bird, previously,

   (E) and compared to the toothless bird previously though oldest it is older

47. **(A)** is the correct answer. Remember, don't eliminate answer choice (A) on a sentence correction problem just because it "sounds funny." In this case, (A) may not be very good, but it is the best of your choices.

48. Movie producers often spend <u>as much or more on advertising</u> a film as they spend on its shooting and production.

   (A) as much or more on advertising

   (B) as much as or more for advertising

   (C) at least as much for the advertisement for

   (D) at least as much on advertising

   (E) at least as much, or more, on the advertising

48. **(D)** is the correct answer. This is a common idiom question on the CLEP. Remember, "as much" needs to be completed with "as," and "more" needs to be completed with "than." However, there is a more succinct way of expressing this idea that "as much as or more than." That way is "at least as much." Eliminate (E) because it is redundant ("or more") and (C) because it is unidiomatic ("for the advertisement for").

SECTION 1

49. The origin of much Appalachian folk music <u>had been</u> the ballad tradition of England and Scotland.

    (A) had been
    (B) is
    (C) comes from
    (D) originated with
    (E) started at

49. **(B)** is the correct answer. Answer choice (A) incorrectly uses the past perfect tense. Answer choices (C), (D), and (E) are redundant, because the verbs repeat the subject ("origin").

50. Those who devised U.S. military policy in Vietnam wanted it <u>to defend South Vietnamese independence</u>, and also as a deterrent to future Communist military action.

    (A) to defend South Vietnamese independence,
    (B) to defend the independence of South Vietnam,
    (C) defending the independence of South Vietnam
    (D) to be defensive of South Vietnam and its independence
    (E) to serve as a defense of South Vietnamese independence

50. **(E)** is the correct answer. This is a parallel construction question. Look beyond the underlined section to find the phrase which you must parallel ("as a deterrent to . . . "). The correct answer must contain "as a defense." Therefore, the answer must be (E).

51. The loss of the use of two fingers on his left hand did not <u>prevent Django Reinhardt to master</u> the art of jazz guitar.

    (A) prevent Django Reinhardt to master
    (B) prevent Django Reinhardt the mastering of
    (C) prevent Django Reinhardt from mastering
    (D) stop Django Reinhardt to master
    (E) stop Django Reinhardt's mastery by

51. **(C)** is the correct answer. In answer choice (A), "prevent . . . to" is unidiomatic. In (B), "prevent . . . the mastering of" is unidiomatic. In (D), "stop . . . to" is unidiomatic. Know what's wrong with (E)? You guessed it! Also, (E) incorrectly states that Django was mastered by the guitar, when in fact the reverse is true: Django mastered the guitar.

QUESTIONS	EXPLANATIONS

52. According to the political scientist Harrison Johnson, modern political discourse <u>is both more divisive and is less substantial than it was</u> at any time during this century.

(A) is both more divisive and is less substantial than it was

(B) is both more divisive and less substantial than it has been

(C) are both more divisive and less substantial than they were

(D) both has been more divisive and less substantive than it has been

(E) was both more divisive and less substantive than it was

52. **(B)** is the correct answer. This is a tough parallelism problem. The proper construction here is "both <u>more</u> divisive and <u>less</u> substantial . . . " The extra "is" in answer choice (A) is not only unnecessary, it is wrong. Answer choice (C) has a subject/verb agreement problem ("discourse were"), answer choice (D) incorrectly uses the present perfect tense, and (E) incorrectly uses the past tense.

53. William Carlos Williams, who was posthumously recognized as one of America's great twentieth-century poets, <u>lived like a relatively obscure</u> country doctor.

(A) lived like a relatively obscure

(B) lived his life in relative obscurity as a

(C) lived as though he were a relatively obscure

(D) was relatively obscure when he was a

(E) was relatively obscure, as a

53. **(B)** is the correct answer. Answer choice (A) is bizarre; how exactly do you live "like a relatively obscure country doctor"? Such a simile might work in a poem, but it is too obscure for CLEP prose. Answer choice (C) makes essentially the same error. Williams didn't have to live "as though" he were an obscure doctor: he was an obscure doctor! The word "posthumously" indicates that Williams was not recognized as a great poet until after his death. Answer choice (B) reflects this information better than do answer choices (D) and (E), and is more concise.

54. Vampires seem to have been characters in our literary tradition <u>forever, their first literary appearance not occurring</u> until the romantic period.

(A) forever, their first literary appearance not occurring

(B) forever, yet they literally appeared first not

(C) forever, even though the first appearance is not

(D) forever; however, their first appearances in literature did not occur

(E) forever; they will not appear in literature

54. **(D)** is the correct answer. Answer choice (A) contains two independent clauses, but lacks a transition that would make it a proper sentence. Answer choice (B) misuses the word "literally" and uses awkward syntax in placing the word "not." Answer choice (C) is vague because it uses the word "the" when "their" would be more appropriate. Answer choice (E) incorrectly uses the future tense.

SECTION 1

QUESTIONS	EXPLANATIONS

QUESTIONS

55. Jesters and minstrels were to their time <u>what stand-up comedians and singer-songwriters are to</u> ours: entertainers whose work occasionally borders on social commentary.

    (A) what stand-up comedians and singer-songwriters are to
    (B) just like stand-up comedians and singer-songwriters are in
    (C) similar to the stand-up comedian and singer-songwriter of
    (D) just like a stand-up comedian and singer-songwriter is to
    (E) what the stand-up comedian or singer-songwriter might be in

EXPLANATIONS

55. **(A)** is the correct answer. It's a typical (A)-type answer, in that it looks horrible. Maintain parallelism: "Jesters and minstrels were <u>to</u> their time what stand-up comedians and singer-songwriters are <u>to</u> ours . . ."

QUESTIONS	EXPLANATIONS

PART II

<u>Questions 56 - 64</u> are based on the following excerpt from a first draft of a magazine article:

(1) *Most people do not know this, but there are a number of mechanisms by which different types of bathroom scales measure weight. (2) In fact, there are four commonly used. (3) The most popular is the spring lever. (4) Should you step on a spring-lever scale, the springs expand and stretch the lever, which pulls the numbered dial to the correct reading. (5) Another you might know is the balance beam. (6) It is like the one used in a doctor's office. (7) To operate it, you slide weights across a beam until the beam is balanced. (8) The beam is balanced when the weights are so placed as to counterbalance what's on the scale.*

(9) *Most electronic scales use a strain-gauge mechanism. (10) Stretched beneath the platform is a small steel beam. (11) When weight is exerted on the platform, the small steel beam bends and stretches a wire, changing its resistance. (12) A computer calculates the resistance and translates it into a weight, which it displays in the read-out window. (13) Another type of electronic scale uses hydraulic pressure. (14) Instead of a steel beam, such a scale use two flexible containers, one full of liquid, the other empty. (15) A computer monitors the flow of fluid from one container to the other. (16) Cold tile floors and excessive humidity from hot showers can affect the accuracy of a scale.*

56. Which of the following is the best way to revise the underlined portion of sentence 1 (reproduced below)?

    Most people do not know this, but there are a number of mechanisms by which different types of bathroom scales measure weight.

    (A) There are
    (B) This is not known to many people, the fact that there is
    (C) Unknown by many, there are
    (D) What many people do not know is that there are
    (E) Many people would not know this; however, there is

56. **(A)** is the correct answer. The most concise answer choice is usually correct.

SECTION 1

QUESTIONS	EXPLANATIONS

57. Which of the following is the best way to revise and combine the underlined portion of sentences 2 and 3 (reproduced below)?

In fact, there are four commonly used. The most popular is the spring lever.

  (A) In fact, there are four, which are used commonly, and most popular

  (B) The fact is that four are common in use, most popularly

  (C) The most popular of all in common usage, of which there are four,

  (D) Four are used in common, and the one that is most popular

  (E) There are four in common usage, the most popular of which

57. **(E)** is the correct answer. In answer choice (B), the phrase "common in use" is unidiomatic. (C) has a vague modifying phrase ("of which there are four"). (D) confuses "common usage" with "used in common"; the two phrases have different meanings. This leaves you with (A) and (E). Go with the stuffier sounding one, (E). The phrase "are used commonly" in (A) is vague; does it mean that they are in common usage or that they are used in a common manner (i.e., in the way commoners would use them)? Don't be a classist snob: pick (E).

58. Which of the following would best replace "Should" at the beginning of sentence 4?

  (A) Whether
  (B) However
  (C) When
  (D) Because
  (E) Until

58. **(C)** is the correct answer. This one is pretty easy. Don't try to read too much into questions; sometimes they're just easy. When you encounter such a question, record the correct answer, say a brief word of gratitude to the higher power of your choice, and move on.

59. Which of the following is the best way to revise and combine sentences 5 and 6 (reproduced below)?

Another you might know is the balance beam. It is like the one used in a doctor's office.

  (A) The balance beam is another one you might know, if you've ever been to a doctor's office.

  (B) Another common mechanism, often used for scales in doctors' offices, is the balance beam.

  (C) When you go to the doctor's office, you might see a balance beam, another popular scale mechanism.

  (D) Do you know about the balance beam, such as is found in a doctor's office?

  (E) As you may know, a doctor's office often has a balance beam scale.

59. **(B)** is the correct answer. Answer choice (A) is too colloquial, as are (D) and (E). Compare (B) and (C); (C) has the phrase "you <u>might</u> see a balance beam," which unnecessarily focuses attention on the question "Under what circumstances might you see one? How might you miss it?" Answer choice (B) skirts the question and gets to the point at hand, which is that such scales are common in doctors' offices.

SECTION 1

60. The use of the word "what's" in sentence 8 is inappropriate because the word is

    (A) incorrectly contracted
    (B) impersonal, when a personal pronoun is required
    (C) not followed by a question mark, as it should be
    (D) too colloquial
    (E) too specific

60. **(D)** is the correct answer. In general, contractions are considered too colloquial for written English, although contracting "not" to the suffix "-n't", as in "don't" and "can't," is arguably acceptable. None of the other answers is even in the ballpark.

61. Which of the following is the best version of sentence 10 (reproduced below)?

    Stretched beneath the platform is a small steel beam.

    (A) (As it is now)
    (B) A small steel beam stretches beneath the platform of a strain-gauge scale.
    (C) The mechanism stretches a small steel beam, beneath the platform.
    (D) This is the kind of scale where a small steel beam is stretched under the platform.
    (E) When a small steel beam is stretched beneath a platform, it is a strain-gauge mechanism.

61. **(B)** is the correct answer. Answer choice (B), while a little longer, is also clearer than (A), and it uses the preferable active voice instead of the passive voice. Answer choice (C) tells us that the mechanism stretches the beam, which is incorrect; the stretched beam is in fact part of the mechanism, not something acted upon by it. Answer choice (D) misuses the word "where," which should be used to indicate location (a scale is not a place, so "where" is the wrong word in this instance). Answer choice (E) tells us that whenever you have a small steel beam stretched beneath a platform, you have a strain-gauge. This is simply untrue; according to the passage, a strain-gauge also requires a wire and a computer.

62. Which of the following statements correctly identifies a grammatical error common to sentences 11 and 12?

    (A) Both are run-on sentences.
    (B) Both are sentence fragments.
    (C) Each contains at least one ambiguous pronoun.
    (D) Each shifts randomly from singular to plural verbs.
    (E) In each, the author shifts from the active to the passive voice.

62. **(C)** is the correct answer. In sentence 11, it is unclear whether the word "its" refers to the bar or the wire. In sentence 12, it is unclear whether "it" refers to the computer or the resistance.

SECTION 1

63. Which of the following is the best way to revise the underlined portion of sentence 14 (reproduced below)?

    Instead of a steel beam, such a scale use two flexible containers, one full of liquid, the other empty.

    (A) Rather than a steel beam, this scale used two flexible containers
    (B) Two flexible containers being used instead of a steel beam,
    (C) With a hydraulic scale, there is no steel beam, just two containers that are flexible,
    (D) Hydraulic scales use two flexible containers,
    (E) It is in the place of a steel beam, the use of two flexible containers,

63. **(D)** is the correct answer. Answer choice (A) unnecessarily shifts the tense of the passage from the present to the past. Answer choice (B) violates the "being" rule. Answer choice (E) begins with an unnecessary and confusing pronoun: to what does "it" refer? Now you've got it down to (C) and (D). (D) is so concise and to the point, how could it be wrong as compared with (C)? Whereas (C) has the awkward construction "with . . . there is," and includes the verbose "containers that are flexible" when "flexible containers" would be both clearer and more concise.

64. The relationship between sentence 16 and the rest of the passage would be strengthened if the author

    (A) used the sentence to start a new paragraph, and then continued with more information on the subject the sentence introduces
    (B) also mentioned, in sentence 16, how temperature and humidity affect each of the four types of scales discussed in the passage
    (C) moved the sentence to the beginning of the passage
    (D) stated which, cold tile floors or excessive humidity, more greatly distorts a scale's accuracy
    (E) deleted the phrase "from hot showers"

64. **(A)** is the correct answer. Sentence 16 introduces a new subject: the accuracy of scales. As such it should start a new paragraph, and should be followed with more information on the subject. Otherwise, you would have a boring, not terribly informative, one-sentence paragraph.

65. Although the guitar is now a mainstay of popular music, only a century ago it was used almost exclusively in flamenco music and obscure classical pieces.

    Begin with Only a century ago the guitar.

    (A) unlike
    (B) but now
    (C) even though
    (D) accordingly
    (E) therefore

65. **(B)** is the correct answer. Your rephrased sentence will probably read: "Only a century ago the guitar was used almost exclusively in flamenco music and obscure classical pieces, but now it is a mainstay of popular music." Of the three available transitions that indicate a reversal—"unlike," "but now," and "even though"—"but now" fits most easily.

SECTION 1

QUESTIONS	EXPLANATIONS

66. We wondered why it was the quarterback, and not the halfback who scored four touchdowns, who received the award for the game's most valuable player.

    Change who received to received.

    (A) why was the quarterback
    (B) why did the quarterback
    (C) why would the quarterback
    (D) why the quarterback
    (E) why, if the quarterback

66. **(D)** is the correct answer. Your rephrased sentence will probably read: "We wondered <u>why the quarterback</u> received the game's most valuable player award, rather than the halfback who scored four touchdowns."

67. Many of the principles found in Enlightenment philosophy were embraced by the framers of the Constitution.

    Begin with Enlightenment philosophers.

    (A) with the framers of the Constitution embracing
    (B) caused the framers of the Constitution to embrace
    (C) and the framers of the Constitution embraced
    (D) of whom the framers of the Constitution embraced
    (E) which the framers of the Constitution embraced

67. **(E)** is the correct answer. Your rephrased sentence will probably read: "Enlightenment philosophers expressed ideas <u>which the framers of the Constitution embraced</u>."

68. The police did not have the manpower necessary to implement a thorough dragnet, and so the two fugitives managed to escape.

    Begin with The two fugitives.

    (A) because they
    (B) resulting from
    (C) as a result of which
    (D) because the police
    (E) since they

68. **(D)** is the correct answer. Your rephrased sentence will probably read: "The two fugitives managed two escape <u>because the police</u> did not have the manpower necessary to implement a thorough dragnet." If you chose answer choice (A) or (E), you fell for the old ambiguous pronoun trick: who would "they" be, the police or the fugitives?

SECTION 1

QUESTIONS	EXPLANATIONS

69. Even though Ralph Ellison completed only one novel during his lifetime, he is nonetheless counted among the great writers of the twentieth century by many.

    Begin with Counted.

    (A) many, even though
    (B) many, Ralph Ellison
    (C) many despite
    (D) many, nonetheless
    (E) many and completing

69. (B) is the correct answer. Your rephrased sentence will probably read: "Counted among the great writers of the twentieth century by <u>many, Ralph Ellison</u> completed only one novel during his lifetime." If you chose (D), you mistakenly assumed that every word in the original sentence must appear in your rephrased sentence.

70. The professor announced that final grades would be based strongly on class participation, and only minimally on test results.

    Replace based strongly with based less.

    (A) as
    (B) and
    (C) opposed to
    (D) but
    (E) than

70. **(E)** is the correct answer. Your rephrased sentence will probably read: "The professor announced that final grades would be based less on test results <u>than</u> on class participation." The word "less" always takes "than" when a comparison is being drawn.

71. Of the three candidates we are currently considering for the job, Bill is certainly the most ambitious but least qualified.

    Change three to two.

    (A) most ambitious but less qualified
    (B) more ambitious and least qualified
    (C) most ambitious, least qualified
    (D) more ambitious, least qualified
    (E) more ambitious but less qualified

71. **(E)** is the correct answer. When comparing three or more, use the superlative ("-est") form. When comparing two, use the comparative ("-er"). The words "most" and "least" are superlative; "more" and "less" are their comparative forms.

72. Major-league baseball teams are allowed to have twenty-five players on their rosters until the first of September, at which time they may expand their rosters to forty players.

    Begin with On the first of September.

    (A) players; before that date,
    (B) players when they may expand
    (C) players, until then
    (D) players, before September first
    (E) players; twenty-five

72. **(A)** is the correct answer. Your rephrased sentence will probably read: "On the first of September baseball teams may expand their rosters to forty <u>players; before that date</u>, they may carry only twenty-five players." Answer choice (C) is close, but would need a semi-colon instead of a comma to make it correct.

SECTION 1

| QUESTIONS | EXPLANATIONS |

73. State law requires candidates to submit petitions with one thousand signatures from residents of each county to qualify for a ballot slot in a state-wide election.

    Begin with <u>*Candidates must*</u>.
    (A) state law requires
    (B) it is required by state law
    (C) according to state law
    (D) state law requirements
    (E) are required by state law

73. **(C)** is the correct answer. Your rephrased sentence will probably read: "Candidates must submit petitions with one thousand signatures from residents of each county in order to qualify for a ballot slot in a state-wide election, <u>according to state law</u>."

74. The professor's book contained a detailed explanation of each of his three important economic theories.

    Change <u>*explanation*</u> *to* <u>*explained*</u>.
    (A) of each in detail
    (B) about each detailed
    (C) in detail of each
    (D) in detail each
    (E) of each detailed

74. **(D)** is the correct answer. Your rephrased sentence will probably read: "The professor's book explained <u>in detail each</u> of his three important economic theories."

SECTION 1

QUESTIONS	EXPLANATIONS

Questions 75 - 83 refer to the following passage.

(1) *All I know about music is that not many people ever really hear it. (2) And even then, on the rare occasions when something opens within, and the music enters, what we mainly hear, or hear corroborated, are personal, private, vanishing evocations. (3) But the man who creates the music is hearing something else, is dealing with the roar rising from the void and imposing order on it as it hits the air. (4) What is evoked in him, then, is of another order, more terrible because it has no words, and triumphant, too, for that same reason. (5) And his triumph, when he triumphs, is ours. (6) I just watched Sonny's face. (7) His face was troubled, he was working hard, but he wasn't with it. (8) And I had the feeling that, in a way, everyone on the bandstand was waiting for him, both waiting for him and pushing him along. (9) But as I began to watch Creole, I realized that it was Creole who held them all back. (10) He had them on a short rein. (11) He was listening to Sonny. (12) He was having a dialogue with Sonny. (13) He wanted Sonny to leave the shoreline and strike out for deep water. (14) He was Sonny's witness that deep water and drowning were not the same thing—he had been there, he knew.*

75. It can be inferred that the narrator is

    (A) listening to a record
    (B) the doorman at a night club
    (C) a clarinetist attending a rehearsal
    (D) an audience member at a concert
    (E) a retired musician dictating his memoir

75. **(D)** is the correct answer. The narrator discusses the differences between audiences and musicians. In sentence 5 he clearly identifies himself with the audience, not with the musicians. He clearly is at a concert (sentences 6 through 14), so neither (A) nor (E) can be correct. Because he has identified himself apart from musicians, answer choice (C) is also wrong. While it is possible that he might be the doorman at a night club, nothing in the passage leads to that inference. The fact that the narrator does seem to be listening intently, and not working, allows us to infer that he is an audience member. This passage, by the way, is excerpted from James Baldwin's short story *Sonny's Blues.*

SECTION 1

QUESTIONS	EXPLANATIONS

76. The author's assertions in sentences 1 and 2 are best characterized by which of the following?

  (A) It is useless to play music for an audience, because audiences do not appreciate music.

  (B) Audiences enjoy music not so much for its own sake as for something mysterious and personal it evokes in them.

  (C) People could be just as entertained contemplating their private thoughts as they are by a concert.

  (D) Audiences do not pay attention to the music when they go to see jazz played in a night club.

  (E) Music is to be valued solely for its therapeutic properties.

76. **(B)** is the correct answer. This is a good paraphrase of the first two sentences. Answer choice (A) amplifies the first sentence beyond recognition; it is too strongly worded to be supported by the passage, as is answer choice (D). The passage offers no basis for the conclusions drawn in answer choices (B) and (E); the word "solely" in (E) is another tip-off that the answer is too strongly worded to be correct.

77. Which of the following best describes the relationship between the first two sentences and sentence 3?

  (A) The first two sentences present an assertion that sentence 3 refutes.

  (B) The first two sentences describe an event, and sentence 3 describes the author's reaction to that event.

  (C) Sentence 3 illustrates a point made in the first two sentences.

  (D) Sentence 3 draws a generalization based on specific points made in the first two sentences.

  (E) Sentence 3 contrasts the experiences of one group with the experiences of another described in the first two sentences.

77. **(E)** is the correct answer. In the first two sentences, the narrator describes how audiences experience music; in sentence 3, he turns to how musicians experience music. Answer choice (E) says just that, although it uses generalizations to do so. Answer choices (A), (B), (C), and (D) all offer plausible relationships between sentences, but they do not describe the relationship between the ones in question. This is typical of the CLEP; when you see answers that are obviously wrong, such as these, do not over-think them in an effort to figure out how they might be correct. Just eliminate them and move on.

78. Which of the following is closest to the meaning of the word "terrible" as it is used in sentence 4?

  (A) frightening
  (B) disgusting
  (C) distasteful
  (D) euphoric
  (E) of poor quality

78. **(A)** is the correct answer. "Frightening" or "terrifying" is a secondary meaning of the word terrible. Answer choices (B), (C), and (E) are all possible meanings of the word "terrible," but they make no sense in the context of sentence 4.

SECTION 1

QUESTIONS	EXPLANATIONS

79. Sonny and Creole are

    (A) actors
    (B) critics
    (C) musicians
    (D) ushers
    (E) bartenders

79. **(C)** is the correct answer. Sentences 6 through 11 make clear that both are performing on a bandstand, with the narrator watching and describing the events.

80. Which of the following best summarizes the event described in sentence 8?

    (A) Sonny finds a solution, which had previously eluded him, to what is troubling him.
    (B) Creole and Sonny enter into a dialogue.
    (C) The band takes a break and leaves the stage.
    (D) The narrator notes an observation that he later decides is incorrect.
    (E) Sonny abandons his work in despair.

80. **(D)** is the correct answer. The narrator states in sentence 8 that he has a feeling that the band is both waiting for Sonny and pushing him along; then, in sentence 9, he reconsiders, and realizes that it is not the entire band but Creole who is setting the pace for the musicians, in particular Sonny. Answer choice (A) picks up a theme mentioned in sentence 7 but bears no relation to what the narrator says in sentence 8. Answer choice (B) literally interprets (and thereby misinterprets) sentence 12; at the very least refers to the wrong sentence. Answer choices (C) and (E) simply have no basis in the narrative.

81. The author uses which of the following for effect in sentences 10, 11, and 12?

    (A) florid descriptive terms
    (B) repetition and clipped cadence
    (C) surreal imagery
    (D) hyperbole
    (E) images of the ocean

81. **(B)** is the correct answer. These short sentences made up of simple words and each beginning with the word "he" have no florid descriptive terms, surreal imagery, or exaggeration. Ocean imagery is used in sentences 13 and 14, but not in 10, 11, and 12.

82. In sentences 9 through 14, the author speculates that Creole is

    (A) angry with Sonny for not trying his hardest
    (B) cajoling Sonny into taking greater chances
    (C) using previous experiences as a swimmer to help Sonny
    (D) intentionally subverting Sonny's performance
    (E) waiting for Sonny to show up so the concert can begin

82. **(B)** is the correct answer. In sentences 9 through 12, the narrator establishes that Creole is controlling the music. In sentences 13 and 14, the narrator uses the metaphor of venturing into deep waters to convey that Creole is coaxing Sonny to work beyond his limitations.

83. In sentences 13 and 14, the mentions of "shoreline" and "deep water" are

    (A) ironic
    (B) contradictory
    (C) metaphoric
    (D) primarily intended as visual imagery
    (E) meant to be interpreted literally

83. **(C)** is the correct answer. As noted in the explanation for question 82, the narrator uses ocean imagery metaphorically.

QUESTIONS	EXPLANATIONS

Questions 84 - 92 refer to the following passage:

(1) *The heavens seem to attract people who do not look at them very seriously. (2) In 1950, Immanuel Velikovsky, a psychoanalyst, wrote a book titled Worlds in Collision. (3) In it, he contended that at the time of the Exodus of the Israelites from Egypt in 1500 B.C., an encounter with a giant comet caused the earth either to slow down suddenly or to stop spinning altogether. (4) Among the consequences were floods, hurricanes, dust storms, fires, boiling seas, rivers the color of blood, the parting of the Red Sea, and the deposition of the manna that sustained the Israelites for forty years. (5) After fifty-two years the comet returned, causing among other things the fall of the walls of Jericho. (6) In certain respects a very learned man, Velikovsky found evidence for these events not only in the Old Testament but also in the literature of other ancient cultures.*

(7) Velikovsky was convinced that the giant comet sprang out of the planet Jupiter, had its two encounters with the earth, had an encounter with Mars and then went on to become what is now the planet Venus. (8) Such a sequence of events, quite apart from what Velikovsky believed were the consequences, calls for the abandonment of an entire edifice of observation and theory that physicists and astronomers have built since Galileo. (9) One can almost admire Velikovsky's imperturbable disregard of it.

84. Which of the following describes the relationship of sentence 1 to the rest of the paragraph?
    (A) It introduces one of the two contrasting groups that the rest of the passage describes.
    (B) It establishes the author's credentials as an expert on the main subject of the passage.
    (C) It explains how the argument that follows is organized.
    (D) It presents an anecdote illustrative of a greater principle discussed later in the passage.
    (E) It presents a generalization of which the rest of the passage is a single example.

84. **(E)** is the correct answer. Velikovsky is, according to the author, someone who does not "look at [the heavens] very seriously." The rest of the passage discusses Velikovsky's book *Worlds in Collision*, in which the author ignores nearly the entire history of astronomy (see sentences 8 and 9) in making his case. Answer choice (A) mentions two contrasting groups, but only one group—those who look at the heavens but not very seriously—is mentioned. Because the author tells us nothing about himself in the first sentence, answer choice (B) must be wrong. Answer choice (C) describes a common type of opening sentence—the type in which the author says "Here's my argument and here's how I intend to prove it"—but sentence 1 is not of this type. Because sentence 1 does not tell us an amusing or instructive story, answer choice (D) cannot be correct.

SECTION 1

85. The purpose of sentence 3 is to

   (A) conclude a point introduced in sentence 2

   (B) establish Velikovsky's credibility in order to later validate his research

   (C) demonstrate that Velikovsky was a Biblical scholar

   (D) initiate a summary of the contents of Velikovsky's book

   (E) suggest that Velikovsky's was the first effort to explain these phenomena scientifically

85. **(D)** is the correct answer. Sentences 3, 4, and 5 lay out the substance of Velikovsky's claims. Because sentence 3 is the first of these, it "initiates a summary of the contents of Velikovsky's book." Answer choice (A) must be wrong because, in sentence 2, the author states a fact that needs no conclusion. Answer choice (B) is a common answer type on the Analyzing Writing section: the type that looks good if you misunderstood the passage. Had you read this passage as pro-Velikovsky, you are likely to have chosen this and several other wrong answers among the questions for this passage. Answer choice (C), similarly, picks up some of the themes of this passage— Velikovsky, the Bible—but puts them together in a way wholly unrelated to the content of the passage. Answer choice (E) is an answer that might appeal to you if you read too much between the lines; just because Velikovsky is the only one mentioned in the passage does not mean he was the first or only to make such an effort.

86. Which of the following best describes the function of sentence 4?

   (A) It describes the effects of an incident that purportedly accounts for an episode of the Bible.

   (B) It details the manner by which the comet described in sentence 3 caused the Biblical events in question.

   (C) It provides examples of occurrences typically synchronous with a comet's passing the Earth.

   (D) It reconciles discrepancies between a Biblical account and the geological record of the Biblical era.

   (E) It contradicts an argument previously made in the passage.

86. **(A)** is the correct answer. Sentence 4 lists events associated with the Exodus of the Israelites as recounted in the Old Testament, and, in sequence with sentence 3, presents Velikovsky's cause-and-effect relationship between the comet and these earthly phenomena. Answer choice (B) is tempting because it touches on many of the points central to the passage, but do not be fooled: sentence 4 does NOT explain how a comet would cause such dramatic phenomena. The end of sentence 3 does, sort of, but the subject really calls for a much more detailed explanation, since it raises many obvious questions (e.g., If the Earth stopped spinning, why didn't it go hurtling into outer space? Or into the Sun? Why didn't everyone fly off the planet and into space? etc.). Answer choice (C) is ridiculous; if such events were common, the Earth would be uninhabitable. Answer choice (D) mentions "the geological record," which is never mentioned in the passage and so cannot be part of the function of sentence 4. And answer choice (E), while it sounds like something a sentence might do, bears no relation to sentence 4, which provides a litany of horrible events associated with the Exodus, not an argument of any quality.

SECTION 1

87. In sentence 6, the effect of using the phrase "In certain respects a very learned man" is to

    (A) imply that that learning is not well evidenced in his astronomical speculations
    (B) establish Velikovsky's credentials as an astronomer and theorist
    (C) indicate the author's ambiguity regarding the validity of Velikovsky's theories
    (D) disparage the profession of psychoanalysis
    (E) clarify a previously mentioned dispute concerning Velikovsky's qualifications

87. **(A)** is the correct answer. Typical of difficult correct answers on this section of the test, the syntax is weird ("that that") and paraphrases abound (Velikovsky's theories are referred to as "astronomical speculations," a phrase that does not appear in the passage). Answer choice (B) would only have appealed to you had you misunderstood the passage as supporting Velikovsky's arguments, which it does not. Answer choice (C) misstates the author's opinion of Velikovsky: the author quite clearly thinks Velikovsky is wrong (see sentences 1, 8, and 9). Answer choice (D) swings too far in the other direction: just because the author thinks Velikovsky's theories about comets are wrong doesn't mean that he disdains psychoanalysis. Because there is no "previously mentioned dispute concerning Velikovsky's qualifications," answer choice (E) must be wrong.

88. Which of the following best describes the main purpose of sentence 6?

    (A) to establish that Velikovsky did not rely exclusively on the Bible, but used numerous other sources
    (B) both to describe Velikovsky's sources and to imply that his reliance on them represents a weakness in his methodology
    (C) to contradict the assertion put forward in sentence 1
    (D) to assert that Velikovsky was not trying to prove a religious point but was rather simply participating in a fundamental scientific inquiry
    (E) to further demonstrate the possibility that rivers, under certain conditions, could turn the color of blood

88. **(B)** is the correct answer. The sentence "describe[s] Velikovsky's sources" ("the Old Testament . . . literature of other ancient cultures") and implies that his ignorance of astronomical observation and theory constitutes a weakness in his argument. This implication is made explicit in sentence 8. Answer choice (A) touches on many of the themes of sentence 6, but the term "numerous" is disputable and a tip-off that (A) is incorrect. This answer is also out-of-synch with the author's tone, which is critical. The author never contradicts the assertion put forward in sentence 1; it is his opinion and he sticks with it, so answer choice (C) is incorrect. Answer choice (D) is included by the test writers to tempt those who hold this opinion; it is certainly not the opinion of the author. Check your opinions at the door when you do Analyzing Writing questions; they will only interfere with your ability to deduce the author's opinions. Sentence 6 never mentions rivers of blood; if you chose this answer, chances are you were taking a blind guess.

SECTION 1

QUESTIONS	EXPLANATIONS

89. The purpose of sentence 8 is to

 (A) commend Velikovsky for his bravery and brinkmanship

 (B) reflect on those theories of the origin of Venus that preceded Velikovsky's

 (C) call into question the validity of the Old Testament as an historical source

 (D) argue that great scientific advances often require one to break with precedent

 (E) indicate a fundamental weakness in Velikovsky's theory

89. **(E)** is the correct answer. That Velikovsky abandons "an entire edifice of observation and theory . . . " is his "fundamental weakness." Answer choices (A) and (D) are included to trap those who misread the passage as supportive of Velikovsky; they are also so similar that neither could be correct without the other also being correct, a surefire tip-off that both answers are wrong. Because "those theories of the origin of Venus that preceded Velikovsky's" are never mentioned, answer choice (B) must be wrong. Answer choice (C) is too strongly worded to be supported by anything (much less sentence 8, which doesn't even mention the Old Testament) in the passage.

90. In sentence 8, the effect of the phrase "quite apart from what Velikovsky believed were the consequences" is to

 (A) indicate that the author feels unqualified to comment on the likelihood of such consequences

 (B) argue that, regardless of those consequences, Velikovsky's work represents a hallmark advance in the field of astronomy

 (C) remind the reader that those consequences are reported in the Old Testament

 (D) summarily dismiss those consequences as also scientifically implausible

 (E) assert that the sequence of events and their consequences must be considered separately

90. **(D)** is the correct answer. From sentence 1 on, the author depicts Velikovsky as a writer whose work is bent on providing a basis for the events of Exodus regardless of the scientific implausibility of his theories. Because the author does not beg a lack of expertise anywhere, or qualify his statements regarding certain subjects, answer choice (A) is unsubstantiated by the passage. Answer choice (B) again is included to attract those who misread the passage. Sentence 8 doesn't even mention the Old Testament, rendering (C) an extremely unlikely answer choice. Answer choice (E) is too strongly worded (especially the word "must") to be supported by the passage.

91. The author's tone throughout the passage is best described as one of

 (A) reverence
 (B) reportorial objectivity
 (C) mean-spirited retaliation
 (D) unbiased curiosity
 (E) mild irony

91. **(E)** is the correct answer. The author is clearly smirking as he writes this, as is most strongly evidenced by sentences 1, 8, and 9. He is certainly not reverent—see sentence 1—nor is he objective or unbiased. However, he does not swing to the other extreme of mean-spirited retaliation, either. There is certainly no evidence that the author is "out to get" Velikovsky or that he has any motivation to do so.

92. Which sentences most clearly indicate the author's attitude toward Velikovsky's work?

 (A) 1, 2, and 3
 (B) 1, 2, and 7
 (C) 1, 8, and 9
 (D) 2, 4, and 5
 (E) 3, 4, and 5

92. **(C)** is the correct answer. See the explanation for question 91, above.

SECTION 1

93. Like many of the nation's great heroes,

    <u>Thomas Jefferson's life</u> has been
             A

    <u>so thoroughly</u> mythologized that <u>it is difficult</u>
       B   C

    to separate biographical fact <u>from</u> fiction.
                                       D

    <u>No error</u>
      E

    93. **(A)** is the correct answer. The modifying phrase "Like many of the nation's great heroes" describes "Thomas Jefferson," not his life. Jefferson's life cannot be like the nation's great heroes: the two are simply not comparable.

94. During <u>yesterday's game</u>, the quarterback
      A   B

    <u>had sustained</u> a crushing blow to the knees,
         C

    rendering him <u>immobile</u> for several minutes.
                    D

    <u>No error</u>
      E

    94. **(C)** is the correct answer. The past perfect ("had sustained") is improperly used here, as it is not used with the simple past, as it always must be. This should read "sustained," not "had sustained."

95. <u>Accepting</u> her fate <u>with all the</u> inner strength
        A   B

    she could muster, <u>the martyr</u> endured <u>her</u>
                    C   D

    execution in tranquil repose. <u>No error</u>
                             E

    95. **(E)** is the correct answer.

96. The teacher, by both <u>constantly</u> cajoling the
                       A

    students <u>to work harder</u> and gradually
            B

    increasing the level of difficulty of their

    assignments, somehow <u>manage</u> to achieve the
                       C

    best improvements in the school system

    <u>year after year</u>. <u>No error</u>
       D   E

    96. **(C)** is the correct answer. In this sentence, the test writers separate the subject and the verb with lots of words, hoping that you will forget to reconnect the two. The subject, "teacher," is singular, and should take the singular verb "manages."

SECTION 1

QUESTIONS	EXPLANATIONS

97. The doctor recommended that the patient

   <u>should</u> cut down her consumption <u>of salty</u>
     A   B

   foods, because the patient <u>was beginning to</u>
                                     C

   <u>show</u> warning signs of hypertension.
     D

   <u>No error</u>
    E

98. The need for a traffic light at <u>the corner of</u>
                                    A

   Elm and Third <u>was amply demonstrated</u> by
                       B

   the two collisions that <u>occurred</u>
                     C

   <u>at that intersection</u> last night. <u>No error</u>
         D   E

99. <u>The necessity of</u> lowering <u>the crime rate</u> in
       A   B

   our neighborhood <u>is a task</u> too great to be
                   C

   handled <u>by a group of</u> resident volunteers
              D

   alone. <u>No error</u>
          E

100. It is <u>better</u> to keep your mouth shut
        A

   <u>and make people</u> wonder whether
         B

   <u>you are ignorant</u> than <u>opening</u> it and
       C   D

   removing all doubt. <u>No error</u>
                  E

---

97. **(A)** is the correct answer. "Recommended . . . should" is redundant; if I'm recommending something, I obviously think you should do it.

98. **(E)** is the correct answer.

99. **(A)** is the correct answer. In this sentence, the subject and predicate don't agree. Is it "the necessity" that "is a task too great . . . ," as the sentence reads? No! "Lowering the crime rate . . . is a task too great . . . ." The phrase "The necessity of" should be deleted.

100. **(D)** is the correct answer. This sentence contains a parallelism error. It should read "It is better <u>to keep your mouth shut</u> . . . than <u>to open it</u> . . . ."

PART III

How to Crack the CLEP General Examination in College Mathematics

9

Overview of the College Mathematics Exam

GOOD NEWS!

The College Mathematics Exam of the CLEP tests nothing that you could not have learned in high school. Undoubtedly, the College Mathematics exam is substantially easier than any course a college would offer. It also takes a lot less time to complete (90 minutes versus 13 weeks). Therefore, if your school awards credit for this exam, you should take it: passing it will save you money, time, and a lot of sweat.

WHAT'S ON THE TEST?

The College Mathematics exam consists of two parts; you will have 45 minutes to take each part. Except for the fact that Part I has thirty-three questions and Part II has thirty-two, there is no difference between the two parts. In 1995 the College Board changed the name of this test from the Mathematics exam to the College Mathematics exam, at which time it eliminated the quantitative comparison section of the exam (i.e., "Which value is greater, the one in Column A or the one in Column B?"). If you have an old CLEP bulletin or have previously studied from an out-of-date test guide, you would have seen this question format. Forget about it; it won't be on your test.

The sixty-five questions you will see will cover the following topics:

According to ETS, "most of the mathematical content [on our tests] is held to topics generally taught prior to the tenth grade."

Topics	# of Questions
Probabilities and Statistics counting and pattern problems probability of a single event probability of compound events mean and median averages	16 or 17
Real Number System prime numbers odd and even numbers factoring and divisibility rational numbers irrational numbers absolute value	13
Functions and Graphs domain and range linear functions composite functions inverse functions	13
Sets intersection and union of sets subsets and Venn diagrams Cartesian product	6 or 7

Topics	# of Questions
Logic	6 or 7
conditional statements	
necessary conditions and sufficient conditions	
negations	
contrapositive, inverse, and converse	
conclusions	
counterexamples	
Miscellaneous Topics	10
number bases	
exponents	
imaginary numbers	

The list above is more daunting than the actual test. A number of the subtopics listed above are tested only once on the exam; some are not tested on every exam. In chapter 10, we review every subject about which you will be asked two or more questions. Subjects that appear only once we review in chapter 12, which gives and explains the answers to the practice test in chapter 11. If you master the material in these reviews, you will know more than enough to get a passing grade on this exam, which is all you need to concern yourself with. At most schools, an 800 and a 500 are worth exactly the same thing: one course credit and a bye on Intro Math.

Before we review the substance of the exam, let's learn a technique that will make this test much easier for you. This technique (in addition to those covered in chapter 2, of course) will help you take advantage of the multiple-choice aspect of this exam, so that your work will be faster and more accurate. It's called "Plugging In."

There are only four answer choices for questions on the CLEP College Mathematics exam. All the other exams have five answer choices per question.

PLUGGING IN

Remember algebra? Algebra was the class in which you spent a lot of time solving for an unknown, usually called x or y. Your teacher probably told you that the final step in solving an algebraic equation was to plug your answers back into the original equation, to make sure that they "worked." Here's a simple example:

$$5x - 2y = x$$
$$4x - 2y = 0$$
$$4x = 2y$$
$$2x = y$$

According to your old algebra teacher, your last step would be to make sure that your solution ($2x = y$) is correct by plugging in values.

Here's how to crack it

♦ Let's make $x = 3$ and $y = 6$ (these are good numbers because they satisfy the equation $2x = y$).

◆ Now plug $x = 3$ and $y = 6$ into the original equation $5x - 2y = x$.

This gives us the equation

$$5(3) - 2(6) = 3$$
$$15 - 12 = 3$$

It works! That means our solution was correct. What if we had made a mistake and come up with an incorrect solution (say, $3x = y$)? We would have plugged in $x = 3$, $y = 9$ and gotten the equation $5(3) - 2(9) = 3$, which simplifies to $3 = -3$. Since this result is untrue, we would have known we had made a mistake.

Here comes the great news: when you see this type of algebra problem on the CLEP (and you will see quite a few, and they will be much tougher than the example above):

◆ Do not try to solve the problem algebraically. Jump immediately to plugging in.

You can do this because the CLEP is a multiple-choice exam, and therefore you already have the correct answer (it's among the answer choices!). All you have to do is find it.

Let's look at an example to see how it works:

> Which of the following equals $x^3 + x^2 - 2x$?
>
> (A) $(x^2 + 1)(x - 2)$
> (B) $(x^2 - x)(x + 2)$
> (C) $(x^2 - 2)(x^2 + x)$
> (D) $-x(x^2 + 2)$

Here's how to crack it

Instead of trying to factor the original equation, plug in a value. Here's how:

◆ Let's make $x = 2$.

This makes the original equation $2^3 + 2^2 - 2(2)$, or $8 + 4 - 4 = 8$.

8 is now your **target**. The correct answer will also have a result of 8.

Now plug 2 in for the variable x in the answer choices:

> (A) $(2^2 + 1)(2 - 2) = (4 + 1)(0) = 0$
> (B) $(2^2 - 2)(2 + 2) = (4 - 2)(4) = (2)(4) = 8$
> (C) $(2^2 - 2)(2^2 + 2) = (4 - 2)(4 + 2) = (2)(6) = 12$
> (D) $-2(2^2 + 2) = -2(4 + 2) = -2(6) = -12$

Only answer choice (B) hits the target of 8. That's because (B) is the correct answer.

Here's another example:

> When $x < -1$, which of the following has the greatest value?
>
> (A) $x + 1$
> (B) x^2
> (C) x^3
> (D) $2x$

Here's how to crack it

◆ Remember that x must be less than –1. Plug in a value that satisfies that condition. We'll pick $x = -3$.

◆ Plug the values into the answer choices:

(A) $x + 1 = -3 + 1 = -2$
(B) $x^2 = (-3)^2 = 9$
(C) $x^3 = (-3)^3 = -27$
(D) $2x = 2(-3) = -6$

The correct answer is (B), because 9 is the greatest of the four values. Had we plugged in –2, –10, or –3,754, the answer would still have been (B). It would have to be, because the correct answer must be correct under all conditions allowed by the problem. When you plug in, plug in numbers that are easy to work with. –3 is a good number to plug in; –3,754 would be a bad number to plug in.

Plugging in is faster and more efficient than conventional algebra, and it helps you avoid the careless mistakes people commonly make when they manipulate algebraic equations.

You can always plug in when a problem has variables in the answer choices. You can also plug in on problems that have unsolvable unknowns. Consider the example below:

Every day, Cindy exercises by jogging from her home to the corner of Main and Elm Streets, then turns around and walks home. Cindy jogs at a rate of 8 miles per hour and walks at a rate of 4 miles per hour. What is Cindy's average rate for her round-trip?

(A) 7

(B) 6

(C) $\dfrac{16}{3}$

(D) $\dfrac{17}{4}$

Be aggressive when you take multiple-choice exams. ETS exams are designed to reward aggressive guessing. If you can eliminate at least one answer choice, make a guess.

Here's how to crack it

In this problem, the "unsolvable unknown" is the distance from Cindy's home to the corner of Main and Elm. Instead of calling this distance x (which is what your old algebra teacher would have wanted you to do), you should plug in a value for the distance. Pick one that makes the problem easy. Plugging in 8 would make this problem very easy: if Main and Elm is 8 miles from Cindy's home, it takes her 1 hour to get there and 2 hours to return. Thus, her round-trip of 16 miles, divided by her time of 3 hours, yields average rate of $\dfrac{16}{3}$ miles per hour. The correct answer, then, is (C).

Plugging in will come in handy on function problems, too. We'll discuss that in the next chapter, when we review functions.

There is one last type of problem in which you can plug in. It's called a "must/always" problem (because it includes an absolute term such as *must*, *always*, *never*, etc.), and it involves a slightly different approach to plugging in. Here's an example:

If *a* and *b* are even integers, which of the following must always be even?

I. $\dfrac{(a+b)}{a}$

II. $a - b$

III. ab

(A) I only
(B) I and II only
(C) II and III only
(D) I, II, and III

Here's how to crack it

On "must/always" questions, you should try to plug in values that satisfy the conditions of the problem (i.e., *a* and *b* must be even) <u>but</u> also provide a counterexample to the "must/always" statement. Look at Roman numeral I. Can we find values that would make $(a+b)/a$ odd? Yes: if $a = 2$ and $b = 4$, $(a + b)/a$ equals 3. Thus, by plugging in, we have proven that Roman numeral I is NOT part of the correct answer. Immediately we can eliminate answer choices (A), (B), and (D) (all of which include Roman numeral I). Hey! Only answer choice (C) remains, so it must be correct. That's the beauty of multiple choice exams: occasionally you will not have to do all the work on a problem in order to find the correct answer, so long as you aggressively eliminate answer choices once you know they are incorrect.

> If your future college gives the same credit for the CLEP exam and the AP exam, take the CLEP: it's much easier!

SUMMARY

1. When you plug in, you change an algebra problem into an easier arithmetic problem.

2. Plug in on problems that have variables in the answer choices. Plug values in for your unknowns, then solve. The result is your **target**.

3. Plug in on problems that have "unsolvable unknowns." Choose a value for the "unsolvable unknown" and solve. Pick a number that makes the arithmetic easiest.

4. Plug in on "must/always" problems. Try to plug in values that provide a counterexample to the "must/always" rule.

> Call your potential schools and ask them about their CLEP policy. Will they give you credit for a good grade? Will a good grade place you out of a class? The admissions or dean's office should know the answer.

10

Math Review

LEARN THIS CHAPTER . . . PASS THE TEST

This chapter reviews every subject about which there are two or more questions on the CLEP College Mathematics exam. Master these and you will certainly get a qualifying grade on the test.

All other subjects covered on the test are reviewed in chapter 12, which contains the explanations for the test questions. While we could have covered them in this chapter, we felt to do so would have created the false impression that you must learn these subjects to succeed on the exam. Rest assured that a thorough understanding of chapters 10 and 12 will lead to a very high CLEP College Mathematics score.

MATHEMATICAL TERMS

TYPES OF NUMBERS

"I know that two and two make four—and should be glad to prove it, too, if I could—though I must say if by any sort of process I could convert two and two into five it would give me much greater pleasure."
—Lord Byron (1788–1824), English poet

- ◆ **Integers** are whole values and can be positive, negative, or 0. Fractions and decimals are not integers.

- ◆ **Rational numbers** are numbers that can be expressed as the ratio of two integers. Whole numbers are rational, as are fractions. Square roots are not rational. A seemingly inordinate number of questions on the math CLEP revolve around the definition of a rational number. Make sure you know it!

- ◆ **Irrational numbers** are numbers that cannot be expressed as the ratio of two integers, such as square roots.

- ◆ **Even numbers** are integers that are divisible by 2. They can be positive, negative, or 0.

- ◆ **Odd numbers** are integers that are not divisible by 2. They can be positive or negative.

- ◆ **Prime numbers** are divisible only by themselves and 1. 2 is the only even prime number. 3, 5, 7, 11, 13, etc., are prime.

- ◆ **Real numbers** are all numbers, rational and irrational, except for imaginary numbers (see below).

- ◆ **Imaginary numbers** are the square roots of negative numbers, e.g. $\sqrt{-9}$. Imaginary numbers are always expressed in terms of i, which is defined as the square root of -1. $\sqrt{-9}$, for example, would be expressed as $(\sqrt{-1})(\sqrt{9}) = 3i$.

- ◆ **Factors** are those positive integers that divide evenly into another integer. The factors of 12 are 1, 2, 3, 4, 6, and 12.

- ◆ **Multiples** are those integers derived by multiplying by an integer. The multiples of 12 are . . . –24, –12, 0, 12, 24, 36, 48 . . .

OTHER IMPORTANT TERMS

The **absolute value** of a number is the distance of that number from 0 on the number line. Simply put, it's the positive value of the number. The symbol for absolute value is two parallel vertical lines surrounding the value in question. for example, $|-5|$ means "the absolute value of –5," which is 5. $|4-6|$ means "the absolute value of 4 – 6, or –2. That value is 2. Note that you perform operations inside an absolute value sign; in the above example, you do NOT change the –6 to a positive 6.

Exponents look like the "4" in the term 2^4. This annotation means "two to the fourth power," or "two times itself four times $(2 \times 2 \times 2 \times 2)$."

The **square root** of a number is the value you would have to square to get that number. Huh? Well, the square root of 9 is 3, because 3^2 equals 9. The symbol for a square root is $\sqrt{}$, as in $\sqrt{9} = 3$.

PROBABILITIES, PATTERNS AND COMBINATIONS, AND STATISTICS

One of the most common types of questions on the College Mathematics exam, and one of the easiest, is the **probability** question. Probabilities questions ask about the likelihood that an event will occur (or that a number of events will occur in sequence). Let's look at an easy example:

> Five slips of paper, numbered 1 through 5, are placed in a hopper. If a person were to draw one slip of paper from the hopper, what is the probability that a slip with the number 4 on it would be drawn?
>
> (A) $\dfrac{1}{2}$
>
> (B) $\dfrac{1}{3}$
>
> (C) $\dfrac{1}{4}$
>
> (D) $\dfrac{1}{5}$

Did you skip chapter 2? If you did, go back and read it! It's crammed with important test-taking tips!

Here's how to crack it

Find the number of possible outcomes of the drawing. There are five: a 1, 2, 3, 4, or 5 could be drawn. Now, how many of those outcomes result in a 4 being drawn? One. Therefore, the probability of a 4 being drawn is 1 in 5, or $\dfrac{1}{5}$. The answer is (D).

The next example is only a little more difficult:

Five slips of paper, numbered 1 through 5, are placed in a hopper. If a person draws two slips of paper from the hopper, without replacing the first slip drawn, what is the probability that the slip with the number 1 on it will be drawn first and that the slip with the number 3 on it will be drawn second?

(A) $\frac{1}{10}$

(B) $\frac{1}{12}$

(C) $\frac{1}{20}$

(D) $\frac{1}{50}$

Here's how to crack it

This problem asks the probability of two events occurring consecutively. Such problems require you to multiply the probability of the two events together. The probability that the 1 would be drawn first is $\frac{1}{5}$; that the 3 would be drawn second is $\frac{1}{4}$ (there are only four numbers left in the hopper after the first drawing, because the problem states that you do not replace the first number after it is drawn). The probability of the two events occurring consecutively, then, is $\frac{1}{5} \times \frac{1}{4} = \frac{1}{20}$. The correct answer is (C). By the way, this works for <u>any</u> number of consecutive events; if the question asked about three events, you would multiply all three of the probabilities together.

Yet another type of probability question gives you two or more chances to achieve a single result. In such a case, you add probabilities. Here's an example:

ETS doesn't write tests for academic institutions only. The company also writes tests for the National Board of Podiatry Examiners, the American Society of Plumbing Engineers, the Institute for Nuclear Power Operations, and the International Council for Shopping Centers.

Five slips of paper, numbered 1 through 5, are placed in a hopper. If a person draws two slip of paper from the hopper, without replacing the first slip drawn, what is the probability that one of the two slips drawn will have the number 2 on it?

(A) $\frac{9}{20}$

(B) $\frac{1}{2}$

(C) $\frac{10}{17}$

(D) $\frac{13}{20}$

Here's how to crack it

This time add the probabilities that the 2 will be drawn ($\frac{1}{5}$ on the first drawing, $\frac{1}{4}$ on the second drawing) to come up with the correct answer, (A).

A slight variation on the probability question is the type that asks how likely it is that something will <u>not</u> happen. The above problem:

> Five slips of paper, numbered 1 through 5, are placed in a hopper. If a person were to draw two slips of paper from the hopper, without replacing the first slip drawn, what is the probability that one of the two slips drawn will <u>not</u> have the number 2 on it?
>
> (A) $\frac{1}{10}$
>
> (B) $\frac{1}{2}$
>
> (C) $\frac{3}{5}$
>
> (D) $\frac{9}{10}$

Here's how to crack it

Here we are looking for two events to occur consecutively (that event is "a 2 is not drawn"), so we multiply the probabilities of the event. They are $\frac{4}{5}$ for the first drawing, and $\frac{3}{4}$ for the second drawing. The answer is (C). A good tip-off as to when you should multiply: if the sum of the probabilities is greater than 1, you should multiply. An event cannot have a probability greater than 1, since 1 means "it happens every single time."

All probabilities questions on the College Mathematics exam fall into one of the categories described above. They will ask about tosses of a coin, rolls of a die, or drawing cards from a deck. Or, they may involve pulling colored marbles or jelly beans from a jar. However, once you get past the superficial details, they are all pretty much the same.

Pattern and combination problems are similar in that they require you to figure out the number of possible outcomes of a series of events. Let's look at an example:

> Of a restaurant's five employees, a manager must pick two to work a certain day. From how many different combinations of employees can the manager choose that day's staff?
>
> (A)   1
> (B)   5
> (C) 10
> (D) 30

Transfer your answers from your test booklet when you have finished a page or section of questions. It saves time and should prevent you from misnumbering your answers.

Here's how to crack it

The easiest way to do these problems is to list all the possibilities. Name the five employees A, B, C, D, and E. Now list all possible combinations of two: AB, AC, AD, and AE (that takes care of all combinations that include A); BC, BD, and BE (that takes care of all combinations that include B); CD and CE; and DE. The total is 10, and the answer is (C).

There is in fact a formula for such problems, but we've found that people make more careless mistakes on tests when they use formulas, so you should do any combination problem you can in the manner described above. On a test, however, you will see a problem with numbers so big that you will not be able to list all the combinations, at which point you will need the formula. See the following example:

> Elvis owns 12 Cadillacs. He plans to race them in groups of three. How many different races can he run without ever repeating the same grouping of three?
>
> (A)   88
> (B)   135
> (C)   220
> (D)   645

Here's how to crack it

Since you won't have time on the test to list what could be 645 different combinations, you should use the following formula:

Always take the path of least resistance on multiple-choice tests. Do not answer the questions that give you trouble until you have answered ALL questions you can answer easily.

$$\frac{(n!)}{[r!(n-r)!]}$$

where n is the number of things in the entire group and r is the number of things in each combination. The exclamation point tells you to perform a factorial. The factorial of x is the product of all numbers between 1 and x, inclusive. In this case, the formula translates to:

$$\frac{(12 \times 11 \times 10 \times 9 \times 8 \times 7 \times 6 \times 5 \times 4 \times 3 \times 2 \times 1)}{(3 \times 2 \times 1)(9 \times 8 \times 7 \times 6 \times 5 \times 4 \times 3 \times 2 \times 1)}$$

The first thing you want to do is to eliminate all the 1's (they have no bearing on the final result) and to cancel out all common factors. In other words, get rid of 9, 8, 7, 6, 5, 4, 3, 2, 1 from both the numerator and the denominator. This will leave you with:

$$\frac{12 \times 11 \times 10}{3 \times 2}$$

Now divide the numerator by $3 \times 2 = 6$, and you get $2 \times 11 \times 10$, or 220. The correct answer is (C).

AVERAGES

The CLEP requires you to know what the arithmetic **mean** and **median** are. The arithmetic **mean** is what we usually call an "average"; it's the sum of a series of numbers divided by the number of members in that series. A bowling average, for example, is the total number of pins knocked down divided by the number of games played. For example, if Adele bowled a 185, a 200, and a 233, her average would be 206, the sum of 185, 200, and 223 (which is 618) divided by the three games she bowled. Her **median** score would be 200. The median is determined by listing all the numbers in a sequence in ascending or descending order and finding the one in the exact middle.

Here's an average question about averages:

> What is the difference between the mean and the median of 24, 27, 31, 37, and 41?
>
> (A) 1
> (B) 2
> (C) 4
> (D) 6

Here's how to crack it

The mean of the numbers listed above is 30 (their sum, 150, divided by 5). The median is 31. Therefore, the difference between the two is 1. The correct answer is (A).

FUNCTIONS AND GRAPHS

A function is a set of instructions that tell you what operation or series of operations to perform. For example:

$$f(x) = 2x + 3$$

tells you to multiply x by 2 and add 3 to the result. $f(5)$, then, would be $2(5) + 3 = 13$.

Some function problems on the College Mathematics test are just that simple. For example:

> If $f(x) = x^2 - 7$, then what is the value of $f(-4)$?
>
> (A) 12
> (B) 9
> (C) 4
> (D) 0

The correct answer is (C), since $(-4)^2 - 7 = 16 - 7 = 9$.

As mentioned earlier, many function problems are tailor-made for plugging in. For example:

> If $f(x) = x^2 - 7$, then $f(x + 1) =$
>
> (A) $x^2 - 6$
> (B) $x^2 - 6x + 6$
> (C) $x^2 + 2x - 6$
> (D) $x^2 + 8$

Whenever possible, use common sense and avoid formulas on math problems. Under test conditions, people sometimes forget, remember incorrectly, or confuse the formulas they've memorized. ETS math problems are designed to reward clear, common-sense thinking.

Here's how to crack it

Rather than work through the algebra (a path fraught with potential careless errors), plug in. Let's make x equal to 4. $f(4) = 16 - 7 = 9$. $f(x + 1) = f(5) = 25 - 7 = 18$. Now we plug 4 into the answer choices:

(A) $x^2 - 6 = 16 - 6 = 10$
(B) $x^2 - 6x + 6 = 16 - 36 + 6 = -14$
(C) $x^2 + 2x - 6 = 16 + 8 - 6 = 18$
(D) $x^2 + 8 = 16 + 8 = 24$

Only answer choice (C) hits our target of 18. Answer choice (C) is correct.

Sometimes the test will require you to work a **compound function**. Compound functions have, as their name implies, two functions for you to work through. For example:

If $f(x) = 3x - 1$ and $g(x) = 2x + 2$, then $g(f(x)) =$

(A) $6x$
(B) $6x - 2$
(C) $6x^2 + 3$
(D) $6x^2 - 2x + 2$

Here's how to crack it

First things first: you must solve compound functions from the inside out. First you solve $f(x)$; then you perform the function g on your result. You should plug in on these problems. Let's make $x = 3$. $f(3) = 9 - 1 = 8$. Now we have to calculate $g(8)$, which equals $2(8) + 2 = 18$. Which of the answers hits our target? Only (A), the correct answer.

The CLEP will ask a couple of questions about **inverse functions**. An inverse function "undoes" another function. Think of a function as something that changes a number's identity, like a magic potion. Its inverse function changes the number back to its original identity: it's the antidote to the potion.

For example, if $f(x) = 2x$, its inverse function g would be $g(x) = \left(\dfrac{x}{2}\right)$. Plug in to see that this is true. Let's make $x = 5$. $f(5) = 2(5) = 10$. $g(10) = \left(\dfrac{10}{2}\right) = 5$. Therefore, $g(f(5)) = 5$.

You can always plug in on inverse function problems. Let's try the following example:

If $f(x) = 3x - 4$, and $g(f(x)) = x$, then $g(x) =$

(A) $4 - 3x$

(B) $\dfrac{(3x - 4)}{3}$

(C) $\dfrac{(4 + 3x)}{4}$

(D) $\dfrac{(x + 4)}{3}$

> Don't be afraid to write in your test booklet. Cross out and circle answers in the booklet. Write out every possible combination in a pattern or probability problem. Redraw geometry problems, map functions, do whatever it takes to make the questions easier. You're the only one who's ever going to use that booklet!

Here's how to crack it

Let's plug in 5 for x. $f(5) = 3(5) - 4 = 11$. $g(x)$ is supposed to reverse the process, so that means that $g(11) = 5$. Which of the four answer choices hits the target of 5 when we plug in $x = 11$?

(A) $4 - 3x = 4 - 33 = -29$

(B) $\dfrac{(3x+4)}{3} = \dfrac{(33-4)}{3} = \dfrac{29}{3}$

(C) $\dfrac{(4+3x)}{4} = \dfrac{(4+33)}{4} = \dfrac{37}{4}$

(D) $\dfrac{(x+4)}{3} = \dfrac{(11+4)}{3} = 5$

The correct answer is (D). All inverse function problems can be done this way.

DOMAIN AND RANGE

The last type of function question involves a function's domain and range. These questions often requires you to identify the graph of a function. The **domain** of a function is the group of numbers the function is being performed on: in other words, all the values x could be in $f(x)$. The **range** of the function is the group of all numbers that make up the results of $f(x)$. Let's take the function $f(x) = 2x$, and let's add the rule that x must be a positive integer less than 5. The **domain** of this function is {1, 2, ,3, 4} and the **range** is {2, 4, 6, 8}. For any function $f(x) = y$, the domain is made up of all possible values of x and the range is made up of all possible values of y. You might remember it this way: one's domain is one's home, or starting point. The range is where the results of $f(x)$ roam (it's also where the buffalo roam; this is a mnemonic device that many have used with great success).

After you've taken our practice exam, read the explanations for all the answers, including the ones for questions you answered correctly. The explanations describe the fastest, most efficient way to do the test problems.

Here's a sample question:

> If $f(x) = x^2$ and the domain of $f(x)$ is all positive real numbers less than 10, then the range of f(x) is all
>
> (A) positive real numbers
> (B) positive real numbers less than 100
> (C) integers less than 10
> (D) integers less than 3

Here's how to crack it

This is basically a vocabulary question. If you know the difference between domain and range, you should see that the correct answer is (B).

Functions can be graphed on a Cartesian grid (see below):

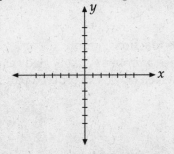

The formula for graphing a function is $f(x) = y$, with the x's plotted along the x-axis and the y's plotted along the y-axis. For example, the graph of $f(x) = 2x$ would look like this:

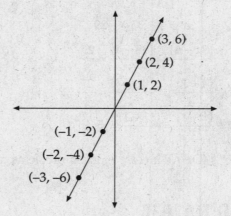

A function may only have one y value assigned to each x; for example, $f(x)$ cannot equal both 2 and –4. Since each x can be assigned only one y value, a graph of a function will pass the "vertical line" test. A vertical line will pass through either no points or one point on the graph of a function, but it will never pass through more than one. Which of the graphs below are functions?

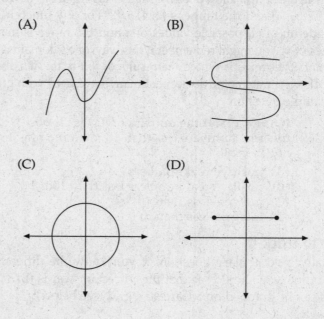

Graphs (A) and (D) are functions; graphs (B) and (C) are not.

Occasionally you will see a problem that is made easier if you remember the old formula $y = mx + b$, in which (x, y) is an ordered pair that satisfies the function

$f(x) = y$, m is the **slope** of the line (its steepness), and b is the **y-intercept** (the value of y when x equals 0). Look at the problem below:

If $f(3) = 9$ and $f(4) = 14$, then $f(6) =$

(A) 16
(B) 19
(C) 24
(D) 38

Here's how to crack it

Because we know that $f(3) = 9$ and $f(4) = 14$, we have two ordered pairs from the graph of function: (3, 9) and (4, 14). Therefore, we can figure out the slope of the line. We do this by calculating its "rise over run," or how much the line goes up divided by how much it goes across. The rise is the difference between the two y coordinates (14 - 9 = 5), the run the difference between the two x coordinates (4 − 3 = 1). The slope of the function is $\dfrac{5}{1} = 5$. Let's plug this into our $y = mx + b$ formula.

$$y = 5x + b$$

Since we have values for x and y (our ordered pairs), we can solve for b. Let's use (3, 9).

$$9 = 5(3) + b$$
$$9 = 15 + b$$
$$-6 = b$$

Now we know that $y = 5x - 6$, which means we can figure out the value of $f(6)$.

$$y = 5(6) - 6$$
$$y = 30 - 6$$
$$y = 24$$

The correct answer is (C). We could have used this same method to find the formula for $f(x)$:

$$y = 5x - 6$$

means that

$$f(x) = 5x - 6.$$

It's just that simple!

SETS

Sets are groups of numbers. They can be huge:

$$S = \{\text{all integers}\}$$

or tiny:

$$S = \{7\}$$

The more you practice taking the exam, the more confident you will be on test day. Take our diagnostic test and do all the College Mathematics questions in the College Board book *The Official Guide to the CLEP*. Your local library should have a copy.

If you're taking more than one exam, bring a snack to have between tests. It will help replenish your energy.

When we compare two or more sets, we sometimes talk of the **union** or **intersection** of them. The union of sets, indicated by the symbol ∪, means "the list of all members of the sets in question." Numbers are listed only once in the union of sets, even if they appear in two or more of the sets in question. The intersection of sets, indicated by the symbol ∩, means "the list of all numbers that all the sets in question hold in common." The union of the sets {1, 2, 3} and {3, 4, 5} is {1, 2, 3, 4, 5}. The intersection of those same two sets is {3}.

Some set questions on the CLEP will involve Venn diagrams. A Venn diagram is a graphic depiction of the relationship between sets. Consider the sets below:

A = {all even integers less than 100}
B = {all multiples of 4 less than 100}
C = {all odd integers less than 100}

A Venn diagram depicting these three sets would look like this:

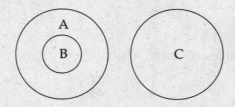

Last (and least, actually) is the Cartesian product of sets. There will probably be only one question on your test about this, but we're including it in the review because no one ever remembers this from school. The Cartesian product of two sets is the list of values you get by multiplying each member of one set by each member of the other. For example, the Cartesian product of

{2, 4, 7}

and

{3, 10}

would be

{6, 12, 21, 20, 40, 70}

LOGIC

Most of the logic on the CLEP exam is easy and self-explanatory. All the logic questions have complete explanations in chapter 12, and none of the logic topics is the subject of more than one question on the test, so we're not going to spend a lot of time on the subject here.

There is one logic subject, however, that may be unfamiliar to you and about which ETS always asks one question. It's called the *contrapositive* and here's how it works:

Let's take a true statement:

> When it rains, the street gets wet.

In logical terms, this could be written:

> When A, then B

The contrapositive, in logical terms, is:

> Not B, then not A

To return to our original statement:

> If the streets are not wet, then it is not raining.

It's just that simple. The contrapositive of a true statement, you should note, is necessarily true. Therefore, if a statement is not necessarily true, it's not the contrapositive. The statement "It is not raining, so the streets cannot be wet," for example, is not necessarily true: the streets could be wet because someone hosed them down, because a fire hydrant is open, or because they are covered with melting snow. Use the "necessarily true" test to eliminate answer choices that cannot be contrapositives.

Don't forget to bring a watch with you to the exam.

SUMMARY

In the immortal words of Porky Pig, "That's all folks!" Take the diagnostic test that follows in chapter 11 and review all the material in chapter 12, "Answers and Explanations..." and you should have a good grasp of the material you need to know to pass the College Mathematics CLEP. For more practice, find a copy of *The Official Handbook for the CLEP Examinations* (College Board) and do all the math problems in its sample test. We strongly advise against practicing with our competitors' guide books, as their facsimile exams are more difficult than the actual exam, and they cover many subjects you will never see on the actual CLEP. Practicing in those books will cause you unnecessary stress.

11

The Princeton Review Sample College Mathematics Exam

PART I

Time—45 minutes

33 questions

Directions: Solve the following problems. Do not spend too much time on any one problem.

Notes: (1) Unless otherwise specified, the domain of any function f is assumed to be the set of all real numbers x for which $f(x)$ is a real number.

(2) i will be used to denote $\sqrt{-1}$.

(3) Figures that accompany the following problems are intended to provide information useful in solving the problems. They are drawn as accurately as possible EXCEPT when it is stated in a specific problem that its figure is not drawn to scale. All figures lie in a plane unless otherwise indicated.

1. If $3x = 12$, and $5y = 25$, then $2x + 8y =$
   (A) 32
   (B) 40
   (C) 48
   (D) 59

2. Which of the following is NOT a number of people among whom 1,365 marbles could be distributed evenly?
   (A) 3
   (B) 5
   (C) 7
   (D) 9

3. If A implies B, B implies C, and C implies D, which of the following is true?
   (A) A implies D.
   (B) B implies A.
   (C) C implies A.
   (D) D implies B.

4. A fair coin is tossed three times. What is the probability that it will come up heads three times in a row?
   (A) $\dfrac{1}{8}$
   (B) $\dfrac{1}{4}$
   (C) $\dfrac{1}{3}$
   (D) $\dfrac{1}{2}$

5. The product of all distinct positive factors of which number below is the greatest?
   (A) 6
   (B) 8
   (C) 11
   (D) 13

6. "If Jim receives a grade of A on the test, I promise to give him a five-dollar reward."

   The promise above would be broken under which of the following conditions?
   (A) Jim does not receive an A, and the speaker does not give him a five-dollar reward.
   (B) Jim does not receive an A, and the speaker gives him a five-dollar reward.
   (C) Jim receives an A, and the speaker does not give him a five-dollar reward.
   (D) Jim receives an A, and the speaker gives him a five-dollar reward.

7. If $3 > x > -4$, which of the following expresses the range of possible values of x^2?
   (A) $-16 < x < 9$
   (B) $-9 < x < 16$
   (C) $0 < x < 16$
   (D) $9 < x < 16$

GO ON TO THE NEXT PAGE.

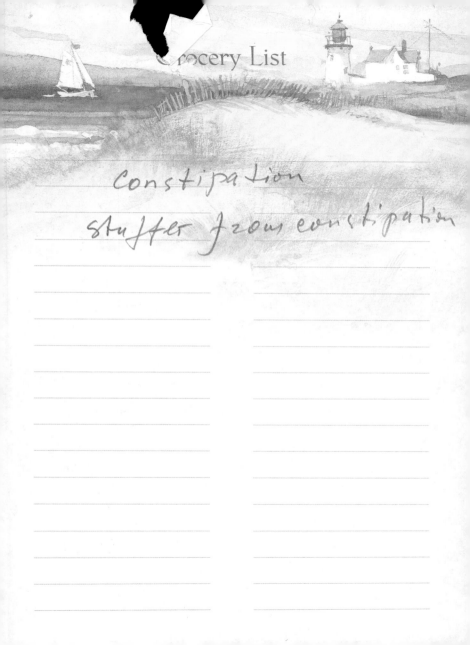

Grocery List

Constipation

stuffer from constipation

8. If a is an even integer and b is an odd integer, which of the following is <u>always</u> an odd integer?

    I. $a + b$

    II. ab

    III. $\dfrac{2a}{b}$

(A) I only
(B) II only
(C) I and II only
(D) II and III only

9. If John, Bill, Joe, Fred, and Luis constitute a basketball team, and if Bill, Henri, Fred, George, Phillipe, and Luis constitute a hockey team, how many players are on both teams?

(A) 0
(B) 1
(C) 2
(D) 3

10. If two fair six-sided dice, with faces numbered 1 through 6, are rolled, what is the probability that <u>neither</u> 3 nor 4 is showing on either die?

(A) $\dfrac{1}{3}$

(B) $\dfrac{4}{9}$

(C) $\dfrac{1}{2}$

(D) $\dfrac{2}{3}$

11. If x is an integer, y is the reciprocal of x, and $4y = -2$, then which of the following is the value of x?

(A) -2

(B) $-\dfrac{1}{2}$

(C) 1

(D) 4

12. If $Q = \{x \mid 0 < x < 99$, and x is the square of an integer$\}$, then Q contains how many elements?

(A) 8
(B) 9
(C) 10
(D) 64

13. If $f(x)$ is a linear function such that $f(4) = 3$ and $f(2) = -1$, then $f(x)$ equals

(A) $x - 1$
(B) $2x - 5$
(C) $x^3 - x^2$
(D) $-2x + 3$

GO ON TO THE NEXT PAGE.

Questions 14 and 15 refer to the table below:

**Daily productivity rates, per employee, for
Company X's five factories**

Factory	Number of Employees	Units Completed per Employee
A	40	18.5
B	20	12
C	25	14
D	50	17.5
E	30	20

14. Which of the factories produces the most units per day?

    (A) A
    (B) B
    (C) C
    (D) D

15. What is the average (arithmetic mean) number of units completed per employee for all five factories combined?

    (A) 16
    (B) 16.5
    (C) 17
    (D) 20

16. A three-person committee is to be chosen from among five candidates. How many different combinations are possible?

    (A) 5
    (B) 10
    (C) 25
    (D) 120

17. Which of the following is equal to $x^4 + 3x^3 - 4x - 12$?

    (A) $(x^2 - 6)(x^2 - 2)$
    (B) $(x^3 + x)(x - 12)$
    (C) $(x^3 - 4)(x + 3)$
    (D) $(x^2 + 5)(x^2 + 7)$

18. Which of the following statements is true?

    (A) The sum of two rational numbers is always greater than either of the numbers.
    (B) The product of two rational numbers is always greater than either of the two numbers.
    (C) The sum of two rational numbers is always rational.
    (D) The square root of a rational number is always rational.

19. If an enclosed garden in 10 feet longer than it is wide, and the perimeter of the garden is 180 feet, then what is the area, in square feet, of the garden?

    (A) 1,000
    (B) 1,200
    (C) 1,600
    (D) 2,000

20. If $\log_2 x = 6$, then $\log_8 x =$

    (A) 2
    (B) 3
    (C) 6
    (D) 12

21. $3(6^{-1}) =$

    (A) 2^{-1}
    (B) 3^{-1}
    (C) 12^{-1}
    (D) 18^{-1}

GO ON TO THE NEXT PAGE.

22. J = {x | x is a rational number}

K = {x | x is an integer}

L = {x | x is an integer and 0 < x < 30}

Which of the Venn diagrams below correctly expresses the relationship between J, K, and L?

(A)

(B)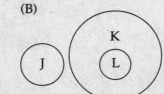

(C)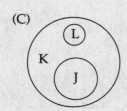

(D)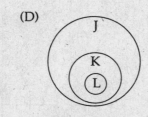

23. If $x < -2$ and $y < 7$, which of the statements below must be true?

(A) $y - x > 9$
(B) $xy < 0$
(C) $x^2 < y^2$
(D) $2x + y < 3$

24. If $f(x) = 3^x$, and $f(y) = 1$, then $y =$

(A) −1
(B) 0
(C) 1
(D) 2

25. Ten slips of paper bearing a number between one and ten are placed in a hopper. No two slips bear the same number. If two slips are drawn from the hopper, what is the probability that the sum of the numbers on those two slips is 15 or greater?

(A) $\dfrac{1}{40}$

(B) $\dfrac{1}{10}$

(C) $\dfrac{2}{9}$

(D) $\dfrac{1}{2}$

26.   I. $\dfrac{8 \times 9}{5}$

   II. $\dfrac{3 - \sqrt{3}}{6}$

   III. $\sqrt{3}$

Which of the above is NOT rational?

(A) I only
(B) I and II only
(C) II and III only
(D) III only

27. A deck of 52 cards contains 13 cards of each of four suits—clubs, spades, diamonds, and hearts. If three cards are drawn from the deck, what is the probability that all three will be of the suit of diamonds?

(A) $\dfrac{11}{850}$

(B) $\dfrac{1}{64}$

(C) $\dfrac{3}{52}$

(D) $\dfrac{1}{13}$

GO ON TO THE NEXT PAGE.

28. A traveler takes a bus from her hometown to another city and returns home by airplane. If the bus averages 50 miles per hour for the trip and the airplane averages 450 miles per hour, what is the traveler's average rate, in miles per hour, for the round trip?

(A)   90
(B) 125
(C) 200
(D) 250

29. Which of the numbers below is NOT an integer?

(A) $\dfrac{10}{2}$

(B) $\sqrt{7}$

(C) $\sqrt{49} \times \sqrt{49} \times \sqrt{49}$

(D) -3

30. In a certain town, 5,326 residents speak Ukrainian and 7,210 speak Russian; some people speak both. If 3,738 residents speak Ukrainian but not Russian, how many residents speak Russian but not Ukrainian?

(A) 6,428
(B) 5,622
(C) 4,105
(D) 3,471

31. A horse breeder owns nine horses. She races them against each other in groups of three. What is the maximum number of races she can run without racing the same group twice?

(A)   28
(B)   84
(C) 504
(D) 729

32. Which of the lines below is perpendicular to the line $4x - y = 6$?

(A) $y = 1$

(B) $y = 0$

(C) $y = 2x + 3$

(D) $y = 8 - \left(\dfrac{1}{4}\right)x$

33.

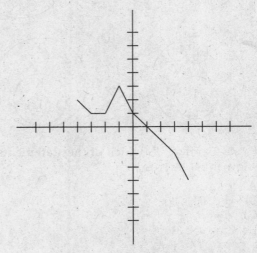

Which of the below expresses the range of $f(x)$, as shown on the Cartesian grid above?

(A) $-4 \le y \le 3$
(B) $-4 \le y \le 4$
(C) $-4 \le x \le 3$
(D) $-4 \le x \le 4$

GO ON TO THE NEXT PAGE.

PART II

Time—45 minutes

32 questions

Directions: Solve the following problems. Do not spend too much time on any one problem.

Notes: (1) Unless otherwise specified, the domain of any function f is assumed to be the set of all real numbers x for which $f(x)$ is a real number.

(2) i will be used to denote $\sqrt{-1}$.

(3) Figures that accompany the following problems are intended to provide information useful in solving the problems. They are drawn as accurately as possible EXCEPT when it is stated in a specific problem that its figure is not drawn to scale. All figures lie in a plane unless otherwise indicated.

34. Rosa has $\frac{1}{2}$ pound of apples. Her friend Malcolm has $\frac{2}{7}$ pound of apples. If they combine their apples, they will collectively have how many pounds of apples?

    (A) $\frac{3}{4}$

    (B) $\frac{11}{14}$

    (C) $\frac{6}{7}$

    (D) $\frac{9}{10}$

35. Which of the following is a counterexample to the statement "For all values n, n is rational when n^2 is rational"?

    (A) $n = 103$
    (B) $n = \sqrt{10}$
    (C) $n = 0$
    (D) $n = -2$

36.

    The number line above is represented by which of the following statements?

    (A) $x < 2$
    (B) $2 < x$ or $x < -7$
    (C) $2 \geq x \geq -7$
    (D) $-7 > x$ and $2 > x$

37. A diner serves five different entrees, three different types of potatoes, and four different green vegetable dishes. How many different combinations of one entree, one potato dish, and one green vegetable dish can the diner serve?

    (A) 60
    (B) 42
    (C) 30
    (D) 24

38. All A are B, and no C are B.

    Which of the following diagrams the statement above?

    (A) 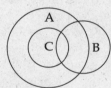   (B)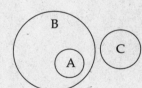

    (C) 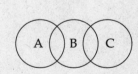   (D)

GO ON TO THE NEXT PAGE.

39. When $x < -1$, which of the values below is always greatest?

    (A) x^3

    (B) $\dfrac{x}{2}$

    (C) $|x|$

    (D) $2x$

40. Which of the numbers below is NOT prime?

    (A) 17
    (B) 23
    (C) 27
    (D) 37

41. The arithmetic mean of 32, 34, x, and y is 20. What is the arithmetic mean of x and y?

    (A) 12
    (B) 10
    (C) 8
    (D) 7

42. If Q = {2, 4, 6, 8, 10, 12} and R = {4, 8, 12, 16, 20}, then Q $\cup$ R has how many elements?

    (A) 3
    (B) 5
    (C) 8
    (D) 10

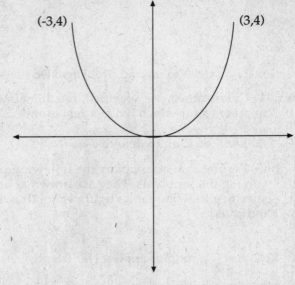

(-3,4)   (3,4)

43. The range of $f(x)$, shown on the Cartesian grid above, is

    (A) $y = 4$
    (B) $-3 < x < 3$
    (C) $-3 < y < 3$
    (D) $0 \le y \le 4$

44. If $1 \le x \le 100$, how many values of x are both the square of an integer and the cube of an integer?

    (A) 3
    (B) 2
    (C) 1
    (D) 0

45. An interior decorator plans to arrange five different figurines on his mantelpiece. How many different ways can the figurines be arranged?

    (A) 120
    (B) 100
    (C) 75
    (D) 25

GO ON TO THE NEXT PAGE.

46. If B = {x, y, z} and C = {f, g}, then how many ordered pairs make up the Cartesian product B × C?

(A) 2
(B) 3
(C) 5
(D) 6

47. The distance from New York to San Francisco is 2,514 miles. Denver is two-thirds of the way from New York to San Francisco. How far, in miles, is Denver from New York?

(A) 1,310
(B) 1,676
(C) 1,823
(D) 2,200

48. If $x > 1$, which of the following has the greatest value?

(A) $x(x - 1)$

(B) $(x + 1)(x - 1)$

(C) x^2

(D) $\left(\dfrac{x^3}{x}\right) - \left(\dfrac{1}{x}\right)$

49. A weather forecaster predicts a 0.3 probability of rain on Monday and a 0.4 probability of rain on Tuesday. If the forecaster is correct, what is the likelihood that it will rain on neither Monday nor Tuesday?

(A) 0.35
(B) 0.42
(C) 0.5
(D) 0.6

50. Which of the following is a complete list of the rational roots of $x^2 - x\sqrt{3} + 5x = 5\sqrt{3}$?

(A) $(-5, \sqrt{3})$
(B) $(-5, -3)$
(C) $(5, -3)$
(D) (-5)

51. A jelly bean jar contains seven red jelly beans, five white jelly beans, and three black jelly beans. If two jelly beans are chosen from the jar at random, without replacing the first, what is the probability that one red and one white jelly bean are the two chosen?

(A) $\dfrac{1}{6}$

(B) $\dfrac{1}{5}$

(C) $\dfrac{2}{7}$

(D) $\dfrac{1}{3}$

52. If $f(x) = x^2 - 2x$, then $f(x + 3) =$
(A) $x^3 + 2x^2 - 6$
(B) $x^2 - 2x - 3$
(C) $x^2 + 2x - 6$
(D) $x^2 + 4x + 3$

GO ON TO THE NEXT PAGE.

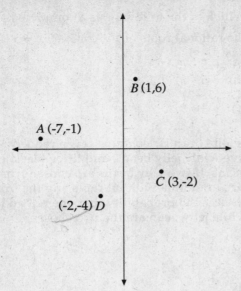

53. In the figure above, which point is on the line $2y - 4x = 8$?

(A) A
(B) B
(C) C
(D) D

54. If $f(x) = 3x - 1$, and $g(x) = x^2$, then $f(g(-2)) =$

(A) −5
(B) −4
(C) 11
(D) 15

55. If B = {$x \mid x$ is an integer greater than 0} and C = {$x \mid x$ is an odd integer less than 100}, which of the below is a subset of B∩C?

(A) {13, 17, 21, 46}
(B) {10, 20, 30}
(C) {−5, −3, 7}
(D) {15}

56. If $f(x)$ is a linear function such that $f(4) = 12$ and $f(-2) = 3$, then $f(9) =$

(A) $\dfrac{39}{2}$

(B) $\dfrac{27}{2}$

(C) 13

(D) 8

57. "When I am hungry, I always eat."

Which of the following correctly states the contrapositive of the statement above?

(A) When I am not hungry, I never eat.
(B) When I am not eating, I am not hungry.
(C) When I am eating, I must be hungry.
(D) When I am not hungry, I sometimes eat.

58. If $f(x) = 2x$ and the range of $(f)x$ is all even positive integers less than 100, then the domain of $(f)x$ is all

(A) positive integers less than 50
(B) even positive integers less than 50
(C) even positive integers less than 100
(D) even positive integers less than 200

59. In a group of 117 people, 67 have brown eyes, 25 have blue eyes, 14 have green eyes, and 11 have hazel eyes. The likelihood that a person chosen at random from the group will have either brown or green eyes is

(A) $\dfrac{2}{3}$

(B) $\dfrac{9}{13}$

(C) $\dfrac{95}{117}$

(D) $\dfrac{11}{12}$

GO ON TO THE NEXT PAGE.

60. If $f(x) = 3x - 2$, and $g(f(x)) = x$, then $g(x) =$

(A) $3x + 2$

(B) $2x - 3$

(C) $\dfrac{x}{3} + 2$

(D) $\dfrac{x+2}{3}$

61. An automobile collector has 30 automobiles with various features. 14 automobiles have automatic transmissions, 18 have power windows, and 21 have power brakes. 7 of the automobiles have all three features; each has at least one of the features. How many automobiles have exactly two of the features?

(A) 5
(B) 7
(C) 8
(D) 9

62. $(3i)(4 - i)(4 + i) =$
(A) $44i$
(B) $51i$
(C) $60i$
(D) $72i$

63. Let S = {9, 11, 13, 16, 81}. What is the sum of the mean and the median of S?

(A) 12
(B) 20
(C) 39
(D) 93

64. Which of the below could be the graph of a linear function?

(A) 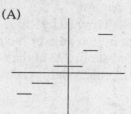   (B)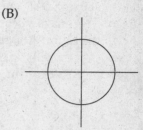

(C) 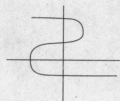   (D)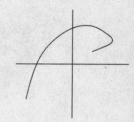

65. In base four, the next whole number greater than 2,133 is

(A) 2,134
(B) 2,140
(C) 2,200
(D) 2,211

STOP

IF YOU FINISH BEFORE TIME IS CALLED, YOU MAY CHECK YOUR WORK ON THIS SECTION ONLY.
DO NOT WORK ON ANY OTHER SECTION IN THE TEST.

SCORING YOUR TEST

This test is a facsimile of the ETS-written CLEP general exam in College Mathematics. Care has been taken to make sure that this test closely resembles the actual exam both in content and format. In other words, when you take the real CLEP, it should look a lot like the test you've just taken.

ETS has never released its scoring methods for the CLEP. ETS states in its literature that, if you get half the raw score points available to you on the test, you should score the national medium—usually between 480 and 500—on a given test.

Your raw score is determined by subtracting 1/3 the number of questions you answer incorrectly from the number of questions you answer correctly. Questions you leave blank are worth 0 points.

Typically, you need about 2/3 of the raw score points available on a test to score in the mid-600s on an ETS test, but, again, this is only speculation regarding the CLEP.

12

Answers and Explanations to the College Mathematics Exam

SECTION 2

QUESTIONS	EXPLANATIONS

Read this entire section, even the explanations for the questions you answered correctly. The material covered in these explanations add up to a pretty thourough review of the material tested on the CLEP. Plus, many explanations contain helpful test-taking tips.

1. If $3x = 12$, and $5y = 25$, then $2x + 8y =$

   (A) 32
   (B) 40
   (C) 48
   (D) 59

1. **(C)** is the correct answer. If $3x = 12$, then $x = 4$. $5y = 25$, so $y = 5$. Therefore, $2x + 8y = 2(4) + 8(5) = 48$. This is an easy problem.

2. Which of the following is NOT a number of people among whom 1,365 marbles could be distributed evenly?

   (A) 3
   (B) 5
   (C) 7
   (D) 9

2. **(D)** is the correct answer. This is a divisibility problem. 1,365 is divisible by 3 because the sum of its digits is divisible by 3; this trick works for 3 and 9 <u>only</u>. 1,365 is divisible by 5 because it ends in a 5 (numbers divisible by 5 end in 0 or 5). To determine divisibility by 7 you have to divide by 7; however, in this problem you need not, because 1,365 is NOT divisible by 9; we know this because the sum of the digits in numbers divisible by 9 is divisible by 9.

3. If A implies B, B implies C, and C implies D, which of the following is true?

   (A) A implies D.
   (B) B implies A.
   (C) C implies A.
   (D) D implies B.

3. **(A)** is the correct answer. In logic, "implies" means "necessitates." Hence, A necessitates B, which necessitates C, which in turn necessitates D. Thus, A implies D. Note that all the other answer choices incorrectly try to reverse the direction. "A implies B" does not mean that "B implies A."

4. A fair coin is tossed three times. What is the probability that it will come up heads three times in a row?

   (A) $\frac{1}{8}$

   (B) $\frac{1}{4}$

   (C) $\frac{1}{3}$

   (D) $\frac{1}{2}$

4. **(A)** is the correct answer. The chance that the coin will come up heads on the first toss is $\frac{1}{2}$. That is true for the second and third tosses as well. To determine the probability that the three will occur consecutively, multiply the three probabilities. $\frac{1}{2} \times \frac{1}{2} \times \frac{1}{2} = \frac{1}{8}$. You could also write out the possibilities: HHH, HHT, HTH, HTT, THH, THT, TTH, TTT.

SECTION 2

5. The product of all distinct positive factors of which number below is the greatest?

   (A) 6
   (B) 8
   (C) 11
   (D) 13

5. **(B)** is the correct answer. All the positive factors of 8 are 1, 2, 4, and 8; their product is 64. 11 and 13, although larger numbers, are prime, so they have only two factors, whose products are, respectively, 11 and 13.

6. "If Jim receives a grade of A on the test, I promise to give him a five-dollar reward."

   The promise above would be broken under which of the following conditions?
   (A) Jim does not receive an A, and the speaker does not give him a five-dollar reward.
   (B) Jim does not receive an A, and the speaker gives him a five-dollar reward.
   (C) Jim receives an A, and the speaker does not give him a five-dollar reward.
   (D) Jim receives an A, and the speaker gives him a five-dollar reward.

6. **(C)** is the correct answer. Don't get thrown on this one. The speaker's promise hinges on the condition that Jim receive an A; without the A grade, there is no promise to break. The answer must be (C) or (D). In (D), the speaker fulfills the promise. The answer must be (C).

7. If $3 > x > -4$, which of the following expresses the range of possible values of x^2?
   (A) $-16 < x < 9$
   (B) $-9 < x < 16$
   (C) $0 < x < 16$
   (D) $9 < x < 16$

7. **(C)** is the correct answer. Remember that x^2 must be greater than or equal to 0. This eliminates (A) and (B), the two most likely careless errors. Since x could equal 0, x^2 could also equal 0. (D), then, is clearly wrong. The answer is (C).

8. If a is an even integer and b is an odd integer, which of the following is <u>always</u> an odd integer?

   I. $a + b$

   II. ab

   III. $\left(\dfrac{2a}{b}\right)$

   (A) I only
   (B) II only
   (C) I and II only
   (D) II and III only

8. **(A)** is the correct answer. Plug in values. Make $a = 2$ and $b = 3$. $a + b = 5$, $ab = 6$, and $\dfrac{2a}{2} = \dfrac{4}{3}$. Only $a + b$ is odd, so Roman numeral I is the only answer that could be correct. Look at the answer choices. The answer to this question must be either "I only" or "none of the above." Since the latter choice is not available, the answer must be "I only."

SECTION 2

QUESTIONS	EXPLANATIONS
9. If John, Bill, Joe, Fred, and Luis constitute a basketball team, and if Bill, Henri, Fred, George, Phillipe, and Luis constitute a hockey team, how many players are on both teams? (A) 0 (B) 1 (C) 2 (D) 3	9. **(D)** is the correct answer. If you got this wrong, you probably were looking for something more complicated than what is being asked. Bill, Fred, and Luis—3 players—are common to both teams. That's all there is to this problem.
10. If two fair six-sided dice, with faces numbered 1 through 6, are rolled, what is the probability that <u>neither</u> 3 nor 4 is showing on either die? (A) $\frac{1}{3}$ (B) $\frac{4}{9}$ (C) $\frac{1}{2}$ (D) $\frac{2}{3}$	10. **(B)** is the correct answer. To figure the probability that 3 and 4 will <u>not</u> come up in a roll of the die, consider the probability that the other numbers—1, 2, 5, and 6—<u>will</u> come up. The probability that a 1, 2, 5, or 6 will appear on the first die is $\frac{4}{6}$, or $\frac{2}{3}$. The same is true, of course, of the second die. The probability that these numbers will appear on both dice is the product of the two probabilities. $\frac{2}{3} \times \frac{2}{3} = \frac{4}{9}$.
11. If x is an integer, y is the reciprocal of x, and $4y = -2$, then which of the following is the value of x? (A) -2 (B) $-\left(\frac{1}{2}\right)$ (C) 1 (D) 4	11. **(A)** is the correct answer. Reciprocals are two numbers which, when multiplied, result in a product of 1. Start calculations on this problem with $4y = -2$. Thus, $y = -\left(\frac{1}{2}\right)$. x, its reciprocal, equals -2.

SECTION 2

12. If $Q = \{x \mid 0 < x < 99$, and x is the square of an integer$\}$, then Q contains how many elements*?

    (A) 8
    (B) 9
    (C) 10
    (D) 64

12. **(B)** is the correct answer. Q is the set of all numbers less than 99 that are also the squares of integers. Thus, $Q = \{1, 4, 9, 16, 25, 36, 49, 64, 81\}$. Q contains 9 elements.

13. If $f(x)$ is a linear function such that $f(4) = 3$ and $f(2) = -1$, then $f(x)$ equals

    (A) $x - 1$
    (B) $2x - 5$
    (C) $x^3 - x^2$
    (D) $-2x + 3$

13. **(B)** is the correct answer. Simply plug the values from the question into the answer choices and choose the one that yields the appropriate results; that is, the answer choice that makes $f(4) = 3$ and makes $f(2) = -1$. (A) indicates that $f(x) = x - 1$. This is impossible because $f(2) = -1$, not 1, as it would if $f(x) = x - 1$. (B) is the only answer choice that makes $f(4) = 3$ and $f(2) = -1$.

SECTION 2

Questions 14 and 15 refer to the table below:

Daily productivity rates, per employee, for Company X's five factories

Factory	Number of Employees	Units Completed per Employee
A	40	18.5
B	20	12
C	25	14
D	50	17.5
E	30	20

14. Which of the factories produces the most units per day?

 (A) A
 (B) B
 (C) C
 (D) D

14. **(D)** is the correct answer. To find the number of units produced each day at each factory, you have to multiply the number of employees by the average number of units produced per employee. Factory D has 50 employees who average 17.5 units per day; therefore, factory D's daily output is $50 \times 17.5 = 875$ units. Note that you do not have to check factory E (it is not among the answer choices). Common sense should tell you that factories B and C, which have fewer employees and a lower unit per employee rate, could not be the correct answers.

15. What is the average (arithmetic mean) number of units completed per employee for all five factories combined?

 (A) 16
 (B) 16.5
 (C) 17
 (D) 20

15. **(C)** is the correct answer. To find the average number of units completed per employee for all five factories, you will have to divide the total number of units produced by the five factories by the total number of employees. Multiply all five sets of numbers, employees and units per day for each factory. A = 740, B = 240, C = 350, D = 875, and E = 600. The company produces 2,885 units. Divide by its 165 employees and you get 17, the average daily output per employee for all five factories.

SECTION 2

16. A three-person committee is to be chosen from among five candidates. How many different combinations are possible?

    (A)   5
    (B)   10
    (C)   25
    (D)   120

16. **(B)** is the correct answer. Assign each of the candidates a letter—call them A, B, C, D, and E. Then, using the blank space provided in the test booklet, list all possible combinations. Start with A and B: ABC, ABD, and ABE. Now move to AC: ACD and ACE. Do not list ACB, as you have already listed this combination once (as ABC). Here are all the combinations: ABC, ABD, ABE, ACD, ACE, ADE, BCD, BCE, BDE, and CDE. There are 10 total. Use this method on all combination problems for which the answer choices are not huge numbers. The method is foolproof and takes less time than you would think.

17. Which of the following is equal to $x^4 + 3x^3 - 4x - 12$?

    (A) $(x^2 - 6)(x^2 - 2)$
    (B) $(x^3 + x)(x - 12)$
    (C) $(x^3 - 4)(x + 3)$
    (D) $(x^2 + 5)(x^2 + 7)$

17. **(C)** is the correct answer. This one can be done by factoring. Look over the answer choices; will x^4 be the product of x^2 and x^2 or x^3 and x? The answer is x^3 and x; the clue is that $x^4 + 3x^3 - 4x - 12$ has an x^3 but no x^2. Thus the answer must be (B) or (C). Expand both, or realize that you will need 4 and 3 to arrive at a result that includes $3x^3$ and $-4x$. However, you could also solve this problem by plugging in. Try $x = 2$. This makes $x^4 + 3x^3 - 4x - 12 = 16 + 24 - 8 - 12 = 20$. When you plug $x = 2$ into the answer choices, only (C) equals 20.

18. Which of the following statements is true?

    (A) The sum of two rational numbers is always greater than either of the numbers.
    (B) The product of two rational numbers is always greater than either of the two numbers.
    (C) The sum of two rational numbers is always rational.
    (D) The square root of a rational number is always rational.

18. **(C)** is the correct answer. (A) is untrue because negative integers are rational. (B) is untrue for the same reason: one positive and one negative disproves this statement. (D) can be disproved by many counterexamples: 5 is rational, its square root is not. However, the sum of two integers, an integer and a fraction, or two fractions will always be rational; therefore, (C) is correct. If you are still confused about this, see the definition of rational numbers on page 124.

SECTION 2

QUESTIONS	EXPLANATIONS

19. If an enclosed garden in 10 feet longer than it is wide, and the perimeter of the garden is 180 feet, then what is the area, in square feet, of the garden?

   (A) 1,000
   (B) 1,200
   (C) 1,600
   (D) 2,000

19. **(D)** is the correct answer. The sides of the rectangle described in problem 19 can be expressed as x and $x + 10$. The perimeter of the garden is the sum of its four sides $x + x + 10 + x + x + 10 = 180$. Simplify this to $4x = 160$. Thus $x = 40$. The sides of the garden are 40 and 50 feet, so its area is $40 \times 50 = 2,000$ square feet.

20. If $\log_2 x = 6$, then $\log_8 x =$

   (A) 2
   (B) 3
   (C) 6
   (D) 12

20. **(A)** is the correct answer. $\log_2 x = 6$ means that $2^6 = x$. Therefore, $x = 64$. The question then asks what is the value of $\log_8 x$. We know that $x = 64$, so we can rewrite this as $\log_8 64 = ?$. Now the question is: 8 to what power equals 64? The answer is 2, which is answer choice (A).

21. $3 (6^{-1}) =$

   (A) 2^{-1}
   (B) 3^{-1}
   (C) 12^{-1}
   (D) 18^{-1}

21. **(A)** is the correct answer. To answer this one correctly, you must know that an exponent of -1 means 1 over the number. In this case, $6^{-1} = \dfrac{1}{6.3} \times \dfrac{1}{6} = \dfrac{1}{2}$, which can be expressed as 2^{-1}.

22. $J = \{x \mid x \text{ is a rational number}\}$
$K = \{x \mid x \text{ is an integer}\}$
$L = \{x \mid x \text{ is an integer and } 0 < x < 30\}$
Which of the Venn diagrams below correctly expresses the relationship between J, K, and L?

   (A)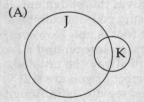

   (B)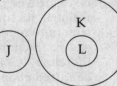

   (C)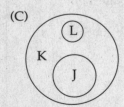

   (D)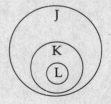

22. **(D)** is the correct answer. Rational numbers are those that can be expressed as the ratio of two integers. Rational numbers include integers and fractions with integer numerators and denominators. Thus, K is a subset of J, and the diagram must show K entirely contained by J. Only (D) does this.

SECTION 2

23. If $x < -2$ and $y < 7$, which of the statements below must be true?

    (A) $y - x > 9$
    (B) $xy < 0$
    (C) $x^2 < y^2$
    (D) $2x + y < 3$

23. **(D)** is the correct answer. (A) can be disproved by making $y = -10$ and $x = -2$. (B) is disproved by the same values. (C) can be disproved by making $x = -6$ and $y = 0$. Thus (D) must be correct.

24. If $f(x) = 3^x$, and $f(y) = 1$, then $y =$

    (A) -1
    (B) 0
    (C) 1
    (D) 2

24. **(B)** is the correct answer. If $f(y) = 1$, then $3^y = 1$. $3^0 = 1$, so y must equal 0. To answer this correctly, you must know that $x^0 = 1$, except when $x = 0$, in which case x^0 is undefined.

25. Ten slips of paper bearing a number between one and ten are placed in a hopper. No two slips bear the same number. If two slips are drawn from the hopper, what is the probability that the sum of the numbers on those two slips is 15 or greater?

    (A) $\dfrac{1}{40}$

    (B) $\dfrac{1}{10}$

    (C) $\dfrac{2}{9}$

    (D) $\dfrac{1}{2}$

25. **(B)** is the correct answer. First, determine the number of possible combinations of two slips of paper. On the first draw, any of the 10 slips may be drawn; on the second, any of the 9 remaining slips. Hence, there are $10 \times 9 = 90$ possible combinations. How many will have a sum of 15 or greater? List them. Assume that on the first draw, a 10 is drawn. On the second draw, a 5, 6, 7, 8, or 9 would satisfy the conditions of the problem. If a 9 is drawn on the first draw, a 6, 7, or 8 on the second draw would satisfy the conditions of the problem. Note that you should count the combination of 10 and 9 only once; because you counted it while assuming that 10 was the first number drawn, you should NOT count it again when assuming that 9 was the first number drawn. Here are all the combinations: 10 and 9, 10 and 8, 10 and 7, 10 and 6, 10 and 5, 9 and 6, 9 and 7, 9 and 8, and 8 and 7. That's a total of 9 combinations, out of 90 possible, for a $\dfrac{1}{10}$ probability.

SECTION 2

QUESTIONS	EXPLANATIONS

26.   I. $\dfrac{8 \times 9}{5}$

   II. $\dfrac{3 - \sqrt{3}}{6}$

   III. $\sqrt{3}$

Which of the above is NOT rational?

(A) I only
(B) I and II only
(C) II and III only
(D) III only

26. **(C)** is the correct answer. A seemingly inordinate number of questions on the math CLEP revolve around the definition of a rational number. Make sure you know it! A rational number is one that can be expressed as the ratio of two integers; it can be an integer or a fraction, but it can't be a square root (by far the most common type of non-rational number, and virtually the only type that shows up on this exam). Neither II nor III is rational, as neither can be simplified so as to eliminate the square roots.

27. A deck of 52 cards contains 13 cards of each of four suits—clubs, spades, diamonds, and hearts. If three cards are drawn from the deck, what is the probability that all three will be of the suit of diamonds?

(A) $\dfrac{11}{850}$

(B) $\dfrac{1}{64}$

(C) $\dfrac{3}{52}$

(D) $\dfrac{1}{13}$

27. **(A)** is the correct answer. There seem to be an inordinate number of questions on the CLEP concerning probabilities and combinations. Master these skills! On the first draw, you have a $\dfrac{13}{52}$, or $\dfrac{1}{4}$ chance of pulling a diamond. OK, so let's say you pulled that diamond. On your second draw, you have a $\dfrac{12}{51}$ chance of pulling a diamond (because there are only 51 cards left in the deck, of which only 12 are diamonds). On the third draw, you'll have an $\dfrac{11}{50}$ chance. Multiply the three probabilities to find the likelihood that the three will occur successively. $\dfrac{1}{4} \times \dfrac{12}{51} \times \dfrac{11}{50} = \dfrac{132}{10,200}$, which reduces to $\dfrac{11}{850}$.

28. A traveler takes a bus from her hometown to another city and returns home by airplane. If the bus averages 50 miles per hour for the trip and the airplane averages 450 miles per hour, what is the traveler's average rate, in miles per hour, for the round trip?

(A)   90
(B)   125
(C)   200
(D)   250

28. **(A)** is the correct answer. Plug in! In this case, plug in a distance between the two cities. Pick a number that makes the problem easy; since the plane averages 450 miles per hour, pick 450. The bus, at 50 miles per hour, will take 9 hours to get from the traveler's hometown to her destination. The plane will take 1 hour to make the return trip. The round trip is 900 miles and takes 10 hours, for an average rate of 90 miles per hour.

SECTION 2

29. Which of the numbers below is NOT an integer?

(A) $\dfrac{10}{2}$

(B) $\sqrt{7}$

(C) $\sqrt{49} \times \sqrt{49} \times \sqrt{49}$

(D) -3

29. (B) is the correct answer. Integers are whole values, positive, negative, and 0. Since $\dfrac{10}{2} = 5$, (A) is an integer. Since $\sqrt{49} = 7$, (C) is an integer.

30. In a certain town, 5,326 residents speak Ukrainian and 7,210 speak Russian; some people speak both. If 3,738 residents speak Ukrainian but not Russian, how many residents speak Russian but not Ukrainian?

(A) 6,428
(B) 5,622
(C) 4,105
(D) 3,471

30. (B) is the correct answer. You can draw an Venn diagram to solve this problem, but it isn't necessary. The 5,326 people in town who speak Ukrainian includes both those who speak only Ukrainian and those who speak both Ukrainian and Russian. Subtract the number who speak only Ukrainian (3,738), and the result is 1,588. That's the number of people who speak BOTH Ukrainian AND Russian. Now, take the number of people who speak Russian (7,210). This number includes those who speak both Russian and Ukrainian AND those who speak only Russian. Subtract out the number of people who speak both languages (1,588) and the result is 5,622, the number of people who speak only Russian.

31. A horse breeder owns nine horses. She races them against each other in groups of three. What is the maximum number of races she can run without racing the same group twice?

(A) 28
(B) 84
(C) 504
(D) 729

31. (B) is the correct answer. To do this problem you need the combinations formula, which is:

$$\frac{(n!)}{\left[r!(n-r)!\right]}$$

where n is the number of things in the entire group and r is the number of things in each combination. In this case, the formula translates to:

$$\frac{(9!)}{\left[3!(9-3)!\right]}$$

or

$$\frac{(9 \times 8 \times 7 \times 6 \times 5 \times 4 \times 3 \times 2 \times 1)}{(3 \times 2 \times 1)(6 \times 5 \times 4 \times 3 \times 2 \times 1)}$$

Now, reduce.

The result is 84.

QUESTIONS	EXPLANATIONS

32. Which of the lines below is perpendicular to the line $4x - y = 6$?

    (A) $y = 1$

    (B) $y = 0$

    (C) $y = 2x + 3$

    (D) $y = 8 - \left(\dfrac{1}{4}\right)x$

32. **(D)** is the correct answer. Rewrite the original equation so that it is in the $y = mx + b$ format. This yields $y = 4x - 6$, which means that the slope of the line created by this equation is 4. A perpendicular line will have a slope that is the negative reciprocal of 4, which is $-\dfrac{1}{4}$. Hence, (D) is your answer.

33.

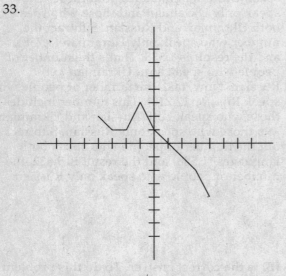

Which of the below expresses the range of $f(x)$, as shown on the Cartesian grid above?

    (A) $-4 \leq y \leq 3$
    (B) $-4 \leq y \leq 4$
    (C) $-4 \leq x \leq 3$
    (D) $-4 \leq x \leq 4$

33. **(A)** is the correct answer. Remember: the domain is the values of x, the range is the values of y. A good mnemonic device is this: one's domain is one's home, or starting point. The range, then, is where you go when you leave home. It is, metaphorically speaking, where the results of $f(x)$, like the buffalo, roam. Since we're looking for the range here, we want a list of all possible values of y; that in itself should eliminate answer choices (C) and (D). Look at the graph again; y clearly never becomes greater than 3. (A) is the correct answer.

SECTION 2

QUESTIONS	EXPLANATIONS

PART II

34. Rosa has $\frac{1}{2}$ pound of apples. Her friend Malcolm has $\frac{2}{7}$ pound of apples. If they combine their apples, they will collectively have how many pounds of apples?

    (A) $\frac{3}{4}$

    (B) $\frac{11}{14}$

    (C) $\frac{6}{7}$

    (D) $\frac{9}{10}$

34. **(B)** is the correct answer. The solution to this problem is $\frac{1}{2}+\frac{2}{7}=\frac{7}{14}+\frac{4}{14}=\frac{11}{14}$. That's all there is to it. Occasionally, the CLEP will throw you a problem so simple that you'll think there's some trick to it, and as a result you might fumble an easy one. If you got this one wrong, you probably tried something more complicated than was necessary; otherwise, you just made a careless addition error.

35. Which of the following is a counterexample to the statement "For all values n, n is rational when n^2 is rational"?

    (A) $n=103$

    (B) $n=\sqrt{10}$

    (C) $n=0$

    (D) $n=-2$

35. **(B)** is the correct answer. $\sqrt{10}$, squared, equals 10, a rational number; however, $\sqrt{10}$ is not rational, and hence is a counterexample to the statement "For all values n, n is rational when n^2 is rational."

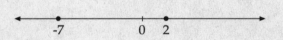

36. The number line above is represented by which of the following statements?

    (A) $x < 2$

    (B) $2 < x$ or $x < -7$

    (C) $2 \geq x \geq -7$

    (D) $-7 > x$ and $2 > x$

36. **(C)** is the correct answer. Go back and look at the number line more closely if you got this wrong. The solid dots on 2 and –7 indicate that x could equal either value; the solid line indicates all other values x could equal. Those values are the ones between –7 and 2, as (C) correctly indicates. Because (A) allows x to equal any value less than 2—for example, –10—it is wrong, since x must be greater than or equal to –7. If you got this one wrong, you either are extremely prone to careless errors or you have fundamental gaps in your knowledge of CLEP-level math, and should review heavily before taking this exam.

QUESTIONS	EXPLANATIONS

37. A diner serves five different entrees, three different types of potatoes, and four different green vegetable dishes. How many different combinations of one entree, one potato dish, and one green vegetable dish can the diner serve?

(A) 60
(B) 42
(C) 30
(D) 24

37. **(A)** is the correct answer. With any of the five different entrees you can have any of the three different potato dishes; therefore, there are 15 (5×3) different combinations of entrees and potatoes. Each of these 15 can be combined with any of the four different green vegetable dishes; therefore yielding 60 (15×4) different possible combinations.

38. All A are B, and no C are B.
Which of the following diagrams the statement above?

(A)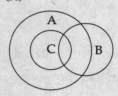

(B)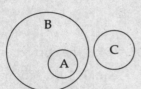

(C)

(D)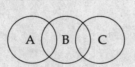

38. **(B)** is the correct answer. The statement "All A are B" tells you that either A equals B or that A is a subset of B. In either case, only answer choice (B) reflects this fact. You don't even need to concern yourself with the statement "no C are B" to get this one right; a rare and beautiful gift to be savored, courtesy of the folks who write the CLEP.

39. When $x < -1$, which of the values below is always greatest?

(A) x^3

(B) $\dfrac{x}{2}$

(C) $|x|$

(D) $2x$

39. **(C)** is the correct answer. Plug in! Let's make $x = -4$. (A) = -64; (B) = -2; (C) = 4 ($|x|$ means that you should find the absolute value of x; absolute value is the distance a number is from 0 on a number line, and, with the exception of $|0|$, it is always positive); and (D) = -8. (C) is the greatest, and is therefore the correct answer! It's just that simple!

SECTION 2

QUESTIONS	EXPLANATIONS

40. Which of the numbers below is NOT prime?

   (A) 17
   (B) 23
   (C) 27
   (D) 37

40. **(C)** is the correct answer. A prime number is one that is divisible only by itself and 1. 27 is also divisible by 3 and 9.

41. The arithmetic mean of 32, 34, x, and y is 20. What is the arithmetic mean of x and y?

   (A) 12
   (B) 10
   (C) 8
   (D) 7

41. **(D)** is the correct answer. The arithmetic mean of a group is its sum divided by the number of members of the group; it is what is most commonly referred to as "the average." The sum of 32, 34, x, and y is $4 \times 20 = 80$. Therefore $x + y = 14$ (the result of subtracting 32 and 34 from 80). The arithmetic mean of x and y, then, is $\frac{14}{2} = 7$.

42. If Q = {2, 4, 6, 8, 10, 12} and R = {4, 8, 12, 16, 20}, then Q $\cup$ R has how many elements?

   (A) 3
   (B) 5
   (C) 8
   (D) 10

42. **(C)** is the correct answer. The symbol $\cup$ represents the union of sets. The union of two sets counts all the elements of each set; elements held in common are not counted twice. Hence, the union of Q and R = {2, 4, 6, 8, 10, 12, 16, 20}, and has 8 elements.

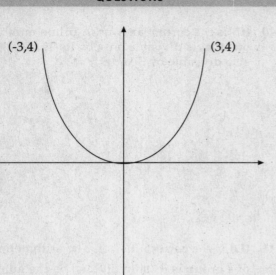

43. The range of $f(x)$, shown on the Cartesian grid above, is

    (A) $y = 4$
    (B) $-3 < x < 3$
    (C) $-3 < y < 3$
    (D) $0 \le y \le 4$

43. **(D)** is the correct answer. Once again: the domain is the values of x, the range is the values of y. Again, a good mnemonic device is this: one's domain is one's home, or starting point. The range is where the results of $f(x)$ roam (it's also where the buffalo roam; again, this is a mnemonic device that many have used with great success). In the Cartesian grid accompanying this problem, y is never greater than 4 and is never less than 0. Answer choice (D) accurately reflects this.

44. If $1 \le x \le 100$, how many values of x are <u>both</u> the square of an integer <u>and</u> the cube of an integer?

    (A) 3
    (B) 2
    (C) 1
    (D) 0

44. **(B)** is the correct answer. The easiest way to do this problem is to list all possible values of x^3 within the parameters of the problem. Those would be: 1, 8, 27, and 64. How many of these numbers are also perfect squares? Two of them (1 and 64). The answer is (B).

SECTION 2

QUESTIONS	EXPLANATIONS

45. An interior decorator plans to arrange five different figurines on his mantelpiece. How many different ways can the figurines be arranged?

   (A) 120
   (B) 100
   (C) 75
   (D) 25

45. **(A)** is the correct answer. The answer to this problem is 5!, which translates to $5 \times 4 \times 3 \times 2 \times 1$. That's because any of the 5 figurines could be in the first position. After the first figurine is chosen, any of the remaining 4 could be in the second position, and so on until you reach the last position.

46. If B = {x, y, z} and C = {f, g}, then how many ordered pairs make up the Cartesian product B $\times$ C?

   (A) 2
   (B) 3
   (C) 5
   (D) 6

46. **(D)** is the correct answer. The Cartesian product of two sets is the number of ordered pairs that can be made taking one element from each set. Since B has 3 elements and C has 2 elements, there are $3 \times 2 = 6$ possible ordered pairs.

47. The distance from New York to San Francisco is 2,514 miles. Denver is two-thirds of the way from New York to San Francisco. How far, in miles, is Denver from New York?

   (A) 1,310
   (B) 1,676
   (C) 1,823
   (D) 2,200

47. **(B)** is the correct answer. All you have to do to get this one is find two-thirds of 2,514.
$$2,514\left(\frac{2}{3}\right) = 1,676.$$

SECTION 2

QUESTIONS	EXPLANATIONS

48. If $x > 1$, which of the following has the greatest value?

(A) $x(x - 1)$

(B) $(x + 1)(x - 1)$

(C) x^2

(D) $\left(\dfrac{x^3}{x}\right) - \left(\dfrac{1}{x}\right)$

48. (C) is the correct answer. Plug in. Let's make $x = 5$. (A) $= 5(4) = 20$; (B) $= 6(4) = 24$; (C) $= 25$; (D) $= 25 - \dfrac{1}{5} =$ a little bit less than 25. The answer is (C). Note that (B) is the difference of perfect squares, meaning it is equal to $x^2 - 1$.

49. A weather forecaster predicts a 0.3 probability of rain on Monday and a 0.4 probability of rain on Tuesday. If the forecaster is correct, what is the likelihood that it will rain on neither Monday nor Tuesday?

(A) 0.35
(B) 0.42
(C) 0.5
(D) 0.6

49. (B) is the correct answer. The probability that it will not rain on Monday is 0.7; that it will not rain on Tuesday, 0.6. The probability that the two will happen consecutively is calculated by multiplying the two.

50. Which of the following is a complete list of the rational roots of $x^2 - x\sqrt{3} + 5x = 5\sqrt{3}$?

(A) $(-5, \sqrt{3})$
(B) $(-5, -3)$
(C) $(5, -3)$
(D) (-5)

50. (D) is the correct answer. Simplify this equation by bringing everything over to one side of the equal sign. The result should be: $x^2 - x\sqrt{3} + 5x - 5\sqrt{3} = 0$. Now, factor. Your result should be $(x + 5)(x - \sqrt{3}) = 0$. The roots are $(-5, \sqrt{3})$ of which only -5 is rational. Backsolving would be another way to solve the problem. Eliminate (A) immediately (it contains an irrational number). Now try the equation in the question with each of the answer choices. The one that satisfies the equation (only -5) is the correct answer.

SECTION 2

QUESTIONS	EXPLANATIONS

51. A jelly bean jar contains seven red jelly beans, five white jelly beans, and three black jelly beans. If two jelly beans are chosen from the jar at random, without replacing the first, what is the probability that one red and one white jelly bean are the two chosen?

(A) $\frac{1}{6}$

(B) $\frac{1}{5}$

(C) $\frac{2}{7}$

(D) $\frac{1}{3}$

51. **(A)** is the correct answer. On the first draw, the chance that a red jelly bean will be drawn is $\frac{7}{15}$. The chance that the second draw will result in a white jelly bean is $\frac{5}{14}$. Multiply the two to determine the probability that they will occur simultaneously; the result is $\frac{1}{6}$. Note that if you reverse the order (white on first draw, red on the second), you get $\frac{5}{15} \times \frac{7}{14}$, and the result is the same.

52. If $f(x) = x^2 - 2x$, then $f(x + 3) =$
    (A) $x^3 + 2x^2 - 6$
    (B) $x^2 - 2x - 3$
    (C) $x^2 + 2x - 6$
    (D) $x^2 + 4x + 3$

52. **(D)** is the correct answer. Plug in. Let $x = 5$. $f(x) = 5^2 - 2(5) = 15$. $f(5 + 3) = f(8) = 64 - 16 = 48$. Now go to the answer choices, and, making sure you substitute 5 (NOT 8) for all the x's, find the answer that yields 48. Answer choice (D) gives you $5^2 = 5^2 + 5(4) + 3 = 48$.

QUESTIONS	EXPLANATIONS

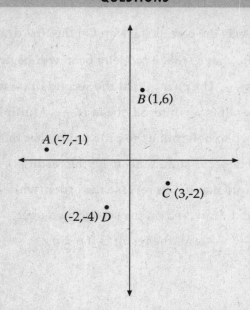

53. In the figure above, which point is on the line $2y - 4x = 8$?

   (A) A
   (B) B
   (C) C
   (D) D

53. **(B)** is the correct answer. The easiest way to do this is to plug each set of ordered pairs into the equation and see which one solves it. The coordinates of (B) are (1,6); the equation, $2y - 3x = 8$, with those coordinates substituted, reads $2(6) - 4(1) = 8$. This is true, which means that B is the correct answer.

54. If $f(x) = 3x - 1$, and $g(x) = x^2$, then $f(g(-2)) =$

   (A) -5
   (B) -4
   (C) 11
   (D) 15

54. **(C)** is the correct answer. First determine the value of $g(-2)$. $g(-2) = (-2)^2 = 4$. Now determine the value of $f(4)$. $f(4) = 3(4) - 1 = 11$.

55. If B = $\{x \mid x$ is an integer greater than 0$\}$ and C = $\{x \mid x$ is an odd integer less than 100$\}$, which of the below is a subset of $B \cap C$?

   (A) $\{13, 17, 21, 46\}$
   (B) $\{10, 20, 30\}$
   (C) $\{-5, -3, 7\}$
   (D) $\{15\}$

55. **(D)** is the correct answer. The symbol $\cap$ indicates the intersection of sets; an intersection of sets is a list of only those elements the two sets hold in common. All of the other choices include either even numbers, which are not included in C, or negative numbers, which are not included in B.

SECTION 2

56. If $f(x)$ is a linear function such that $f(4) = 12$ and $f(-2) = 3$, then $f(9) =$

   (A) $\dfrac{39}{2}$

   (B) $\dfrac{27}{2}$

   (C) 13

   (D) 8

56. **(A)** is the correct answer. Since $f(x)$ is a linear function, it can be expressed in the form $y = m(x) + b$. We know that (4, 12) and (−2, 3) are two points on the line; because we have two points, we can figure out the slope (m) of the line. The slope $= \left(\dfrac{(12 - 3)}{(4 - (-2))} \right) = \dfrac{9}{6} = \dfrac{3}{2}$. Now that we have a value for m, we have 3 of our 4 variables and can solve for b. Using the ordered pair (4, 12), we have $12 = \dfrac{3}{2(4 + b)}$. b, therefore, equals 6. Now we know that $f(x) = \dfrac{3}{2(x) + 6}$. What is the value of $f(9)$? $f(9) = \dfrac{3}{2(9) + 6} = \dfrac{39}{2}$.

57. "When I am hungry, I always eat."

   Which of the following correctly states the contrapositive of the statement above?

   (A) When I am not hungry, I never eat.
   (B) When I am not eating, I am not hungry.
   (C) When I am eating, I must be hungry.
   (D) When I am not hungry, I sometimes eat.

57. **(B)** is the correct answer. The contrapositive of the statement "If A, then B" is "If not B, then not A." In the statement "When I am hungry, I always eat," "When I am hungry" is A and "I always eat" is B. The contrapositive, "If not B, then not A," translates to "If I am not eating, then I am not hungry." Answer choice (B) is the only one that comes close to saying this; in fact, with a few minor changes, that is exactly what it says.

SECTION 2

58. If $f(x) = 2x$ and the range of $(f)x$ is all even positive integers less than 100, then the domain of $(f)x$ is all

    (A) positive integers less than 50
    (B) even positive integers less than 50
    (C) even positive integers less than 100
    (D) even positive integers less than 200

58. **(A)** is the correct answer. Given that $f(x) = 2x$, the range of $f(x)$ is all possible values of $2x$. We are told that $2x$ can equal any positive integer less than 100. x, then, can equal any positive integer less than 50.

59. In a group of 117 people, 67 have brown eyes, 25 have blue eyes, 14 have green eyes, and 11 have hazel eyes. The likelihood that a person chosen at random from the group will have either brown or green eyes is

    (A) $\dfrac{2}{3}$

    (B) $\dfrac{9}{13}$

    (C) $\dfrac{95}{117}$

    (D) $\dfrac{11}{12}$

59. **(B)** is the correct answer. Since the question asks the probability that one or another thing will happen, you need to add the two probabilities together. The likelihood that a person with brown eyes would be chosen at random is $\dfrac{67}{117}$; the likelihood a person with green eyes will be chosen is $\dfrac{14}{117}$. The sum of these is $\dfrac{81}{117}$, which reduces to $\dfrac{9}{13}$.

60. If $f(x) = 3x - 2$, and $g(f(x)) = x$, then $g(x) =$

    (A) $3x + 2$

    (B) $2x - 3$

    (C) $\dfrac{x}{3} + 2$

    (D) $\dfrac{x+2}{3}$

60. **(D)** is the correct answer. Plug in. Let's make $x = 5$. $f(5) = 3(5) - 2 = 13$. Because $g(f(x)) = x$, we know that $g(13) = 5$; that is, is simply reverses the process of $(f)x$. All that's left to do, then, is to plug 13 into the answer choices and see which one yields 5. Because only (D) does, (D) must be the correct answer.

SECTION 2

QUESTIONS	EXPLANATIONS

61. An automobile collector has 30 automobiles with various features. 14 have automatic transmissions, 18 have power windows, and 21 have power brakes. 7 of the automobiles have all three features; each has at least one of the features. How many automobiles have exactly two of the features?

    (A) 5
    (B) 7
    (C) 8
    (D) 9

61. **(D)** is the correct answer. Add the number of automobiles with each of the three features. $14 + 18 + 21 = 53$. This number is greater than 30, the number of automobiles in the collection, because some automobiles are being counted two or three times (since some have two or three of the features). We know that 7 automobiles have all three features; those cars are being counted three times in our total of 53. Since we only want to count them once, we subtract $2 \times 7 = 14$ from our total, leaving a result of 39. That number is still 9 greater than 30, because 9 cars are still being counted twice: those are the cars with exactly two of the features.

62. $(3i)(4 - i)(4 + i) =$

    (A) $44i$
    (B) $51i$
    (C) $60i$
    (D) $72i$

62. **(B)** is the correct answer. First off, you have to remember that $i = \div -1$. Note that $(4 - i)(4 + i)$ is the difference of perfect squares, which means it equals $4^2 - i^2$. This, in turn, equals $16 - (-1) = 17$. This simplifies $(3i)(4 - i)(4 + i)$ to $(3i)17$. The answer is $51i$.

63. Let $S = \{9, 11, 13, 16, 81\}$. What is the sum of the mean and the median of S?

    (A) 12
    (B) 20
    (C) 39
    (D) 93

63. **(C)** is the correct answer. The mean of 9, 11, 13, 16, and 81 is the sum of the numbers (130) divided by 5, which equals 26. The median is 13 (to determine the median, list all the numbers in ascending, or descending, order; the number in the exact middle of the list is the median). The sum of the two is 39.

SECTION 2

QUESTIONS	EXPLANATIONS

64. Which of the below could be the graph of a linear function?

(A)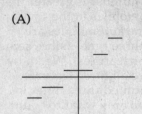

(B)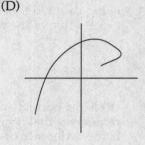

(C)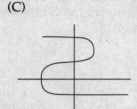

(D)

64. **(A)** is the correct answer. A graph of a linear equation must pass the vertical line test; that is, any vertical line drawn on the Cartesian grid should intersect the graph of a linear equation no more than once. (B), (C), and (D) all fail this test.

65. In base four, the next whole number greater than 2,133 is
   (A) 2,134
   (B) 2,140
   (C) 2,200
   (D) 2,211

65. **(C)** is the correct answer. In base four, the only digits are 0, 1, 2, and 3. Starting from 0, the numbers in base 4 are 0, 1, 2, 3, 10, 11, 12, 13, 20, etc. When you get to 33, the next number is 100. If you were ever taught this, it may all be coming back to you right about now. If you have no idea what this is all about, don't worry; there may be no question on your test about this, and there certainly won't be more than one, so you can just plan to skip it. Remember, you don't have to get anywhere near all these questions right to receive credit for the CLEP at most schools that accept the College Mathematics test. Anyway, since there is no 4 in base 4, you should immediately eliminate answer choices (A) and (B). Chances are if you got that far, you knew how to do this problem and got it right.

PART IV

How to Crack the CLEP General Examination In Humanities

13

Overview of the
Humanities Exam

WHAT'S ON THE TEST?

The CLEP General Examination in Humanities consists of 150 questions covering general knowledge of art history, music, and literature. It also includes a very few questions about film, dance, and architecture. Here's the breakdown, by percentage and number, of the subjects tested:

SUBJECT	% OF TEST	# OF QUESTIONS
Fine Arts	50	75
Visual Arts (painting, sculpture, etc.)	25	35 to 40
Music	15	20 to 25
Architecture	5	7 to 8
Film and Dance	5	7 to 8
Literature	50	75
Poetry	15 to 20	20 to 30
Fiction	10 to 15	15 to 25
Drama	5 to 10	7 to 15
Nonfiction	5 to 10	7 to 15
Philosophy	5	7 to 8

Call your potential schools and ask them about their CLEP policy. Will they give you credit for a good grade? Will a good grade place you out of a class? The admissions office or the dean's office should know the answer.

HOW IS THE TEST STRUCTURED?

The test is divided into two parts (called, appropriately, Part I and Part II) of seventy-five questions each. There are no special questions that appear only on one part of the test: the two sections are, in terms of structure and the type of material tested, identical. You will be allowed 45 minutes for each section, during which time you will only be allowed to work on that particular section.

TYPES OF QUESTIONS

Half the questions (seventy-five of the 150) fall under the category of "trivial pursuit"; they simply test your ability to regurgitate factual information, mostly the names of artists, writers, etc. and their works. For example:

Who wrote *Romeo and Juliet*, *Hamlet*, and *Othello*?

(A) Arthur Miller
(B) Bertolt Brecht
(C) Anton Chekov
(D) Tennessee Williams
(E) William Shakespeare

Thirty percent of the questions (forty-five total) test your ability to recognize techniques and styles of famous writers, painters, sculptors, or eras/countries. Some will require you to know definitions of common literary/artistic terms. For example:

The narrative technique most prominently featured in James Joyce's *Ulysses* is

(A) Dickensian realism
(B) stream of conscious
(C) first-person omniscient
(D) melodrama
(E) flashback

Which of the following would represent an anachronism?

(A) A photograph taken at night.
(B) A novel in which a romantic story is told in a historical setting.
(C) A painting of Alexander the Great driving an automobile.
(D) A piece of music that changes tempo several times.
(E) A dance recital performed without music.

Familiarize yourself thoroughly with all question formats BEFORE you take the exam. You want to spend your test time deciding which answer is correct, not reading directions.

The remaining 20 percent (thirty questions) tests your ability to understand and interpret paintings, poems, etc. that you may never have seen before. Because these questions involve recognizing styles in works you are not expected to be familiar with, none of these questions will deal with types of works you cannot experience during the test; in other words, none of these questions will be about music, film, or dance.

A typical question of this type may ask you to read a poem. Accompanying questions may ask you to identify the poem's main theme and to identify the definition of difficult or unconventionally used words in the poem, or to interpret the meaning of a line or image. For example:

Methought I saw my late espoused saint

Brought to me like Alcestis from the grave,

Whom Jove's great son to her glad husband gave,

Rescued from Death by force, though pale and faint.

The "saint" mentioned in the first line, above, is the poet's

(A) wife
(B) mother
(C) guardian angel
(D) muse
(E) imagination

The answers to the questions above are: (E), (B), (C), and (A).

MAKING THE GRADE

No school requires a perfect score on the General Examination in Humanities of those seeking college credit for the test. In fact, most require only that you receive the equivalent of a C grade. Most schools set that score between the high 400's and 500. To receive this grade, you only need to achieve a raw score of approximately 75. As far as most schools are concerned, a 500 is exactly as valuable as an 800. For each, you will receive the exact same number of credits toward your degree.

A FAIR TEST

ETS writes a lot of "tricky" exams. The PSAT, SAT, GRE, and GMAT are all ETS exams on which the test writers often set out to confound the test taker. Oddly worded questions coupled with answer choices that appear correct at first glance (such answer choices touch on many of the same themes as the correct answer, but typically include an overgeneralization or an error on a tangential point) conspire to make the test taker's job much more difficult than it has to be. If you've ever taken one of these exams—and you almost certainly have—you may well have some anxiety about the CLEP Humanities exam.

> Be aggressive when you take multiple choice exams. ETS exams are designed to reward aggressive guessing. If you can eliminate at least one answer choice, make a guess.

Well, rest easy. The good news is that the CLEP Humanities test includes none of the tricks you've come to know and hate on other ETS exams. Questions on the CLEP are worded in a straightforward manner, usually in as few words as possible. Answer choices are straightforward: if you are familiar with the subject being tested, there will almost certainly be either an obvious correct answer or four obvious incorrect answers.

For example, a CLEP question about the cubist painter Paul Cézanne might look like this:

Which of the following is the French post-impressionist whose pronounced use of geometric shapes has led historians to dub him "the father of cubism"?

(A) Jean-Honoré Fraggonard
(B) Paul Cézanne
(C) Jacques Louis David
(D) Le Corbusier
(E) Arthur Rimbaud

Here's how to crack it

This is not a difficult question if your art history is solid. Fraggonard and David are both painters from the early 19th century, far too early for either to be considered the father of a twentieth-century art movement. Rimbaud was a famous poet, not a painter, and Le Corbusier was a famous architect.

What you will *not* see on the test is a question such as this:

> Which of the following is the French post-impressionist whose pronounced use of geometric shapes has led many to dub him "the father of cubism"?
>
> (A) Georges Braques
> (B) Paul Cézanne
> (C) Pablo Picasso
> (D) Claude Monet
> (E) Camille Pisarro

Here's how to crack it

This question is much more difficult, because both Braques and Picasso are strongly associated with cubism (in fact, either could arguably be called the "father of cubism"), while Monet and Pisarro are both prominent French post-impressionists. The first version of the question is designed to reward you for general knowledge of nineteenth-century French art; the latter version requires you to have much more specific knowledge of the same topic. To repeat, questions on the CLEP Humanities exam are, fortunately, of the former type.

This principle holds true for the art history identifications as well, of which there will be approximately twenty on your test. Art history IDs present you with five paintings, sculptures, works of architecture, etc., each image representing an answer choice. These images are followed by three questions asking you for an identification. For example, a display of five paintings might be followed by questions asking you to identify which is by Cézanne, which is by Rembrandt, and which is by Michelangelo. Or, the same five paintings might be followed by questions asking you to identify which painting is by a French post-impressionist, which is by a Dutch Renaissance painter, and which is by an Italian Renaissance painter. In either case, the identifications will not be tricky. When asked to identify a Cézanne, you will not be presented with a Cézanne and four paintings that look like Cézannes but just happen to be painted by somebody else. Furthermore, the Cézanne you are asked to identify will be typical of his work, not some anomaly in his oeuvre. The governing principle, then, is this: if you know that Cézanne is a post-impressionist, and if you know what post-impressionist paintings look like, you will be able to pick out the Cézanne from the group, because the other four paintings will be of identifiably different styles.

CLEP Humanities test booklets are printed on heavy, glossy paper, so that the art reproductions are clear. All other tests are printed on newsprint. You can easily write on the glossy paper with pencil. Mark up your booklet: cross out wrong answers and circle questions you want to come back to later. Take control of the test, don't let it control you.

TEST-TAKING TECHNIQUES

Remember the basic test-taking techniques we covered in chapter 2?

- ◆ Do not rush in an effort to finish this exam.
- ◆ Never spend an inordinate amount of time on any one question.
- ◆ Guess if you can eliminate even one answer choice.

In addition, there are several advanced techniques for cracking the Humanities test.

COMMON SENSE GOES A LONG WAY

As previously mentioned, the CLEP is a fair test. It wants to reward you for what you know. It also tries to reward you for common sense. For example:

> A chord made up of a root note, a major third above the root, and a major fifth above the root is called a _____ chord.
>
> (A) minor
> (B) diminished
> (C) whole tone
> (D) major
> (E) augmented

The answer to this question is (D), a major chord. This would be totally obvious if you have training in music; if not, common sense might tell you that a chord with two major intervals in it is probably a major chord. But you might also have a moment of doubt, during which you might think, "Sure that's what I think it's called, but is that what someone who has studied at a conservatory for five years would call it? Maybe they have a secret name for such chords that only they know!" Fearing that the answer "major chord" is too obvious, you might then desperately guess one of the other four answer choices.

At this point you would have overthought the question. You would have wasted the extra time you spent thinking these paranoid thoughts, and on top of that, you would have chosen an incorrect answer. Remember, this is a straightforward test. This test does not try to trick you; it simply tries to figure out what you recognize and what you don't. Don't get cute when you're guessing, or you will get burned.

CONSIDER THE CONTEXT

Context clues are all over this test. Use them. A quote from *Hamlet*, for example, might allude to the murder of somebody's father, the theme of revenge, or the contemplative and indecisive nature of the main character. Without ever mentioning Hamlet or the name of any character in the play, the quote will drop hints for those who know the play's main themes that this is a quote from *Hamlet*. Again, don't suspect that such context clues are there to fool you. If you pick up on one, you know enough to answer the accompanying question correctly.

CALL IT DIVERSE, CALL IT P.C., BUT WHATEVER YOU CALL IT...

Did you skip chapter 2? If you did, go back and read it! It's crammed with important test-taking tips!

This test tries not to fall into the trap of presenting the artistic achievements of the western world as solely the domain of white men. Do NOT choose the name of every woman, black, Latino, etc. you recognize. BUT you should be aware that a number of questions will address them. Women and minority artists make good guesses when all else fails.

TAILOR YOUR SUBJECT REVIEW TO THE TEST

What you will need to know and be able to recognize in order to pass the CLEP Humanities exam are the general characteristics of art, writing, etc., of the major historical periods and art movements, and the names of the artists associated with each. You will also need to know basic definitions for terms commonly used when discussing each of the major subject areas. Even a perfunctory review of this material would take up an entire book, so rather than provide one, this book provides (at the end of this chapter) a bibliography of sources in which you will be able to find this information easily. All books listed should be available at your local library. Also, after you take the practice exam in this book, read the entire section explaining the correct and incorrect answers for each question; if you know all the material covered in that section, you will undoubtedly do well on the CLEP. Read even those explanations accompanying questions you answered correctly; the descriptions of wrong answers form the basis of a good general review.

Visual arts is the single most frequently tested subject on this exam, with between thirty-five and forty questions. Dance or film are the least frequently tested, with about four questions each. Do NOT start studying film and dance until you have made a thorough review of art history (no matter how much more you prefer movie theaters to art museums). A solid review of art history, music, poetry, and fiction will yield enough knowledge to pass this exam without any review whatsoever of philosophy, dance, film, nonfiction, or drama. Look back at the subject breakdown at the beginning of this chapter when planning your review sessions.

A GENERAL OUTLINE OF WHAT YOU ARE EXPECTED TO KNOW

FINE ARTS: VISUAL ARTS

You will need to be able to recognize and distinguish among artworks from the classical world and artworks from the following periods and styles: medieval, High Renaissance, mannerism, baroque, romanticism, impressionism, post-impressionism, cubism, and modern art. You will need to know the names of the most famous artists of each of these periods, and will almost certainly be expected to recognize a famous work by each of the following artists: Leonardo da Vinci, Michelangelo, Rembrandt, Van Gogh, and Picasso. You will probably see one or more works from the Vatican collection, perhaps from the ceiling of the Sistine Chapel (Michelangelo) or from the Stanza della Segnatura (Raphael). You will almost certainly be asked to identify a sculpture by Rodin as well.

You will be quizzed on basic vocabulary, such as the terms used to describe different types of artwork—*mosaic, triptych, diptych, mural, fresco,* etc.—and terms used to describe different techniques—*chiaroscuro, abstraction, vanishing point,* etc.

> "I don't very much enjoy looking at paintings in general. I know too much about them. I take them apart."
> —Georgia O'Keeffe (1887–1986), U.S. artist

From the non-Western world, you will have to be able to recognize artwork from Africa, Mesoamerica, and Oceania. As previously stated, these will not be tricky: you will not be asked to differentiate between a Dogon mask and a Dan mask. You will probably not even be asked to differentiate between an African mask and an Oceanic mask, which have much more recognizable differences. You may have to identify a Native American or Eskimo work. You will have to be able to recognize Japanese painting and, perhaps, Indian sculpture.

FINE ARTS: MUSIC

You will need to be aware of the major characteristics of music from the following periods: Medieval (Gregorian chants), Renaissance, Baroque, Classical, Romantic, and Twentieth Century. You will need to know the following major composers:

- ◆ Baroque: Bach, Handel, Vivaldi
- ◆ Classical: Haydn, Mozart, Beethoven (know that Beethoven simultaneously marks the end of the Classical period and the beginning of the Romantic period)
- ◆ Romantic: Brahms, Puccini, Verdi, Wagner
- ◆ Twentieth century: Stravinsky

You will need to know the following about opera: most of the great operas were composed during the Classical and Romantic periods. Mozart's operas are generally considered to represent the high water-mark of Classical opera. Romantic opera is typified by the works of Verdi and Puccini. German High Romanticism is typified in the works of Wagner. You will need to know the names of the most famous operas by these composers.

You will need to know the major types of composition: *symphony*, *concerto*, *overture*, *quartet*, and *sonata*. You will need to know about various musical instruments, both classical and popular, and know the definitions of commonly used musical terms, such as *coda*, *clef*, *key*, *meter*, and *vocal register*. You will need to recognize descriptions of one or more ethnic, folk, or popular music form.

FINE ARTS: ARCHITECTURE, FILM AND DANCE

You will only see fifteen questions about all three of these subjects combined. Make sure you know the absolute basics of architecture: that you can recognize the Parthenon, a Gothic cathedral, and works by Frank Lloyd Wright. Film and dance questions are a crapshoot. For film, you will probably have to identify a famous director and know the definition of a term such as *montage* or *synchronous sound*. You may need to be able to recognize an important film genre, such as *film noir*. For dance, you will probably have to define one or two ballet terms and recognize the name of a famous ballet or dancer.

LITERATURE: POETRY

You should be familiar with the most famous work or works of the following poets: Geoffrey Chaucer (*The Canterbury Tales*), William Shakespeare, John Donne, John Milton (*Paradise Lost*), Alexander Pope, William Blake, Robert Burns, William Wordsworth, John Keats, Emily Dickinson, Walt Whitman,

Lewis Carroll, William Butler Yeats, Robert Frost, and T.S. Eliot. For those for whom this list is too long, here's a short list: Shakespeare, Milton, Keats, Frost, and Eliot are most important for the purposes of the CLEP. Rest assured, however, that questions about most of the poets on the long list will appear on the CLEP.

Fortunately, the CLEP focuses almost entirely on English-language poets, so you need not spend a lot of time studying foreign-language poets. Nonetheless, know the names Dante, Baudelaire, Rimbaud, and Goethe, and be able to identify their major works.

Know the vocabulary of poetry: be able to define terms such as *strophe*, *stanza*, *verse*, *quatrain*, *couplet*, and *iambic pentameter*. Know the major poetic devices, such as *metaphor*, *simile*, *irony*, and *hyperbole*.

A disproportionate share of the third type of CLEP Humanities question, the type that asks you to interpret a work of art you may never have seen before, are poetry questions. Read the poems carefully and do NOT try to read between the lines: answers to ETS questions can't be too subtle or there would be a lot of angry calls to Princeton Junction, New Jersey, every time test scores are sent out. The correct answer may very well call for you to know the definition of a difficult word, but it will not call for you to make a chancy interpretation of a poem (if you find yourself thinking "This poem *might* be about . . .," then you are wandering too far afield).

> "We make out of the quarrel with others, rhetoric, but out of the quarrel with ourselves, poetry."
> —W. B. Yeats (1865–1939), Irish poet

LITERATURE: FICTION

You will need to be familiar with the following writers and their major works: Daniel Defoe, Jonathan Swift (*Gulliver's Travels*), Nathaniel Hawthorne (*The Scarlet Letter*), James Fenimore Cooper, Edgar Allen Poe, Herman Melville (*Moby Dick*), Charles Dickens, Mark Twain (especially *Huckleberry Finn*), Joseph Conrad, Jack London, William Faulkner, F. Scott Fitzgerald, James Joyce, John Steinbeck, and Ernest Hemingway. Know the great women novelists: the Brontes, Jane Austen, Virginia Woolf, Zora Neale Hurston (*Their Eyes Were Watching God*). Know also the great African-American twentieth-century novelists: Hurston, Richard Wright (especially *Native Son*), Ralph Ellison (*Invisible Man*), James Baldwin. Know the following non-English language writers: Albert Camus, Cervantes, Fyodor Dostoyevsky, Leo Tolstoy, Franz Kafka, and Voltaire. Be familiar with the plots of these author's major books, as you will have to identify at least a couple of them.

Know the difference between various fiction formats: *epic*, *novel*, *novella*, and *short story*. Know the difference between such genres as *allegory*, *satire*, *romance*, *parody*, *picaresque*, and *farce*. Know the difference between *first person* and *third person* narration. Know the difference between a *symbol*, a *metaphor*, and a *simile*.

LITERATURE: DRAMA

The Greek tragedies and Shakespeare's plays are the two most likely subjects of CLEP drama questions. Know the plots of the *Oresteia* and *Prometheus Bound* (Aeschylus), the *Oedipus* plays (Sophocles), *Medea*, *Electra*, and *The Bacchae* (Euripides), as well as the comedies *Lysistrata*, *The Frogs*, and *The Clouds* (Aristophanes). Know the plots of all Shakespeare's major tragedies: *Hamlet*,

Othello, Macbeth, Romeo and Juliet, Julius Caesar and *King Lear*. Be familiar with his great histories and comedies as well. Other playwrights whom you might encounter on the CLEP include: Moliere, Henrik Ibsen, Edmond Rostand (*Cyrano de Bergerac*), Oscar Wilde, Samuel Beckett (*Waiting for Godot, Endgame*), Eugene Ionesco, Eugene O'Neill, and Tennessee Williams.

Know what differentiates a tragedy, comedy, and history. Many of the terms you need to learn for fiction are applicable to drama as well (*farce, parody*, etc.).

LITERATURE: PHILOSOPHY AND NON-FICTION

The barrier between philosophy and non-fiction is a thin one on the CLEP. Among the two topics, expect approximately eighteen questions. Be familiar with the "greatest hits" of ancient history: *The Peloponnesian War* (Thucydides), *The Histories* (Heroditus), and *Twelve Caesars* (Suetonius). Know the autobiographies of St. Augustine (*Confessions*) and Jean Jacques Rousseau (*Confessions*), the essays of Montaigne, and the writings of Karl Marx.

In the field of philosophy, know the great philosophers of antiquity (Plato and Aristotle) as well as the major schools of antiquity (Stoicism, Cynicism, Epicureanism, etc.) Be familiar with these western philosophers: Thomas Hobbes (*The Leviathan*), Niccolo Macchiavelli (*The Prince*), John Locke, Rene Descartes, Jean Jacques Rousseau, Immanuel Kant, Georg W. F. Hegel, and Friedrich Nietzsche. Know also the major tenets of these Eastern philosophies/religions: Hinduism, Taoism, Confucianism, Buddhism, and Islam.

BIBLIOGRAPHY

General information can be found in any good desk reference, such as *The New York Public Library Desk Reference* (Webster's New World). For art history, we recommend *Art Through the Ages* by Horst de la Croix and Richard G. Tansey (HBJ); and *History of Art* by H.W. Janson (Prentice Hall). For music, look at *The Concise Oxford History of Music* (Oxford University Press) and the *New Harvard Dictionary of Music* (Harvard University Press). A good source for poetry studies is *The Top 500 Poems* edited by William Harmon (Columbia University Press); there are also many "How to Understand Poetry" books on the shelves and most are quite good. *The Norton Introduction to Poetry* and *The Norton Introduction to Fiction* both include long indexes with definitions of important terms in their respective fields. Finally, the best source for condensed information on any of these topics are college outlines. These books are basically equivalent to Cliff Notes (or Monarch Notes), but for an entire college course instead of a single book. The *Harper Collins College Outline* series is a good one. You would go broke buying all the books you need to ace this exam, so study at the library.

14

The Princeton Review
Sample Humanities Exam

PART I

Time—45 minutes

75 questions

Directions: Each of the questions or incomplete statements below is followed by five suggested answers or completions. Select the one that is best in each case.

1. A creature with the body of a lion and the head of a man is called a

   (A) minotaur
   (B) sphinx
   (C) cyclops
   (D) shrew
   (E) centaur

2. Which of the following is a woodwind instrument?

   (A) bassoon
   (B) timpani
   (C) mandolin
   (D) cello
   (E) tuba

3. A Roman philosopher arguing that wealth, health, and good fortune are immaterial, that only matters of vice and virtue are important, and that personal tragedy should therefore be borne impassively would likely be of which school?

   (A) Stoicism
   (B) Epicureanism
   (C) Manicheanism
   (D) Existentialism
   (E) Neoplatonism

4. *Pilgrim's Progress* and *Animal Farm* are two examples of a narrative form in which events contain a sustained reference to a second set of events or meanings. This form of narrative is called

   (A) comedy
   (B) tragedy
   (C) history
   (D) allegory
   (E) melodrama

Questions 5 and 6 refer to the following lines.

"April is the cruellest month, breeding
Lilacs out of the dead land, . . ."

5. The lines above open

   (A) Stevens' *Thirteen Ways of Looking at a Blackbird*
   (B) Blake's *London*
   (C) Shelly's *Adonais*
   (D) Coleridge's *Kubla Khan*
   (E) Eliot's *The Waste Land*

6. The line "April is the cruellest month" alludes to the first lines of

   (A) *The Aenead*
   (B) the prologue to *The Canterbury Tales*
   (C) *The Fairie Queene*
   (D) *Ode on a Grecian Urn*
   (E) *The Flowers of Evil*

GO ON TO THE NEXT PAGE.

7. The term *pieta* describes a depiction of

   (A) the Virgin Mary mourning over Jesus'
       body
   (B) the martyrdom of a saint
   (C) a main altar of a cathedral
   (D) a scene from Greek mythology
   (E) an episode from the Old Testament

8. Who wrote *The Marriage of Heaven and Hell*
   and *Songs of Innocence and Experience*?

   (A) Henry Wadsworth Longfellow
   (B) Rudyard Kipling
   (C) Alexander Pope
   (D) Jonathan Swift
   (E) William Blake

9. Ernest Hemingway once said, "All American
   literature comes from one book. . . ." The book
   to which he was referring is

   (A) *Clarissa*
   (B) *Typee*
   (C) *The Scarlet Letter*
   (D) *The Adventures of Huckleberry Finn*
   (E) *Uncle Tom's Cabin*

10. Which of the following is NOT part of the
    interior of a Gothic cathedral?

    (A) entablature
    (B) transept
    (C) choir
    (D) nave
    (E) apse

Questions 11 to 13 are based on the passages below:

   (A) "From Stettin in the Baltic to Trieste in
       the Adriatic, an iron curtain has
       descended across the Continent.
       Behind that line lie all the capitals of
       the ancient states of Central and
       Eastern Europe."
   (B) "The New Frontier of which I speak is not
       a set of promises - it is a set of chal-
       lenges. It sums up not what I intend to
       offer the American people, but what I
       intend to ask of them."
   (C) "An epidemic of indiscriminate assault
       upon character does not good, but very
       great harm. The soul of every scoun-
       drel is gladdened whenever an honest
       man is assailed . . . ."
   (D) "I said then, and I say now, that while
       there is a lower class, I am in it, while
       there is a criminal element, I am of it,
       and while there is a soul in prison, I am
       not free . . . ."
   (E) "When we let freedom ring, when we let
       it ring from every village and every
       hamlet, from every state and every
       city, we will be able to speed up that
       day when all God's children . . . will be
       able to join hands and sing . . . 'Free at
       last! Free at last! Thank God almighty,
       we are free at last.'"

Which of the above is an excerpt from a
speech by:

11. John F. Kennedy?

12. Martin Luther King?

13. Winston Churchill?

GO ON TO THE NEXT PAGE.

Questions 14 to 16 refer to illustrations (A) through (E):

(A)

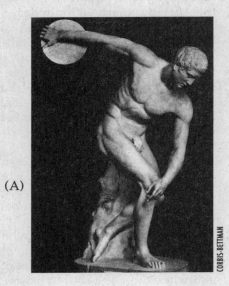

CORBIS-BETTMAN

(B)

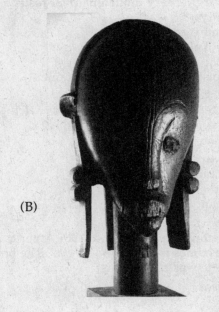

COURTESY OF THE METROPOLITAN MUSEUM OF ART

(C)

CORBIS-BETTMAN

GO ON TO THE NEXT PAGE.

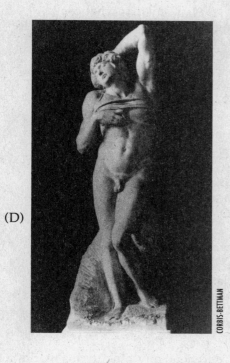

(D)

CORBIS-BETTMAN

(E)

CORBIS-BETTMAN

14. Which is by Michelangelo?

15. Which is by Auguste Rodin?

16. Which is a Gabon carving?

GO ON TO THE NEXT PAGE.

17. Mozart's *The Magic Flute (Die Zauberflöte)* is a(n)

    (A) cantata
    (B) opera
    (C) oratorio
    (D) symphony
    (E) concerto

18. The movies *The Bicycle Thief*, *Open City*, and *Germany Year Zero* all belong to what category?

    (A) film noir
    (B) American avant-garde
    (C) screwball comedy
    (D) documentary
    (E) Italian neorealist

19. Bigger Thomas is the central character of what novel?

    (A) *Light in August*
    (B) *Portnoy's Complaint*
    (C) *Native Son*
    (D) *Gravity's Rainbow*
    (E) *Pride and Prejudice*

20. This twentieth-century masterpiece draws on Slavic folk melodies, among other sources. With its abrupt transitions between seemingly unrelated segments, this work was once considered so radical that its debut in 1913 precipitated a riot.

    The musical piece described above is

    (A) Richard Strauss' *Also Sprach Zarathustra*
    (B) Johann Sebastian Bach's *Mass in B Minor*
    (C) Franz Liszt's *Les Preludes*
    (D) Johnannes Brahms' *Violin Concerto in D Major*
    (E) Igor Stravinsky's *The Rites of Spring*

Questions 21 and 22 refer to the following:

> ". . . say first what cause
> Moved our grand parents, in that happy state
> Favored of Heav'n so highly, to fall off
> From their Creator, and transgress his will
> For one restraint, lords of the world besides?
> Who first seduced them to that foul revolt?
> Th'infernal serpent. . . ."

21. The lines above are from

    (A) *The Inferno*
    (B) *Paradise Lost*
    (C) *The Faerie Queene*
    (D) *Mac Flecknoe*
    (E) *Othello*

22. The words "that foul revolt" refer to

    (A) the betrayal of Regan and Goneril
    (B) Satan's rebellion in Heaven
    (C) the fall of Adam and Eve
    (D) the crucifixion of Jesus
    (E) the American Revolution

23. "If I reprehend anything in this world, it is the use of my oracular tongue, and a nice derangement of epitaphs."

    The speech above, from Sheridan's *The Rivals*, is an example of

    (A) gallicism
    (B) dithyramb
    (C) pun
    (D) haiku
    (E) malapropism

GO ON TO THE NEXT PAGE.

24. Which of the following composers was most responsible for transforming the symphony from its pre-classical *sinfonia* form to its classical form?

    (A) Antonio Vivaldi
    (B) Arnold Schönberg
    (C) Franz Josef Haydn
    (D) Ludwig van Beethoven
    (E) Charles Gounod

25. The use of tiny dots to create an image in painting, a technique exemplified by the work of Georges Seurat, is called

    (A) chiaroscuro
    (B) cartooning
    (C) pointillism
    (D) foreshortening
    (E) etching

26. Fill in the blank below:

    A(n) _____ is episodic and has a rogue or misfit for a hero. The wandering hero serves as a prism through which readers can view many strata of society.

    (A) historical novel
    (B) myth
    (C) novella
    (D) epic
    (E) picaresque novel

Questions 27 to 29 are based on the following lists of titles:

    (A) *Troilus and Criseyde, Parliement of Foules, Canterbury Tales*
    (B) *The Rape of the Lock, An Essay on Man, An Essay on Criticism*
    (C) *Moll Flanders, Robinson Crusoe, Roxana*
    (D) *No Exit, Nausea, Being and Nothingness*
    (E) *Martin Chuzzlewit, Bleak House, Great Expectations*

27. Which are by Jean-Paul Sartre?

28. Which are by Alexander Pope?

29. Which are by Charles Dickens?

Questions 30 to 32 are based on illustrations (A) through (E):

(A)

(B)

(C)

GO ON TO THE NEXT PAGE.

(D)

CORBIS-BETTMAN

(E)

THE BETTMAN ARCHIVE

30. Which depicts a gathering of great philosophers?

31. Which depicts the carnage caused by the Spanish Civil War?

32. Which depicts the creation of Adam?

GO ON TO THE NEXT PAGE.

33. This pair, director and actor, collaborated on over a dozen movies. In such films as *Stagecoach* and *The Man Who Shot Liberty Valence*, their work set the standard for American Westerns.

    These two men are

    (A) Frank Capra and Jimmy Stewart
    (B) Billy Wilder and Jack Lemmon
    (C) John Ford and John Wayne
    (D) Ernst Lubitsch and Melvyn Douglas
    (E) Mack Sennett and Fatty Arbuckle

34. Caryatids and atlantes are

    (A) types of ribbing used to decorate vaulted arches
    (B) sculpted human figures used as architectural supports
    (C) different types of Oceanic masks
    (D) ornaments found on Egyptian sarcophagi
    (E) brushes used in oil painting

Questions 35 to 37 refer to the poem below:

That time of year thou mayst in me behold
When yellow leaves, or none, or few, do hang
Upon those boughs which shake against the cold,
Bare ruin'd choirs where late the sweet birds sang.
In me thou see'st the twilight of such day
As after sunset fadeth in the west,
Which by and by black night doth take away,
Death's second self, that seals up all in rest.
In me thou see'st the glowing of such fire,
That on the ashes of his youth doth lie,
As the deathbed whereon it must expire,
Consum'd with that which it was nourish'd by.
This thou perceiv'st, which makes thy love more strong.
To love that well which thou must leave ere long.

35. The poem above follows what verse form?

    (A) terza rima
    (B) English sonnet
    (C) elegaic stanza
    (D) rhyme royal
    (E) Spenserian stanza

36. The main theme of the poem is

    (A) aging
    (B) autumn
    (C) birds
    (D) fire
    (E) nighttime

37. This poem was written by

    (A) Percy Bysshe Shelley
    (B) William Wordsworth
    (C) John Donne
    (D) William Shakespeare
    (E) Emily Dickinson

GO ON TO THE NEXT PAGE.

38. Who wrote *Cannery Row*, *Of Mice and Men*, and *The Grapes of Wrath*?

    (A) Samuel Richardson
    (B) John Steinbeck
    (C) Virginia Woolf
    (D) James Baldwin
    (E) William Faulkner

39. "Through pity and fear, [tragedy] achieves the purgation of such emotions."

    The passage above, from Aristotle's *Poetics*, describes

    (A) catharsis
    (B) denouement
    (C) farce
    (D) irony
    (E) hubris

40. Which of the following lists the instrumentation of a classical string quartet?

    (A) violin, viola, cello, bass
    (B) two violins, viola, cello
    (C) two violas, violin, cello
    (D) viola, cello, guitar, bass
    (E) violin, mandolin, cello, guitar

41. Fill in the blank below:

    Lenin wrote: "It is impossible to fully understand Marx's *Capital*, particularly its first chapter, without preliminary study and complete understanding of _____."

    (A) Kierkegaard's *Sickness Unto Death*
    (B) Hegel's *Logic*
    (C) Aquinas' *Summa Theologica*
    (D) Plato's *Phaedrus*
    (E) Kant's *Critique of Pure Reason*

42. Which of the following genres of music is indigenous to and most closely associated with Louisiana?

    (A) polka and polonaise
    (B) raga and flamenco
    (C) chamber and comic opera
    (D) Cajun and zydeco
    (E) motet and chanson

43. What twentieth-century U.S. dramatist wrote *Mourning Becomes Electra* based on Aeschylus' *Oresteia*?

    (A) Eugene O'Neill
    (B) Lillian Hellman
    (C) Thornton Wilder
    (D) Clifford Odets
    (E) Arthur Miller

44. The framers of the U.S. Constitution drew most heavily from the work of a seventeenth-century English philosopher, particularly from his *Two Treatises on Government*. This philosopher is

    (A) David Hume
    (B) John Calvin
    (C) Immanuel Kant
    (D) John Locke
    (E) Benedict Spinoza

45. Whose works, which included *The Protestant Ethic and the Spirit of Capitalism*, laid the foundation for modern sociology?

    (A) Margaret Mead
    (B) Dag Hammarskjöld
    (C) Rainer Maria Rilke
    (D) Max Weber
    (E) François Truffaut

GO ON TO THE NEXT PAGE.

Questions <u>46</u> to <u>48</u> are based on illustrations (A)
through (E):

(A)

(B)

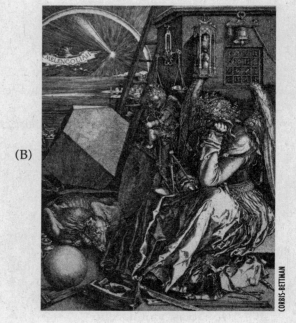

(C)

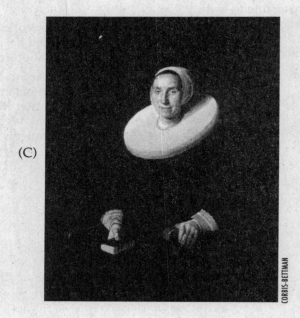

GO ON TO THE NEXT PAGE.

(D)

(E)

46. Which is a mosaic?

47. Which is an engraving?

48. Which is a diptych?

GO ON TO THE NEXT PAGE.

Questions 49 to 51 refer to the following lines:

(A) "Sitting beside the road, watching the wagon mount the hill toward her, Lena thinks, 'I have come from Alabama: a fur piece . . . .'"

(B) "Ships at a distance have every man's wish on board. For some they come in with the tide. For others they sail forever on the horizon, never out of sight, never landing . . . ."

(C) "In a village of La Mancha the name of which I have no desire to recall, there lived not so long ago one of those gentlemen who always have a lance in the rack, an ancient buckler, a skinny nag, and a greyhound for the chase."

(D) "Someone must have been telling lies about Joseph K., for without having done anything wrong he was arrested one fine morning."

(E) "Hopping a freight out of Los Angeles at high noon one day in late September 1955 I got on a gondola and lay down with my duffel bag under my head and my knees crossed and contemplated the clouds . . . ."

49. Which opens Franz Kafka's *The Trial*?

50. Which opens Zora Neale Hurston's *Their Eyes Were Watching God*?

51. Which are from Cervantes' *Don Quixote*?

52. All of the following terms are used to describe female vocal registers EXCEPT:

(A) alto
(B) contralto
(C) mezzo-soprano
(D) tenor
(E) soprano

53. Statues of the Buddha usually depict him

(A) lying on his back
(B) seated in the lotus position
(C) dancing, with one leg off the ground
(D) on horseback
(E) as a child

54. Architectural drawings used to show how a finished building will look to passersby are called

(A) turrets
(B) presentation drawings
(C) engravings
(D) blueprints
(E) hieroglyphs

55. "Magnificent, My nose! . . . You pug, you knob, you button-head,
Know that I glory in this nose of mine,
For a great nose indicates a great man . . . ."

The lines above are spoken by the title character of

(A) *Hedda Gabbler*
(B) *Waiting for Godot*
(C) *Cyrano de Bergerac*
(D) *Othello*
(E) *The Misanthrope*

GO ON TO THE NEXT PAGE.

56. "One is not born, but rather becomes, a woman."

    The quote above comes from Simone de Beauvoir's classic work of feminist literature entitled

    (A) *Common Sense*
    (B) *The Lottery*
    (C) *The Feminine Mystique*
    (D) *Little Women*
    (E) *The Second Sex*

57. "It is necessary that the prince should know how to color his nature well, and how to be a great hypocrite and dissembler."

    Who wrote the sentence above?

    (A) Friedrich Nietzsche
    (B) Aristotle
    (C) Plato
    (D) Albert Camus
    (E) Niccolo Machiavelli

58. The works of Beckett, Genet, and Ionesco typify what twentieth-century form of theater in which nearly anonymous characters participate in meaningless and often illogical activities?

    (A) Restoration comedy
    (B) drawing-room comedy
    (C) theater of the absurd
    (D) theater of cruelty
    (E) epic

Questions 59 and 60 refer to the lines of poetry below.

"Turning and turning in the widening gyre
The falcon cannot hear the falconer;
Things fall apart; the center cannot hold . . ."

59. The lines above were written by

    (A) Robert Browning
    (B) Robert Frost
    (C) William Butler Yeats
    (D) William Carlos Williams
    (E) Elizabeth Bishop

60. The poem they open is called

    (A) *The Second Coming*
    (B) *Howl*
    (C) *Lycidas*
    (D) *Auguries of Innocence*
    (E) *The Rape of the Lock*

GO ON TO THE NEXT PAGE.

Questions 61 to 63 refer to illustrations (A) through (E):

(A)

(B)

(C)

GO ON TO THE NEXT PAGE.

(D)

CORBIS-BETTMAN

(E)

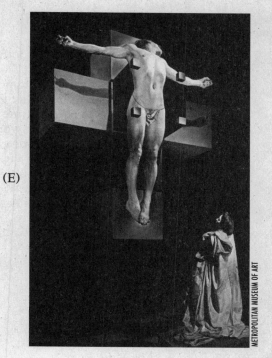

METROPOLITAN MUSEUM OF ART

61. Which is representative of fifteenth-century Flemish painting?

62. Which is representative of seventeenth-century Dutch painting?

63. Which was painted during the twentieth century?

GO ON TO THE NEXT PAGE.

Questions 64 to 66 refer to these lines from Shakespeare's plays:

(A) "How sharper than a serpent's tooth it is
To have a thankless child!"

(B) "Tomorrow, and tomorrow, and tomorrow
Creeps in this petty pace from day to day
To the last syllable of recorded time . . . ."

(C) "If music be the food of love, play on;
Give me excess of it, that, surfeiting,
The appetite may sicken, and so die."

(D) "O that this too sullied flesh would melt,
Thaw, and resolve itself into a dew,
Or that the Everlasting had not fixed
His canon 'gainst self-slaughter . . . ."

(E) "I am not only witty in myself, but the
cause that wit is in other men."

64. Which is spoken by Falstaff?

65. Which is spoken by Macbeth?

66. Which is spoken by King Lear?

67. An orchestral piece of several movements in which a solo instrumentalist is featured for the entire piece is called a(n)

(A) tone poem
(B) concerto
(C) chanson
(D) string quartet
(E) opera buffa

Questions 68 to 70 concern the poem below:

Loveliest of Trees
Loveliest of trees, the cherry now
Is hung with bloom along the bough,
And stands about the woodland ride
Wearing white for Eastertide.
Now of my threescore years and ten,
Twenty will not come again,
And take from seventy springs a score,
It only leaves me fifty more.
And since to look at things in bloom
Fifty springs are little room,
About the woodlands I will go
To see the cherry hung with snow.

68. How many years old is the narrator of this poem?

(A) Twenty
(B) Fifty
(C) Sixty
(D) Seventy
(E) It is impossible to tell.

69. At what time of year does the poem take place?

(A) winter
(B) spring
(C) summer
(D) fall
(E) It is impossible to tell.

70. Which of the following most closely approximates the meaning of the word "ride" as it is used in line 3 of the poem?

(A) tree
(B) cherry blossom
(C) carriage
(D) roadway
(E) snowfall

GO ON TO THE NEXT PAGE.

71. Michelangelo's fresco *The Last Judgement* is located in the

    (A) Louvre
    (B) Sistine Chapel
    (C) Palace at Versailles
    (D) National Gallery in Washington, DC
    (E) Westminster Abbey

72. Describing humanity's natural state, what philosopher speculated: "No arts; no letters; no society; and which is worst of all, continual fear and danger of violent death; and the life of man, solitary, nasty, brutish, and short."?

    (A) Martin Heidegger
    (B) Thomas Hobbes
    (C) Jeremy Bentham
    (D) Saint Augustine
    (E) John Stuart Mills

73. "Early to bed and early to rise,
    Makes a man healthy, wealthy, and wise."

    The couplet above originally appeared in

    (A) *Poor Richard's Almanac*
    (B) Aesop's *Fables*
    (C) *Essays* by Montaigne
    (D) *Confessions of Jean-Jacques Rousseau*
    (E) *The Analects of Confucius*

74. Who composed the scores for the ballets *Swan Lake* and *The Nutcracker Suite*?

    (A) George Frideric Handel
    (B) Felix Mendelssohn
    (C) Gustav Holst
    (D) Peter Ilyich Tchaikovsky
    (E) Domenico Scarlatti

75. Twyla Tharp is a famous

    (A) modern choreographer
    (B) screenwriter
    (C) sheet-metal sculptor
    (D) eighteenth-century polemicist
    (E) nineteenth-century fictional heroine

GO ON TO THE NEXT PAGE.

PART II

Time—45 minutes

75 questions

Directions: Each of the questions or incomplete statements below is followed by five suggested answers or completions. Select the one that is best in each case.

76. Perhaps France's greatest novelist, this author created detailed, often scathing, portrayals of the bourgeois society to which he belonged and which he loved. His works, collectively known as "La Comédie Humaine," include *Père Goriot* and *Cousin Bette*.

    The author described above is

    (A) Arthur Rimbaud
    (B) Emile Zola
    (C) Honoré de Balzac
    (D) Francois Rabelais
    (E) Albert Camus

77. Beethoven's Third Symphony is also referred to as

    (A) the "Jupiter"
    (B) *Das Lied van der Erde*
    (C) *Music for Royal Fireworks*
    (D) the "Eroica"
    (E) *Die Schöne Müllerin*

78. Tom, a warehouse worker, who writes poetry; Laura, his shy, crippled sister; their mother, a well-meaning but shrill and foolish Southern emigre and a "gentleman caller" make up the list of characters in

    (A) *The Glass Menagerie*
    (B) *The Iceman Cometh*
    (C) *Our Town*
    (D) *The Crucible*
    (E) *A Raisin in the Sun*

79. Which of the following was <u>not</u> an Italian Renaissance painter?

    (A) Corregio
    (B) Raphal Sanzio
    (C) Titian
    (D) Giorgio de Chirico
    (E) Michelangelo

<u>Questions 80 to 82</u> refer to the following lines of poetry:

(A) "But at my back I always hear
Time's winged chariot hurrying near,
And yonder all before us lie
Deserts of vast eternity."

(B) "Because I could not stop for Death—
He kindly stopped for me—
The Carriage held but just Ourselves—
And Immortality . . . ."

(C) "O my Luve's like a red, red rose,
That's newly sprung in June:
O my Luve's like the melodie
That's sweetly played in tune! . . ."

(D) "O Captain! my Captain! rise up and hear the bells.
Rise up—for you the flag is flung—for you the bugle trills . . . ."

(E) "One, two! One, two! And through and through
The vorpal blade went snicker-snack!
He left it dead, and with its head
He went galumphing back."

80. Which excerpt contains examples of onomatopoeia?

81. Which excerpt contains two similes?

82. Which excerpt contains an example of personification?

GO ON TO THE NEXT PAGE.

83. Born in Holland, this painter used utilized vibrant colors and short, thick brush strokes in his Expressionistic works. He often juxtaposed complementary colors, such as the blue and orange in his *The Starry Night*, to dynamic effect.

   The artist referred to in the passage above is

   (A) Vincent van Gogh
   (B) Sandro Botticelli
   (C) Jasper Johns
   (D) Jan Vermeer
   (E) Edvard Munch

84. This 1516 description of "Erewhon" is actually a philosophical treatise on equality, freedom, and the nature of a perfect society. It is

   (A) Rousseau's *The Social Contract*
   (B) Swift's *A Modest Proposal*
   (C) Buber's *I and Thou*
   (D) More's *Utopia*
   (E) Darwin's *On the Origins of Species*

85. A childhood burglary of a pear orchard and a chance hearing of children singing "Take it and read" are central turning points in which autobiography of religious conversion?

   (A) *The Autobiography of Benjamin Franklin*
   (B) *The Confessions of St. Augustine*
   (C) *The Life and Times of Frederick Douglass*
   (D) *Confessions of an English Opium Eater*
   (E) Plato's *Apology*

86. Which is <u>not</u> an eighteenth-century novelist?

   (A) Daniel DeFoe
   (B) Henry Fielding
   (C) George Bernard Shaw
   (D) Lawrence Sterne
   (E) Samuel Richardson

<u>Questions 87 to 89</u> refer to the following lists of opera titles:

   (A) *Rigoletto, Aida, Il Trovatore*
   (B) *Faust, Romeo et Juliet*
   (C) *La Nozze de Figaro, Don Giovanni, The Abduction from the Seraglio*
   (D) *La Boheme, Madama Butterfly, Tosca*
   (E) *Lucia di Lammermoor, L'elisir d'amore*

Which of the above were composed by:

87. Mozart?

88. Puccini?

89. Verdi?

GO ON TO THE NEXT PAGE.

Questions 90 to 92 refer to illustrations (A) through (E):

(A)

(B)

(C)

GO ON TO THE NEXT PAGE.

(D)

THE BETTMAN ARCHIVE

(E)

CORBIS-BETTMAN

90. Which was designed by Antonio Gaudi?

91. Which is a Mayan temple?

92. Which is a Gothic cathedral?

GO ON TO THE NEXT PAGE.

93. His Samurai films served as the basis for the Westerns *High Plains Drifter* and *The Magnificent Seven*. His *Hidden Fortress* strongly influenced George Lucas' *Star Wars* trilogy.

The film director described above is

(A) Lo Wei
(B) Zhang Yimou
(C) Akira Kurosawa
(D) Yasujiro Ozu
(E) Kenji Mizoguchi

94. The style of singing associated with elegant, pleasing melodies, simple rhythms and harmonies, and the straightforward depiction of a single, simple emotion is called _____ singing.

(A) bel canto
(B) madrigal
(C) recitative
(D) tarantella
(E) octave

95. Leonardo da Vinci's painting *La Gioconda* is more commonly referred to as the

(A) *Birth of Venus*
(B) *Last Supper*
(C) *Mona Lisa*
(D) *Blue Boy*
(E) *Burghers of Calais*

96. Who wrote *Lady Chatterley's Lover, Sons and Lovers*, and *The Rainbow*?

(A) Isaac Bashevis Singer
(B) Thomas Wolfe
(C) Ernest Hemingway
(D) Charlotte Brontë
(E) D. H. Lawrence

97. "The woods are lovely, dark, and deep,
But I have promises to keep,
And miles to go before I sleep,
And miles to go before I sleep."

These lines were written by

(A) Edwin Arlington Robinson
(B) Robert Frost
(C) Lord Byron
(D) Gerard Manley Hopkins
(E) Samuel Johnson

98. The effort to depict a subject from many different viewpoints simultaneously is characteristic of what style of painting?

(A) Romanticism
(B) Northern Renaissance
(C) Italian Baroque
(D) Realism
(E) Cubism

99. This 1855 volume marked the arrival of free verse as an important form in American poetry. It was regularly rewritten, reedited, and expanded by its author until his death in 1892.

The collection described above is

(A) Pound's *Cantos*
(B) Masters' *Spoon River Anthology*
(C) Ovid's *Metamorphosis*
(D) Whitman's *Leaves of Grass*
(E) Wordsworth's *Lyrical Ballads*

GO ON TO THE NEXT PAGE.

Questions 100 to 102 refer to the following groups of people:

(A) Dashiell Hammett, James M. Cain, Jim Thompson
(B) O. Henry, John Cheever, Edgar Allan Poe
(C) Isaac Asimov, Ray Bradbury, Ursula K. LeGuin
(D) Alvin Ailey, Merce Cunningham, George Ballanchine
(E) Preston Sturges, Busby Berkeley, Howard Hawks

100. Which is a group of "pulp fiction" writers?

101. Which is a group of writers most famous for their short stories?

102. Which is a group of choreographers?

103. "Did he live his life again in every detail of desire, temptation, and surrender during that supreme moment of complete knowledge? He cried in a whisper at some image, at some vision—he cried out twice, a cry that was no more than a breath:
'The horror! The horror!'"

The passage above is from

(A) *Heart of Darkness*
(B) *To the Lighthouse*
(C) *Les Misérables*
(D) *A Harlot High and Low*
(E) *Moll Flanders*

GO ON TO THE NEXT PAGE.

Questions <u>104 to 106</u> are based on the illustrations
below:

(A)

(B)

(C)

(D)

(E)

104. Which is by Henry Moore?

105. Which is from Medieval Europe?

106. Which is by a French post-impressionist?

GO ON TO THE NEXT PAGE.

107. Compared with the capital of a Doric column, the capital of an Ionic column is

    (A) smaller
    (B) closer to the shaft
    (C) more ornate
    (D) lighter in color
    (E) less prominently displayed

108. Which of the following is <u>not</u> a property of a musical tone?

    (A) duration
    (B) timbre
    (C) syncopation
    (D) pitch
    (E) intensity

109. An extreme exaggeration, used to literary effect, is called a(n)

    (A) euphony
    (B) anachronism
    (C) allusion
    (D) parable
    (E) hyperbole

<u>Questions 110 to 112</u> refer to the following groups of fictional characters:

    (A) Queequeg, Starbuck, Captain Ahab, Tashtego, Ishmael
    (B) Natty Bumppo, Cora Munro, Alice Munro, Major Duncan Hayward
    (C) Mr. Allworthy, Blifil, Sophia Western, Molly Seagrim, Lady Bellaston
    (D) Phillip Pirrip, Miss Havisham, Magwitch, Estella
    (E) Flora, Miles, Peter Quint, Miss Jessel

110. Which appear in *The Last of the Mohicans*?

111. Which appear in *Moby Dick*?

112. Which appear in *Great Expectations*?

113. A family crisis results in Nora's realization that her husband Torvald condescends and belittles her. At the play's conclusion, she leaves him.

    The play described above is

    (A) *The Winter's Tale*
    (B) *Medea*
    (C) *Camille*
    (D) *A Doll's House*
    (E) *Man and Superman*

Questions 114 to 116 are based on the illustration below:

THE METROPOLITAN MUSEUM OF ART

114. The work pictured above was painted by

(A) Sandro Botticelli
(B) Andy Warhol
(C) Albrecht Dürer
(D) Donatello
(E) Jacques Louis David

115. It is most closely associated what painting style?

(A) Abstract Expressionism
(B) Neoclassicism
(C) Dadaism
(D) Neo-Primitivism
(E) Photo Realism

116. The subject of the painting is the

(A) rape of the Sabine women
(B) great Roman orator Cicero
(C) death of Socrates
(D) adoration of the Magi
(E) Council of Trent

117. In classical ballet, a three-part dance in which two performers perform an addagio duet, then dance solo, and then conclude with another duet is called a

    (A) pas de deux
    (B) polonaise
    (C) par terre
    (D) pirouette
    (E) plié

118. This French "synthetic cubist" painted geometrical shapes and incorporated imagery from billboards, posters, neon lights, and, most often, machinery.

    The sentence above describes

    (A) Gustave Courbet
    (B) Claude Monet
    (C) Antoine-Jean Gros
    (D) Ferdinand Leger
    (E) Jacques Louis David

119. The Parthenon is located

    (A) atop Mount Vesuvius
    (B) next to the Sistine Chapel
    (C) on the Athenian Acropolis
    (D) along the North Sea shore
    (E) on the island of Crete

120. This composer revolutionized opera by stressing the role of the orchestra instead of that of the singer. His experiments in harmonics paved the way for twentieth-century atonality, and can be heard in his *Tristan und Isolde*, *Parsifal*, and *Ring Cycle*. He is _____.

    (A) Robert Schumann
    (B) Richard Wagner
    (C) Johannes Brahms
    (D) Ludwig van Beethoven
    (E) Carl Maria von Weber

Questions 121 to 123 are based on the poem below:

On First Looking into Chapman's Homer
Much have I traveled in the realms of gold,
And many goodly states and kingdoms seen;
Round many western islands have I been
Which bards in fealty to Apollo hold.
Oft of one wide expanse had I been told
That deep-browed Homer ruled as his demesne,
Yet did I never breathe its pure serene
Till I heard Chapman speak it loud and bold.
Then felt I like some watcher of the skies
When a new planet swims into his ken;
Or like stout Cortez when with eagle eyes
He stared at the Pacific - and all his men
Looked at each other with a wild surmise-
Silent, upon a peak in Darien.

121. In line 4, the word "fealty" is closest in meaning to

    (A) lofty reams
    (B) distance
    (C) anger
    (D) loyalty
    (E) contentedness

122. The "wide expanse" referred to in line 5 is

    (A) the Mediterranean Sea
    (B) the library
    (C) the Pacific Ocean
    (D) *The Odyssey*
    (E) the mountains of Mexico

123. The poem above was written by

    (A) John Keats
    (B) Ben Jonson
    (C) Edgar Allan Poe
    (D) Adrienne Rich
    (E) Paul Verlaine

GO ON TO THE NEXT PAGE.

124. Who starred in the movies *City Lights, Modern Times, The Great Dictator,* and *The Gold Rush*?

(A) W.C. Fields
(B) Robert Redford
(C) Charlie Chaplin
(D) Buster Keaton
(E) Victor Mature

125. The "one-point" technique, used to create linear perspective in paintings, is most closely associated with which of the following periods in Western art history?

(A Modernism
(B) The Italian Renaissance
(C) Early medieval
(D) Gothic
(E) Surrealism

126. The numbers in the music staff above are used to indicate _____.

(A) meter signature
(B) key
(C) harmonics
(D) clef
(E) instrumentation

127. What epic poem recounts the history of the Trojan War?

(A) *The Divine Comedy*
(B) *Adonais*
(C) *The Iliad*
(D) *Candide*
(E) *Samson Agonistes*

Questions 128 to 130 refer the following:

(A) A self-described "Dust Bowl refugee," this singer and songwriter composed union anthems and other famous songs of protest, including "This Land is Your Land."

(B) This master of the Mississippi Delta blues is generally recognized as the blues' most haunting guitar player and singer. His compositions that, decades later, became hits for rock bands include: "Crossroads" (for Cream), "Love in Vain" and "Stop Breaking Down" (both for the Rolling Stones).

(C) Composer of numerous movie and theater scores, this songwriter wrote many standards, among which are "White Christmas," "God Bless America," "Alexander's Ragtime Band," and "There's No Business Like Show Business."

(D) Known as "the father of Bluegrass music," this singer and songwriter conceived of and, with Lester Flatt and Earl Scruggs, perfected all the elements of that genre.

(E) His name practically synonymous with ragtime music, this pianist and composer also wrote an opera, *Tremonisha*.

Which of the above describes:

128. Irving Berlin?

129. Scott Joplin?

130. Woody Guthrie?

GO ON TO THE NEXT PAGE.

131. The fugue is most closely associated with which of the following musical terms?

(A) monophony
(B) precipitato
(C) program music
(D) counterpoint
(E) atonality

132. This style of art, of which Andy Warhol was a practitioner, uses commercial culture as its subject matter and sometimes as its raw materials.

The sentence above describes

(A) Surrealism
(B) Pop Art
(C) Constructivism
(D) Minimalism
(E) Art Deco

133. Upton Sinclair's muckraking classic *The Jungle* is about

(A) garment industry sweatshops
(B) the dangers of nuclear power
(C) Chicago's meat-packing industry
(D) the battle to control water rights in California
(E) the making of the movie *The African Queen*

Questions 134 to 136 refer to the following groups of people:

(A) J. M. W. Turner, William Hogarth, Thomas Gainsborough
(B) Roy Lichtenstein, Edward Hopper, Robert Rauschenberg
(C) Edouard Manet, Camille Pissarro, Edgar Degas
(D) Hans Holbein, Peter Brueghel the Elder, Albrecht Durer
(E) Salvador Dali, Rene Magritte, Max Ernst

134. Which is a group of surrealists?

135. Which is a group of impressionists?

136. Which is a group of English artists?

GO ON TO THE NEXT PAGE.

137. "Do not go gentle into that good night. . .
Rage, rage against the dying of the light."

These lines were written by

(A) Dylan Thomas
(B) Langston Hughes
(C) Marianne Moore
(D) W. H. Auden
(E) Alfred, Lord Tennyson

138. All of the following are jazz musicians/
composers of the twentieth century EXCEPT:

(A) Duke Ellington
(B) Aubrey Beardsley
(C) Thelonius Monk
(D) John Coltrane
(E) Jelly Roll Morton

139. The hero of what book encounters the
Lilliputians, the Brobdingnagians, the Yahoos,
and the Houynhms?

(A) *Moby Dick*
(B) *Shipwrecked*
(C) *Robinson Crusoe*
(D) *A Tale of Two Cities*
(E) *Gulliver's Travels*

Questions 140-141 refer to the dramatic speech
below:

". . . Have you eyes,
And do not see your own damnation? Eyes,
And cannot see whose company you keep?
Whose son are you? I tell you, you have sinned—
And do not know it—against your own on earth
And in the grave. A swift and two-edged sword,
Your mother's and your father's curse, shall sweep you
Out of this land. Those clear-seeing eyes
Shall then be darkened . . . ."

140. The subject of the speech above is

(A) Agamemnon
(B) Orestes
(C) Clytemnestra
(D) Antigone
(E) Oedipus

141. The speaker is

(A) Iphigenia
(B) Odysseus
(C) Electra
(D) Teiresias
(E) Achilles

GO ON TO THE NEXT PAGE.

142. A sequence of brief film clips, conventionally used to show the passing of time, is called a

    (A) montage
    (B) trailer
    (C) gaffer
    (D) splice
    (E) crane shot

143. The process of decorating a manuscript with drawings or paintings is called

    (A) illumination
    (B) fluting
    (C) camposanto
    (D) rustication
    (E) palazzo

144. Which of the following was written earliest?

    (A) *The Love Song of J. Alfred Prufrock*
    (B) *Paradise Lost*
    (C) *The Divine Comedy*
    (D) *Songs of Innocence and Experience*
    (E) *Sailing to Byzantium*

145. The bodhrán, the harp, the uillean pipes, and the tin whistle are instruments associated with the music of what nation?

    (A) Bali
    (B) Lithuania
    (C) Germany
    (D) Mexico
    (E) Ireland

146. Fill in the blanks

    A line of iambic pentameter is made up of _____ feet of _____ syllables.

    (A) three . . . three
    (B) four . . . two
    (C) four . . . three
    (D) five . . . two
    (E) five . . . three

147. This 1982 Nobel prize-winning author's novels of "magical realism," among which are *One Hundred Years of Solitude* and *Love in the Time of Cholera*, have earned him international acclaim.

    The author described above is

    (A) Dylan Thomas
    (B) Gabriel Garcia Marquez
    (C) Russell Banks
    (D) William Kennedy
    (E) Elie Wiesel

148. Which of the following painters was the closest contemporary of James Joyce?

    (A) Henri Matisse
    (B) Eugene Delacroix
    (C) Franz Hals
    (D) Anthony Van Dyck
    (E) Caravaggio

149. A supernatural event that helps move the plot of a story or drama along is called a(n)

    (A) caesura
    (B) parody
    (C) spoonerism
    (D) deus ex machina
    (E) trochee

150. The technique of painting on plaster is called

    (A) gisant
    (B) striation
    (C) fresco
    (D) pastel
    (E) dry point

STOP

IF YOU FINISH BEFORE TIME IS CALLED, YOU MAY CHECK YOUR WORK ON THIS SECTION ONLY.
DO NOT WORK ON ANY OTHER SECTION IN THE TEST.

NO TEST MATERIAL ON THIS PAGE.

SCORING YOUR TEST

This test is a facsimile of the ETS-written CLEP general exam in Humanities. Care has been taken to make sure that this test closely resembles the actual exam both in content and format. In other words, when you take the real CLEP, it should look a lot like the test you've just taken.

ETS has never released its scoring methods for the CLEP. ETS states in its literature that, if you get half the raw score points available to you on the test, you should score the national medium–usually between 480 and 500–on a given test.

Your raw score is determined by subtracting 1/4 the number of questions you answer incorrectly from the number of questions you answer correctly. Questions you leave blank are worth 0 points.

Typically, you need about 2/3 of the raw score points available on a test to score in the mid-600s on an ETS test, but, again, this is only speculation regarding the CLEP.

15

Answers and Explanations to the Humanities Exam

SECTION 3

Read this entire section, even the explanations for the questions you answered correctly. The material covered in these explanations add up to a pretty thorough review of the material tested on the CLEP. Plus, many explanations contain helpful test-taking tips.

1. A creature with the body of a lion and the head of a man is called a

   (A) minotaur
   (B) sphinx
   (C) cyclops
   (D) shrew
   (E) centaur

1. **(B)** is the correct answer. A minotaur has the head of a bull and the body of a human; in Greek mythology, Theseus kills a minotaur in the Cretan labyrinth. A cyclops is a one-eyed giant; Polyphemus, who eats most of Odysseus' crew in *The Odyssey*, is a cyclops. A shrew is a woman of violent temper and foul disposition. A centaur has the body of a horse and the torso and head of a human.

2. Which of the following is a woodwind instrument?

   (A) bassoon
   (B) timpani
   (C) mandolin
   (D) cello
   (E) tuba

2. **(A)** is the correct answer. A timpani is a large kettle drum with a pedal that facilitates changes in its tone. A mandolin is a small stringed instrument commonly used in Italian folk music and American bluegrass. A cello is a stringed instrument larger than a viola and smaller than a bass. A tuba is a large brass instrument.

3. A Roman philosopher arguing that wealth, health, and good fortune are immaterial, that only matters of vice and virtue are important, and that personal tragedy should therefore be borne impassively would likely be of which school?

   (A) Stoicism
   (B) Epicureanism
   (C) Manicheanism
   (D) Existentialism
   (E) Neoplatonism

3. **(A)** is the correct answer. Epicureans believed that pleasure is the highest good and were thus the near-opposites of the Stoics. The Manicheans were third-century Persians whose central tenet was that the world was dualistic, divided between good and evil. They were not present in Rome. Existentialism is a twentieth-century school of philosophy, much too late to be the correct answer to this question, as is Neoplatonism, which developed in the third-century.

4. *Pilgrim's Progress* and *Animal Farm* are two examples of a narrative form in which events contain a sustained reference to a second set of events or meanings. This form of narrative is called

   (A) comedy
   (B) tragedy
   (C) history
   (D) allegory
   (E) melodrama

4. **(D)** is the correct answer. Go back and reread this question if you got this one wrong. You almost certainly made a careless error. Comedy, tragedy, and history are the three categories of Shakespearean drama; melodrama is a type of drama in which emotions, cause and effect, etc., are noticeably exaggerated. *Pilgrim's Progress* is an allegory of personal spiritual development; *Animal Farm* is an allegory of the Soviet revolution.

SECTION 3

QUESTIONS	EXPLANATIONS

<u>Questions 5 and 6</u> refer to the following lines:

"April is the cruellest month, breeding
Lilacs out of the dead land . . ."

5. The lines above open

    (A) Stevens' *Thirteen Ways of Looking at a Blackbird*
    (B) Blake's *London*
    (C) Shelly's *Adonais*
    (D) Coleridge's *Kubla Khan*
    (E) Eliot's *The Waste Land*

5. **(E)** is the correct answer. The fact that this poem doesn't rhyme is a tip-off that it is probably modern. Blake's poetry almost always rhymes, as do Shelly's and Coleridge's. Had you known this, you should have eliminated (B), (C), and (D) and guessed among (A) and (E).

6. The line "April is the cruellest month" alludes to the first lines of

    (A) *The Aenead*
    (B) the prologue to *The Canterbury Tales*
    (C) *The Fairie Queene*
    (D) *Ode on a Grecian Urn*
    (E) *The Flowers of Evil*

6. **(B)** is the correct answer. Chaucer's *Canterbury Tales* begins "Whan that April with his shoures sote / The droughte of Marche hath perced to the rote . . . ." Chaucer evokes the positive aspects of spring as a time of rebirth; Eliot's poem gives spring a decidedly more pessimistic spin, and by alluding to Chaucer's poem intensifies the differences between his poem and Chaucer's. Of the other answer choices, only *The Aenead* begins with a line you would be expected to recognize: "I sing of arms and the man . . . ."

7. The term *pieta* describes a depiction of

    (A) the Virgin Mary mourning over Jesus' body
    (B) the martyrdom of a saint
    (C) a main altar of a cathedral
    (D) a scene from Greek mythology
    (E) an episode from the Old Testament

7. **(A)** is the correct answer. A good way to remember this is to realize that "pieta" is Italian for both "pity" and "piety." What could be more pitiable than the image of Mary mourning over her crucified son? The religious subject is certainly evocative of piety. When guessing, remember that the answer to a question like this one would have to be a subject so common in Italian sculpture and painting that it was given its own name. Thus, (A) and (B) are better guesses than (D) or (E), which, while not infrequent subjects of Italian art, are certainly less common than are images of Catholic iconography.

SECTION 3

8. Who wrote *The Marriage of Heaven and Hell* and *Songs of Innocence and Experience*?

    (A) Henry Wadsworth Longfellow
    (B) Rudyard Kipling
    (C) Alexander Pope
    (D) Jonathan Swift
    (E) William Blake

8. **(E)** is the correct answer. This is one of those trivial pursuit questions that you either know or you don't. Nothing tricky here: these are among Blake's most famous works.

9. Ernest Hemingway once said, "All American literature comes from one book. . . ." The book to which he was referring is

    (A) *Clarissa*
    (B) *Typee*
    (C) *The Scarlet Letter*
    (D) *The Adventures of Huckleberry Finn*
    (E) *Uncle Tom's Cabin*

9. **(D)** is the correct answer. (C) and (E) would be decent guesses; *Typee* is too obscure a work (it is by Melville, the author of *Moby Dick*) and *Clarissa* is by the Englishman Samuel Richardson, so it would be a very unlikely source of American literature. Twain's *Huckleberry Finn* is highly regarded in nearly all critical circles; its themes of freedom, equality, and self-reliance are among the reasons it is considered a source of much American literature that followed it.

10. Which of the following is NOT part of the interior of a Gothic cathedral?

    (A) entablature
    (B) transept
    (C) choir
    (D) nave
    (E) apse

10. **(A)** is the correct answer. Entablature is the term used to describe the entire structure above a column in a classical order; the entablature usually includes the architrave, frieze, and cornice. The transept of a cathedral corresponds to the cross arms of a crucifix, after which the floor plan of a Gothic cathedral is modeled. The choir is the rectangular area in which the choir sits. The nave is the center aisle. The apse is the vaulted recess at the end of the choir.

SECTION 3

QUESTIONS	EXPLANATIONS

Questions 11 to 13 are based on the passages below:

(A) "From Stettin in the Baltic to Trieste in the Adriatic, an iron curtain has descended across the Continent. Behind that line lie all the capitals of the ancient states of Central and Eastern Europe."

(B) "The New Frontier of which I speak is not a set of promises – it is a set of challenges. It sums up not what I intend to offer the American people, but what I intend to ask of them."

(C) "An epidemic of indiscriminate assault upon character does not good, but very great harm. The soul of every scoundrel is gladdened whenever an honest man is assailed . . . ."

(D) "I said then, and I say now, that while there is a lower class, I am in it, while there is a criminal element, I am of it, and while there is a soul in prison, I am not free . . . ."

(E) "When we let freedom ring, when we let it ring from every village and every hamlet, from every state and every city, we will be able to speed up that day when all God's children . . . will be able to join hands and sing . . . 'Free at last! Free at last! Thank God almighty, we are free at last.'"

Which of the above is an excerpt from a speech by:

11. John F. Kennedy?

12. Martin Luther King?

13. Winston Churchill?

11. **(B)** is the correct answer. The term "New Frontier" should have been your tip-off that this quote is Kennedy's.

12. **(E)** is the correct answer. This is from King's famous "I Have a Dream" speech.

13. **(A)** is the correct answer. Churchill coined the term "Iron Curtain."

Answer choice (C) is from a speech by Theodore Roosevelt, in which he attacked irresponsible muckraking journalists. Answer choice (D) is from a speech by Eugene Debs, a Socialist who ran for the presidency several times at the turn of the twentieth century.

SECTION 3

Questions 14 to 16 refer to illustrations (A) through (E) [see exam]:

14. Which is by Michelangelo?

14. **(D)** is the correct answer. This sculpture, *The Bound Slave,* is on the tomb of Jules II, on exhibit in the Louvre in Paris.

15. Which is by Auguste Rodin?

15. **(C)** is the correct answer. This sculpture is Rodin's portrait of the French novelist Honoré de Balzac.

16. Which is a Gabon carving?

16. **(B)** is the correct answer. This head was carved by an artist of the Fang tribe. Answer choice (A) is a Greek sculpture called *Discobolos*. (E) is Greenough's famous statue of George Washington.

17. Mozart's *The Magic Flute (Die Zauberflöte)* is a(n)
    - (A) cantata
    - (B) opera
    - (C) oratorio
    - (D) symphony
    - (E) concerto

17. **(B)** is the correct answer. Another trivial pursuit question. Remember that Mozart is most famous for symphonies, operas, and concertos. The correct answer was most likely to be one of those three.

18. The movies *The Bicycle Thief, Open City*, and *Germany Year Zero* all belong to what category?
    - (A) film noir
    - (B) American avant-garde
    - (C) screwball comedy
    - (D) documentary
    - (E) Italian neorealist

18. **(E)** is the correct answer. Italian neorealism is a film movement that hit its peak right after World War II; it emphasized gritty realism, often using non-actors in starring roles and filming on location in such war-demolished locales as Berlin. Film noir is a stylized American form most often associated with hard-boiled gangster movies; *The Maltese Falcon* is a prime example. The American avant-garde is typified by nonlinear, non-narrative experimental filmmaking, and is typified by the works of Stan Brakhage and Kenneth Anger. Screwball comedy, as its name implies, is a form of high-energy, wacky comedy in which events usually get way out of hand; Preston Sturges' movies, such as *Hail the Conquering Hero*, typify the genre. Documentaries are nonfiction films.

SECTION 3

QUESTIONS	EXPLANATIONS

19. Bigger Thomas is the central character of what novel?

   (A) *Light in August*
   (B) *Portnoy's Complaint*
   (C) *Native Son*
   (D) *Gravity's Rainbow*
   (E) *Pride and Prejudice*

19. **(C)** is the correct answer. Bigger Thomas is the antihero of Richard Wright's moving, disturbing tale of poverty, alienation, and remorseless murder. *Light in August* is by William Faulkner; *Portnoy's Complaint* is by Phillip Roth; *Gravity's Rainbow* is by Thomas Pynchon; and *Pride and Prejudice* is by Jane Austen.

20. This twentieth-century masterpiece draws on Slavic folk melodies, among other sources. With its abrupt transitions between seemingly unrelated segments, this work was once considered so radical that its debut in 1913 precipitated a riot.

   The musical piece described above is

   (A) Richard Strauss' *Also Sprach Zarathustra*
   (B) Johann Sebastian Bach's *Mass in B Minor*
   (C) Franz Liszt's *Les Preludes*
   (D) Johnannes Brahms' *Violin Concerto in D Major*
   (E) Igor Stravinsky's *The Rites of Spring*

20. **(E)** is the correct answer. The fact that *The Rites of Spring* instigated a riot is one of the most commonly cited facts about the piece. The question mentions the twentieth century, which should have helped you eliminated Bach, Brahms, and Liszt.

SECTION 3

QUESTIONS	EXPLANATIONS

Questions 21 and 22 refer to the following:

> ". . . say first what cause
> Moved our grand parents, in that happy state
> Favored of Heav'n so highly, to fall off
> From their Creator, and transgress his will
> For one restraint, lords of the world besides?
> Who first seduced them to that foul revolt?
> Th'infernal serpent . . . ."

21. The lines above are from

    (A) *The Inferno*
    (B) *Paradise Lost*
    (C) *The Faerie Queene*
    (D) *Mac Flecknoe*
    (E) *Othello*

21. **(B)** is the correct answer. *Paradise Lost* is Milton's epic poem about the fall of Adam and Eve ("our grand parents"). The phrases "in that happy state," "favored of Heav'n," and "transgress his will" should be tip-offs that this is the tale of Adam and Eve, first in Eden, then banished from it. *The Inferno* is the first part of Dante's *Divine Comedy* trilogy, in which the poet visits hell. *The Faerie Queene* is Spenser's epic allegory of moral virtues. *Mac Flecknoe* is Dryden's satiric jab at his contemporary, Thomas Shadwell. *Othello* is a Shakespearean tragedy.

22. The words "that foul revolt" refer to

    (A) the betrayal of Regan and Goneril
    (B) Satan's rebellion in Heaven
    (C) the fall of Adam and Eve
    (D) the crucifixion of Jesus
    (E) the American Revolution

22. **(C)** is the correct answer. Answer choice (A) refers to Shakespeare's *King Lear*. (B) describes an event mentioned in *Paradise Lost*, but the context should tell you that Milton is here referring to Eve's eating the apple ("Who . . . seduced them . . . ? Th'infernal serpent . . .."). (E) cites an event that occurred over a century after the writing of *Paradise Lost*.

23. If I reprehend anything in this world, it is the use of my oracular tongue, and a nice derangement of epitaphs."

The speech above, from Sheridan's *The Rivals*, is an example of

    (A) gallicism
    (B) dithyramb
    (C) pun
    (D) haiku
    (E) malapropism

23. **(E)** is the correct answer. The speech cited is by Mistress Malaprop, the character whose name has become synonymous with the comical misuse of language. Gallicism is a term of French origin. A dithyramb is a wild Greek choral song, usually in honor of Dionysus or Bacchus. A pun is a humorous, clever play on words; not an unwitting one, as is a malapropism. Haiku is a Japanese form of three-line poetry.

SECTION 3

QUESTIONS	EXPLANATIONS

24. Which of the following composers was most responsible for transforming the symphony from its pre-classical *sinfonia* form to its classical form?

    (A) Antonio Vivaldi
    (B) Arnold Schönberg
    (C) Franz Josef Haydn
    (D) Ludwig van Beethoven
    (E) Charles Gounod

24. **(C)** is the correct answer. The classical period in music begins in the eighteenth century and ends in the early nineteenth century with Beethoven, who simultaneously marks the beginning of the romantic period. The transition from pre-classical to classical was largely facilitated by Haydn, who wrote over 100 symphonies. Schönberg was a twentieth-century composer; Gounod was a French romantic most famous for his opera *Faust*. Vivaldi was a baroque composer, most famous for *The Four Seasons*, which are concerti.

25. The use of tiny dots to create an image in painting, a technique exemplified by the work of Georges Seurat, is called

    (A) chiaroscuro
    (B) cartooning
    (C) pointillism
    (D) foreshortening
    (E) etching

25. **(C)** is the correct answer. The use of tiny dots, or points, in painting is called (not surprisingly) pointillism. Chiaroscuro is the counterbalancing of light and dark. Cartooning is a technique of reproducing a sketch through the use of a grid. Foreshortening is the technique of distorting an image in order to reproduce the effect of three-dimensionality in a painting. An etching is a type of engraving.

26. Fill in the blank below:

    A(n) _____ is episodic and has a rogue or misfit for a hero. The wandering hero serves as a prism through which readers can view many strata of society.

    (A) historical novel
    (B) myth
    (C) novella
    (D) epic
    (E) picaresque novel

26. **(E)** is the correct answer. A historical novel is one based on a historical event. A myth is a legend, usually with some basis in history. A novella is a short novel; the term is often associated with works in French and Italian. An epic is a grand-scale work that usually tells of a heroic adventure resulting in (1) a major transformation of the hero, and (2) some major event in a society's history, such as its founding or destruction.

SECTION 3

Questions 27 to 29 are based on the following lists of titles:

(A) *Troilus and Criseyde, Parlement of Foules, Canterbury Tales*

(B) *The Rape of the Lock, An Essay on Man, An Essay on Criticism*

(C) *Moll Flanders, Robinson Crusoe, Roxana*

(D) *No Exit, Nausea, Being and Nothingness*

(E) *Martin Chuzzlewit, Bleak House, Great Expectations*

27. Which are by Jean-Paul Sartre?

28. Which are by Alexander Pope?

29. Which are by Charles Dickens?

27. **(D)** is the correct answer. These are Sartre's most famous works. *No Exit* is a play about hell (or something very much like it); *Nausea* is a major existentialist novel; *Being and Nothingness* is one of existentialism's major philosophical works.

28. **(B)** is the correct answer. These are three of Pope's most famous works. Pope wrote his greatest works in the early eighteenth century.

29. **(E)** is the correct answer. Other famous novels by Dickens include *Oliver Twist, David Copperfield,* and *A Tale of Two Cities.*

Answer choice (A) is a list of works by the Medieval English poet Geoffrey Chaucer; (C) is a list of works by the English novelist Daniel DeFoe.

SECTION 3

QUESTIONS	EXPLANATIONS

<u>Questions 30 to 32</u> are based on illustrations (A) through (E) [see exam]:

30. Which depicts a gathering of great philosophers?

30. **(A)** is the correct answer. Raphael's *The School of Athens* depicts all the great philosophers of antiquity. At the center are Plato, pointing toward the sky to symbolize his idealism, and Aristotle, pointing to the ground to indicate his pragmatism.

31. Which depicts the carnage caused by the Spanish Civil War?

31. **(C)** is the correct answer. Picasso's *Guernica* is painted in black, white, and gray to evoke newspaper photography. It is one of his masterpieces.

32. Which depicts the creation of Adam?

32. **(E)** is the correct answer. This famous detail is from Michelangelo's ceiling paintings at the Sistine Chapel in Rome. The painting is usually referred to by the title *The Creation of Adam.*

Answer choice (B) is by Rembrandt and is called *Syndics of the Cloth Guild*, although most people call it "The Dutch Masters," after the cigar company that appropriated the image. Answer choice (D) is called *The Raft of the Medusa* and is by Théodore Géricault.

33. This pair, director and actor, collaborated on over a dozen movies. In such films as *Stagecoach* and *The Man Who Shot Liberty Valence*, their work set the standard for American Westerns.

These two men are

(A) Frank Capra and Jimmy Stewart
(B) Billy Wilder and Jack Lemmon
(C) John Ford and John Wayne
(D) Ernst Lubitsch and Melvyn Douglas
(E) Mack Sennett and Fatty Arbuckle

33. **(C)** is the correct answer. Frank Capra is most famous for directing tales of greatness about common Americans, such as *It's a Wonderful Life* and *Mr. Smith Goes to Washington* (both of which star Jimmy Stewart). Billy Wilder is most famous for writing and directing caustic comedies, such as *The Apartment* (which stars Jack Lemmon). Ernst Lubitsch is famous for his sophisticated comedies, such as *To Be or Not to Be* and *Ninotchka* (the latter stars Melvyn Douglas). Mack Sennett and Fatty Arbuckle collaborated on numerous early silent comedy shorts.

34. Caryatids and atlantes are
(A) types of ribbing used to decorate vaulted arches
(B) sculpted human figures used as architectural supports
(C) different types of Oceanic masks
(D) ornaments found on Egyptian sarcophagi
(E) brushes used in oil painting

34. **(B)** is the correct answer. Another trivial pursuit question. If you recognized the Greek roots of these words, that might have helped you eliminate answer choices (C) and (D).

SECTION 3

Questions 35 to 37 refer to the poem below:

That time of year thou mayst in me behold
When yellow leaves, or none, or few, do hang
Upon those boughs which shake against the cold,
Bare ruin'd choirs where late the sweet birds sang.
In me thou see'st the twilight of such day
As after sunset fadeth in the west,
Which by and by black night doth take away,
Death's second self, that seals up all in rest.
In me thou see'st the glowing of such fire,
That on the ashes of his youth doth lie,
As the death-bed whereon it must expire,
Consum'd with that which it was nourish'd by.
This thou perceiv'st, which makes thy love more strong.
To love that well which thou must leave ere long.

35. The poem above follows what verse form?

   (A) terza rima
   (B) English sonnet
   (C) elegaic stanza
   (D) rhyme royal
   (E) Spenserian stanza

35. **(B)** is the correct answer. Terza rima is composed of three-line iambic pentameter stanzas and uses a very difficult, interlocking rhyme scheme. Dante's *Divine Comedy* is composed in terza rima form. An elegaic stanza consists of four lines of iambic pentameter with alternating rhyme. Rhyme royal has seven iambic pentameter lines. A Spenserian stanza has nine lines of iambic pentameter and uses a rhyme scheme so challenging that little other than Spenser's *Faerie Queene* has even been written in the form. English sonnet is the form of Shakespeare's sonnets, of which this is one; English sonnets are divided into three four–line stanzas (called quatrains) and a closing couplet.

36. The main theme of the poem is

   (A) aging
   (B) autumn
   (C) birds
   (D) fire
   (E) nighttime

36. **(A)** is the correct answer. This question requires some interpretation of the poem, unless you have previously studied it and remember its theme. The poet compares himself to a tree in the throws of autumnal decay; to the last flickers of daylight; and to the dying embers of a fire. While the poet mentions autumn, birds, fire, and nighttime, none of these is his main theme. Aging, and the effect the imminence of death has on love, is.

37. This poem was written by

   (A) Percy Bysshe Shelley
   (B) William Wordsworth
   (C) John Donne
   (D) William Shakespeare
   (E) Emily Dickinson

37. **(D)** is the correct answer. This is one of Shakespeare's most famous sonnets. If you guessed Dickinson, you should read some of her poetry, as this sonnet is not at all characteristic of her work.

SECTION 3

QUESTIONS	EXPLANATIONS

38. Who wrote *Cannery Row*, *Of Mice and Men*, and *The Grapes of Wrath*?

(A) Samuel Richardson
(B) John Steinbeck
(C) Virginia Woolf
(D) James Baldwin
(E) William Faulkner

38. **(B)** is the correct answer. These, along with *East of Eden*, are Steinbeck's most famous works. Samuel Richardson was a seventeenth-century novelist who wrote *Clarissa* and *Pamela*. Virginia Woolf was a twentieth-century novelist whose great works include *To the Lighthouse* and *Mrs. Dalloway*. James Baldwin was a twentieth-century African-American author who wrote *Go Tell It on the Mountain* and *Notes of a Native Son*. William Faulkner was a twentieth-century American novelist; his works include *As I Lay Dying*, *The Sound and the Fury*, and *Light in August*.

39. "Through pity and fear, [tragedy] achieves the purgation of such emotions."

The passage above, from Aristotle's *Poetics*, describes

(A) catharsis
(B) denouement
(C) farce
(D) irony
(E) hubris

39. **(A)** is the correct answer. Aristotle explains his theories of drama in his *Poetics*. In this passage he describes catharsis, the emotional release one gets from watching another's misfortunes artfully and didactically presented. Denouement is the term used to describe all the events following the climax of a drama, novel, film, etc. Farce is a type of broad comedy. Irony is a comic tool in which the literal meaning of what is being said is somehow subverted. Hubris is the excessive pride to which Aristotle partially ascribes the fall of heroes in Greek tragedies.

40. Which of the following lists the instrumentation of a classical string quartet?

(A) violin, viola, cello, bass
(B) two violins, viola, cello
(C) two violas, violin, cello
(D) viola, cello, guitar, bass
(E) violin, mandolin, cello, guitar

40. **(B)** is the correct answer. Trivial pursuit territory. Answer choice (E) would make for a particularly awful sounding ensemble.

41. Fill in the blank below:

Lenin wrote: "It is impossible to fully understand Marx's *Capital*, particularly its first chapter, without preliminary study and complete understanding of _____."

(A) Kierkegaard's *Sickness Unto Death*
(B) Hegel's *Logic*
(C) Aquinas' *Summa Theologica*
(D) Plato's *Phaedrus*
(E) Kant's *Critique of Pure Reason*

41. **(B)** is the correct answer. This question is asking, in a roundabout way, whether you know that Marx based much of his thinking on the works of Hegel. Kierkegaard was an early existentialist. Aquinas was one of the great fathers of the Catholic church, and thus an extremely unlikely hero to Marx or Lenin, both of whom were atheists. Plato was one of antiquity's two most important philosophers, the other being Aristotle. Kant was an immensely influential philosopher whose philosophy stands in many ways in direct contrast with Hegel's.

QUESTIONS	EXPLANATIONS

42. Which of the following genres of music is indigenous to and most closely associated with Louisiana?

    (A) polka and polonaise
    (B) raga and flamenco
    (C) chamber and comic opera
    (D) Cajun and zydeco
    (E) motet and chanson

42. **(D)** is the correct answer. Cajun is the name of an ethnic group living in southern Louisiana, after whom the musical genre is named. Zydeco is a musical gumbo of funk, rhythm and blues, and New Orleans-style rock-and-roll. Polkas and polonaises are native to Poland (*polonaise* is French for "Polish"). Ragas are from India, flamenco from Spain. Chamber music and comic opera are two forms of European classical music. Motet and chanson are types of Renaissance songs.

43. What twentieth-century U.S. dramatist wrote *Mourning Becomes Electra* based on Aeschylus' *Oresteia*?

    (A) Eugene O'Neill
    (B) Lillian Hellman
    (C) Thornton Wilder
    (D) Clifford Odets
    (E) Arthur Miller

43. **(A)** is the correct answer. Another trivial pursuit question. This is O'Neill's most famous work; he also wrote *Anna Christie*, *A Long Day's Journey into Night*, and *The Iceman Cometh*. Lillian Hellman wrote *Watch on the Rhine* and *The Little Foxes*. Thornton Wilder wrote *Our Town*. Clifford Odets wrote *Waiting for Lefty* and *Golden Boy*. Arthur Miller wrote *The Crucible* and *Death of a Salesman*.

44. The framers of the U.S. Constitution drew most heavily from the work of a seventeenth-century English philosopher, particularly from his *Two Treatises on Government*. This philosopher is

    (A) David Hume
    (B) John Calvin
    (C) Immanuel Kant
    (D) John Locke
    (E) Benedict Spinoza

44. **(D)** is the correct answer. David Hume was an English empiricist who argued against proofs of the existence of God. John Calvin was a fatalist theologian and founder of Calvinism. Immanuel Kant was the German founder of "critical philosophy." Benedict Spinoza was a Dutch philosopher and proponent of "monism."

45. Whose works, which included *The Protestant Ethic and the Spirit of Capitalism*, laid the foundation for modern sociology?

    (A) Margaret Mead
    (B) Dag Hammarskjöld
    (C) Rainer Maria Rilke
    (D) Max Weber
    (E) François Truffaut

45. **(D)** is the correct answer. Margaret Mead was an important anthropologist. Dag Hammarskjöld was a diplomat. Rilke was a German poet. Truffaut was a French film director associated with the French New Wave of the late 1950s and early 1960s.

SECTION 3

QUESTIONS	EXPLANATIONS

Questions 46 to 48 are based on illustrations (A) through (E) [see exam]:

46. Which is a mosaic?

46. **(D)** is the correct answer. A mosaic is an artwork made of embedded pieces of stone or glass.

47. Which is an engraving?

47. **(B)** is the correct answer. An engraving is a print made from a metal plate onto which a design, illustration, etc., has been incised. This engraving is by the famous engraver Albrecht Dürer.

48. Which is a diptych?

48. **(A)** is the correct answer. A diptych is any two-paneled artwork, usually an altarpiece.

Answer choice (C) is a portrait in oil paint of *A Lady with a Bible* by Frans Hals. Answer choice (E) is an ancient Sumerian figurine dating to approximately 2100 B.C. Looks good for its age, doesn't it?

SECTION 3

Questions 49 to 51 refer to the following lines:

(A) "Sitting beside the road, watching the wagon mount the hill toward her, Lena thinks, 'I have come from Alabama: a fur piece . . . .'"

(B) "Ships at a distance have every man's wish on board. For some they come in with the tide. For others they sail forever on the horizon, never out of sight, never landing . . . ."

(C) "In a village of La Mancha the name of which I have no desire to recall, there lived not so long ago one of those gentlemen who always have a lance in the rack, an ancient buckler, a skinny nag, and a greyhound for the chase."

(D) "Someone must have been telling lies about Joseph K., for without having done anything wrong he was arrested one fine morning."

(E) "Hopping a freight out of Los Angeles at high noon one day in late September 1955 I got on a gondola and lay down with my duffel bag under my head and my knees crossed and contemplated the clouds . . . ."

49. Which opens Franz Kafka's *The Trial*?

49. **(D)** is the correct answer. Joseph K. is the main character of Kafka's *The Trial*, in which he is tried by a mysterious justice system for crimes the nature of which he never learns.

50. Which opens Zora Neale Hurston's *Their Eyes Were Watching God*?

50. **(B)** is the correct answer. Zora Neale Hurston's *Their Eyes Were Watching God* is one of the greatest achievements in fiction of the Harlem Renaissance. This sentence opens Spike Lee's *She's Gotta Have It*. Hurston's novel inspired Alice Walker's *The Color Purple*.

51. Which are from Cervantes' *Don Quixote*?

51. **(C)** is the correct answer. "La Mancha" should have served as your context clue. The Broadway musical based on *Don Quixote* is tiled *Man of La Mancha*.

Answer choice (A) is the opening sentence of William Faulkner's *Light in August*. Answer choice (E) is the opening line of Jack Kerouac's *The Dharma Bums*.

SECTION 3

QUESTIONS	EXPLANATIONS

52. All of the following terms are used to describe female vocal registers EXCEPT:

    (A) alto
    (B) contralto
    (C) mezzo-soprano
    (D) tenor
    (E) soprano

52. **(D)** is the correct answer. *Tenor* is a term used to describe a male vocal register.

53. Statues of the Buddha usually depict him

    (A) lying on his back
    (B) seated in the lotus position
    (C) dancing, with one leg off the ground
    (D) on horseback
    (E) as a child

53. **(B)** is the correct answer. A trivial pursuit question. In the lotus position, the Buddha is seated, legs crossed, face forward, palms upward on his knees, his middle fingers and thumbs touching.

54. Architectural drawings used to show how a finished building will look to passersby are called

    (A) turrets
    (B) presentation drawings
    (C) engravings
    (D) blueprints
    (E) hieroglyphs

54. **(B)** is the correct answer. A turret is a small tower. An engraving is a piece of art work created through a process of incising the work onto a surface and then printing a copy off that surface. Blueprints are floor plans and do not show how a finished building will look from the street, as presentation drawings do. Hieroglyphs are symbols used by the ancient Egyptians as an alphabet.

55. "Magnificent,
My nose! . . . You pug, you knob, you button-
   head,
Know that I glory in this nose of mine,
For a great nose indicates a great man . . . ."

The lines above are spoken by the title character of

    (A) *Hedda Gabbler*
    (B) *Waiting for Godot*
    (C) *Cyrano de Bergerac*
    (D) *Othello*
    (E) *The Misanthrope*

55. **(C)** is the correct answer. The reference to the speaker's nose, and particularly to its prominence, should have tipped you off that this passage is from *Cyrano de Bergerac*, in which the main character has an almost unfeasibly large nose. *Hedda Gabbler* is a play by Ibsen. *Waiting for Godot* is a play by Samuel Beckett. *Othello* is by Shakespeare, *The Misanthrope* by Molière.

56. "One is not born, but rather becomes, a woman."

The quote above comes from Simone de Beauvoir's classic work of feminist literature entitled

    (A) *Common Sense*
    (B) *The Lottery*
    (C) *The Feminine Mystique*
    (D) *Little Women*
    (E) *The Second Sex*

56. **(E)** is the correct answer. *Common Sense* is a Revolutionary War tract by the polemicist Thomas Paine. *The Lottery* is a short story by Shirley Jackson. *The Feminine Mystique* is a classic work of feminist literature, but it is by Betty Friedan, not Simone de Beauvoir. *Little Women* is a novel by Louisa May Alcott.

SECTION 3

QUESTIONS	EXPLANATIONS

57. "It is necessary that the prince should know how to color his nature well, and how to be a great hypocrite and dissembler."

Who wrote the sentence above?

(A) Friedrich Nietzsche
(B) Aristotle
(C) Plato
(D) Albert Camus
(E) Niccolo Machiavelli

57. **(E)** is the correct answer. The reference to "the prince" is your context clue that this passage is from Machiavelli's *The Prince*, the classic philosophical work on cynical realpolitik.

58. The works of Beckett, Genet, and Ionesco typify what twentieth-century form of theater in which nearly anonymous characters participate in meaningless and often illogical activities?

(A) Restoration comedy
(B) drawing-room comedy
(C) theater of the absurd
(D) theater of cruelty
(E) epic

58. **(C)** is the correct answer. Restoration comedy, as its name implies, was popular during the English Restoration (ca. 1660 - named after the Restoration of the monarchy after Cromwell's failed attempt at a Republic). Drawing-room comedies are English plays of the late-nineteenth century typified by the works of Oscar Wilde. *Theater of cruelty* is a term coined by the French experimental dramatist Antonin Artaud to describe his work. *Epic* refers to any theatrical work of extraordinary length and scope.

Questions 59 and 60 refer to the lines of poetry below.

"Turning and turning in the widening gyre
The falcon cannot hear the falconer;
Things fall apart; the center cannot hold . . ."

59. The lines above were written by

(A) Robert Browning
(B) Robert Frost
(C) William Butler Yeats
(D) William Carlos Williams
(E) Elizabeth Bishop

59. **(C)** is the correct answer. These are the opening lines of one of Yeats' most famous poems.

60. The poem they open is called

(A) *The Second Coming*
(B) *Howl*
(C) *Lycidas*
(D) *Auguries of Innocence*
(E) *The Rape of the Lock*

60. **(A)** is the correct answer. *Howl* is one of the great works of Beat poetry; it is by Allen Ginsberg. *Lycidas* is a long eulogy written by John Milton. *Auguries of Innocence* is a collection of aphorisms by William Blake; it begins with the famous lines "To see a World in a Grain of Sand / And a Heaven in a Wild Flower, / Hold Infinity in the palm of your hand / And Eternity in an hour." *Thirteen Waysof Looking at a Blackbird* is a poem by Wallace Stevens, a twentieth-century American poet.

SECTION 3

Questions 61 to 63 refer to illustrations (A) through (E) [see exam]:

61. Which is representative of fifteenth-century Flemish painting?

62. Which is representative of seventeenth-century Dutch painting?

63. Which was painted during the twentieth century?

61. **(B)** is the correct answer. The painting is *The Last Supper*, by Dirk Bouts. The elongated figures and over-lit faces are the stylistic giveaway of fifteenth-century Flemish painting.

62. **(C)** is the correct answer. This is Rembrandt's *Christ and the Woman of Samaria*. Dark backgrounds and dramatic chiaroscuro are hallmarks of seventeenth-century Dutch painting and particularly of Rembrandt's work.

63. **(E)** is the correct answer. This is *Crucifixion* by Salvador Dali, a prominent Surrealist painter.

Answer choice (A) is *The Last Supper* by Andrea del Castagno, a fifteenth-century Italian painter. Answer choice (D) is *La Repos de La Saints Famille en Egypt* by Jean Honore Fragonard, a late rococo French painter.

SECTION 3

QUESTIONS

<u>Questions 64 to 66</u> refer to these lines from Shakespeare's plays:

(A) "How sharper than a serpent's tooth it is
To have a thankless child!"

(B) "Tomorrow, and tomorrow, and tomorrow
Creeps in this petty pace from day to day
To the last syllable of recorded time . . . ."

(C) "If music be the food of love, play on;
Give me excess of it, that, surfeiting,
The appetite may sicken, and so die."

(D) "O that this too sullied flesh would melt,
Thaw, and resolve itself into a dew,
Or that the Everlasting had not fixed
His canon 'gainst self-slaughter . . . ."

(E) "I am not only witty in myself, but the
cause that wit is in other men."

64. Which is spoken by Falstaff?

65. Which is spoken by Macbeth?

66. Which is spoken by King Lear?

67. An orchestral piece of several movements in which a solo instrumentalist is featured for the entire piece is called a(n)

(A) tone poem
(B) concerto
(C) chanson
(D) string quartet
(E) opera buffa

EXPLANATIONS

64. **(E)** is the correct answer. This is the only line among the five answer choices spoken in prose, not verse. Falstaff, a comic character featured in several of Shakespeare's plays, speaks in prose. The content of the line further gives away that it is the speech of a comic character.

65. **(B)** is the correct answer. This is one of the most famous lines from *Macbeth*.

66. **(A)** is the correct answer. The phrase "a thankless child" is the tip-off that this line belongs to King Lear, who is betrayed by his two daughters after he has divided his worldly possessions between them.

Answer choice (C) is the opening line of *The Twelfth Night*; answer choice (D) is spoken by Hamlet.

67. **(B)** is the correct answer. A tone poem is a piece intended to evoke a particular mood or visual image. A chanson is a type of Renaissance song. A string quartet is a piece composed for a string quartet. An opera buffa is a dramatic musical piece with no spoken dialogue.

SECTION 3

QUESTIONS	EXPLANATIONS

Questions 68 to 70 concern the poem below:

Loveliest of Trees

Loveliest of trees, the cherry now
Is hung with bloom along the bough,
And stands about the woodland ride
Wearing white for Eastertide.
Now of my threescore years and ten,
Twenty will not come again,
And take from seventy springs a score,
It only leaves me fifty more.
And since to look at things in bloom
Fifty springs are little room,
About the woodlands I will go
To see the cherry hung with snow.

68. How many years old is the narrator of this poem?

   (A) Twenty
   (B) Fifty
   (C) Sixty
   (D) Seventy
   (E) It is impossible to tell.

68. **(A)** is the correct answer. The poet says "Now of my threescore years and ten, / Twenty will not come again. . ." meaning he expects to live seventy years and has already lived twenty of them.

69. At what time of year does the poem take place?

   (A) winter
   (B) spring
   (C) summer
   (D) fall
   (E) It is impossible to tell.

69. **(B)** is the correct answer. In the first stanza, the poet tells us that the cherry trees are in bloom. He also tells us that it is Eastertime. In the third stanza, he mentions that he has only fifty springs left in his life. It is springtime. Don't be fooled by the allusions to snow and white; white is the color of cherry blossoms in bloom.

70. Which of the following most closely approximates the meaning of the word "ride" as it is used in line 3 of the poem?

   (A) tree
   (B) cherry blossom
   (C) carriage
   (D) roadway
   (E) snowfall

70. **(D)** is the correct answer. Substitute the answer choices for the word. Answers (B) and (E) really make no sense. If you have never seen the word "ride" used this way before, guess among answer choices (A), (C), and (D).

SECTION 3

71. Michelangelo's fresco *The Last Judgement* is located in the

    (A) Louvre
    (B) Sistine Chapel
    (C) Palace at Versailles
    (D) National Gallery in Washington, D.C.
    (E) Westminster Abbey

71. **(B)** is the correct answer. Trivial pursuit stuff. The National Gallery would be a bad guess, as there are very few works by the Grand Masters in the United States; they were all snatched up by collectors long before there was a U.S.

72. Describing humanity's natural state, what philosopher speculated: "No arts; no letters; no society; and which is worst of all, continual fear and danger of violent death; and the life of man, solitary, nasty, brutish, and short"?

    (A) Martin Heidegger
    (B) Thomas Hobbes
    (C) Jeremy Bentham
    (D) Saint Augustine
    (E) John Stuart Mills

72. **(B)** is the correct answer. This is *the* famous quote from Hobbes' *Leviathan*, a pessimistic philosophical treatise on the nature of man and government. Memorize the phrase "nasty, brutish, and short" and associate it with Thomas Hobbes, and you will know all you need to know about Hobbes for the purposes of the CLEP.

73. "Early to bed and early to rise, Makes a man healthy, wealthy, and wise."

    The couplet above originally appeared in

    (A) *Poor Richard's Almanac*
    (B) Aesop's *Fables*
    (C) *Essays* by Montaigne
    (D) *Confessions of Jean-Jacques Rousseau*
    (E) *The Analects of Confucius*

73. **(A)** is the correct answer. *Poor Richard's Almanac*, written by Benjamin Franklin, is full of such maxims.

74. Who composed the scores for the ballets *Swan Lake* and *The Nutcracker Suite*?

    (A) George Frederick Handel
    (B) Felix Mendelssohn
    (C) Gustav Holst
    (D) Peter Ilyich Tchaikovsky
    (E) Domenico Scarlatti

74. **(D)** is the correct answer. Handel was a late baroque composer famous for oratorios, operas and orchestral suites. Mendelssohn was a nineteenth-century German composer. Holst was a modern composer who helped develop polytonality; his most famous work is *The Planets*. Scarlatti was an eighteenth-century composer best known for his harpsichord pieces.

75. Twyla Tharp is a famous

    (A) modern choreographer
    (B) screenwriter
    (C) sheet-metal sculptor
    (D) eighteenth-century polemicist
    (E) nineteenth-century fictional heroine

75. **(A)** is the correct answer. Trivial pursuit stuff. Once choreographer for the Stuttgart Ballet, with her own dance troupe Twyla Tharp choreographed *The Catherine Wheel* to music by Talking Heads' David Byrne; she has also choreographed pieces to Beach Boys music.

SECTION 3

PART II

76. Perhaps France's greatest novelist, this author created detailed, often scathing, portrayals of the bourgeois society to which he belonged and which he loved. His works, collectively known as "La Comédie Humaine," include *Père Goriot* and *Cousin Bette*.

The author described above is

(A) Arthur Rimbaud
(B) Emile Zola
(C) Honoré de Balzac
(D) Francois Rabelais
(E) Albert Camus

76. **(C)** is the correct answer. Rimbaud is a famous Symbolist poet; his works include *Illuminations* and *A Season in Hell*. Zola was a great French novelist but not the one described in the question; he wrote *Germinal*. Rabelais wrote an early French novel, the bawdy *Gargantua and Pantagruel*. Camus was a French existentialist; he wrote *The Stranger*, *The Plague*, and *The Myth of Sisyphus*.

77. Beethoven's *Third Symphony* is also referred to as

(A) the "Jupiter"
(B) *Das Lied von der Erde*
(C) *Music for Royal Fireworks*
(D) the "Eroica"
(E) *Die Schöne Müllerin*

77. **(D)** is the correct answer. "The Jupiter Symphony" is Mozart's *Symphony Number 41*. *Das Lied van der Erde* is a vocal work by Gustav Mahler. *Music for Royal Fireworks* is by Handel. *Die Schöne Müllerin* is a song cycle by Schubert.

78. Tom, a warehouse worker who writes poetry; Laura, his shy, crippled sister; their mother, a well-meaning but shrill and foolish Southern woman; and a "gentleman caller" make up the list of characters in

(A) *The Glass Menagerie*
(B) *The Iceman Cometh*
(C) *Our Town*
(D) *The Crucible*
(E) *A Raisin in the Sun*

78. **(A)** is the correct answer. *The Glass Menagerie* is by Tennessee Williams. *The Iceman Cometh* is by Eugene O'Neill; *Our Town* is by Thornton Wilder; *The Crucible* is by Arthur Miller; and *A Raisin in the Sun* is by Lorraine Hansberry.

79. Which of the following was NOT an Italian Renaissance painter?

(A) Corregio
(B) Raphael Sanzio
(C) Titian
(D) Giorgio de Chirico
(E) Michelangelo

79. **(D)** is the correct answer. De Chirico was one of the forerunners of surrealism; he is a twentieth-century artist. Be aware that the Teenage Mutant Ninja Turtles are named after Renaissance painters; this information would have helped you eliminate (B) and (E).

SECTION 3

Questions 80 to 82 refer to the following lines of poetry:

(A) "But at my back I always hear
Time's winged chariot hurrying near,
And yonder all before us lie
Deserts of vast eternity."

(B) "Because I could not stop for Death—
He kindly stopped for me—
The Carriage held but just Ourselves—
And Immortality . . . ."

(C) "O my Luve's like a red, red rose,
That's newly sprung in June:
O my Luve's like the melodie
That's sweetly played in tune!"

(D) "O Captain! my Captain! rise up and hear
the bells.
Rise up—for you the flag is flung—for you
the bugle trills . . . ."

(E) "One, two! One, two! And through and
through
The vorpal blade went snicker-snack!
He left it dead, and with its head
He went galumphing back."

80. Which excerpt contains examples of onomatopoeia?

80. **(E)** is the correct answer. Onomatopoeia is the use of words to imitate sounds and actions, such as "snicker-snack" and "galumphing" in answer choice (E). This bit of poetry is by Lewis Carroll (from *Jabberwocky*).

81. Which excerpt contains two similes?

81. **(C)** is the correct answer. A simile is a comparison of two things, usually including the word "like" or "as." The first and third lines of answer choice (C) each contain a simile. These lines were composed by Robert Burns.

82. Which excerpt contains an example of personification?

82. **(B)** is the correct answer. Personification is the ascription of human characteristics to nonhuman beings or entities. When Emily Dickinson writes that death "kindly stopped for me," she is personifying a natural force.

Answer choice (A) is from Andrew Marvell's *To His Coy Mistress*; answer choice (D) is from Walt Whitman's *O Captain! My Captain!*, a eulogy for Abraham Lincoln.

SECTION 3

QUESTIONS	EXPLANATIONS

83. Born in Holland, this painter utilized vibrant colors and short, thick brush strokes in his Expressionistic works. He often juxtaposed complementary colors, such as the blue and orange in his *The Starry Night*, to dynamic effect.

The artist referred to in the passage above is

(A) Vincent van Gogh
(B) Sandro Botticelli
(C) Jasper Johns
(D) Jan Vermeer
(E) Edvard Munch

83. **(A)** is the correct answer. "Vibrant color," "thick brush strokes," "blue and orange," "*Starry Night*"—these are all clues pointing to van Gogh. Boticelli was a Renaissance painter; he painted *The Birth of Venus*. Jasper Johns was a twentieth-century American, famous for paintings of the American flag. Jan Vermeer was a seventeenth-century Dutch painter. Munch was a Norwegian Expressionist; he is most famous for *The Scream (a.k.a The Shriek)*.

84. This 1516 description of "Erewhon" is actually a philosophical treatise on equality, freedom, and the nature of a perfect society. It is

(A) Rousseau's *The Social Contract*
(B) Swift's *A Modest Proposal*
(C) Buber's *I and Thou*
(D) More's *Utopia*
(E) Darwin's *On the Origins of Species*

84. **(D)** is the correct answer. Rousseau's *The Social Contract* is a treatise on the nature of man and society and the source of his concept of "the noble savage." Swift's *A Modest Proposal* is a masterpiece of satire, in which he suggests the solution to poverty is eating one's young. Buber's *I and Thou* is a philosophical work on the relationship between humans and God. Darwin's *On the Origin of Species* is the seminal work in the theory of evolution.

85. A childhood burglary of a pear orchard and a chance hearing of children singing "Take it and read" are central turning points in which autobiography of religious conversion?

(A) *The Autobiography of Benjamin Franklin*
(B) *The Confessions of St. Augustine*
(C) *The Life and Times of Frederick Douglass*
(D) *Confessions of an English Opium Eater*
(E) Plato's *Apology*

85. **(B)** is the correct answer. St. Augustine's autobiography has many overtones of allegory; his theft in the pear orchard, for example, is meant to be read as analogous to the temptation of Eve in the Garden of Eden.

86. Which is NOT an eighteenth-century novelist?

(A) Daniel DeFoe
(B) Henry Fielding
(C) George Bernard Shaw
(D) Lawrence Sterne
(E) Samuel Richardson

86. **(C)** is the correct answer. DeFoe wrote *Robinson Crusoe* and *Moll Flanders*. Fielding wrote *Tom Jones*. Sterne wrote *Tristram Shandy*. Richardson wrote the insufferable *Clarissa*. Shaw was a turn-of-the-century dramatist.

SECTION 3

QUESTIONS	EXPLANATIONS

<u>Questions 87 to 89</u> refer to the following lists of opera titles:

(A) *Rigoletto, Aida, Il Trovatore*
(B) *Faust, Romeo et Juliet*
(C) *La Nozze de Figaro, Don Giovanni, The Abduction from the Seraglio*
(D) *La Boheme, Madama Butterfly, Tosca*
(E) *Lucia di Lammermoor, L'elisir d'amore*

Which of the above were composed by:

87. Mozart?

87. **(C)** is the correct answer. Of Mozart's operas, be sure you are familiar with the following titles: *The Marriage of Figaro* (*La Nozze de Figaro* in Italian), *Don Giovanni*, and *The Magic Flute* (*Die Zauberflote* in German). Mozart composed operas in both German and Italian; his operatic works are considered the greatest achievement of the Classical period of operatic composition.

88. Puccini?

88. **(D)** is the correct answer. The three titles listed in answer choice (D) are among Puccini's most famous works; others include *Turandot* and *Manon Lescaut*. Giacomo Puccini composed during the Romantic period. His works incorporate much of what is pleasing of the more lyrical Classical opera style and thus remain quite popular today.

89. Verdi?

89. **(A)** is the correct answer. Like Puccini, Verdi wrote in a style that captured both the melodicism of Classical opera and the high drama of Romantic opera. He is considered by many to be the greatest Italian operatic composer. Among his masterpieces not mentioned in the answer choice: *La Traviata, La Forza del Destino* (immortalized on TV's "The Odd Couple"), and adaptations of Shakespeare's *Macbeth, Othello*, and *Falstaff*. Answer choice (B) is a list of operas by the French Romantic Charles Gounod; *Faust* is the only Gounod opera you would be expected to recognize. Answer choice (E) is a list of operas by Gaetano Donizetti. While considered a major composer by opera fans, he is definitely second-tier by CLEP standards and will never be the answer to a CLEP Humanities question.

SECTION 3

QUESTIONS	EXPLANATIONS

Questions 90 to 92 refer to illustrations (A) through (E) [see exam]:

90. Which was designed by Antonio Gaudi?

90. **(E)** is the correct answer. This building is *Casa Mila* in Barcelona. The "dripping wax" effect was Gaudi's specialty.

91. Which is a Mayan temple?

91. **(C)** is the correct answer.

92. Which is a Gothic cathedral?

92. **(A)** is the correct answer. This is the cathedral at Cologne, begun in A.D. 1248.

Answer choice (B) is The Crystal Cathedral in Garden Grove, CA. Answer choice (D) is a Japanese shrine.

93. His Samurai films served as the basis for the Westerns *High Plains Drifter* and *The Magnificent Seven*. His *Hidden Fortress* strongly influenced George Lucas' *Star Wars* trilogy.

The film director described above is

(A) Lo Wei
(B) Zhang Yimou
(C) Akira Kurosawa
(D) Yasujiro Ozu
(E) Kenji Mizoguchi

93. **(C)** is the correct answer. Lo Wei is a Hong Kong director who directed several Bruce Lee movies. Zhang Yimou is from mainland China; he directed *Raise the Red Lantern* and *Farewell My Concubine*. Ozu was a great Japanese director of domestic dramas, such as *Tokyo Story*. Mizoguchi is also a famous Japanese filmmaker, but not the one described in the question.

94. The style of singing associated with elegant, pleasing melodies, simple rhythms and harmonies, and the straightforward depiction of a single, simple emotion is called _____ singing.

(A) bel canto
(B) madrigal
(C) recitative
(D) tarantella
(E) octave

94. **(A)** is the correct answer. A madrigal is a type of Renaissance/baroque song. Recitative is the term for "sung dialogue" (as opposed to arias, duets, etc.) in an opera. A tarantella is a type of ethnic Italian dance. An octave is the interval between one musical note and the one an eighth above or below it; it is also the term used to describe all the notes between and including two such tones.

SECTION 3

QUESTIONS	EXPLANATIONS

95. Leonardo da Vinci's painting *La Gioconda* is more commonly referred to as the

    (A) *Birth of Venus*
    (B) *Last Supper*
    (C) *Mona Lisa*
    (D) *Blue Boy*
    (E) *Burghers of Calais*

95. **(C)** is the correct answer. *The Birth of Venus* is by Boticelli. *The Last Supper* is also by Leonardo da Vinci. *Blue Boy* is by Gainsborough. *The Burghers of Calais* is a famous sculpture by Auguste Rodin. *La Gioconda* is Italian for "the gypsy."

96. Who wrote *Lady Chatterley's Lover*, *Sons and Lovers*, and *The Rainbow*?

    (A) Isaac Bashevis Singer
    (B) Thomas Wolfe
    (C) Ernest Hemingway
    (D) Charlotte Brontë
    (E) D. H. Lawrence

96. **(E)** is the correct answer. Trivial pursuit territory. Singer is a Nobel Prize-winning novelist. Wolfe was an American who wrote *Look Homeward, Angel* and *You Can't Go Home Again*. Hemingway wrote *For Whom the Bell Tolls*, *A Farewell to Arms*, and *The Old Man and the Sea*. Brontë wrote *Jane Eyre*.

97. "The woods are lovely, dark, and deep,
But I have promises to keep,
And miles to go before I sleep,
And miles to go before I sleep."

These lines were written by

    (A) Edwin Arlington Robinson
    (B) Robert Frost
    (C) Lord Byron
    (D) Gerard Manley Hopkins
    (E) Samuel Johnson

97. **(B)** is the correct answer. These are among Frost's most famous lines. Learn to recognize them, as there is a good chance you will see them somewhere on the CLEP.

98. The effort to depict a subject from many different viewpoints simultaneously is characteristic of what style of painting?

    (A) Romanticism
    (B) Northern Renaissance
    (C) Italian Baroque
    (D) Realism
    (E) Cubism

98. **(E)** is the correct answer. Cubism developed at the turn of the twentieth century. Romanticism emphasized nature and atmosphere; a late-eighteenth century movement, it was strictly representational (as were all the other wrong answer choices here). Northern Renaissance refers to the art of Northern Europe during the 15th and 16th centuries; Italian Baroque refers to the works of such sixteenth- and seventeenth-century artists as Caravaggio. Realism was a nineteenth-century French movement.

99. This 1855 volume marked the arrival of free verse as an important form in American poetry. It was regularly rewritten, reedited, and expanded by its author until his death in 1892.

The collection described above is
    (A) Pound's *Cantos*
    (B) Masters' *Spoon River Anthology*
    (C) Ovid's *Metamorphosis*
    (D) Whitman's *Leaves of Grass*
    (E) Wordsworth's *Lyrical Ballads*

99. **(D)** is the correct answer. Pound and Masters were twentieth-century poets. Ovid was a poet of Roman antiquity. Wordsworth was English, not American.

SECTION 3

QUESTIONS	EXPLANATIONS

Questions 100 to 102 refer to the following groups of people:

(A) Dashiell Hammett, James M. Cain, Jim Thompson

(B) O. Henry, John Cheever, Edgar Allan Poe

(C) Isaac Asimov, Ray Bradbury, Ursula K. LeGuin

(D) Alvin Ailey, Merce Cunningham, George Ballanchine

(E) Preston Sturges, Busby Berkeley, Howard Hawks

100. Which is a group of "pulp fiction" writers?

100. **(A)** is the correct answer. The term "pulp fiction" refers to a type of mid-twentieth century American crime story, so called because the magazines and books in which they appeared were printed on cheap pulp paper. Such stories and novels depicted the world as unjust and violent, and its characters are either duplicitous con artists or naïve dupes. Hammett wrote *The Glass Key*, *The Maltese Falcon*, and the *Thin Man* stories, among others. Among Cain's most famous works are *The Postman Always Rings Twice* and *Double Indemnity*. Thompson wrote *The Getaway*, *The Killer Inside Me*, and *The Grifters*, among others.

101. Which is a group of writers most famous for their short stories?

101. **(B)** is the correct answer. O. Henry (1862 - 1910) wrote over 300 short stories, the most famous of which is "The Gift of the Magi." John Cheever, also famous for his novels, wrote moralistic stories largely set in late twentieth-century American suburbia. Poe is a nineteenth-century American best known for his Gothic horror tales, such as "The Fall of the House of Usher" and "The Tell-Tale Heart."

102. Which is a group of choreographers?

102. **(D)** is the correct answer. Alvin Ailey founded the a dance troupe in the 50s that has since become world renowned, particularly for its incorporation of African themes into modern dance. Merce Cunningham is an innovator in *avant garde* dance. George Balanchine choreographed over 100 ballets for the New York City Ballet.

Answer choice (C) is a list of famous science fiction authors. Asimov is among the most prolific authors of all-time; his best known science fiction work is *The Foundation Trilogy*. Bradbury wrote *Fahrenheit 451* and *The Martian Chronicles*. LeGuin wrote *The Left Hand of Darkness* and *The Lathe of Heaven*.

Answer choice (E) is a list of Hollywood comedy directors. Sturges wrote and directed *The Lady Eve* and *Hail the Conquering Hero*. Berkeley was famous for extravagant romantic comedies that featured dance, such as *42nd Street*. Hawks directed *His Girl Friday* and *Bringing Up Baby*; he is also famous for his work in Westerns and drama.

SECTION 3

103. "Did he live his life again in every detail of desire, temptation, and surrender during that supreme moment of complete knowledge? He cried in a whisper at some image, at some vision—he cried out twice, a cry that was no more than a breath:
'The horror! The horror!'"

The passage above is from

(A) *Heart of Darkness*
(B) *To the Lighthouse*
(C) *Les Misérables*
(D) *A Harlot High and Low*
(E) *Moll Flanders*

103. **(A)** is the correct answer. This excerpt is from the climactic scene of *Heart of Darkness*, the death of Kurtz. If you've ever seen the movie *Apocalypse Now*, which is loosely based on Conrad's novella, you should have recognized Kurtz's dying words; they are spoken in the film by Marlon Brando.

Questions 104 to 106 are based on the illustrations below [see exam]:

104. Which is by Henry Moore?

104. **(A)** is the correct answer. This abstract sculpture, with its curved edges and massive forms, is typical of Moore's work.

105. Which is from medieval Europe?

105. **(E)** is the correct answer. The image, of the Madonna and child, is typical of medieval art in its seeming lack of concern for realistic perspective, its use of rounded, stylized forms, and its emphasis on iconography.

106. Which is by a French post-impressionist?

106. **(C)** is the correct answer. This painting is by Paul Cézanne, a French post-Impressionist.

Illustration (B) depicts an African sculpture carved by a Senufo artist.

Illustration (D) depicts a painting by Henri Hayden, a twentieth-century French cubist painter; his paintings are less representational than are those of the post-Impressionists.

107. Compared with the capital of a Doric column, the capital of an Ionic column is

(A) smaller
(B) closer to the shaft
(C) more ornate
(D) lighter in color
(E) less prominently displayed

107. **(C)** is the correct answer. This is the obligatory question about Greek columns. Ionic columns are the ones whose capitals - the ornamentation up top - have all the fancy curlicues.

SECTION 3

108. Which of the following is NOT a property of a musical tone?

    (A) duration
    (B) timbre
    (C) syncopation
    (D) pitch
    (E) intensity

108. **(C)** is the correct answer. Syncopation is a property of rhythm, and only has meaning in the context of a series of tones. Duration is the length of a tone; timbre is the quality that distinguishes a C sharp played on a trumpet from the exact same note played on a clarinet; pitch is the note value of the tone, as indicated on a musical staff; and intensity is its volume.

109. An extreme exaggeration, used to literary effect, is called a(n)

    (A) euphony
    (B) anachronism
    (C) allusion
    (D) parable
    (E) hyperbole

109. **(E)** is the correct answer. Euphony is the use, usually in poetry, of words that sound good together. An anachronism is a chronological error in a piece of art; for example, when clocks strike in *Julius Caesar* (the play set in a time predating the invention of clocks). An allusion is a reference to a familiar event, person, or work of literature. A parable is a story that illustrates a moral.

Questions 110 to 112 refer to the following groups of fictional characters:

    (A) Queequeg, Starbuck, Captain Ahab, Tashtego, Ishmael
    (B) Natty Bumppo, Cora Munro, Alice Munro, Major Duncan Heyward
    (C) Mr. Allworthy, Blifil, Sophia Western, Molly Seagrim, Lady Bellaston
    (D) Phillip Pirrip, Miss Havisham, Magwitch, Estella
    (E) Flora, Miles, Peter Quint, Miss Jessel

110. Which appear in *The Last of the Mohicans*?

110. **(B)** is the correct answer. See the explanation for question 112.

111. Which appear in *Moby Dick*?

111. **(A)** is the correct answer. See the explanation for question 112.

112. Which appear in *Great Expectations*?

112. **(D)** is the correct answer. Answer choice (C) is a list of characters from *Tom Jones*. Answer choice (E) is a list of characters from *The Turn of the Screw*.

113. A family crisis results in Nora's realization that her husband Torvald condescends toward and belittles her. At the play's conclusion, she leaves him.

    The play described above is

    (A) *The Winter's Tale*
    (B) *Medea*
    (C) *Camille*
    (D) *A Doll's House*
    (E) *Man and Superman*

113. **(D)** is the correct answer. Be familiar with the plot of Ibsen's *A Doll's House*. Because the play is about the self-actualization of a subjugated woman, it is very popular with test-writers looking to balance out male-dominated tests with female names, themes, etc. (even though it was written by a man).

SECTION 3

QUESTIONS	EXPLANATIONS

Questions 114 to 116 are based on the illustration below [see exam]:

114. The work pictured above was painted by

    (A) Sandro Botticelli
    (B) Andy Warhol
    (C) Albrecht Dürer
    (D) Donatello
    (E) Jacques Louis David

114. **(E)** is the correct answer. Jacques Louis David painted The Death of Socrates in 1787. Socrates, one of the most influential figures in the history of philosophy, was tried and convicted of corrupting the morals of youths, and was sentenced to death. David depicts Socrates' followers attempting to convince their mentor to seek an alternative to his punishment, but Socrates insists on abiding by the sentence, which he agrees is unjust. He is shown willingly reaching for the deadly cup of hemlock. Boticelli and Donatello are painters of the High Renaissance. Andy Warhol is an American Pop artist from the last half of the twentieth century. Albrecht Dürer is a sixteenth century German painter and engraver.

115. It is most closely associated what painting style?

    (A) Abstract Expressionism
    (B) Neo-Classicism
    (C) Dadaism
    (D) Primitivism
    (E) Photo Realism

115. **(B)** is the correct answer. David's paintings are most closely associated with the Neo-Classical movement. Like the Neo-Classicists, David chose subjects that glorified ancient Greece and Rome. David is not considered only a Neo-Classicist because he developed stylistic innovations that fed later Romantic movements, but it is with the Neo-Classicists that his work is most closely associated. Abstract Expressionism is a mid-twentieth century movement that emphasizes texture and color and de-emphasizes subject matter. Dadaism is an early twentieth-century movement that focused on the absurdities of life in the expanding industrial world; Dadaists would exhibit urinals in galleries and draw mustaches on reproductions of the Mona Lisa. The term 'primitivism' is used to describe the works of artists of many periods; such works typically demonstrate the artist's enthusiasm and lack of formal training. Photo Realism, as its name implies, is a movement in which artists tried to recreate, on canvas, reality as it is depicted in photographs.

116. The subject of the painting is the

    (A) rape of the Sabine women
    (B) great Roman orator Cicero
    (C) death of Socrates
    (D) adoration of the Magi
    (E) Council of Trent

116. **(C)** is the correct answer. See the explanation for question 114 for further details.

SECTION 3

QUESTIONS	EXPLANATIONS

117. In classical ballet, a three-part dance in which two performers perform an adagio duet, then dance solo, and then conclude with another duet is called a

(A) pas de deux
(B) polonaise
(C) par terre
(D) pirouette
(E) plié

117. **(A)** is the correct answer. A polonaise is a type of Polish dance. Par terre is the term for any dance steps performed on the floor (as opposed to airborne steps). A pirouette is a dance movement in which the dancer twirls. A plié is a bend at the knees.

118. This French "synthetic cubist" painted geometrical shapes and incorporated imagery from billboards, posters, neon lights, and, most often, machinery.

The sentence above describes

(A) Gustave Courbet
(B) Claude Monet
(C) Antoine-Jean Gros
(D) Ferdinand Leger
(E) Jacques Louis David

118. **(D)** is the correct answer. Trivial pursuit territory again. Courbet painted in the nineteenth century, predating synthetic cubism by almost thirty years. Monet was an impressionist. Gros and David were classicists from the early nineteenth century.

119. The Parthenon is located

(A) atop Mount Vesuvius
(B) next to the Sistine Chapel
(C) on the Athenian Acropolis
(D) along the North Sea shore
(E) on the island of Crete

119. **(C)** is the correct answer. Mount Vesuvius is a volcano; the Parthenon would not have lasted so long there. The Sistine Chapel is in Rome; the Parthenon is in Greece.

120. This composer revolutionized opera by stressing the role of the orchestra instead of that of the singer. His experiments in harmonics paved the way for twentieth-century atonality, and can be heard in his *Tristan und Isolde*, *Parsifal*, and *Ring Cycle*. He is _____.

(A) Robert Schumann
(B) Richard Wagner
(C) Johannes Brahms
(D) Ludwig van Beethoven
(E) Carl Maria von Weber

120. **(B)** is the correct answer. Schumann, Brahms, and Beethoven all wrote either no operas or operatic works of relatively little consequence. Weber is a great German opera composer, but not the one described in question 120.

SECTION 3

QUESTIONS	EXPLANATIONS

Questions 121 to 123 are based on the poem below:

On First Looking into Chapman's Homer

Much have I traveled in the realms of gold,
And many goodly states and kingdoms seen;
Round many western islands have I been
Which bards in fealty to Apollo hold.
Oft of one wide expanse had I been told
That deep-browed Homer ruled as his demesne,
Yet did I never breathe its pure serene
Till I heard Chapman speak it loud and bold.
Then felt I like some watcher of the skies
When a new planet swims into his ken;
Or like stout Cortez when with eagle eyes
He stared at the Pacific—and all his men
Looked at each other with a wild surmise—
Silent, upon a peak in Darien.

121. In line 4, the word "fealty" is closest in meaning to

    (A) lofty reams
    (B) distance
    (C) anger
    (D) loyalty
    (E) contentedness

121. **(D)** is the correct answer. "Fealty" is a term for loyalty often found in chivalric literature.

122. The "wide expanse" referred to in line 5 is

    (A) the Mediterranean Sea
    (B) the library
    (C) the Pacific Ocean
    (D) *The Odyssey*
    (E) the mountains of Mexico

122. **(D)** is the correct answer. The "wide expanse" in question is one ruled by Homer, the blind Greek poet credited with both *The Iliad* and *The Odyssey*. This expanse, then, would be his epic poems.

123. The poem above was written by

    (A) John Keats
    (B) Ben Jonson
    (C) Edgar Allan Poe
    (D) Adrienne Rich
    (E) Paul Verlaine

123. **(A)** is the correct answer. Adrienne Rich's poetry is much more modern in style than this poem; Verlaine's, more wildly imagistic. You should probably have been able to eliminate these two. Poe also should have seemed an unlikely candidate, because this poem isn't very scary.

SECTION 3

124. Who starred in the movies *City Lights*, *Modern Times*, *The Great Dictator*, and *The Gold Rush*?

  (A) W.C. Fields
  (B) Robert Redford
  (C) Charlie Chaplin
  (D) Buster Keaton
  (E) Victor Mature

124. **(C)** is the correct answer. These are Chaplin's most famous movies. Fields was a comedian who achieved movie fame in *The Bank Dick* and *It's A Gift*, among others. Redford is a movie star of the 1970s, 1980s, and 1990s. Keaton was a contemporary of Chaplin's; his most famous movies are *The General*, *Steamboat Bill Junior*, and *The Cameraman*. Victor Mature was a star in the 1940s and 1950s; he was a kinder, gentler version of Robert Mitchum.

125. The "one-point" technique, used to create linear perspective in paintings, is most closely associated with which of the following periods in Western art history?

  (A Modernism
  (B) the Italian Renaissance
  (C) Early medieval
  (D) Gothic
  (E) Surrealism

125. **(B)** is the correct answer. One-point perspective, in which one point in the background of a painting is used as a "vanishing point" (all objects growing proportionally smaller as they approach the point), is most closely associated with the Italian Renaissance. The use of this technique clearly separates works of this period from the medieval works that preceded them; medieval artists were generally more concerned with the religious significance of their images than with their realism, and perspective in their works is often distorted and bizarre.

126. The numbers in the music staff above are used to indicate _____.

  (A) meter signature
  (B) key
  (C) harmonics
  (D) clef
  (E) instrumentation

126. **(A)** is the correct answer. The key is indicated by the # sign. The clef is indicated by the treble clef symbol to the far left of the staff. Harmonics and instrumentation are not indicated in the staff shown in question 126. Meter signature is also sometimes referred to as the time signature.

127. What epic poem recounts the history of the Trojan War?

  (A) *The Divine Comedy*
  (B) *Adonais*
  (C) *The Iliad*
  (D) *Candide*
  (E) *Samson Agonistes*

127. **(C)** is the correct answer. *The Divine Comedy* recounts the poet Dante's allegorical visits to hell, purgatory, and heaven. *Adonais* is Shelley's eulogy for his friend, John Keats. *Candide* is a satirical novella by Voltaire about the title character's search for "the best of all possible worlds;" *Samson Agonistes* is John Milton's play about the death of Samson.

SECTION 3

QUESTIONS	EXPLANATIONS

Questions 128 to 130 refer the following:

(A) A self-described "Dust Bowl refugee," this singer and songwriter composed union anthems and other famous songs of protest, including "This Land is Your Land."

(B) This master of the Mississippi Delta blues is generally recognized as the blues' most haunting guitar player and singer. His compositions that, decades later, became hits for rock bands include: "Crossroads" (for Cream), "Love in Vain" and "Stop Breaking Down" (both for The Rolling Stones).

(C) Composer of numerous movie and theater scores, this songwriter wrote many standards, among which are "White Christmas," "God Bless America," "Alexander's Ragtime Band," and "There's No Business Like Show Business."

(D) Known as "the father of Bluegrass music," this singer and songwriter conceived of and, with Lester Flatt and Earl Scruggs, perfected all the elements of that genre.

(E) His name practically synonymous with ragtime music, this pianist and composer also wrote an opera, *Tremonisha*.

Which of the above describes:

128. Irving Berlin?

129. Scott Joplin?

130. Woody Guthrie?

128. **(C)** is the correct answer. See answer to question 130.

129. **(E)** is the correct answer. See answer to question 130.

130. **(A)** is the correct answer. Answer choice (B) describes Robert Johnson. Answer choice (D) describes Bill Monroe.

SECTION 3

QUESTIONS	EXPLANATIONS

131. The fugue is most closely associated with which of the following musical terms?

   (A) monophony
   (B) *precipitato*
   (C) program music
   (D) counterpoint
   (E) atonality

131. **(D)** is the correct answer. A fugue is, by definition, a contrapuntal composition. Monophony (meaning "a single voice") would be a close opposite to a fugue. *Precipitato* means "hurried," which a fugue may be but doesn't necessarily have to be. Program music is music intended to evoke a specific story or image. Atonality is characteristic of music that defies the conventions associated with "pleasing" Western harmonics.

132. This style of art, of which Andy Warhol was a practitioner, uses commercial culture as its subject matter and sometimes as its raw materials.

The sentence above describes

   (A) Surrealism
   (B) Pop Art
   (C) Constructivism
   (D) Minimalism
   (E) Art Deco

132. **(B)** is the correct answer. Surrealism depicted seemingly unrelated images, often intended to portray subconscious thoughts. Constructivism was a Russian movement emphasizing the free use of geometric shapes. Minimalism was an American movement; its paintings are often of one or two colors and are nonrepresentational. Art deco was a design movement of the 1920s and 1930s, characterized by its use of slender, sleek forms.

133. Upton Sinclair's muckraking classic *The Jungle* is about

   (A) garment industry sweatshops
   (B) the dangers of nuclear power
   (C) Chicago's meat-packing industry
   (D) the battle to control water rights in California
   (E) the making of the movie *The African Queen*

133. **(A)** is the correct answer. Trivial pursuit territory again. The battle to control water rights in California is a subtext of the movie *Chinatown*; the making of the movie *The African Queen* is the subject of the movie *White Hunter, Black Heart*.

SECTION 3

QUESTIONS	EXPLANATIONS

Questions 134 to 136 refer to the following groups of people:

(A) J.M.W. Turner, William Hogarth, Thomas Gainsborough

(B) Roy Lichtenstein, Edward Hopper, Robert Rauschenberg

(C) Edouard Manet, Camille Pissarro, Edgar Degas

(D) Hans Holbein, Pieter Brueghel the Elder, Albrecht Dürer

(E) Salvador Dali, René Magritte, Max Ernst

134. Which is a group of surrealists?

134. **(E)** is the correct answer. Surrealism is a twentieth-century art movement grounded in dream imagery; Dali's *Persistence of Memory* and *Eggs on a Plate* and Magritte's *Son of Man*, which depicts a man in a bowler, his face obscured by an apple suspended in midair, are among the most famous works of the movement.

135. Which is a group of impressionists?

135. **(C)** is the correct answer. French Impressionism stands as one of art history's most prominent and influential movements. Painters such as Manet, Pisarro, and Degas, believing that the invention of the camera had liberated them from the task of strictly representational painting, placed a new emphasis on the effects of light and movement on their subjects; they also rejected their predecessors focus on classical and mythic subjects, preferring instead to paint everyday people and objects. Impressionism arguably marks the starting point of the abstract art movements that dominated the twentieth century.

136. Which is a group of English artists?

136. **(A)** is the correct answer. Turner (1775 - 1851) is best remembered for his landscapes and seascapes. Hogarth (1697 - 1764) was a great painter and engraver. Gainsborough is best known for his portrait *Blue Boy*. Answer choice (B) is a list of post-World War II American artists. Answer choice (D) is a list of early Renaissance artists.

SECTION 3

QUESTIONS	EXPLANATIONS

137. "Do not go gentle into that good night . . .
Rage, rage against the dying of the light."

These lines were written by

(A) Dylan Thomas
(B) Langston Hughes
(C) Marianne Moore
(D) W. H. Auden
(E) Alfred, Lord Tennyson

137. **(A)** is the correct answer. These are among the most famous lines written by Dylan Thomas. Know them, because you are likely to see them on the CLEP.

138. All of the following are jazz musicians/composers of the twentieth century EXCEPT:

(A) Duke Ellington
(B) Aubrey Beardsley
(C) Thelonius Monk
(D) John Coltrane
(E) Jelly Roll Morton

138. **(B)** is the correct answer. Aubrey Beardsley was a late nineteenth-century British graphic artist.

139. The hero of what book encounters the Lilliputians, the Brobdingnagians, the Yahoos, and the Houynhms?

(A) *Moby Dick*
(B) *Shipwrecked*
(C) *Robinson Crusoe*
(D) *A Tale of Two Cities*
(E) *Gulliver's Travels*

139. **(E)** is the correct answer. This is something that is very likely to come up on the CLEP. You should make sure you are familiar with the basic plot points of *Gulliver's Travels* before you take the CLEP.

SECTION 3

Questions 140 to 141 refer to the dramatic speech below:

". . . Have you eyes,
And do not see your own damnation? Eyes,
And cannot see whose company you keep?
Whose son are you? I tell you, you have sinned—
And do not know it—against your own on earth
And in the grave. A swift and two-edged sword,
Your mother's and your father's curse, shall sweep you
Out of this land. Those clear-seeing eyes
Shall then be darkened . . . ."

140. The subject of the speech above is

(A) Agamemnon
(B) Orestes
(C) Clytemnestra
(D) Antigone
(E) Oedipus

140. **(E)** is the correct answer. Agamemnon was the leader of the Greek army in Troy; on his return home he was murdered by his wife Clytemnestra, a murder later avenged by Orestes, their son. Antigone is the younger daughter of Oedipus and his wife/mother (ick!), Jocasta. Oedipus was the hero/king, abandoned in his infancy, who unwittingly killed his father (whom he mistook for a bandit) and married his mother, thereby bringing a curse upon the city of Thebes.

141. The speaker is

(A) Iphigenia
(B) Odysseus
(C) Electra
(D) Teiresias
(E) Achilles

141. **(D)** is the correct answer. Teiresias was the blind soothsayer of Thebes, on whose shoulders falls the unpleasant duty of telling Oedipus that he has killed his father and married his mother. Iphigenia and Electra were daughters of Agamemnon and Clytemnestra (see explanation for question 140). Odysseus was a Greek hero of the Trojan War; his twenty years of wandering after the war are the subject of Homer's *The Odyssey*. Achilles was the nearly invincible Greek hero of the Trojan War; a weakness in his heel proved his undoing.

142. A sequence of brief film clips, conventionally used to show the passing of time, is called a

(A) montage
(B) trailer
(C) gaffer
(D) splice
(E) crane shot

142. **(A)** is the correct answer. A trailer is a short advertisement for a film, shown either on television or at a movie theater before the feature. A gaffer is a technical foreman who works at a film shoot. A splice is how two pieces of film, shot at different times, are connected. A crane shot is a camera shot taken from a crane; usually, the camera swoops down or up, to great dramatic effect.

SECTION 3

QUESTIONS	EXPLANATIONS

143. The process of decorating a manuscript with drawings or paintings is called

    (A) illumination
    (B) fluting
    (C) *camposanto*
    (D) rustication
    (E) *palazzo*

143. **(A)** is the correct answer. Fluting is the term for the ornamental grooves in a column. *Canposanto* is an Italian term for a cemetery near a church. Rustication is a masonry process. *Palazzo* is the Italian word for palace.

144. Which of the following was written earliest?

    (A) *The Love Song of J. Alfred Prufrock*
    (B) *Paradise Lost*
    (C) *The Divine Comedy*
    (D) *Songs of Innocence and Experience*
    (E) *Sailing to Byzantium*

144. **(C)** is the correct answer. *The Divine Comedy* (ca. 1310) predates *Paradise Lost* (1667) by more than 300 years. Then comes *Songs of Innocence and Experience* (1789-94). *Sailing to Byzantium* and *Prufrock* are twentieth-century compositions.

145. The bodhrán, the harp, the uillean pipes, and the tin whistle are instruments associated with the music of what nation?

    (A) Bali
    (B) Lithuania
    (C) Germany
    (D) Mexico
    (E) Ireland

145. **(E)** is the correct answer. Pure trivial pursuit. If your hunch was that "bodhrán" and "uillean pipes" looked like Irish terms, your hunch was correct, and you should have gone with it.

146. Fill in the blanks:

A line of iambic pentameter is made up of _____ feet of _____ syllables.

    (A) three . . . three
    (B) four . . . two
    (C) four . . . three
    (D) five . . . two
    (E) five . . . three

146. **(D)** is the correct answer. An iamb contains two syllables, one stressed and one unstressed. The prefix "pent-" should have tipped you off that a pentameter is made up of five feet.

147. This 1982 Nobel prize-winning author's novels of "magical realism," among which are *One Hundred Years of Solitude* and *Love in the Time of Cholera*, have earned him international acclaim.

The author described above is

    (A) Dylan Thomas
    (B) Gabriel Garcia Marquez
    (C) Russell Banks
    (D) William Kennedy
    (E) Elie Wiesel

147. **(B)** is the correct answer. Dylan Thomas was a Welsh poet, dramatist, and short story writer. Russell Banks is a contemporary American novelist, as is William Kennedy. Elie Wiesel is a famous chronicler of the Holocaust and a novelist.

SECTION 3

148. Which of the following painters was the closest contemporary of James Joyce?

    (A) Henri Matisse
    (B) Eugène Delacroix
    (C) Franz Hals
    (D) Anthony Van Dyck
    (E) Caravaggio

148. **(A)** is the correct answer. Eugène Delacroix (1798-1863), Franz Hals (1580?-1666), Anthony Van Dyck (1599-1641), Caravaggio (1565?-1609), James Joyce (1882-1941), Henri Matisse (1869-1954).

149. A supernatural event that helps resolve a story or drama is called a(n)

    (A) caesura
    (B) parody
    (C) spoonerism
    (D) deus ex machina
    (E) trochee

149. **(D)** is the correct answer. A caesura is a pause in a line of verse, usually occurring in the middle of a line. A parody is a humorous imitation, usually of a more serious work. A spoonerism is the transposition of the initial sounds of two words, usually to humorous effect. A trochee is a two-beat metrical foot, containing a stressed syllable followed by an unstressed syllable.

150. The technique of painting on plaster is called

    (A) gisant
    (B) striation
    (C) fresco
    (D) pastel
    (E) dry point

150. **(C)** is the correct answer. Gisant is a type of statue that appears on a tomb. Striation is the process of grooving or striping a surface. Pastel describes either a soft color or a chalk-like substance used to create works of art in such colors. Dry point is an engraving technique.

PART **V**

How to Crack the CLEP General Examination in Social Sciences

16

Overview of the Social Sciences Exam

WHAT'S ON THE TEST?

The CLEP General Examination in Social Sciences consists of 125 questions covering general knowledge of American history, European history, world history, government, political science, sociology, economics, psychology, geography, and anthropology. As you might guess from the breadth of subjects covered, the General Examination is extremely general in its focus; no subject is tested in extensive detail. Here's the breakdown, by percentage and number, of the subjects tested:

SUBJECT	% OF TEST	# OF QUESTIONS
History	40	50
U.S. History	17	20 to 22
Western Civilization	15	8 to 20
World Civilization	8	10
Social Sciences	60	75
Government & Political Science	13	13 to 15
Sociology	11	13
Psychology	10	12 to 13
Economics	10	12 to 13
Geography	10	12 to 13
Anthropology	6	7 to 8

Call your potential schools and ask them about their CLEP policy. Will they give you credit for a good grade? Will a good grade place you out of a class? The admissions or dean's office should know the answer.

The exam tests familiarity with terminology, methodology, theories, generalizations, and principles; the ability to apply those theories, generalizations, and principles to specific situations or historical incidents; and the ability to read and interpret charts and graphs. All of these are tested on a fundamental level only; anything you need to know to pass this exam can be found in a high school text book.

HOW IS THE TEST STRUCTURED?

The test is divided into two parts (called, appropriately, Part I and Part II) of sixty-two or sixty-three questions. There are no special questions that appear only on one part of the test: the two sections are, in terms of structure and the type of material tested, identical. You will be allowed forty-five minutes for each section, during which time you will only be allowed to work on that particular section.

MAKING THE GRADE

No school requires a perfect score on the General Examination in Social Sciences of those seeking college credit for the test. In fact, most require only that you receive the equivalent of a C grade. Most schools set that score between the high 400's and 500. To receive this grade, you only need to achieve a raw score of approximately sixty-three.

Therefore, as we discussed in chapter 2, don't rush to finish this exam, getting questions wrong in your hurry. As far as most schools are concerned, a 500 is exactly as valuable as an 800. For each, you will receive the exact same number of credits toward your degree.

Your best hope for increasing your chances of guessing correctly is to have a firm grasp of the material. However, knowing some governing principles of the test helps. The next section lays out some of the basic rules ETS follows when choosing the questions and answer choices that appear on this test.

A FAIR TEST

ETS writes a lot of "tricky" exams. The PSAT, SAT, GRE, and GMAT are all ETS exams on which the test writers often set out to confound the test taker. Oddly worded questions coupled with answer choices that appear correct at first glance (such answer choices touch on many of the same themes as the correct answer, but typically include an overgeneralization or an error on a tangential point) conspire to make the test taker's job much more difficult than it has to be. If you've ever taken one of these exams—and you almost certainly have—you may well have some anxiety about the CLEP Social Sciences exam.

Well, rest easy. The good news is that the CLEP Social Sciences test includes none of the tricks you've come to know and hate on other ETS exams. Questions on the CLEP are worded in a straightforward manner, usually in as few words as possible. Answer choices are straightforward: if you are familiar with the subject being tested, there will almost certainly be either an obvious correct answer or four obvious incorrect answers.

For example, a CLEP question about government might look like this:

A presidential veto can be overridden by a
Congressional vote of

(A) a simple majority in one house
(B) a simple majority in both houses
(C) a two-thirds majority in one house, a
        simple majority in the other
(D) a two-thirds majority in both houses
(E) unanimity in both houses

Here's how to crack it

This is not a difficult question if you're up on your American government; it deals with a government issue that is frequently in the news. Even if you did not know the correct answer (which is (D)), you should have been able to hazard a pretty good guess using the process of elimination.

> Be aggressive when you take multiple choice exams. ETS exams are designed to reward aggressive guessing. If you can eliminate at least one answer choice, make a guess.

Here's how you might have thought it through: since a simple majority is required to pass a bill, and since it is harder to override a veto than to pass a bill, you should have been able to eliminate answer choices (A) and (B). Answer choice (E) would make an override impossible, so the answer has to be (C) or (D).

What you will NOT see is a question such as this:

> Which section of the U.S. Constitution prohibits the formation of a new state within the jurisdiction of any current state?
>
> (A) Article IV, Section 1
> (B) Article IV, Section 2
> (C) Article IV, Section 3
> (D) Article VI
> (E) Article VII

Familiarize yourself thoroughly with all question formats BEFORE you take the exam. You want to spend your test time deciding which answer is correct, not reading directions.

This question requires a degree of familiarity with detail far beyond the scope of the CLEP Social Sciences exam. As you study, remember that the test is designed to reward you for a solid general knowledge of the many subjects it tests. Because even a perfunctory review of this material would take up an entire book, this book provides a bibliography (at the end of this chapter) of sources in which you will be able to find this information easily. All books listed should be available at your local library.

MAXIMIZE YOUR STRENGTHS AND MINIMIZE YOUR WEAKNESSES

As we said in chapter 2, tailor your approach to maximize your strengths and minimize your weaknesses. Suppose you are strong in the field of American history, and weak in anthropology. You want to make sure that you answer every single American history-related question, and you certainly do not want to miss an American history question in order to work on an anthropology question. If question 61 asks about Asmat headhunting practices, and question 62 asks about the Battle of Lexington, you should skip question 61 and go straight to question 62. Save those questions in your areas of weakness for last; that way, if you never get to them, you will have minimized your losses.

COMMON SENSE GOES A LONG WAY

As previously mentioned, the CLEP is a fair test. It wants to reward you for what you know. It also tries to reward you for common sense. For example:

> In a traditional society, socialization is primarily the function of
>
> (A) secondary schools
> (B) television and radio
> (C) the government
> (D) the military
> (E) the family

The answer to this question is (E). Socialization is the process by which individuals learn how to function within society; traditional societies are those organized primarily around family and religion. Even without knowledge of these terms, you might well have guessed (E), because common sense should tell you that an individual's family is the single most important source of social attitudes. However, had you let the terms "traditional society" and "socialization" scare you into thinking that the correct answer relied on arcane technical knowledge, you might have been tempted to guess one of the less obvious answers, perhaps suspecting that answer choice (E) was a trick answer.

At this point you would have overthought the question. You would have wasted the extra time you spent thinking these paranoid thoughts, and on top of that you would have chosen an incorrect answer. Remember, this is a straightforward test. This test does not try to trick you; it simply tries to figure out what you recognize and what you don't. Don't get cute when you're guessing, or you will get burned.

TAILOR YOUR SUBJECT REVIEW TO THE TEST

United States history is the single most frequently tested (between twenty and twenty-two questions) subject on this exam. Anthropology is the least frequently tested (seven or eight questions). Do NOT start studying anthropology until you have made a thorough review of U.S. history. A solid review of U.S. and European history, government, and any other two social sciences (except anthropology) will yield enough knowledge to pass this exam. Look back at the subject breakdown at the beginning of this chapter when planning your review sessions.

Did you skip chapter 2? If you did, go back and read it! It's crammed with important test-taking tips!

After you take the practice exam in this book, read the entire section explaining the correct and incorrect answers for each question; if you know all the material covered in that section, you will undoubtedly do well on the CLEP. Read even those explanations accompanying questions you answered correctly; the descriptions of wrong answers form the basis of a good general review.

A GENERAL OUTLINE OF WHAT YOU ARE EXPECTED TO KNOW

U.S. History

While the General Examination won't ask you about any of the minutiae of U.S. history, there are plenty of important events, all of which are fair game for the test. Be sure you know who the colonists were and why they came, the major reasons for their split with England, and major events of the Revolutionary War. You should have a general knowledge of the causes and major events of the following: the War of 1812; the Louisiana Purchase; the issues surrounding slavery and how they brought about the Civil War; the Reconstruction Era; the westward expansion, the decimation of Native American populations, the railroad, late nineteenth century industrialization and the labor movement; World

War I; Prohibition and the "gangster era"; the Great Depression and the New Deal; World War II; the Cold War; the Civil Rights and women's movements; the Vietnam War; and the Nixon administration and the Watergate scandal. You might be asked a question or two about American culture: music, literature, television, film, radio, etc.

WESTERN CIVILIZATION

The eighteen to twenty questions on this subject could cover just about anything a good generalist would be expected to know. In other words, while you won't need to know the names of officials in Napoleon's government, you will need to know who Napoleon was and why he was a significant historical figure. Questions in this subject category will go as far back as ancient Greece and Rome. They will also cover the medieval period, the Renaissance, and the rest of the modern era right up to the present day. There is not enough space here even to list all the subjects you could be asked about; just rest assured that if you have a good general knowledge of Western history's "greatest hits," these questions will be a breeze; if you do not, it's time for you to crack some books. These questions may include one or two about Western culture: philosophy, poetry, literature, the fine arts, etc.

WORLD CIVILIZATION

This is where ETS covers the non-Western world. Expect questions about the culture and history of Japan, China, Russia, Africa, Central America, and South America. As there are only ten questions for this entire subject, expect no more than one or two questions about any one of these cultures. Historical events, religions and philosophies, art and literature, and the influences of cultures upon one another are all fair game for these questions.

"History . . . is, indeed, little more than the register of the crimes, follies, and misfortunes of mankind."
—Edward Gibbon, author, *The Decline and Fall of the Roman Empire*

GOVERNMENT/POLITICAL SCIENCE

Most of the government/political science questions are about American government. You should have a good general grasp of the Constitution, particularly the powers it gives to the executive, legislative, and judicial branches, as well as the major amendments: the Bill of Rights and the thirteenth, fourteenth, nineteenth, twenty-second, twenty-fifth an twenty-sixth. Know about general trends among populations in political behavior and voting: what influences their vote and party affiliation, etc. Know about the mechanisms for and the major issues surrounding international politics, and know the differences between different types of representative and nonrepresentative governments.

SOCIOLOGY AND PSYCHOLOGY

Psychology and sociology share a large gray area, and some questions on this test properly fall under both categories. The two categories together will make up 21 percent of the exam.

Most sociology questions are definition-related; you will be asked what terms such as "role conflict," "extended family," and "deferred gratification" mean. The test will include questions about the mechanisms of social inclusion and stratification, deviance and conformity, hierarchical structures, demographics, and social structure. One question will ask about proper scientific methodology. You need to know who Max Weber was (he was the father of modern sociology, author of *The Protestant Ethic and the Spirit of Capitalism*).

Psychology questions, like sociology questions, are largely definition-related. You will need to know terms such as "introversion," "id," and "moral relativism." The test will include questions about the best known theories of Freud, Jung, Pavlov, Skinner, and Piaget. You will also need to have general knowledge of the mechanisms governing individual personality and group dynamics, socialization and nonconformity, the learning process, and aging.

ECONOMICS

The CLEP covers both macroeconomics (the study of the economy as a whole) and microeconomics (the study of those forces acting on individual participants in the economy). You will need to know about the Federal Reserve Board, monetary and fiscal policy, competitive markets and monopolies, international trade, the law of supply and demand, and opportunity cost. You will need to know the difference between absolute advantage and comparative advantage. You will need to know how to read graphs indicating equilibrium between supply and demand and depicting production-possibility curves.

GEOGRAPHY

Geography questions require a basic knowledge of differences in weather, climate, and terrain among various regions of the world, and the effects of these differences on various cultures.

ANTHROPOLOGY

Anthropology questions require a basic understanding of prehistoric society and early forms of societal organization such as pastoral, slash-and-burn, and hunter-gatherer. Questions test basic terminology of both physical and cultural anthropology.

"If economists could manage to get themselves thought of as humble, competent people on a level with dentists, that would be splendid."
—John Maynard Keynes (1883–1946), British economist

BIBLIOGRAPHY

There are too few questions on any one subject to justify intensive study for this exam; take it if you think you know enough to pass, otherwise just resign yourself to the fact that you will have to take the commensurate course at college. If you need to bone up on just one subject, the best sources for condensed information are college outlines. These books are basically equivalent to Cliff Notes (or Monarch Notes), but for an entire college course instead of a single book. The **HarperCollins College Outline** series is a good one. You would go broke buying all the books you need to ace this exam, so study at the library. You might also check out the popular **Don't Know Much About History** (Avon) when you review U.S. history; it hits all the major topics and is a fun, easy read.

17

The Princeton Review
Sample Social Sciences Exam

PART I

Time—45 minutes

55 questions

Directions: Each of the questions or incomplete statements below is followed by five suggested answers or completions. Select the one that is best in each case.

1. Before the President of the United States can sign a bill into law,
   (A) the bill must be passed by one house of Congress, but not necessarily by both
   (B) similar versions of the bill, although not necessarily identical, must be passed by both houses of Congress
   (C) identical versions of the bill must be passed by both houses of Congress
   (D) a majority of Cabinet members must approve the bill for the President's signature
   (E) the Supreme Court must first assure the constitutionality of the bill

2. A double-blind experiment is one in which members of the control and experimental groups
   (A) know which group they are assigned to, but the data collector does not
   (B) know which group they are assigned to, as does the data collector
   (C) do not know which group they are assigned to, but the data collector knows
   (D) do not know which group they are assigned to, nor does the data collector know
   (E) are told prior to the experiment that they are assigned to the group opposite to the one they are actually assigned to

3. Lyndon Johnson's antipoverty, pro-civil rights program was called the
   (A) Marshall Plan
   (B) New Deal
   (C) Fourteen Points Plan
   (D) Domino Theory
   (E) Great Society

4. Adam Smith was a proponent of
   (A) Keynesian economics
   (B) laissez-faire economics
   (C) mercantilism
   (D) feudalism
   (E) communism

5. The study of population trends is called
   (A) demography
   (B) genetics
   (C) biology
   (D) epistemology
   (E) epidemiology

6. The term *gross reserve requirement* refers to the
   (A) limit on how much the Federal Reserve may raise or lower interest rates during any given month
   (B) amount government must spend annually on foreign aid
   (C) percentage of the value of an investment that a stock market investor is allowed to borrow from a stock broker
   (D) percentage of total deposits that banks are required to maintain in cash holdings
   (E) tax rate at which government expenditures and government income reach parity

7. Following the Civil War, most freed slaves
   (A) joined the pioneering movement as it headed West
   (B) stayed in the South and worked as sharecroppers
   (C) moved to the North and took professions
   (D) took work building the nation's growing railroad system
   (E) were given property in the South by the federal government

GO ON TO THE NEXT PAGE.

8. The Japanese invasion of China ultimately helped the cause of the Chinese Communist Revolution because

(A) the Communists' refusal to fight the Japanese later resulted in Japanese military support for the revolution

(B) Communist efforts against the Japanese won them greater popular support in China

(C) the Communists were able to watch idly as the Japanese decimated the Republican army

(D) the United States provided the Communists, with whom it was united against a common enemy, with a large supply of arms and supplies once World War II started

(E) Japan's friendly relations with Russia resulted in the dissemination of Communist propaganda in China

9. The continents of Europe and Asia are

(A) separated by the Mediterranean Sea
(B) separated by the Atlantic Ocean
(C) separated by the Pacific Ocean
(D) separated by the Elbe River
(E) not separated by a body of water

10. The first public health law was passed in England in 1848, largely in response to conditions caused by the

(A) bubonic plague
(B) Napoleonic wars
(C) population shift toward the countryside
(D) growing popularity of the automobile
(E) industrial revolution

11. Herdspeople and simple agriculturists sometimes form rank societies, in which members have equal access to

(A) economic resources and power, but not to prestige

(B) economic resources, but not to power or prestige

(C) prestige, but not to power or economic resources

(D) prestige and power, but not to economic resources

(E) power, but not to economic resources or prestige

12. Which section of the U.S. Constitution prohibits the states from infringing upon the constitutional rights of U.S. citizens?

(A) the body
(B) the Tenth Amendment
(C) the Fourteenth Amendment
(D) the Eighteenth Amendment
(E) the Nineteenth Amendment

13. The Haymarket Square Riot was a turning point in the

(A) Communist takeover of Hungary
(B) origins of World War I
(C) French Revolution
(D) history of U.S. labor unions
(E) Cold War

14. During which of the following sleep stages is dreaming thought to occur?

(A) Rapid Eye Movement sleep
(B) Stage One sleep
(C) Stage Two sleep
(D) Stage Three sleep
(E) Stage Four sleep

GO ON TO THE NEXT PAGE.

Question 15 refers to the chart below:

WIDGET PRODUCTION AT ACME, INC.		
Number of employees	Daily production	Average daily production per employee
10	110	11
11	132	13
12	180	15
13	195	15
14	203	14.5
15	216	14
16	216	13.5

15. The downward trend in average daily production per employee for the thirteenth through the sixteenth employee illustrates the law of

(A) diminishing returns
(B) planned obsolescence
(C) stagflation
(D) progressive taxation
(E) comparative advantage

16. Joan of Arc played a major role in

(A) changing the momentum of the Hundred Years' War
(B) the early development of monastic Christian life
(C) the spread of agricultural technology throughout France
(D) expelling the Vikings from Normandy
(E) expanding Charlemagne's realm of power

17. The theory asserting that the language we speak organizes our thoughts and perceptions of the world is called

(A) linguistic relativity
(B) social deviance
(C) mixed motive conflict
(D) conflict theory
(E) cultural diffusion

18. The Dead Sea can sustain only a very few forms of life primarily because

(A) it is too shallow
(B) its waters are too cold
(C) it is so heavily salinated
(D) the atmosphere surrounding it is too heavily polluted
(E) those forms of life it does support are voracious predators

THE POLITICAL QUADRILLE
Music by Dred Scott

Reprinted by permission of the Library of Congress

19. The cartoon above makes the observation that

(A) the Reconstruction Era provided minorities with a political voice for the first time in U.S. history
(B) Dred Scott was an influential statesman who orchestrated peaceful agreements among political rivals
(C) the Supreme Court decision on *Dred Scott* resulted in strange political alliances during the 1860 U.S. presidential election
(D) African-American music is the primary source of all American popular music
(E) the *Dred Scott* decision ushered in for the first time an era in which politicians were more concerned with average citizens than with the powerful

GO ON TO THE NEXT PAGE.

20. The most important commodities of the trans-Saharan trade route during the Middle Ages were

    (A) gold and salt
    (B) art and textiles
    (C) spices and wine
    (D) livestock and wood
    (E) produce and coal

21. Which of the following is NOT an example of conformity?

    (A) A committee member changes his vote in order to join the majority.
    (B) A customer waits in line to be served.
    (C) A pet owner trains his dog to bite people dressed in blue.
    (D) A soldier performs an act he feels is morally wrong because he is ordered to.
    (E) A diner waits to see what everyone else at the table orders before ordering her meal.

22. The population of a state determines the number of its representatives

    (A) on the President's cabinet
    (B) among the federal judiciary
    (C) in the Senate
    (D) in the House of Representatives
    (E) on congressional conference committees

23. Thomas Jefferson opposed some of Alexander Hamilton's policies because Jefferson feared that those policies would

    (A) favor the wealthy and elite at the expense of the less well-off
    (B) result in a powerless Federal government
    (C) unfairly benefit the South at the expense of the North
    (D) assist the French in their revolution
    (E) lead to a Burr presidency

24. A society in which the main sources of employment are information and service industries is called

    (A) pastoral
    (B) agrarian
    (C) pluralistic
    (D) industrial
    (E) postindustrial

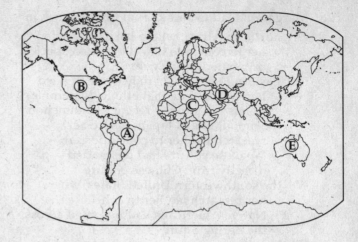

25. Which of the five locations, shown on the map above, has the heaviest annual rainfall?

    (A) A
    (B) B
    (C) C
    (D) D
    (E) E

GO ON TO THE NEXT PAGE.

26. Margaret Mead is best known for her work in

    (A) northern Africa, where her research led her to conclude that the human species originated near Egypt
    (B) Eastern Europe, where her research led her to conclude that ethnic discrimination is a relatively recent phenomenon
    (C) the mountains of Japan, where her research led her to conclude that Japanese culture had descended directly from Chinese culture
    (D) the southwestern United States, where her research led her to conclude that Native Americans had migrated across the Bering Strait
    (E) New Guinea, where her research led her to conclude that gender roles are primarily determined by culture, not biology

27. The first major Protestant break from the Catholic Church was instigated in Germany in 1517 by

    (A) Joseph Smith
    (B) John Knox
    (C) Martin Luther
    (D) Immanuel Kant
    (E) John Calvin

28. Among the President's advisors, the secretary of state's authority is most likely to be threatened by the

    (A) secretary of commerce
    (B) secretary of health and human resources
    (C) vice president
    (D) chief justice of the Supreme Court
    (E) national security advisor

29. Monetarists believe that the money supply should

    (A) be altered monthly in response to the health of the economy
    (B) be permanently set at a fixed level
    (C) be increased until a zero-level of unemployment is reached
    (D) grow and shrink at the exact rate of population growth
    (E) grow at a constant, predictable rate

30. Contemporaneous written records of Mayan civilization

    (A) did not exist, because the Mayans did not have a written language
    (B) were mostly preserved by Mayans, who hid them from invading Spanish forces
    (C) were preserved by Spanish historians who accompanied the conquistadors
    (D) were largely destroyed by the Spanish, who hoped to supplant indigenous Mayan culture with Christianity
    (E) were destroyed by the Mayans in order to prevent the Spaniards from seeing Mayan holy texts

31. Following a policy of appeasement, Western governments did not react with military force to Hitler's annexation of

    (A) Belgium
    (B) Holland
    (C) Poland
    (D) the Alsace-Lorraine region
    (E) the Sudetenland in Czechoslovakia

32. According to Freud, the conscience resides in the

    (A) id
    (B) Eros
    (C) ego
    (D) Thanatos
    (E) superego

33. Ancestor worship and the belief that all natural objects possess a soul is characteristic of

    (A) Shintoism
    (B) Zen Buddhism
    (C) Islam
    (D) Judaism
    (E) Catholicism

GO ON TO THE NEXT PAGE.

34. All of the following facilitated the French sale of the Louisiana Territory to the United States EXCEPT

(A) an epidemic of yellow fever among the French in modern Haiti and the Dominican Republic
(B) the absence of a French military presence in the New World
(C) France's need for funds to support a European military campaign
(D) a threatened military alliance between the U.S. and Great Britain against France
(E) the slave revolt against the French in modern Haiti

35. "No arts; no letters; no society; and which is worst of all, continual fear and danger of violent death; and the life of man, solitary, nasty, brutish, and short."

The quotation above, describing human relations outside the protection of the state, is from a work by

(A) Thomas Hobbes
(B) Rene Descartes
(C) John Locke
(D) John Stuart Mill
(E) Jean-Jacques Rousseau

36. The forums in which the purchase of labor, raw materials, equipment, and land by producers is conducted are called

(A) currency exchanges
(B) input markets
(C) output markets
(D) monopolies
(E) oligopolies

37. The Supreme Court decision *Brown v. Board of Education* concerned

(A) segregation
(B) school prayer
(C) the theory of evolution
(D) free speech
(E) privacy

38. The world's most populous city is

(A) London
(B) Bangkok
(C) Moscow
(D) Chicago
(E) Mexico City

39. All of the following lived during the Renaissance period EXCEPT

(A) Copernicus
(B) Leonardo da Vinci
(C) Giuseppe Garibaldi
(D) Nicolo Macchiavelli
(E) Vasco da Gama

40. Which of the following is true about the internment of Japanese Americans by the United States during World War II?

(A) Only 2,000 Japanese Americans were relocated.
(B) Many of those relocated were known dissidents.
(C) Some of those who were relocated later served in the U.S. armed forces.
(D) Congress passed a law requiring the relocation of all aliens during the war.
(E) Those who were relocated eventually recovered their homes and possessions.

41. The concept of private land ownership is most likely to be found among a group of

(A) nomadic herdsmen
(B) food collectors
(C) agriculturalists
(D) horticulturalists
(E) pastoralists

42. A person who believes both in elected government and collective ownership of a society's resources and industries would most likely be

(A) a democratic socialist
(B) an anarchist
(C) a fascist
(D) a free-market capitalist
(E) a republican

GO ON TO THE NEXT PAGE.

43. "These people were among the most militant of the ancient world. Males entered a military-style troop at the age of seven, joined the army at age twenty, and served until the age of sixty. The women enjoyed more rights than their counterparts elsewhere and could even hold property, but were still primarily regarded as producers of future warriors."

The passage above describes the

(A) Spartans
(B) Athenians
(C) Phoenicians
(D) Trojans
(E) Sumerians

44. Which of the following is true of language development in children?

(A) Children enter a babbling phase between the ages of eighteen and twenty-four months.
(B) It is substantially similar among children of different cultures and languages.
(C) Modern psychology holds that the development of language is the result of operant conditioning.
(D) Children of different cultures differ in when they begin to use language by as much as three years.
(E) Children begin to understand sentences at the same time they begin to speak in sentences.

45. When a market is in equilibrium, a subsequent increase in supply will usually result in

(A) a decrease in demand
(B) an increase in per-unit price
(C) a decrease in per-unit price
(D) inflation
(E) a lack of consumer confidence

46. The Constitution empowers the President to do all of the following EXCEPT

(A) declare war
(B) make treaties
(C) grant reprieves and pardons
(D) command the armed forces
(E) appoint ambassadors

47. The belief that one's own culture is morally superior to others is called

(A) normative behavior
(B) social Darwinism
(C) cultural relativism
(D) xenophobia
(E) ethnocentrism

48. Before the construction of the Panama Canal, ships traveling from New York to San Francisco usually sailed

(A) below the southern tip of Africa
(B) below the southern tip of South America
(C) above the northern tip of Canada
(D) above the northern tip of Europe and Asia
(E) through a difficult network of lakes and canals across the northern border of the United States

49. "The supreme good is like water
which nourishes all things without trying to.
It is content with the low places that people disdain.
Thus it is like the Tao."
The lines above were written by

(A) Mohammed
(B) Confucius
(C) Lao-tzu
(D) Moses
(E) Saint Paul

GO ON TO THE NEXT PAGE.

Question 50 refers to the chart below:

AMERICAN OPINION OF THE PRESIDENT'S CHARACTER 1964-1984 (Percentage answering "yes")					
The President is	1964	1969	1973	1980	1984
trustworthy	73%	48%	30%	65%	58%
capable	70%	59%	67%	34%	55%
compassionate	66%	52%	48%	64%	53%

50. Which of the following can be inferred from the above?

(A) Presidents don't have to be considered compassionate in order to win elections.
(B) The Watergate scandal affected the public perception of Nixon's capability to serve as president.
(C) Every president between Kennedy and Bush has suffered from a lack of public trust.
(D) Public perception of Nixon's trustworthiness dropped during his tenure.
(E) Ronald Reagan was the most popular president of the last 30 years.

51. There is a positive correlation between improvement of one's social class and all of the following EXCEPT

(A) level of education
(B) life span
(C) number of children borne
(D) mental health
(E) physical health

52. Which of the following lists the reigns of Augustus Caesar, Caligula, Claudius, Julius Caesar, Nero, and Tiberius in chronological order?

(A) Caligula, Nero, Julius Caesar, Claudius, Augustus Caesar, Tiberius
(B) Augustus Caesar, Caligula, Tiberius, Julius Caesar, Nero, Claudius
(C) Julius Caesar, Caligula, Claudius, Nero, Tiberius, Augustus Caesar
(D) Tiberius, Nero, Julius Caesar, Augustus Caesar, Claudius, Caligula
(E) Julius Caesar, Augustus Caesar, Tiberius, Caligula, Claudius, Nero

53. The inflation rate is defined as the average annual increase in

(A) unemployment
(B) gross national product
(C) amount of leisure time available to the average citizen
(D) prices
(E) disparity between the wealthiest and poorest members of a society

54. Fill in the blanks:

The Sherman Anti-Trust Act, used for its first decade as a weapon against _____, later became the government's most effective tool against _____.

(A) political parties . . . lobbyists
(B) unethical gold speculators . . . corrupt bankers
(C) proponents of slavery . . . carpetbaggers
(D) subversive propagandists . . . government censorship
(E) labor unions . . . corporate monopolies

55. Political revolutions most often occur in societies when

(A) social conditions are extremely poor and the government is extremely oppressive
(B) social conditions remain the same for extended periods of time
(C) new racial or ethnic groups are introduced
(D) elections have recently been held, with inconclusive results
(E) social conditions improve somewhat, but not as quickly as the majority wishes

56. One major difference between operant and Pavlovian conditioning is that

(A) operant conditioning never uses food as a stimulus
(B) operant responses are voluntary, while Pavlovian responses are involuntary
(C) Pavlovian conditioning is permanent
(D) an operant response is instantaneous, while a Pavlovian response follows a long delay
(E) Pavlovian stimuli are always sonic

GO ON TO THE NEXT PAGE.

57. The boycott of the Montgomery bus system by African Americans
    - (A) occurred at the height of the civil rights movement of the mid-1960s
    - (B) was led by Malcolm X
    - (C) was instigated by the arrest of Rosa Parks
    - (D) lasted for three weeks and failed to achieve its goal
    - (E) was staged to protest the assassination of Martin Luther King

58. The debate over whether genetics or upbringing is the most prominent influence on intelligence and behavior is characterized by the phrase
    - (A) "mind over matter"
    - (B) "man against machine"
    - (C) "nature versus nurture"
    - (D) "feast or famine"
    - (E) "the individual good versus the general good"

59. The field of paleoanthropology is primarily concerned with the study of the
    - (A) history of all species during the Paleozoic period
    - (B) emergence and evolution of the human species
    - (C) extinction of the dinosaurs
    - (D) variations in population growth rates among different contemporary human populations
    - (E) contemporary primitive populations of the South Pacific

60. The area of Australia is approximately
    - (A) one-third the area of mainland China
    - (B) the same as the area of India
    - (C) the same as the area of the forty-eight contiguous United States
    - (D) twice the area of Texas
    - (E) three times the area of Canada

61. In his play *The Crucible*, Arthur Miller compares the Salem Witch Trials of the seventeenth century to the
    - (A) Red Scare of the 1950s
    - (B) events leading up to World War I
    - (C) Communist Revolution in the Soviet Union
    - (D) Supreme Court decision *Marbury v. Madison*
    - (E) fall of the Roman Empire

62. The Muslim influence on medieval Spain resulted in all of the following EXCEPT
    - (A) banking and credit systems
    - (B) terrace farming
    - (C) development of the sciences
    - (D) heightened religious intolerance
    - (E) irrigation

63. The demise of the castle as an effective defensive structure was brought about primarily by the development of
    - (A) the catapult
    - (B) the submarine
    - (C) gunpowder weapons
    - (D) armor
    - (E) the airplane

GO ON TO THE NEXT PAGE.

PART II

Time—45 minutes

62 questions

Directions: Each of the questions or incomplete statements below is followed by five suggested answers or completions. Select the one that is best in each case.

64. World War I is often said to have led directly to World War II because

   (A) border skirmishes between France and Spain were never resolved during the first war
   (B) the victors neglected to disarm Germany after the war
   (C) the harshness of the Treaty of Versailles created widespread resentment among the German people
   (D) the cost of the war led directly and immediately to the Great Depression
   (E) the postwar European map contained too many large and powerful nations

65. A Mercator projection map distorts which of the following geographical features?

   (A) the intensity of climatic shifts between regions
   (B) the area of land masses
   (C) the uniformity of ocean currents
   (D) the isolation, by region, of the world's languages
   (E) the amount of rainfall near the equator

66. The Supreme Court decision *Marbury v. Madison* established the principle of

   (A) one man, one vote
   (B) separate but equal
   (C) no taxation without representation
   (D) gerrymandering
   (E) judicial review

67. Which of the following is least likely to result in an increase in aggregate demand?

   (A) a decrease in income taxes
   (B) an increase in interest rates
   (C) an increase in the federal budget
   (D) an increase in net exports
   (E) an increase in government entitlement payments

68. The process by which a minority group modifies its distinctive characteristics in order to conform with a dominant society is called

   (A) resocialization
   (B) cultural lag
   (C) cohabitation
   (D) assimilation
   (E) a folkway

69. The Sixth Amendment of the U.S. Constitution guarantees a criminal defendant all of the following EXCEPT:

   (A) the right to confront prosecution witnesses
   (B) bail will not be excessive
   (C) a speedy, public trial
   (D) a defense lawyer
   (E) a jury trial

70. The Missouri Compromise established

   (A) Missouri, and all subsequent states, as "slave-free" territories
   (B) the boundaries of all future states located within the Louisiana Territory
   (C) the rights of riverboat proprietors to transact business along the Mississippi River
   (D) more democratic means of determining the size of each state's congressional delegation
   (E) Missouri's southern border as the dividing line between "free" and "slave" states

GO ON TO THE NEXT PAGE.

71. A society's culture is said to be integrated when
    (A) it is practiced only by the ruling elite of the society
    (B) it requires certain practices of men only, and other practices of women only
    (C) it is shared by two or more ethnic groups, even if those groups do not interact
    (D) different aspects of the culture are consistent with, as opposed to contradictory to, one another
    (E) religious, military, and government positions of authority are largely held by the same people or class

72. Developmental psychologists use the term instrumental aggression to refer to behavior in which an aggressor
    (A) hurts someone by accident
    (B) acts to achieve a goal
    (C) reacts to an attack with greater force than the attacker used
    (D) attacks with a weapon
    (E) repeatedly attacks the same person without provocation

73. "From Stettin in the Baltic to Trieste in the Adriatic, an iron curtain has descended across the Continent. Behind that line lie all the capitals of the ancient states of Central and Eastern Europe."

    The quotation above is from a speech by whom, and to what situation was the speaker referring?

    (A) Georges Clemenceau, the outbreak of World War I
    (B) Benito Mussolini, the Nazi invasion of Poland
    (C) Woodrow Wilson, the Russian Revolution
    (D) Winston Churchill, the Soviet takeover of Eastern Europe
    (E) George Bush, the fall of the Berlin Wall

74. In 1912, the last Manchu emperor abdicated the Chinese throne. His government was replaced by
    (A) a dictatorship, led by Chou En-lai
    (B) a Communist government, led by Mao Tse-Tung
    (C) a Republic, led by Yuan Shih-k'ai
    (D) a Socialist democracy, led by Ho Chi Minh
    (E) a monarchy, led by Sun Yat-sen

75. Australia has summer when the United States has winter because, relative to the United States, Australia is
    (A) closer to the Arctic Circle
    (B) across the international date line
    (C) across the equator
    (D) closer to the equator
    (E) more humid

76. The power of an executive to reject parts of a legislative bill while enacting others is called
    (A) an executive agreement
    (B) a policy shift
    (C) a pocket veto
    (D) a line-item veto
    (E) a plea bargain

77. All of the following are actions the Federal Reserve Board might take to invigorate a sluggish economy EXCEPT
    (A) lowering bank reserve requirements
    (B) selling government securities on the open market
    (C) buying bonds on the open market
    (D) encouraging member banks to make more loans
    (E) lowering the discount rate

GO ON TO THE NEXT PAGE.

78. The Potsdam Declaration of World War II

    (A) stated that Germany had an irrevocable right to the Alsace-Lorraine region
    (B) announced Italy's intention to enter the war
    (C) served as the framework for the European peace treaty following the war
    (D) warned the Japanese that failure to surrender would result in "prompt and utter destruction"
    (E) outlined the plan for U.S. entry into the war in Europe

79. The principle of the fundamental attribution error states that a person will tend to judge others' behavior

    (A) based on a realistic assessment of how he or she would behave under similar circumstances
    (B) less accurately than that person judges his or her own behavior
    (C) leniently, especially if such behavior has no adverse effect on the person judging it
    (D) by stricter standards than that person judges himself or herself
    (E) arbitrarily and without reference to any moral or ethical standards

80. Civilization probably began in

    (A) North America
    (B) western Europe
    (C) Mesopotamia and the Nile Valley
    (D) New Guinea and Australia
    (E) the British isles

81. A group of influential people who hold sway over government, economic, and military activity is called a

    (A) silent majority
    (B) proletariat
    (C) counterculture
    (D) political party
    (E) power elite

82. An individual's status in a caste system is primarily

    (A) earned through good deeds
    (B) bought with cash, goods, and services
    (C) decided, upon reaching adulthood, by a religious leader
    (D) assigned arbitrarily
    (E) ascribed by birth

83. Jean Piaget is best known for his work in the field of

    (A) cultural anthropology
    (B) semiotic literary criticism
    (C) revisionist history
    (D) free market economics
    (E) developmental psychology

84. Between 1649 and 1660, the English government was a

    (A) monarchy, under Charles I
    (B) monarchy, under Elizabeth I
    (C) monarchy, under Henry VIII
    (D) commonwealth, under Oliver Cromwell
    (E) commonwealth, under Winston Churchill

85. The Mississippi River creates borders between all the following pairs of states EXCEPT

    (A) Mississippi and Arkansas
    (B) Tennessee and Arkansas
    (C) Texas and Arkansas
    (D) Illinois and Missouri
    (E) Illinois and Iowa

86. Turkey was ruled from the fourteenth to the early twentieth century by the

    (A) Ottoman empire
    (B) Mughal dynasty
    (C) Safavids
    (D) Shah of Iran
    (E) Holy Roman Empire

87. The primary reason for U.S. involvement in Vietnam was

    (A) the necessity to protect massive oil reserves which were the United States' primary source of energy
    (B) the fear that a Communist takeover of Vietnam would lead to a Communist takeover of the entire region
    (C) the desire to protect one of the region's only long-standing democratic regimes
    (D) to establish a base from which an offensive attack could be launched against Communist China
    (E) to protect American business interests in the region

GO ON TO THE NEXT PAGE.

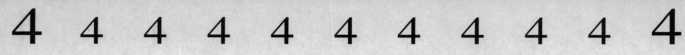

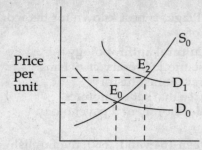

88. The graph above demonstrates that, when demand increases and supply stays constant in an economy in equilibrium,

    (A) both equilibrium price and equilibrium quantity rise
    (B) equilibrium price rises and equilibrium quantity falls
    (C) equilibrium price stays constant and equilibrium quantity rises
    (D) equilibrium price falls and equilibrium quantity rises
    (E) both equilibrium price and equilibrium quantity stay constant

89. When a public opinion poll proves inaccurate, the problem is usually that

    (A) the polling organization surveyed too large a group
    (B) data collectors misrecorded responses
    (C) the poll was taken in person, rather than by phone
    (D) the population surveyed did not constitute a representative sample
    (E) respondents weren't interested in the survey topic

90. Who among the following is NOT associated with the Romantic period?

    (A) William Wordsworth
    (B) Daniel Defoe
    (C) George Noel Gordon, Lord Byron
    (D) Percy Bysshe Shelley
    (E) John Keats

91. Peasants are distinguished from subsistence farmers by the fact that peasants

    (A) form completely autonomous communities
    (B) participate in extra-agricultural social groups, such as guilds and churches
    (C) must produce excess crops in order to pay rent to a landlord
    (D) have great opportunity to rise through the hierarchy of the societies in which they reside
    (E) exist only under a monarchical form of government

92. Which of the following pieces of legislation posed the greatest threat to the U.S. Constitution's guarantee of freedom of the press?

    (A) the Alien and Sedition Acts
    (B) the National Industrial Recovery Act
    (C) the Civil Rights Act of 1964
    (D) the Census Act
    (E) the Federal Securities Act

93. The term *ethnic group* is used to describe a group with

    (A) a shared culture
    (B) shared physical characteristics
    (C) a shared economic status
    (D) differing physical characteristics
    (E) differing religious beliefs

94. Overwhelming and irrational fear associated with a particular thing or experience is called a

    (A) mesomorph
    (B) fetish
    (C) premoral stage
    (D) phobia
    (E) separation anxiety

GO ON TO THE NEXT PAGE.

95. Which of the following statements about the U.S. government is true?

(A) The Federal Bureau of Investigation is an agency of the judicial branch.
(B) A tie vote in the Senate is broken by the Speaker of the House.
(C) Appropriations bills must originate in the Senate.
(D) A congressional bill can become law without the president's signature.
(E) Congress nominates candidates for the Supreme Court.

96. An Islamic religious war is called a

(A) mosque
(B) salaam
(C) halal
(D) Koran
(E) jihad

97. The value of all goods and services produced by an economy when its labor, natural, and capital resources are employed to capacity is referred to by economists as the

(A) aggregate supply demand curve
(B) cross-price elasticity formula
(C) feedback effect
(D) Laspeyres price index
(E) potential gross national product

98. The North Atlantic Treaty Organization (NATO) was formed in

(A) 1865
(B) 1914
(C) 1932
(D) 1949
(E) 1972

99. Great Britain and France are separated by the

(A) Pacific Ocean
(B) Nile River
(C) Mediterranean Sea
(D) English Channel
(E) Arctic Ocean

100. The Lend-Lease Act allowed Franklin Roosevelt to

(A) place additional judges favorable to his policies on the Supreme Court
(B) assist the Allies without violating the U.S. policy of neutrality
(C) provide equipment to farmers who would otherwise have been unable to harvest crops
(D) create jobs for artists during the Depression
(E) establish a fund to insure bank deposits of up to $100,000

101. All of the following are physiological motives EXCEPT

(A) hunger
(B) fatigue
(C) curiosity
(D) thirst
(E) pain

102. Fill in the blanks:

Groups are _____ likely than individuals to make risky decisions and take risky actions, because of a phenomenon called _____.

(A) more . . . laissez-faire leadership
(B) more . . . the diffusion of responsibility
(C) less . . . empathy
(D) less . . . rationalization
(E) less . . . the division of labor

103. A government with both a symbolic royal head of state and elected leaders who are empowered to govern is called

(A) a dictatorship
(B) an absolute monarchy
(C) a constitutional monarchy
(D) a junta
(E) a totalitarian regime

GO ON TO THE NEXT PAGE.

104. The division of labor by gender is
    (A) universal to all cultures
    (B) found in primitive societies, but disappears as societies advance
    (C) not as common worldwide as is the division of labor by race and class
    (D) primarily isolated among most cultures to food-gathering activities
    (E) determined solely by biological capacity

105. The term Manifest Destiny refers to the idea that
    (A) the Marxist Revolution in the Soviet Union was inevitable
    (B) all events are preordained in the Calvinist universe
    (C) the United States in the nineteenth century had a sacred right to all of North America
    (D) every United States resident has the inalienable right to life, liberty, and the pursuit of happiness
    (E) the Roman Empire was fated to fall

106. All of the following countries fought successful revolutionary wars against European colonists during the early nineteenth century except
    (A) Argentina
    (B) Brazil
    (C) Chile
    (D) Bolivia
    (E) Peru

107. A drop in the value of the American dollar against foreign currencies would most probably result in
    (A) an increase in American tariffs on imported goods
    (B) more Americans taking vacations abroad
    (C) a pronounced long-term worldwide recession
    (D) increased American investment in foreign businesses and property
    (E) an increase in American exports

108. Which of the following countries is not located in the Middle East?
    (A) Syria
    (B) Egypt
    (C) Jordan
    (D) Algeria
    (E) Israel

109. The first western settlements in Australia were made up largely of
    (A) German speculators
    (B) American farmers
    (C) Norwegian fishermen
    (D) British prisoners
    (E) French gold prospectors

110. Interest groups such as Environmental Action and Americans for Constitutional Action rate members of Congress primarily on the basis of
    (A) how closely the legislator's voting record conforms to the group's politics
    (B) how many pieces of legislation a member of Congress introduces in a year
    (C) the amount of money legislators accept in donations from political action groups
    (D) the legislators' level of experience in state and local politics
    (E) the member of Congress' attendance record

111. According to Carl Gustav Jung, the collective unconscious is comprised of
    (A) the male and female aspects of one's personality
    (B) memories from the first three months of an individual's life
    (C) those rules regulating socialization in a given society
    (D) behavior patterns and memories inherited from one's ancestors
    (E) learned responses to dangerous stimuli

112. The United States foreign policy stating that its government would not tolerate European interventions in the Americas is called the
    (A) Mayflower Compact
    (B) Quartering Act
    (C) Truman Doctrine
    (D) Monroe Doctrine
    (E) Pentagon Papers

GO ON TO THE NEXT PAGE.

113. A household made up of a father, mother, their children and their grandchildren, and the father's brother is called

(A) a nuclear family
(B) an extended family
(C) a nontraditional family
(D) a patriarchal society
(E) a matriarchal society

114. The Buddha Gautama, founder of Buddhism, lived in

(A) India, during the sixth century B.C.
(B) Thailand, during the third century B.C.
(C) the Philippines, during the first century B.C.
(D) China, during the third century
(E) Japan, during the fifteenth century

115. One major difference between peasants and serfs during medieval times is that serfs

(A) had more money and were therefore considered somewhat better off than peasants
(B) were not free to move from the area in which they lived and worked
(C) commonly received education, health care, and other amenities not available to peasants
(D) were allowed by law to buy the land they worked
(E) worked for the Church, whereas peasants worked for the king

116. Max Weber argued that Calvinist Protestantism was instrumental in the development of

(A) liberation theology, because of its doctrines of compassion
(B) capitalism, because it instilled a work ethic in its adherents
(C) democracy, because of its emphasis on free will
(D) charity, because of its emphasis on self-betterment through good deeds
(E) communism, because it stressed the group over the individual

117. The United States and Japan were able to establish friendly relations quickly after World War II primarily because

(A) the strength of Japan's economy made Japan a desirable trading partner for the U.S.
(B) their differences during the war had been only minor
(C) the U.S. wished to take advantage of Japan's military strength in the region
(D) the two shared a common enemy, the Soviet Union
(E) the U.S., as a gesture of peace, restored the sovereignty of the emperor immediately after the war

118. The Sugar Act, passed by the British Parliament in 1764, was intended to

(A) increase the amount of sugar imported from Britain by its Asian colonies
(B) shift the world production center of sugar from the Old World to the New World
(C) raise revenue to offset the costs of the French and Indian War
(D) provide the colonies with a greater measure of self-government
(E) impose punitive measures on the American colonies to discourage their growing independence

119. The population of the United States is most heavily concentrated

(A) along the coast of the Gulf of Mexico, from New Orleans to Tampa
(B) on the northeast coast, from Boston to Washington D.C.
(C) along the entire length of the Pacific Coast, from San Diego to Seattle
(D) in the western mountain region, from Denver to Salt Lake City
(E) along the Mississippi River, from Memphis to St. Louis

GO ON TO THE NEXT PAGE.

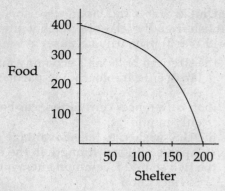

120. The production possibility curve for society X, illustrated above, indicates that

    (A) society X cannot produce adequate amounts of both food and shelter
    (B) society X would be best served by producing 150 units of shelter and 150 units of food
    (C) in order to produce 200 units of shelter, society X would have to forego the production of food
    (D) in order to produce 350 units of food, society X would have to forego the production of shelter
    (E) society X could simultaneously produce 400 units of food and 200 units of shelter

121. "Until philosophers are kings, or the kings and princes of the world have the spirit and power of philosophy . . . cities will never have rest from their evils."

    The quotation above is from

    (A) Aristotle's *Ethics*
    (B) Ralph Waldo Emerson's *Politics*
    (C) Jonathan Swift's *A Modest Proposal*
    (D) John Locke's *Second Treatise of Government*
    (E) Plato's *Republic*

122. The political party with which a citizen chooses to be affiliated is most powerfully influenced by that citizen's

    (A) religion
    (B) family
    (C) economic status
    (D) level of education
    (E) personal encounters with politicians

123. The process that causes people in a large crowd to lose some of their inhibitions is called

    (A) deindividuation
    (B) reciprocity
    (C) group polarization
    (D) guilt complex
    (E) aphasia

124. All of the following are Romance languages EXCEPT

    (A) Portuguese
    (B) German
    (C) Italian
    (D) French
    (E) Spanish

125. In the U.S., the Radical Republicans of the nineteenth century campaigned most vigorously for

    (A) the dismantling of the federal government
    (B) a punitive Reconstruction
    (C) annexing Texas
    (D) the maintenance of slavery in Southern states
    (E) territorial expansion into Canada

STOP

IF YOU FINISH BEFORE TIME IS CALLED, YOU MAY CHECK YOUR WORK ON THIS SECTION ONLY.
DO NOT WORK ON ANY OTHER SECTION IN THE TEST.

NO TEST MATERIAL ON THIS PAGE.

SCORING YOUR TEST

This test is a facsimile of the ETS-written CLEP general exam in Social Sciences. Care has been taken to make sure that this test closely resembles the actual exam both in content and format. In other words, when you take the real CLEP, it should look a lot like the test you've just taken.

ETS has never released its scoring methods for the CLEP. ETS states in its literature that, if you get half the raw score points available to you on the test, you should score the national medium—usually between 480 and 500—on a given test.

Your raw score is determined by subtracting 1/4 the number of questions you answer incorrectly from the number of questions you answer correctly. Questions you leave blank are worth 0 points.

Typically, you need about 2/3 of the raw score points available on a test to score in the mid-600s on an ETS test, but, again, this is only speculation regarding the CLEP.

18

Answers and Explanations to the Social Sciences Exam

SECTION 4

Read this entire section even the explanations for the questions you answered correctly. The material covered in these explanations add up to a pretty thorough review of the material tested on the CLEP. Plus, many explanations contain helpful test-taking tips.

1. Before the President of the United States can sign a bill into law,
   (A) the bill must be passed by one house of Congress, but not necessarily by both
   (B) similar versions of the bill, although not necessarily identical, must be passed by both houses of Congress
   (C) identical versions of the bill must be passed by both houses of Congress
   (D) a majority of cabinet members must approve the bill for the President's signature
   (E) the Supreme Court must first assure the constitutionality of the bill

1. **(C)** is the correct answer. Both houses of Congress must pass the identical bill in order for it to reach the President's desk. Members of both houses meet in a conference committee in an effort to hammer out their differences so that identical versions of a bill might be proposed on the floors of both houses. The amendment procedure often makes it necessary for conference committees to meet many times to reconcile differences between the various versions of a bill.

2. A double-blind experiment is one in which members of the control and experimental groups
   (A) know which group they are assigned to, but the data collector does not
   (B) know which group they are assigned to, as does the data collector
   (C) do not know which group they are assigned to, but the data collector knows
   (D) do not know which group they are assigned to, nor does the data collector know
   (E) are told prior to the experiment that they are assigned to the group opposite to the one they are actually assigned to

2. **(D)** is the correct answer. A blind is a device used to limit bias in experiments. When the subjects of an experiment, both the experimental group and the control group, are unaware of the condition assigned to them, those groups are said to be blind. A double-blind experiment takes the added precaution of not telling the data collectors which group is which, thereby lessening the possibility that the data collector might bias his/her observations in order to obtain the desired results (i.e., those that support the experimental hypothesis).

SECTION 4

QUESTIONS	EXPLANATIONS

3. Lyndon Johnson's antipoverty, pro-civil rights program was called the

   (A) Marshall Plan
   (B) New Deal
   (C) Fourteen Points Plan
   (D) Domino Theory
   (E) Great Society

3. **(E)** is the correct answer. The Marshall Plan was a post-World War II assistance program for Europe. The U.S. provided funds for countries to rebuild, and in return those countries became America's allies in its battle against Communism. The New Deal was Franklin D. Roosevelt's program of recovery from the Great Depression. The Fourteen Points Plan was Woodrow Wilson's blueprint for peace following World War I. The Domino Theory dominated U.S. foreign policy for decades; it held that Communist expansion had to be entirely contained, because once one country fell to Communist rule, others would fall as a consequence - just like dominoes!

4. Adam Smith was a proponent of

   (A) Keynesian economics
   (B) laissez-faire economics
   (C) mercantilism
   (D) feudalism
   (E) communism

4. **(B)** is the correct answer. Smith's *The Wealth of Nations* argues that an open marketplace with each individual pursuing his/her own interests will result in the greatest benefit to a nation. Keynesian economics, named after John Maynard Keynes, argues that the government must play a regulatory role in the economy. Mercantilism also held that the government should play a role in the economy, primarily a supportive and protectionist role.

5. The study of population trends is called

   (A) demography
   (B) genetics
   (C) biology
   (D) epistemology
   (E) epidemiology

5. **(A)** is the correct answer. Genetics is the study of heredity. Biology is the study of living matter, particularly with regard to life/death cycles, reproduction, and self-nourishment. Epistemology is the study of methods and capacities of human knowledge. Epidemiology is the study of how diseases are transmitted within a population.

6. The term *gross reserve requirement* refers to the

   (A) limit on how much the Federal Reserve may raise or lower interest rates during any given month
   (B) amount government must spend annually on foreign aid
   (C) percentage of the value of an investment that a stock market investor is allowed to borrow from a stock broker
   (D) percentage of total deposits that banks are required to maintain in cash holdings
   (E) tax rate at which government expenditures and government income reach parity

6. **(D)** is the correct answer. The Federal Reserve determines what amount of their assets banks must hold in reserve. When the percentage is relatively low, it allows banks to invest and lend more and should, accordingly, result in economic growth.

SECTION 4

7. Following the Civil War, most freed slaves

   (A) joined the pioneering movement as it headed West
   (B) stayed in the South and worked as sharecroppers
   (C) moved to the North and took professions
   (D) took work building the nation's growing railroad system
   (E) were given property in the South by the federal government

7. **(B)** is the correct answer. Although the Homestead Act of 1867 was designed to give former slaves the opportunity to buy land at bargain basement rates, very few had even the little amount of money necessary to become property holders. The land was subsequently bought up by the wealthy, who often turned around and rented it, at steep rates, to farmers too poor to buy their own property. The resulting system was known as tenant farming or sharecropping. Tenants would work a piece of land and turn over 50 percent of their crop to their landlord. Often other expenses, such as rent for a rundown shack, overpriced groceries available only through the land owner, etc., devoured all other income a sharecropper might earn. The system was designed to keep the poor in poverty, and was very effective at this.

8. The Japanese invasion of China ultimately helped the cause of the Chinese Communist Revolution because

   (A) the Communists' refusal to fight the Japanese later resulted in Japanese military support for the revolution
   (B) Communist efforts against the Japanese won them greater popular support in China
   (C) the Communists were able to watch idly as the Japanese decimated the Republican army
   (D) the United States provided the Communists, with whom it was united against a common enemy, with a large supply of arms and supplies once World War II started
   (E) Japan's friendly relations with Russia resulted in the dissemination of Communist propaganda in China

8. **(B)** is the correct answer. Prior to the Japanese invasion, Republican forces primarily preoccupied themselves with fighting the Communists; in fact, some argue that it was this emphasis on fighting Communism that provided Japan an easy opportunity to invade and occupy parts of China. Thereafter, the Republic and Communists formed an extremely uneasy alliance to fight the Japanese. During the ensuing battles, the Communists showed themselves to be dedicated patriots, thus earning much needed public sympathy for their cause. The U.S. did provide weapons to the Republican army, but never to the Communists. As far as Japan and Russia having friendly relations, forget about it: they fought a war in 1904, and the Russians were willing to fight them again in 1945. They didn't make up during the years in between.

9. The continents of Europe and Asia are

   (A) separated by the Mediterranean Sea
   (B) separated by the Atlantic Ocean
   (C) separated by the Pacific Ocean
   (D) separated by the Elbe River
   (E) not separated by a body of water

9. **(E)** is the correct answer. Technically speaking, the two continents aren't separated at all, which is why many geographers refer to the two by the single name "Eurasia."

SECTION 4

10. The first public health law was passed in England in 1848, largely in response to conditions caused by the
    (A) bubonic plague
    (B) Napoleonic wars
    (C) population shift toward the countryside
    (D) growing popularity of the automobile
    (E) industrial revolution

10. **(E)** is the correct answer. The industrial revolution led to greater concentration of populations in squalid urban neighborhoods. Such living conditions, along with poor working conditions, long hours, and poverty, conspired to create major public health problems. Edwin Chadwick campaigned tirelessly, and his efforts resulted in the installation of public sewage systems and running water in many towns and cities. Other industrial nations quickly followed suit. The bubonic plague occurred in the fourteenth century. During the 1800s, the English population shifted toward cities, not toward the countryside. Automobiles did not become popular and affordable until well into the twentieth century.

11. Herdspeople and simple agriculturists sometimes form rank societies, in which members have equal access to
    (A) economic resources and power, but not to prestige
    (B) economic resources, but not to power or prestige
    (C) prestige, but not to power or economic resources
    (D) prestige and power, but not to economic resources
    (E) power, but not to economic resources or prestige

11. **(A)** is the correct answer. In rank societies, no limitations are placed on personal wealth or on power, which in anthropological terms means the ability to make somebody else do what you don't want to do (by threat of force). Prestige, however, comes in the form of access to certain positions in society and is determined by birth. In a rank society, only certain members may become chief or priests. In such societies, all members, including the chief, usually perform the same work. The chief and other ranking members are usually entitled to acts of deference, such as bowing, by their inferiors in rank. Rank societies are more stratified than egalitarian societies (no limits on access to power, prestige, or wealth) and less stratified than class or caste societies (limited access to power, prestige, and wealth for those of lower classes).

SECTION 4

12. Which section of the U.S. Constitution prohibits the states from infringing upon the constitutional rights of U.S. citizens?

    (A) the body
    (B) the Tenth Amendment
    (C) the Fourteenth Amendment
    (D) the Eighteenth Amendment
    (E) the Nineteenth Amendment

12. **(C)** is the correct answer. The original intent of the Bill of Rights was to guarantee that the federal government would not infringe on the rights of individuals (the framers were especially wary of a powerful central government, having just gained independence from a monarchy). In the post-Civil War era, the federal government moved to make sure that the states would not refuse newly freed slaves their constitutional rights. Hence, the Fourteenth Amendment (1868), which states in part: "No State shall make or enforce any law which shall abridge the privileges or immunities of citizens of the United States; nor shall any State deprive any person of life, liberty, or property, without due process of law . . . ." The body of the Constitution lays out the structure of the federal government and enumerates the powers of its various offices. The Tenth Amendment returns to the states any powers not specifically granted the federal government in the Constitution. The Eighteenth Amendment prohibited the sale of "intoxicating liquors" in the U.S. The Nineteenth Amendment gave women the right to vote.

13. The Haymarket Square Riot was a turning point in the

    (A) Communist takeover of Hungary
    (B) origins of World War I
    (C) French Revolution
    (D) history of U.S. labor unions
    (E) Cold War

13. **(D)** is the correct answer. The day before the riot, Knights of Labor union members demonstrated for an eight-hour workday at the McCormick Reaper Company in Chicago. During the demonstration union members attacked strikebreakers and were in turn attacked by police who fired into the crowd, killing six strikers and wounding many more. The next day, members of the Knights of Labor gathered in Haymarket Square to protest this incident of police brutality. At that demonstration, someone—purportedly an anarchist labor agitator, but nobody knows for sure—threw a bomb into the crowd, killing seven police officers and precipitating a riot. The resulting bad publicity, spread in no small part by the enemies of organized labor, caused the demise of the nation's first powerful union.

SECTION 4

14. During which of the following sleep stages is dreaming thought to occur?

    (A) Rapid Eye Movement sleep
    (B) Stage One sleep
    (C) Stage Two sleep
    (D) Stage Three sleep
    (E) Stage Four sleep

14. **(A)** is the correct answer. Stages One through Four are the stages of non-dream sleep. Stage One is the period of lightest sleep, Stage Four the heaviest. Rapid Eye Movement (REM) sleep, so called because of the tendency of sleepers in this stage to move their eyes rapidly beneath their closed eyelids, occurs approximately every ninety minutes during normal sleep. It is during this time that people are thought to dream; experimental evidence includes electroencephalogram (EEG) tests demonstrating increased mental activity during the REM stage.

WIDGET PRODUCTION AT ACME, INC.		
Number of employees	Daily production	Average daily production per employee
10	110	11
11	132	13
12	180	15
13	195	15
14	203	14.5
15	216	14
16	216	13.5

15. The downward trend in average daily production per employee for the thirteenth through the sixteenth employee illustrates the law of

    (A) diminishing returns
    (B) planned obsolescence
    (C) stagflation
    (D) progressive taxation
    (E) comparative advantage

15. **(A)** is the correct answer. Up to a certain point, adding laborers increases a factory's total output <u>and</u> its per employee output. At that point, however, the factory and laborers can no longer both work at peak efficiency. While overall production may increase, per employee production decreases; this decrease occurs by definition at the point of diminishing returns.

SECTION 4

16. Joan of Arc played a major role in

    (A) changing the momentum of the Hundred Years' War
    (B) the early development of monastic Christian life
    (C) the spread of agricultural technology throughout France
    (D) expelling the Vikings from Normandy
    (E) expanding Charlemagne's realm of power

16. **(A)** is the correct answer. The Hundred Years' War between France and England was going badly for France when Joan of Arc, a peasant girl, had a vision from heaven telling her that she had been chosen to save France. Her actions revived the French army at a fortuitous time, as the English army was overextended and weakening. Several battles later, large portions of France had been liberated from the English. Joan was eventually captured by the British, who turned her over to the Inquisition. Joan was burned at the stake for heresy. She was later canonized by the Roman Catholic church.

17. The theory asserting that the language we speak organizes our thoughts and perceptions of the world is called

    (A) linguistic relativity
    (B) social deviance
    (C) mixed motive conflict
    (D) conflict theory
    (E) cultural diffusion

17. **(A)** is the correct answer. Social deviance is a term describing actions that are counter to societal norms. A mixed motive conflict is one between parties in which no one wishes to be the absolute victor or loser (and so a compromise is sought). Conflict theory holds that conflict motivates most human behavior; its source is Karl Marx's work. Cultural diffusion describes the process by which ideas, styles, and other nonmaterial entities spread between and within societies.

18. The Dead Sea can sustain only a very few forms of life primarily because

    (A) it is too shallow
    (B) its waters are too cold
    (C) it is so heavily salinated
    (D) the atmosphere surrounding it is too heavily polluted
    (E) those forms of life it does support are voracious predators

18. **(C)** is the correct answer. The Dead Sea has one of the highest salt contents of any body of water on Earth.

SECTION 4

QUESTIONS	EXPLANATIONS

THE POLITICAL QUADRILLE
Music by Dred Scott

Reprinted by permission of the Library of Congress.

19. The cartoon above makes the observation that

(A) the Reconstruction Era provided minorities with a political voice for the first time in U.S. history

(B) Dred Scott was an influential statesman who orchestrated peaceful agreements among political rivals

(C) the Supreme Court decision on *Dred Scott* resulted in strange political alliances during the 1860 U.S. presidential election

(D) African-American music is the primary source of all American popular music

(E) the *Dred Scott* decision ushered in for the first time an era in which politicians were more concerned with average citizens than with the powerful

19. **(C)** is the correct answer; the cartoon shows the Republicans courting women and minorities (none of whom were allowed to vote, and yet the Republicans won anyway) and the Democrats courting big money and Southern "white trash." The picture of Lincoln and the mention of the *Dred Scott* decision (1857) should have tipped you off that (A) is wrong; Reconstruction began after the Civil War and Lincoln's assassination (1865). Scott was a slave who had sued for his liberty, won, then lost on appeal. The final appeal, to the Supreme Court, resulted in an aggressively pro-slavery decision that left the Civil War inevitable and imminent.

20. The most important commodities of the trans-Saharan trade route during the Middle Ages were

(A) gold and salt
(B) art and textiles
(C) spices and wine
(D) livestock and wood
(E) produce and coal

20. **(A)** is the correct answer. Gold was an important component of export trade and so was necessary to anyone who wanted to import anything of value. Salt, in the days before refrigeration, was the method of preserving food and as such was extremely valuable.

SECTION 4

QUESTIONS	EXPLANATIONS

21. Which of the following is NOT an example of conformity?

   (A) A committee member changes his vote in order to join the majority.
   (B) A customer waits in line to be served.
   (C) A pet owner trains his dog to bite people dressed in blue.
   (D) A soldier performs an act he feels is morally wrong because he is ordered to.
   (E) A diner waits to see what everyone else at the table orders before ordering her meal.

21. **(C)** is the correct answer. In answer choices (A) and (E), the person acting is allowing his/her actions to be influenced by what others are doing, which is one form of conformity. In answer choices (B) and (D), the person acting is conforming to societal/hierarchical norms. Conformity is an act intended to bring a person closer to the social norm in order to gain acceptance or anonymity. Answer choice (C) describes an act with quite a different, antisocial intent.

22. The population of a state determines the number of its representatives

   (A) on the President's cabinet
   (B) among the federal judiciary
   (C) in the Senate
   (D) in the House of Representatives
   (E) on congressional conference committees

22. **(D)** is the correct answer. Every state is represented by two Senators, regardless of its size. In the House of Representatives, however, representation is proportional to a state's population. Because representatives represent smaller constituencies, the House is considered the legislative body closer and more responsive to the will of the people. For this reason, the Constitution vests in it the power to initiate spending bills. The Senate, considered the more elite institution, was given the patrician duty of approving ambassadors and judges.

23. Thomas Jefferson opposed some of Alexander Hamilton's policies because Jefferson feared that those policies would

   (A) favor the wealthy and elite at the expense of the less well-off
   (B) result in a powerless Federal government
   (C) unfairly benefit the South at the expense of the North
   (D) assist the French in their revolution
   (E) lead to a Burr presidency

23. **(A)** is the correct answer. Hamilton supported a strong federal government as a protector of the interests of the rich and powerful; Jefferson wanted less federal government and looked to policies that would protect the rights of individuals, particularly against the rich and powerful. The other answer choices get history all wrong; Jefferson feared that Hamilton would make the Federal government too powerful and it was Jefferson, not Hamilton, who supported the French Revolution; Hamilton opposed it. Hamilton's banking policies, implemented during the Washington administration, strongly favored the moneyed interests of the North at the expense of the South. As far as Hamilton and Burr were concerned, the two were mortal enemies; Burr ultimately killed Hamilton in a duel. Also, Jefferson and Burr were Democrats, Hamilton a Federalist, so they were of opposing political parties.

SECTION 4

24. A society in which the main sources of employment are information and service industries is called

    (A) pastoral
    (B) agrarian
    (C) pluralistic
    (D) industrial
    (E) postindustrial

24. **(E)** is the correct answer. Postindustrial society is considered the next advancement beyond industrial society, in which the society's source of wealth and employment is primarily manufacturing. Pastoral societies are relatively underdeveloped and are centered on the domestication of animals. Nomads are often pastoral. Agrarian societies center around agriculture. A pluralistic society is one in which people of different ethnicities and cultures coexist without relinquishing their distinctive identities.

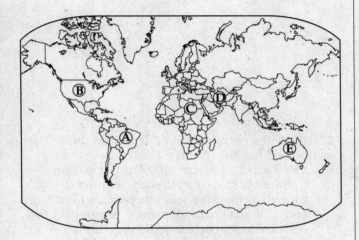

25. Which of the five locations, shown on the map above, has the heaviest annual rainfall?

    (A) A
    (B) B
    (C) C
    (D) D
    (E) E

25. **(A)** is the correct answer, in the Brazilian rain forest. Answer choice (B) is in the desert in Arizona; answer choice (C) is in the Sahara Desert; (D), in northern Iran, where rainfall is light; and (E) is in the Great Victoria Desert of Australia.

QUESTIONS	EXPLANATIONS

26. Margaret Mead is best known for her work in

(A) northern Africa, where her research led her to conclude that the human species originated near Egypt

(B) Eastern Europe, where her research led her to conclude that ethnic discrimination is a relatively recent phenomenon

(C) the mountains of Japan, where her research led her to conclude that Japanese culture had descended directly from Chinese culture

(D) the southwestern United States, where her research led her to conclude that Native Americans had migrated across the Bering Strait

(E) New Guinea, where her research led her to conclude that gender roles are primarily determined by culture, not biology

26. **(E)** is the correct answer. Mead is primarily known for such works as *Growing Up in New Guinea* (1928) and *Coming of Age in Samoa* (1931). Like the work of most ground-breaking scientists, Mead's has since come under tremendous scrutiny and some of it has been pretty well disproven. Still, both her successful contributions to the field and the attention she drew with her unconventional (particularly for her time) assertions continue to exert a major impact on anthropology. Many people who know nothing else about the field know that Margaret Mead was a famous anthropologist.

27. The first major Protestant break from the Catholic Church was instigated in Germany in 1517 by

(A) Joseph Smith
(B) John Knox
(C) Martin Luther
(D) Immanuel Kant
(E) John Calvin

27. **(C)** is the correct answer. In 1517, Luther posted his Ninety-Five Theses, in which he listed ninety-five criticisms of the Roman Catholic Church. Corruption within the Church at the time was rampant and flagrant, and Luther's criticisms aimed squarely at this corruption, particularly the practice of selling indulgences (absolution of sins) without assigning penance or expecting contrition. Although he originally intended to remain within the Church, Luther's rebellion quickly snowballed, resulting in a Lutheran Church and, soon thereafter, numerous Protestant denominations. Joseph Smith founded the Mormon faith. John Knox was a Scottish adherent of John Calvin's church (the Calvinists). Immanuel Kant was a great eighteenth-century German philosopher.

SECTION 4

28. Among the president's advisors, the secretary of state's authority is most likely to be threatened by the

   (A) secretary of commerce
   (B) secretary of health and human resources
   (C) vice president
   (D) chief justice of the Supreme Court
   (E) National security advisor

28. **(E)** is the correct answer. The National security advisor chairs the National Security Council, created in 1947 to deal with the consequences of the impending Cold War. Over time the NSA has gained increasing power in steering foreign policy. Henry Kissinger, Zbignew Brzezinski, John Poindexter, and Brent Scowcroft all occasionally usurped the secretary of state's authority to steer U.S. foreign policy. The secretaries of commerce and HHR both deal almost exclusively with domestic policies. The vice president has no defined duties other than presiding over the Senate, and a v.p.'s powers are basically those the president allows. The chief justice is not a presidential advisor.

29. Monetarists believe that the money supply should

   (A) be altered monthly in response to the health of the economy
   (B) be permanently set at a fixed level
   (C) be increased until a zero-level of unemployment is reached
   (D) grow and shrink at the exact rate of population growth
   (E) grow at a constant, predictable rate

29. **(E)** is the correct answer. Monetarists generally favor as little government intervention as possible; they believe that unpredictable shifts in the monetary supply result in economic instability, and point to inflation rates during the postwar period (a period of increased government economic intervention) as proof. Accordingly, most monetarists believe that constant and regular growth of the money supply would most likely result in economic stability and health.

30. Contemporaneous written records of Mayan civilization

   (A) did not exist, because the Mayans did not have a written language
   (B) were mostly preserved by Mayans, who hid them from invading Spanish forces
   (C) were preserved by Spanish historians who accompanied the conquistadors
   (D) were largely destroyed by the Spanish, who hoped to supplant indigenous Mayan culture with Christianity
   (E) were destroyed by the Mayans in order to prevent the Spaniards from seeing Mayan holy texts

30. **(D)** is the correct answer. Although the conquistadors and other Western interlopers in the New World were primarily interested in gaining wealth, they were also genuinely interested in spreading Christianity. In their zealousness to do so, they destroyed many of the documents that, had they survived, would today better illuminate the lives of the 100 million Native Americans who populated North and South America prior to Western exploration (many of whom died as a result of the introduction to their population of European diseases such as smallpox.) We include this last factoid not to be politically correct, but because it is very likely that there will be a question about this fact on your CLEP).

SECTION 4

31. Following a policy of appeasement, Western governments did not react with military force to Hitler's annexation of

    (A) Belgium
    (B) Holland
    (C) Poland
    (D) the Alsace-Lorraine region
    (E) the Sudetenland in Czechoslovakia

31. **(E)** is the correct answer. After uniting Austria with Germany, Hitler annexed the Sudetenland, claiming that the German-speaking population there wanted and deserved autonomy. Western governments should by then have understood Hitler's expansionist goals, but wary of confrontation, they chose to allow the annexation. The hope was that Hitler would be satisfied with what he had gotten and not go looking for more. It was an awful miscalculation. Not long after, Hitler annexed the rest of Czechoslovakia with no pretext, and soon invaded Poland, thus beginning World War II.

32. According to Freud, the conscience resides in the

    (A) id
    (B) Eros
    (C) ego
    (D) Thanatos
    (E) superego

32. **(E)** is the correct answer. Freud's theory of personality holds that humans have two basic, conflicting urges, one to procreate (Eros) and one to destroy (Thanatos). Personality develops to regulate these urges. The id is the part of one's personality that seeks immediate and total gratification. The superego, which develops through socialization, imposes order via the conscience (the knowledge that some actions and thoughts are both wrong and socially unacceptable) and the ego ideal (one's idealized self-image). Mediating between id and superego is the ego, which most closely corresponds to one's apparent personality.

33. Ancestor worship and the belief that all natural objects possess a soul is characteristic of

    (A) Shintoism
    (B) Zen Buddhism
    (C) Islam
    (D) Judaism
    (E) Catholicism

33. **(A)** is the correct answer. Shintoism, the native religion of Japan, is an animistic religion. It holds that the spirits of trees, weather, etc., influence earthly events, as do the spirits of ancestors after death.

SECTION 4

QUESTIONS	EXPLANATIONS

34. All of the following facilitated the French sale of the Louisiana Territory to the United States EXCEPT

   (A) an epidemic of yellow fever among the French in modern Haiti and the Dominican Republic

   (B) the absence of a French military presence in the New World

   (C) France's need for funds to support a European military campaign

   (D) a threatened military alliance between the U.S. and Great Britain against France

   (E) the slave revolt against the French in modern Haiti

34. **(B)** is the correct answer. The French had military units in the U.S. (they held New Orleans) and in St. Domingue, the island today known as the Dominican Republic (the eastern half of the island) and Haiti (the western half). That military presence was greatly diminished, however, by the slave revolt in Haiti and an epidemic of yellow fever (answer choices A and E). Napoleon decided to withdraw from the New World entirely in order to redeploy his troops in Europe, which he hoped to conquer. Jefferson engineered the beginnings of an alliance with Great Britain against the French, further encouraging Napoleon to cut his losses in the New World and concentrate his efforts elsewhere.

35. "No arts; no letters; no society; and which is worst of all, continual fear and danger of violent death; and the life of man, solitary, nasty, brutish, and short."

The quotation above, describing human relations outside the protection of the state, is from a work by

   (A) Thomas Hobbes
   (B) Rene Descartes
   (C) John Locke
   (D) John Stuart Mill
   (E) Jean-Jacques Rousseau

35. **(A)** is the correct answer. Hobbes was a defender of absolute monarchy. His thoughts on the subject are recorded in his classic tome *The Leviathan*, in which he compares the state to a human body, with the monarch as the head. Descartes is famous as a scientist and for his observation "I think, therefore I am," a cornerstone of ontology. John Locke opposed Hobbes, claiming that a ruler's authority came from the consent of the governed and not, as Hobbes had claimed, from God. Mill was a utilitarian philosopher, whose goal was to determine "the greatest good for the greatest number of people." Rousseau wrote *The Social Contract*, an influential philosophical work which followed in the tradition Locke had established.

36. The forums in which the purchase of labor, raw materials, equipment, and land by producers is conducted are called

   (A) currency exchanges
   (B) input markets
   (C) output markets
   (D) monopolies
   (E) oligopolies

36. **(B)** is the correct answer. The term input market refers to those markets in which producers buy what they need to produce goods, which they sell in output markets. A monopoly is a firm that controls the market for an entire good; an oligopoly is like a monopoly, except that control of the market is spread among a very few firms. A currency exchange is a market in which different foreign currencies are bought and sold.

SECTION 4

QUESTIONS	EXPLANATIONS

37. The Supreme Court decision *Brown v. Board of Education* concerned

    (A) segregation
    (B) school prayer
    (C) the theory of evolution
    (D) free speech
    (E) privacy

37. **(A)** is the correct answer. *Brown v. Board of Education* is the landmark decision that struck down the court's previous approval (*Plessy v. Ferguson*) of "separate but equal" facilities for blacks and whites in the South.

38. The world's most populous city is

    (A) London
    (B) Bangkok
    (C) Moscow
    (D) Chicago
    (E) Mexico City

38. **(E)** is the correct answer. Mexico City's population in 1992 was 23 million and it is still growing at a fast rate. Second is Sao Paolo, Brazil, with over 20 million. It, too, is growing quickly and could someday overtake Mexico City. Moscow has a population of about 7 million; it has the largest population of the four incorrect answer choices.

39. All of the following lived during the Renaissance period EXCEPT

    (A) Copernicus
    (B) Leonardo da Vinci
    (C) Giuseppe Garibaldi
    (D) Nicolo Macchiavelli
    (E) Vasco da Gama

39. **(C)** is the correct answer. Garibaldi was a mid–nineteenth-century revolutionary who was instrumental in uniting Italy. All of the others listed in the answer choices lived during the last part of the fifteenth century and the first half of the sixteenth century. Copernicus demonstrated that Earth circles the Sun, not vice versa, as had been believed. Leonardo was a master artist, scientist, and inventor. Macchiavelli wrote the definitive work on realpolitik, *The Prince*. Vasco da Gama sailed around the Cape of Good Hope, thereby establishing a sea route to India.

40. Which of the following is true about the internment of Japanese Americans by the United States during World War II?

    (A) Only 2,000 Japanese Americans were relocated.
    (B) Many of those relocated were known dissidents.
    (C) Some of those who were relocated later served in the U.S. armed forces.
    (D) Congress passed a law requiring the relocation of all aliens during the war.
    (E) Those who were relocated eventually recovered their homes and possessions.

40. **(C)** is the correct answer; this is a pretty p.c. question, typical of the CLEP. It's a question that makes a point, the point being that Americans should hang their heads in shame over this sorry chapter in our history. Over 100,000 Japanese Americans were relocated, and most if not all lost their homes and possessions. The relocation was mandated by presidential order; Congress was compliant in that it never acted to stop it, but that was the extent of congressional participation. There were not 100,000 Japanese American dissidents in the U.S. before the war, nor even half that many, making answer choice (B) incorrect.

SECTION 4

41. The concept of private land ownership is most likely to be found among a group of

    (A) nomadic herdsmen
    (B) food collectors
    (C) agriculturalists
    (D) horticulturalists
    (E) pastoralists

41. **(C)** is the correct answer. Nomadic herdsmen and pastoralists both travel the countryside, usually caring for animals. While they generally regard livestock as private property, they do not regard the land as being ownable. Food collectors (such as hunter-gatherers) and horticulturalists (many of whom practice "slash and burn") usually settle for brief periods of time, until the land can no longer support them, and then move on. Agriculturalists are generally sedentary, and it is among them that the notion of private land ownership is most likely to be common.

42. A person who believes both in elected government and collective ownership of a society's resources and industries would most likely be

    (A) a democratic socialist
    (B) an anarchist
    (C) a fascist
    (D) a free-market capitalist
    (E) a republican

42. **(A)** is the correct answer. Anarchists believe in as little government as possible; fascists believe that the government should control as much as possible. Free-market capitalists believe that the government should leave the economic sector of society alone, but do not necessarily have a preference about their nation's form of government. Republicans believe in elected, centralized government, but do not necessarily have a preference about their nation's economic system.

43. "These people were among the most militant of the ancient world. Males entered a military-style troop at the age of seven, joined the army at age twenty, and served until the age of sixty. The women enjoyed more rights than their counterparts elsewhere and could even hold property, but were still primarily regarded as producers of future warriors."

    The passage above describes the

    (A) Spartans
    (B) Athenians
    (C) Phoenicians
    (D) Trojans
    (E) Sumerians

43. **(A)** is the correct answer. After the Messenian slaves revolted against Spartan rule, Spartan society was regeared almost entirely toward the development of skillful, ruthless warriors. Boys were forced to fend for themselves from an early age and were responsible for their own clothing and sustenance. Service in the armed forces for all but a few lasted a lifetime. The nation's commerce and industry were left to area residents who were not Spartan, as the Spartans felt their army could spare no citizen.

SECTION 4

44. Which of the following is true of language development in children?

    (A) Children enter a babbling phase between the ages of eighteen and twenty-four months.
    (B) It is substantially similar among children of different cultures and languages.
    (C) Modern psychology holds that the development of language is the result of operant conditioning.
    (D) Children of different cultures differ in when they begin to use language by as much as three years.
    (E) Children begin to understand sentences at the same time they begin to speak in sentences.

44. **(B)** is the correct answer. Children of different cultures and languages generally start babbling at the same time (between the ages of six and twelve months) and generally make similar babbling noises ("gaga," "baba," and "deedee" are common). Other developmental periods—when children start using their first words, when they start to form sentences, etc.—generally occur at the same stage regardless of language or culture. Answer choice (C) is incorrect because there is of yet no unified theory as to how children learn language; the operant theory, put forward by B.F. Skinner, has been largely rejected. Answer choice (E) is incorrect because observation shows children understand sentences long before they can speak them.

45. When a market is in equilibrium, a subsequent increase in supply will usually result in

    (A) a decrease in demand
    (B) an increase in per-unit price
    (C) a decrease in per-unit price
    (D) inflation
    (E) a lack of consumer confidence

45. **(C)** is the correct answer. When a market is in equilibrium, an increase in supply will usually cause producers to lower prices in an effort to sell their product. Demand should remain stable, although it may well increase, depending on the nature of the product (i.e., is it something you can stockpile?) and how low prices fall.

46. The Constitution empowers the President to do all of the following EXCEPT

    (A) declare war
    (B) make treaties
    (C) grant reprieves and pardons
    (D) command the armed forces
    (E) appoint ambassadors

46. **(A)** is the correct answer. Only Congress has the right to declare war.

47. The belief that one's own culture is morally superior to others is called

    (A) normative behavior
    (B) social Darwinism
    (C) cultural relativism
    (D) xenophobia
    (E) ethnocentrism

47. **(E)** is the correct answer. Normative behavior is behavior that conforms to social norms (sorry, there's no other succinct way to put it). Social Darwinism is the belief that society performs in a Darwinist fashion, facilitating the success of "fitter" humans and the failure of those "less fit." Cultural relativism, the exact opposite of ethnocentrism, is the belief that cultures can only be judged relative to each other and that none are better or worse. Xenophobia is the fear of foreigners.

SECTION 4

QUESTIONS

EXPLANATIONS

48. Before the construction of the Panama Canal, ships traveling from New York to San Francisco usually sailed

    (A) below the southern tip of Africa
    (B) below the southern tip of South America
    (C) above the northern tip of Canada
    (D) above the northern tip of Europe and Asia
    (E) through a difficult network of lakes and canals across the northern border of the United States

48. **(B)** is the correct answer. The northern routes mentioned above are impassable most times of the year because of ice. Sailing below Africa would be taking the long way around. There is no such network of lakes and canals as described in answer choice (E).

49. "The supreme good is like water which nourishes all things without trying to. It is content with the low places that people disdain. Thus it is like the Tao."

    The lines above were written by

    (A) Mohammed
    (B) Confucius
    (C) Lao-tzu
    (D) Moses
    (E) Saint Paul

49. **(C)** is the correct answer. Lao-tzu is the author of the *Tao Te Ching*, the central book of the Chinese philosophy of Taoism (Tao means "the way"). A contemporary of Confucius, Lao-tzu set his focus on the spiritual realm and humanity's place in creation, as opposed to Confucius, whose interests lay mainly with the mundane.

Question 50 refers to the chart below:

AMERICAN OPINION OF THE PRESIDENT'S CHARACTER 1964-1984 (Percentage answering "yes")					
The President is	1964	1969	1973	1980	1984
trustworthy	73%	48%	30%	65%	58%
capable	70%	59%	67%	34%	55%
compassionate	66%	52%	48%	64%	53%

50. Which of the following can be inferred from the above?

    (A) Presidents don't have to be considered compassionate in order to win elections.
    (B) The Watergate scandal affected the public perception of Nixon's capability to serve as president.
    (C) Every president between Kennedy and Bush has suffered from a lack of public trust.
    (D) Public perception of Nixon's trustworthiness dropped during his tenure.
    (E) Ronald Reagan was the most popular president of the last 30 years.

50. **(D)** is the correct answer. 1969 and 1973 are both years during Nixon's tenure. While 48 percent of the public considered Nixon trustworthy in 1969, only 30 percent felt the same way in 1974. Don't try to read between the lines too much on inference questions; the correct answer will be indisputable based on the statistics presented. Answer choice (B) is a case in point; it tries to bait you with a generalization about the Watergate scandal. Note, however, that public perception of Nixon's capability actually increased between the 1969 and 1973 polls. Even if it hadn't, there would be no way, based on this polling data, to conclude that Watergate (as opposed to some other event, such as the withdrawal from Vietnam) was the cause of change in public perception of his capability to serve as president.

SECTION 4

51. There is a positive correlation between improvement of one's social class and all of the following EXCEPT

    (A) level of education
    (B) life span
    (C) number of children borne
    (D) mental health
    (E) physical health

51. **(C)** is the correct answer. Sociological studies show that the better one's class status, the more likely one is to achieve a higher level of education and live a longer, healthier life. Improvement in class status correlates negatively with the number of children borne; the better one's status gets, the fewer children one is likely to have.

52. Which of the following lists the reigns of Augustus Caesar, Caligula, Claudius, Julius Caesar, Nero, and Tiberius in chronological order?

    (A) Caligula, Nero, Julius Caesar, Claudius, Augustus Caesar, Tiberius
    (B) Augustus Caesar, Caligula, Tiberius, Julius Caesar, Nero, Claudius
    (C) Julius Caesar, Caligula, Claudius, Nero, Tiberius, Augustus Caesar
    (D) Tiberius, Nero, Julius Caesar, Augustus Caesar, Claudius, Caligula
    (E) Julius Caesar, Augustus Caesar, Tiberius, Caligula, Claudius, Nero

52. **(E)** is the correct answer. Julius Caesar was named dictator for life in 44 B.C., effectively if not actually bringing the Roman Republic to an end. A power struggle after his assassination resulted in Octavian (renamed Augustus Caesar) gaining control. He ruled from 27 B.C. until his death in A.D. 14. Tiberius ruled from A.D. 14 to A.D. 37 and was succeeded by Caligula, "the monster." Claudius followed (A.D. 41 to A.D. 54) with a reign that generated a number of Robert Graves books and a really good PBS series. Nero ruled, poorly, until his death in A.D. 68. A good and surprisingly entertaining source of information about the Caesars is Suetonius' *The Twelve Caesars*, a contemporary history. It gets a little dull after Nero dies, but up to that point it's a hoot and a half.

53. The inflation rate is defined as the average annual increase in

    (A) unemployment
    (B) gross national product
    (C) amount of leisure time available to the average citizen
    (D) prices
    (E) disparity between the wealthiest and poorest members of a society

53. **(D)** is the correct answer. Inflation refers to an increase in the cost of goods, which is measured by price indices. The consumer price index (CPI) is the price index most commonly referenced in the media; it measures the cost of living for the average consumer. Other price indices measure the cost of raw goods, labor, etc.

SECTION 4

54. Fill in the blanks:

The Sherman Anti-Trust Act, used for its first decade as a weapon against _____, later became the government's most effective tool against _____.

(A) political parties . . . lobbyists

(B) unethical gold speculators . . . corrupt bankers

(C) proponents of slavery . . . carpetbaggers

(D) subversive propagandists . . . government censorship

(E) labor unions . . . corporate monopolies

54. **(E)** is the correct answer. The Sherman Anti-Trust Act of 1890 was designed to protect trade against unfair restraints. It was vaguely worded and left much discretion in the hands of the government, which at the time was extremely friendly to big business interests, regardless of ethics. The government initially refused to use the act to break up monopolies; further, it decided that unions were an unfair restraint against trade, and used the law to crush strikes with federal troops. The law's first application was to break a railway strike; not long after, the Supreme Court ruled that the law could not be used against manufacturers, thereby excluding a large number of corporate monopolies from its scope. Twelve years later, Teddy Roosevelt turned the law against a number of corporate trusts. At the same time, he stopped the practice of using federal troops against striking workers, thereby affording the unions the opportunity to grow.

55. Political revolutions most often occur in societies when

(A) social conditions are extremely poor and the government is extremely oppressive

(B) social conditions remain the same for extended periods of time

(C) new racial or ethnic groups are introduced

(D) elections have recently been held, with inconclusive results

(E) social conditions improve somewhat, but not as quickly as the majority wishes

55. **(E)** is the correct answer. According to historian Crane Brinton, revolutions usually occur not when conditions are at their worst but rather when they start to get better. Citizens under extremely repressive governments are usually too frightened to revolt, much as they may secretly wish to.

SECTION 4

56. One major difference between operant and Pavlovian conditioning is that

   (A) operant conditioning never uses food as a stimulus
   (B) operant responses are voluntary, while Pavlovian responses are involuntary
   (C) Pavlovian conditioning is permanent
   (D) an operant response is instantaneous, while a Pavlovian response follows a long delay
   (E) Pavlovian stimuli are always sonic

56. **(B)** is the correct answer. Operant conditioning involves training an animal that a certain behavior, such as pressing a bar, is rewarded (usually with food, water, or some other basic need). Pavlovian conditioning involves pairing an unconditioned stimulus, such as food, with a conditioned stimulus, such as a bell (while the stimulus can be sonic, it need not necessarily be). The unconditioned stimulus must evoke an unconditioned response (the classic example is salivation). In time, the subject of Pavlovian conditioning will salivate in response to the conditioned stimulus. That response is, of course, involuntary (just try to voluntarily salivate—it's not easy!). Pavlovian conditioning is not permanent; when the conditioned stimulus is not paired with the unconditioned stimulus, the conditioned response will eventually disappear in a process called *extinction*. Pavlovian responses are instantaneous.

57. The boycott of the Montgomery bus system by African Americans

   (A) occurred at the height of the civil rights movement of the mid-1960s
   (B) was led by Malcolm X
   (C) was instigated by the arrest of Rosa Parks
   (D) lasted for three weeks and failed to achieve its goal
   (E) was staged to protest the assassination of Martin Luther King

57. **(C)** is the correct answer. The Montgomery boycott occurred in 1956; it and *Brown v. Board of Education* are the starting points of the Civil Rights movement. The boycott also brought Martin Luther King (1929-1968) to national prominence. Twenty-seven years old at the time, King was pastor of Parks' church. Although clearly groomed for greatness—his grandfather had led the protests resulting in Atlanta's first black high school, his father was a minister and community leader, and King had already amassed impressive academic credentials (Morehead College, Crozier Theological Seminary, University of Pennsylvania, and finally, a Ph.D. from Boston University)—the yearlong bus boycott gave him his first national podium. King organized peaceful protests based in principle on his studies of Thoreau and Gandhi, and in these protests he saw the springboard to the national civil rights movement he would spearhead for the next decade (until his assassination).

SECTION 4

QUESTIONS	EXPLANATIONS

58. The debate over whether genetics or upbringing is the most prominent influence on intelligence and behavior is characterized by the phrase

    (A) "mind over matter"
    (B) "man against machine"
    (C) "nature versus nurture"
    (D) "feast or famine"
    (E) "the individual good versus the general good"

58. **(C)** is the correct answer. The "nature versus nurture" debate is one that is constantly played out in sociology.

59. The field of paleoanthropology is primarily concerned with the study of the

    (A) history of all species during the Paleozoic period
    (B) emergence and evolution of the human species
    (C) extinction of the dinosaurs
    (D) variations in population growth rates among different contemporary human populations
    (E) contemporary primitive populations of the South Pacific

59. **(B)** is the correct answer. Paleoanthropology is one discipline in the field of physical anthropology. Physical anthropology differs from cultural anthropology in that the former primarily studies the biological history of humanity, while the latter studies human cultural artifacts. Another major discipline within the field of physical anthropology is the study of human variation, or why and in what ways contemporary human populations vary biologically.

60. The area of Australia is approximately

    (A) one-third the area of mainland China
    (B) the same as the area of India
    (C) the same as the area of the forty-eight contiguous United States
    (D) twice the area of Texas
    (E) three times the area of Canada

60. **(C)** is the correct answer; both Australia and the forty-eight contiguous United States are approximately 3 million square miles in area. China has an area of approximately 3.5 million square miles; India, 1.3 million square miles; Texas, 250,000 square miles; and Canada, nearly 4 million square miles.

SECTION 4

QUESTIONS	EXPLANATIONS

61. In his play *The Crucible*, Arthur Miller compares the Salem witch trials of the seventeenth century to the

 (A) Red Scare of the 1950s
 (B) events leading up to World War I
 (C) Communist Revolution in the Soviet Union
 (D) Supreme Court decision *Marbury v. Madison*
 (E) fall of the Roman Empire

61. **(A)** is the correct answer. During the 1950s, fear of being labeled "Communist" grew so great in the U.S. that many industries established blacklists barring from work anyone under even the slightest of suspicion of Communist ties. People who had attended one socialist rally twenty years prior, people who were friends with socialists, people who had signed petitions supporting liberal causes suddenly found themselves without work or credit. The House Un-American Activities Committee and Senate committees chaired by Joseph McCarthy called hundreds of witnesses in their efforts to uproot Communism from the government and the entertainment industry. Attacks on the entertainment industry hit Miller where he lived, and he responded with a play purportedly about the hysteria that led to the Salem witch trials, but which was clearly about McCarthy's crusade. Even if you are not familiar with the play, you should have been able to guess this one by choosing the answer choice most clearly analogous to the Salem witch trials. The Russian Revolution is the allegorical subject of Orwell's *Animal Farm*.

62. The Muslim influence on medieval Spain resulted in all of the following except

 (A) banking and credit systems
 (B) terrace farming
 (C) development of the sciences
 (D) heightened religious intolerance
 (E) irrigation

62. **(D)** is the correct answer. The Muslims, who held Spain for several centuries and remained there after the Catholic Church regained control, had established a tradition of religious tolerance unmatched in the rest of Europe. Muslims, Jews, and Christians were free to practice their faiths. Dedication to the arts and sciences was also a hallmark of medieval Muslim society, and the Muslims were responsible for many of the advances made in physics, mathematics, medicine, and philosophy during the Middle Ages.

63. The demise of the castle as an effective defensive structure was brought about primarily by the development of

 (A) the catapult
 (B) the submarine
 (C) gunpowder weapons
 (D) armor
 (E) the airplane

63. **(C)** is the correct answer. Cannons provided for the first time an effective offense against castle walls, while the development of muskets proved a great equalizer among combatants.

SECTION 4

PART II

64. World War I is often said to have led directly to World War II because

    (A) border skirmishes between France and Spain were never resolved during the first war

    (B) the victors neglected to disarm Germany after the war

    (C) the harshness of the Treaty of Versailles created widespread resentment among the German people

    (D) the cost of the war led directly and immediately to the Great Depression

    (E) the postwar European map contained too many large and powerful nations

64. **(C)** is the correct answer. The victors of World War I sought terms of reparation so harsh that few robust nations could have met them, much less one that had just fought a losing war. The Treaty of Versailles eviscerated (but did not disband) the German army and navy, forced Germany to cede land and accept an occupational force, and demanded reparations Germany could not afford. The result was a resentful German public much more open to Hitler's message than it might otherwise have been. Answer choice (E), by the way, is totally incorrect; in fact, the postwar map included too many small, fragile nations, all of which Hitler easily rolled over once he began his conquests.

65. A Mercator projection map distorts which of the following geographical features?

    (A) The intensity of climatic shifts between regions

    (B) The area of land masses

    (C) The uniformity of ocean currents

    (D) The isolation, by region, of the world's languages

    (E) The amount of rainfall near the equator

65. **(B)** is the correct answer. The Mercator projection map is the flat map that makes Greenland look like it's really, really big. That's because the Mercator map makes no adjustment for the fact that the world is round; thus, those land masses near the poles, where longitude and latitude lines bunch up, appear much larger than they actually are.

66. The Supreme Court decision *Marbury v. Madison* established the principle of

    (A) one man, one vote

    (B) separate but equal

    (C) no taxation without representation

    (D) gerrymandering

    (E) judicial review

66. **(E)** is the correct answer. In *Marbury v. Madison*, Justice John Marshall declared a section of the Judiciary Act of 1789 unconstitutional, thereby establishing as precedent the Supreme Court's power to overturn legislation on the basis of unconstitutionality. "One man, one vote," if you add the qualifiers "white" and "property-holding"' to the word "man," is the principle by which nascent American democracy was governed. The principle of "separate but equal" was established by *Plessy v. Ferguson*, later to be overturned by *Brown v. Board of Education*. "No taxation without representation" was a rallying cry of the American Revolution. Gerrymandering is the practice of drawing voting districts in such a way as to create artificial majorities or to give one party an unfair advantage in state legislative elections, typically by trying to concentrate all those supporting the opposition party in as few districts as possible.

SECTION 4

67. Which of the following is least likely to result in an increase in aggregate demand?

    (A) a decrease in income taxes
    (B) an increase in interest rates
    (C) an increase in the Federal budget
    (D) an increase in net exports
    (E) an increase in government entitlement payments

67. **(B)** is the correct answer. Aggregate demand is the sum of consumer spending, investment, government spending, and the trade balance (value of exports minus value of imports). Anything that increases consumer spending (answers (A), (E)), government spending (C), or favorably shifts the balance of trade (D) increases aggregate demand. An increase in interest rates generally will result in a decrease in consumer spending. It may result in an increase in investment spending, but that result will be a zero-sum gain, not a net increase.

68. The process by which a minority group modifies its distinctive characteristics in order to conform with a dominant society is called

    (A) resocialization
    (B) cultural lag
    (C) cohabitation
    (D) assimilation
    (E) a folkway

68. **(D)** is the correct answer. Socialization is the process of altering one's basic values and attitudes; it can be either voluntary (e.g., converting to a new religion) or involuntary (e.g., incarceration). Cultural lag describes the difference in time between changes in the material culture (e.g., technology) and the non-material (e.g., attitudinal) adjustments to those changes. Cohabitation is the term used to describe an intimate relationship between a non-married couple sharing a living space. Folkways are those activities that are routine to a culture's daily life.

69. The Sixth Amendment of the U.S. Constitution guarantees a criminal defendant all of the following EXCEPT:

    (A) the right to confront prosecution witnesses
    (B) bail will not be excessive
    (C) a speedy, public trial
    (D) a defense lawyer
    (E) a jury trial

69. **(B)** is the correct answer. The constitutional prohibition against excessive bail is part of the Eighth Amendment, which also prohibits cruel and unusual punishment.

70. The Missouri Compromise established

    (A) Missouri, and all subsequent states, as "slave-free" territories
    (B) the boundaries of all future states located within the Louisiana Territory
    (C) the rights of riverboat proprietors to transact business along the Mississippi River
    (D) more democratic means of determining the size of each state's congressional delegation
    (E) Missouri's southern border as the dividing line between "free" and "slave" states

70. **(E)** is the correct answer. The Missouri Compromise, devised by Henry Clay and signed into law in 1820, was intended to fend off an immediate confrontation over slavery in new territories, which, with the Louisiana Purchase, had suddenly become a major issue. With both sides intransigent on the issue of slavery, the compromise bought the country some time but, of course, proved no permanent solution to the crisis that ultimately led to the Civil War.

SECTION 4

QUESTIONS	EXPLANATIONS

71. A society's culture is said to be integrated when
   (A) it is practiced only by the ruling elite of the society
   (B) it requires certain practices of men only, and other practices of women only
   (C) it is shared by two or more ethnic groups, even if those groups do not interact
   (D) different aspects of the culture are consistent with, as opposed to contradictory to, one another
   (E) religious, military, and government positions of authority are largely held by the same people or class

71. **(D)** is the correct answer. The term integrated culture is used by anthropologists to describe the fact that component parts of a culture work in harmony with one another. If that seems kind of obvious, remember that the study of anthropology is the study of human culture, and that it describes a lot of things we take for granted precisely because we, and the dictates of our lives, are the subjects of that study.

72. Developmental psychologists use the term instrumental aggression to refer to behavior in which an aggressor
   (A) hurts someone by accident
   (B) acts to achieve a goal
   (C) reacts to an attack with greater force than the attacker used
   (D) attacks with a weapon
   (E) repeatedly attacks the same person without provocation

72. **(B)** is the correct answer. Instrumental aggression is aggressive behavior used as a means toward an end. For example, a child wishing to get to the head of a line may attempt to intimidate those children ahead of him into letting him have his way. Developmental psychologists differentiate instrumental aggression from exploratory aggression, in which a child hurts another unintentionally while exploring and learning, and from hostile aggression, in which a child hurts another with the main goal of inflicting pain (perhaps in retribution for an embarrassment).

73. "From Stettin in the Baltic to Trieste in the Adriatic, an iron curtain has descended across the Continent. Behind that line lie all the capitals of the ancient states of Central and Eastern Europe."

   The quotation above is from a speech by whom, and to what situation was the speaker referring?
   (A) Georges Clemenceau, the outbreak of World War I
   (B) Benito Mussolini, the Nazi invasion of Poland
   (C) Woodrow Wilson, the Russian Revolution
   (D) Winston Churchill, the Soviet takeover of Eastern Europe
   (E) George Bush, the fall of the Berlin Wall

73. **(D)** is the correct answer. The quote is from a famous speech given by Churchill after World War II. The phrase "iron curtain" stuck and became the preeminent metaphor for the divide between the Western market democracies and the Eastern Soviet client states.

SECTION 4

74. In 1912, the last Manchu emperor abdicated the Chinese throne. His government was replaced by

    (A) a dictatorship, led by Chou En-lai
    (B) a Communist government, led by Mao Tse-Tung
    (C) a Republic, led by Yuan Shih-k'ai
    (D) a Socialist democracy, led by Ho Chi Minh
    (E) a monarchy, led by Sun Yat-sen

74. **(C)** is the correct answer. This is a question you might have to answer by process of elimination. The Communist revolution didn't succeed in China until 1949, and both Chou En-lai and Mao Tse-Tung were prominent Communist leaders. Ho Chi Minh was a Vietnamese hero and once ruled North Vietnam, but never China. The Emperor was replaced by a republic which, after the demise of Yuan Shih-k'ai, was led by the more famous (in the West, anyway) Chiang Kai-shek.

75. Australia has summer when the United States has winter because, relative to the United States, Australia is

    (A) closer to the Arctic Circle
    (B) across the international date line
    (C) across the equator
    (D) closer to the equator
    (E) more humid

75. **(C)** is the correct answer. The equator is the dividing line for the seasons. The earth spins on an axis which tilts towards and away from the sun. Summer occurs in the Northern Hemisphere when the northern end of the axis is tilted toward the sun, bringing the Northern Hemisphere more directly into the sun's rays. When the northern end of the axis tilts away from the sun, the Southern Hemisphere receives the sun's rays more directly.

76. The power of an executive to reject parts of a legislative bill while enacting others is called

    (A) an executive agreement
    (B) a policy shift
    (C) a pocket veto
    (D) a line-item veto
    (E) a plea bargain

76. **(D)** is the correct answer. A line-item veto allows a chief executive to veto parts of a bill while maintaining others. An executive agreement is an agreement between the president and another nation's head of state and has the force of law, even though it does not require congressional approval. Policy shift is a term used to describe what happens when a government policy changes. A pocket veto occurs when the president does not sign a bill within ten days of its arrival on his desk AND Congress adjourns during that ten-day period. A plea bargain is a way for a criminal defendant to avoid trial by pleading guilty to lesser charges.

SECTION 4

QUESTIONS	EXPLANATIONS

77. All of the following are actions the Federal Reserve Board might take to invigorate a sluggish economy EXCEPT

   (A) lowering bank reserve requirements

   (B) selling government securities on the open market

   (C) buying bonds on the open market

   (D) encouraging member banks to make more loans

   (E) lowering the discount rate

77. **(B)** is the correct answer. The Federal Reserve Board would likely pursue one or more strategies for introducing more money into the marketplace if it were attempting to invigorate a sluggish economy. Lowering reserve requirements would allow banks to lend proportionally more of their holdings; lowering the discount rate would make it cheaper for banks to borrow from the Fed, thereby spurring loans to businesses and private citizens; and encouraging banks to make more loans would also, presumably, increase the number of loans made and hence the amount of money in the economy. When the Fed buys bonds on the open market, it puts more money into the market. When it sells securities, conversely, it takes money out of the economy.

78. The Potsdam Declaration of World War II

   (A) stated that Germany had an irrevocable right to the Alsace-Lorraine region

   (B) announced Italy's intention to enter the war

   (C) served as the framework for the European peace treaty following the war

   (D) warned the Japanese that failure to surrender would result in "prompt and utter destruction"

   (E) outlined the plan for U.S. entry into the war in Europe

78. **(D)** is the correct answer. At Potsdam, President Truman, along with Chiang Kai-Shek and Winston Churchill, issued a veiled ultimatum (the Potsdam Declaration) to the Japanese. The document did not specifically mention the atomic bomb, although in retrospect it is clear that it threatened. The CLEP may ask a question regarding Truman's reasons for dropping the bomb. Here are some common answers: Truman wished to avert a ground war, as there was evidence that such a war would have been both long and bloody. Furthermore, he wanted to end the war with Japan before the Soviet Union got involved; Truman was already looking ahead and seeing the Cold War, with the Soviet Union as the greatest future threat to U.S. security. Truman saw Hiroshima and Nagasaki as opportunities to demonstrate to the U.S.S.R. both U.S. might and the nation's willingness to use it. Finally, contemporary science knew relatively little about radiation and its terrible effects on life, so that Truman's decision was in part informed by the fact that he was ill-informed.

SECTION 4

79. The principle of the fundamental attribution error states that a person will tend to judge others' behavior

    (A) based on a realistic assessment of how he or she would behave under similar circumstances
    (B) less accurately than that person judges his or her own behavior
    (C) leniently, especially if such behavior has no adverse effect on the person judging it
    (D) by stricter standards than that person judges himself or herself
    (E) arbitrarily and without reference to any moral or ethical standards

79. **(D)** is the correct answer. Psychologists have discovered that people err in their assessment of causal relations depending on their own situation, demonstrating a bias toward themselves and a corresponding lack of charity toward others. Hence, we tend to judge others more harshly than they deserve and ourselves less harshly than we deserve. Common sense should have helped you eliminate answer choices (A) and (B), as each indicates a wisdom one should have learned through personal experience that humans don't have. Answer choice (E) also defies common sense and should be eliminated.

80. Civilization probably began in

    (A) North America
    (B) western Europe
    (C) Mesopotamia and the Nile Valley
    (D) New Guinea and Australia
    (E) the British Isles

80. **(C)** is the correct answer. Mesopotamia is what the Greeks called the region between the Tigris and Euphrates Rivers (in parts of modern day Iraq, Syria, and Turkey). The land was unusually fertile—it is also referred to as "the Fertile Crescent"—and therefore well-suited for agriculture. So too was the Nile Valley. Not surprisingly, two of the great early civilizations were Egypt (Nile Valley) and Persia (Mesopotamia).

81. A group of influential people who hold sway over government, economic, and military activity is called a

    (A) silent majority
    (B) proletariat
    (C) counterculture
    (D) political party
    (E) power elite

81. **(E)** is the correct answer. Silent majority is a term coined by Richard Nixon to describe those who supported his Vietnam policy but did not demonstrate, as did its opponents. Proletariat is a term used to describe those who work as wage earners at jobs that require manual or physical labor. A counterculture is a group organized around activities that greatly differ from cultural norms. A political party is a group of people who are organized around similar beliefs and who nominate and support candidates for public office.

82. An individual's status in a caste system is primarily

    (A) earned through good deeds
    (B) bought with cash, goods, and services
    (C) decided, upon reaching adulthood, by a religious leader
    (D) assigned arbitrarily
    (E) ascribed by birth

82. **(E)** is the correct answer. A caste system is an extremely stratified and rigid system of determining one's status in society. Status, through caste membership, is determined by the caste of one's parents. South Africa during the apartheid era was a classic caste system, and conspicuous remnants of India's caste system (officially outlawed in 1949) remain to this day.

SECTION 4

QUESTIONS	EXPLANATIONS

83. Jean Piaget is best known for his work in the field of

   (A) cultural anthropology
   (B) semiotic literary criticism
   (C) revisionist history
   (D) free market economics
   (E) developmental psychology

83. **(E)** is the correct answer. Piaget (1896-1980) studied children at various ages in his efforts to understand intelligence and the learning process. He theorized that children pass through four stages of cognitive development, progressing from ignorance to progressively more comprehensive and complex understandings of the world around them.

84. Between 1649 and 1660, the English government was a

   (A) monarchy under Charles I
   (B) monarchy under Elizabeth I
   (C) monarchy under Henry VIII
   (D) commonwealth under Oliver Cromwell
   (E) commonwealth under Winston Churchill

84. **(D)** is the correct answer. Civil war, a result of heavy taxes and religious disputes, interrupted royal control of England in 1649. From the various factions opposed to the king, Oliver Cromwell, a Calvinist, emerged as ruler. Cromwell ruled, capably, until his death, at which point popular sentiment swung back toward the monarchy, leading to the restoration of the crown. Charles II was recalled from exile and resumed the English monarchy, which has continued uninterrupted ever since.

85. The Mississippi River creates borders between all the following pairs of states EXCEPT

   (A) Mississippi and Arkansas
   (B) Tennessee and Arkansas
   (C) Texas and Arkansas
   (D) Illinois and Missouri
   (E) Illinois and Iowa

85. **(C)** is the correct answer. The Mississippi River cuts through Louisiana to the Mississippi-Arkansas border. The Mississippi runs along Arkansas' eastern border; Arkansas shares its southwestern border with Texas.

86. Turkey was ruled from the fourteenth to the early twentieth century by the

   (A) Ottoman empire
   (B) Mughal dynasty
   (C) Safavids
   (D) Shah of Iran
   (E) Holy Roman empire

86. **(A)** is the correct answer. The Ottoman empire grew from the victories of Osman, who through conquest unified the nomadic tribes of Turkey near the turn of the fourteenth century. The empire is known for its highly developed bureaucratic government, its military, and the flourishing of Islamic culture the empire oversaw during the sixteenth century. The Mughal dynasty ruled India from the beginning of the sixteenth century to the middle of the nineteenth century. The Safavids ruled Iran. The Ottoman, Mughal, and Safavid empires are known as the "Gunpowder Empires," because their ascendance was facilitated by the development of gunpowder weapons. Shah is a title that has been used by a number of Iranian rulers, including Mughal emperors. The Holy Roman empire was a Germanic empire that ruled from the tenth century until it was officially disbanded by Napoleon in the early nineteenth century.

SECTION 4

QUESTIONS	EXPLANATIONS

87. The primary reason for U.S. involvement in Vietnam was

    (A) the necessity to protect massive oil reserves which were the United States' primary source of energy

    (B) the fear that a Communist takeover of Viet nam would lead to a Communist takeover of the entire region

    (C) the desire to protect one of the region's only long-standing democratic regimes

    (D) to establish a base from which an offensive attack could be launched against Communist China

    (E) to protect American business interests in the region

87. **(B)** is the correct answer. Throughout the Cold War, United States foreign policy subscribed to the Domino Theory, which stated that the fall of one country to Communism would quickly lead to the fall of many others in the same region. Otherwise, Vietnam held no real strategic value to the United States; the U.S. had established a presence in the region through alliances with South Korea, Thailand, Japan, Taiwan, the Philippines, etc. The Vietnamese government that the U.S. supported was a right-wing government that had been installed with the help of the CIA; it was not a flourishing democracy.

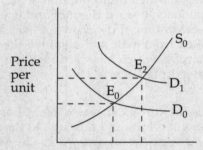

88. The graph above demonstrates that when demand increases and supply stays constant in an economy in equilibrium,

    (A) both equilibrium price and equilibrium quantity rise

    (B) equilibrium price rises and equilibrium quantity falls

    (C) equilibrium price stays constant and equilibrium quantity rises

    (D) equilibrium price falls and equilibrium quantity rises

    (E) both equilibrium price and equilibrium quantity stay constant

88. **(A)** is the correct answer. In the graph, supply remains at a constant rate (S_0) while demand shifts to the right (from D_0 to D_1). The result is a shift in the point of equilibrium (from E_0 to E_1) such that both the price per unit and the number of units sold increases. You don't really need the chart to figure out the answer to this one, just pure common sense. The law of supply and demand tells you that if demand increases and the supply stays constant, the price of an item will increase. Only answer choice (A) provides you that option.

89. When a public opinion poll proves inaccurate, the problem is usually that

    (A) the polling organization surveyed too large a group

    (B) data collectors misrecorded responses

    (C) the poll was taken in person, rather than by phone

    (D) the population surveyed did not constitute a representative sample

    (E) respondents weren't interested in the survey topic

89. **(D)** is the correct answer. The accuracy of a poll depends in large part on how well the survey sample matches the population at large. With a good representative sample, a small group—fewer than 2,000—can accurately reflect the opinions of America's 200,000,000 eligible voters. Other important factors in determining the accuracy of a poll include the wording of the questions and the tone of voice of the interviewer.

SECTION 4

QUESTIONS	EXPLANATIONS

90. Who among the following is NOT associated with the Romantic period?

    (A) William Wordsworth
    (B) Daniel Defoe
    (C) George Noel Gordon, Lord Byron
    (D) Percy Bysshe Shelley
    (E) John Keats

90. **(B)** is the correct answer. Defoe wrote *Robinson Crusoe* in 1745. The Romantic period, marked by a love of nature and an emphasis on the primacy of human beings and individual experience, began around 1800 and ran through the first three-quarters of the century.

91. Peasants are distinguished from subsistence farmers by the fact that peasants

    (A) form completely autonomous communities
    (B) participate in extra-agricultural social groups, such as guilds and churches
    (C) must produce excess crops in order to pay rent to a landlord
    (D) have great opportunity to rise through the hierarchy of the societies in which they reside
    (E) exist only under a monarchical form of government

91. **(D)** is the correct answer. Peasantry is a class development that accompanies the rise of the standard of living in pre-commercial societies. As standards of living rise and more and better goods are sought by more people, intercommunity trade evolves and, *voilà*, commerce has begun. With commerce come such developments as private property and the need for excess wealth (for trade). Peasants help create excess wealth by producing more crops than they need to survive, and turning over the excess to the landowner as rent. The landowner, in turn, uses the crops for trade.

92. Which of the following pieces of legislation posed the greatest threat to the U.S. Constitution's guarantee of freedom of the press?

    (A) the Alien and Sedition Acts
    (B) the National Industrial Recovery Act
    (C) the Civil Rights Act of 1964
    (D) the Census Act
    (E) the Federal Securities Act

92. **(A)** is the correct answer. The Alien and Sedition Acts, enacted during John Adams' administration, allowed the government to deport foreigners it suspected of threatening national security, and also allowed the government to fine or imprison those who wrote "falsely and maliciously" against the government. It was used by the government to silence newspapers and journals critical of its policies. The National Industrial Recovery Act and the Federal Securities Act were both New Deal programs; the former was designed to revitalize industry, the latter established a body to police trading on Wall Street. The Civil Rights Act of 1964 guaranteed a slate of rights to minorities and women; the Census Act established the national census in 1790.

93. The term ethnic group is used to describe a group with

    (A) a shared culture
    (B) shared physical characteristics
    (C) a shared economic status
    (D) differing physical characteristics
    (E) differing religious beliefs

93. **(A)** is the correct answer. Ethnic groups often share national origin, language, religion, practices, and beliefs. Race refers to a group with shared physical characteristics. Class refers to a group with a shared economic status.

SECTION 4

QUESTIONS	EXPLANATIONS

94. Overwhelming and irrational fear associated with a particular thing or experience is called a

    (A) mesomorph
    (B) fetish
    (C) premoral stage
    (D) phobia
    (E) separation anxiety

94. **(D)** is the correct answer. Yes, occasionally the CLEP will give you a question that is this easy. A mesomorph is a stocky, muscular body. A fetish is a sexual preoccupation with an object, such as an article of clothing. The premoral stage is that period of life preceding awareness of moral concerns. Separation anxiety is an overwhelming fear associated with the loss of an "attachment figure" (e.g., a family, a car, etc.).

95. Which of the following statements about the U.S. government is true?

    (A) The Federal Bureau of Investigation is an agency of the judicial branch.
    (B) A tie vote in the Senate is broken by the Speaker of the House.
    (C) Appropriations bills must originate in the Senate.
    (D) A congressional bill can become law without the president's signature.
    (E) Congress nominates candidates for the Supreme Court.

95. **(D)** is the correct answer; if the President fails to sign a bill for ten days and Congress remains in session for that ten-day period, that bill becomes law without the President's signature. The FBI is part of the executive branch of government. A tie vote in the Senate is broken by the vice president. Appropriations bills must originate in the House of Representatives. The President nominates candidates for the Supreme Court, who must then be approved by the Senate.

96. An Islamic religious war is called a

    (A) mosque
    (B) salaam
    (C) halal
    (D) Koran
    (E) jihad

96. **(E)** is the correct answer. A mosque is an Islamic temple. *Salaam* is the Arabic word for "peace." *Halal* is the term used to describe Islamic dietary law. The *Koran* is Islam's holy book.

97. The value of all goods and services produced by an economy when its labor, natural, and capital resources are employed to capacity is referred to by economists as the

    (A) aggregate supply demand curve
    (B) cross-price elasticity formula
    (C) feedback effect
    (D) Laspeyres price index
    (E) potential gross national product

97. **(E)** is the correct answer. Most economists use the terms potential-level GNP, natural-level GNP, and full employment-level GNP interchangeably.

98. The North Atlantic Treaty Organization (NATO) was formed in

    (A) 1865
    (B) 1914
    (C) 1932
    (D) 1949
    (E) 1972

98. **(D)** is the correct answer. The CLEP doesn't expect you to memorize dates, but it does expect you to know why NATO was formed and thus know the approximate date of its origin. NATO was organized in the wake of World War II and in reaction to the fear of Soviet expansion after the war. In that context, only answer choice (D), 1949, makes sense.

SECTION 4

QUESTIONS	EXPLANATIONS

99. Great Britain and France are separated by the

    (A) Pacific Ocean
    (B) Nile River
    (C) Mediterranean Sea
    (D) English Channel
    (E) Arctic Ocean

99. **(D)** is the correct answer. If this one stumped you, spend some time studying a map of the world.

100. The Lend-Lease Act allowed Franklin Roosevelt to

    (A) place additional judges favorable to his policies on the Supreme Court
    (B) assist the Allies without violating the U.S. policy of neutrality
    (C) provide equipment to farmers who would otherwise have been unable to harvest crops
    (D) create jobs for artists during the Depression
    (E) establish a fund to insure bank deposits of up to $100,000

100. **(B)** is the correct answer. The Lend-Lease Act was passed in late 1940, over a year before the U.S. became involved in World War II. Roosevelt was anxious to help the Allies in any way possible, but was handcuffed by an isolationist Congress. Lend-Lease provided him a means, because it allowed him to lend or lease military equipment to the British. Roosevelt tried to pack the Supreme Court but was rebuked by Congress. Roosevelt did create New Deal programs for farmers, but never the one specifically described in answer choice (C). Answer choice (D) describes one function of the WPA (Works Progress Administration), which attempted to create jobs to offset the massive unemployment caused by the Great Depression. Answer choice (E) describes the FDIC (Federal Deposit Insurance Corporation).

101. All of the following are physiological motives EXCEPT

    (A) hunger
    (B) fatigue
    (C) curiosity
    (D) thirst
    (E) pain

101. **(C)** is the correct answer. A physiological motive is one driven by biological need, such as the need for sustenance, sleep, or the need to avoid pain. Curiosity is an effectance motive, which seem instinctive but are in fact learned. They are called "effectance motives" because they allow an individual to have an effect on the environment (others include activity, exploration, and manipulation).

102. Fill in the blanks:

Groups are _____ likely than individuals to make risky decisions and take risky actions, because of a phenomenon called _____.

    (A) more . . . laissez-faire leadership
    (B) more . . . the diffusion of responsibility
    (C) less . . . empathy
    (D) less . . . rationalization
    (E) less . . . the division of labor

102. **(B)** is the correct answer. A group of soldiers, business executives, etc., is more likely to follow a risky course of action than would be any single group member. This is because participation in the group allows each member to feel less responsibility in the case of failure. The consensus-building process that groups undergo may also suppress dissent and consideration of the possible drawbacks of a risky plan. Accordingly, a group is less likely to consider those drawbacks than would be an individual.

SECTION 4

QUESTIONS	EXPLANATIONS

103. A government with both a symbolic royal head of state and elected leaders who are empowered to govern is called

    (A) a dictatorship
    (B) an absolute monarchy
    (C) a constitutional monarchy
    (D) a junta
    (E) a totalitarian regime

103. **(C)** is the correct answer. England is a prime example of a constitutional monarchy. The queen is the country's symbolic leader, but real power resides with the prime minister and members of Parliament, who are elected officials.

104. The division of labor by gender is

    (A) universal to all cultures
    (B) found in primitive societies, but disappears as societies advance
    (C) not as common worldwide as is the division of labor by race and class
    (D) primarily isolated among most cultures to foodga thering activities
    (E) determined solely by biological capacity

104. **(A)** is the correct answer. Anthropologists have yet to discover a society in which work was not clearly divided along gender lines. Even in advanced societies, women are still primarily responsible for child rearing and still do proportionally little of the hunting and heavy manual work. Answer choice (C) is incorrect because, while there are classless societies and societies free of ethnic prejudice (some societies, after all, are entirely made up of one ethnic group), there are no societies in which the division of labor is not determined in part by gender. (D) is incorrect because child rearing and cooking are primarily female jobs; mining, wood work, and warfare are primarily the work of males. Biological capacity plays a role in determining the division of work by gender, but it is not the only consideration; social concerns and biases also play a part.

105. The term Manifest Destiny refers to the idea that

    (A) the Marxist Revolution in the Soviet Union was inevitable
    (B) all events are preordained in the Calvinist universe
    (C) the United States in the nineteenth century had a sacred right to all of North America
    (D) every United States resident has the inalienable right to life, liberty, and the pursuit of happiness
    (E) the Roman Empire was fated to fall

105. **(C)** is the correct answer. The term Manifest Destiny was coined by the journalist John L. O'Sullivan and was quickly picked up in political discourse, as it captured perfectly the expansionist mood of the era. If you didn't know exactly what Manifest Destiny was but knew that it had to do with U.S. history, you should have eliminated (A) and (E) and guessed among the remaining three. You might also have eliminated (B), preferring to guess only among those answer choices that specifically mentioned the U.S.

SECTION 4

QUESTIONS	EXPLANATIONS

106. All of the following countries fought successful revolutionary wars against European colonists during the early nineteenth century except

    (A) Argentina
    (B) Brazil
    (C) Chile
    (D) Bolivia
    (E) Peru

106. **(B)** is the correct answer. Argentina declared its independence from Spain in 1816, and José de San Martín, one of the new nation's most powerful generals, led a force across the border to liberate Chile. Símon Bolívar led revolutions leading to the liberation of Columbia, Venezuela, Ecuador, Panama, and Bolivia. Brazil's declaration of independence was nonviolent; in fact, the independent state declared Dom Pedro, the son of the last Portuguese governor of the colony, the emperor of Brazil.

107. A drop in the value of the American dollar against foreign currencies would most probably result in

    (A) an increase in American tariffs on imported goods
    (B) more Americans taking vacations abroad
    (C) a pronounced long-term worldwide recession
    (D) increased American investment in foreign businesses and property
    (E) an increase in American exports

107. **(E)** is the correct answer. A drop in the value of the dollar against foreign currencies would (all other things being equal) make American goods cheaper abroad. As a result, American goods would be in greater demand overseas. The downside of a devaluation of the dollar is that it makes imports and overseas travel and investment more expensive.

108. Which of the following countries is not located in the Middle East?

    (A) Syria
    (B) Egypt
    (C) Jordan
    (D) Algeria
    (E) Israel

108. **(D)** is the correct answer. The Middle East is the region stretching from the eastern and southeastern shore of the Mediterranean Sea across the Arabian peninsula. Algeria is on the north coast of Africa across the Mediterranean from Spain and France. It is much too far west to be considered part of the Middle East.

109. The first western settlements in Australia were made up largely of

    (A) German speculators
    (B) American farmers
    (C) Norwegian fishermen
    (D) British prisoners
    (E) French gold prospectors

109. **(D)** is the correct answer. In 1770, the British claimed Australia, even though it was already inhabited by 300,000 aborigines. British prisons were overcrowded, and Britain's practice of sending prisoners to the American colonies ended with the American Revolution. The British chose Australia as the new site of their penal colony, and started sending prisoners there in 1788. Australia's economic value became apparent over the course of the next century, and soon many British speculators were moving to Australia in hopes of striking it rich. Some even hired prisoners to tend their sheep.

SECTION 4

110. Interest groups such as Environmental Action and Americans for Constitutional Action rate members of Congress primarily on the basis of

    (A) how closely the legislator's voting record conforms to the group's politics
    (B) how many pieces of legislation a member of Congress introduces in a year
    (C) the amount of money legislators accept in donations from political action groups
    (D) the legislator's level of experience in state and local politics
    (E) the member of Congress' attendance record

110. **(A)** is the correct answer; a number of special interest groups in Washington give legislators grades—usually between zero and 100—based on how closely their voting records match the group's political objectives. Consumer advocates, anti-federalists, gun lobbyists, environmentalists, and just about every other group you can imagine rate legislators and publicize the results. Such numbers provide Congress–watchers and potential campaign donors a quick reference for identifying who is on which side of the issues.

111. According to Carl Gustav Jung, the collective unconscious is comprised of

    (A) the male and female aspects of one's personality
    (B) memories from the first three months of an individual's life
    (C) those rules regulating socialization in a given society
    (D) behavior patterns and memories inherited from one's ancestors
    (E) learned responses to dangerous stimuli

111. **(D)** is the correct answer; according to Jung, people have two levels of unconscious. In their personal unconscious reside all repressed memories, forgotten thoughts and experiences, etc. In their collective unconscious reside those memories that are inherited. Jung argued that different societies with no means of contact understood various symbols the same way and constructed similar myths because they shared this unconscious with the primitive humans from which humanity is thought to have evolved. This concept, while popular, remains controversial many decades after its formulation. Jung theorized that human personality encompassed both a male and female aspect, which he called *animus* and *anima*, respectively.

SECTION 4

QUESTIONS	EXPLANATIONS

112. The United States foreign policy stating that its government would not tolerate European interventions in the Americas is called the

(A) Mayflower Compact
(B) Quartering Act
(C) Truman Doctrine
(D) Monroe Doctrine
(E) Pentagon Papers

112. **(D)** is the correct answer. The Monroe Doctrine was asserted by President James Monroe in 1823. It also stated the U.S. interest in the affairs of other nations in its hemisphere and has been invoked as recently as the 1980s, to justify U.S. interference in Nicaragua, El Salvador, and Panama. The Mayflower Compact was a declaration of self-government, signed by nearly all the adult male Pilgrims who arrived at Plymouth on the Mayflower. The Quartering Act was a pre-Revolutionary British law requiring American colonists to quarter British soldiers on demand. The Truman Doctrine declared U.S. support for people of other nations fighting against Communist takeovers; it was the linchpin of the U.S. containment policy toward Communism. The Pentagon Papers were secret files leaked to the press; they revealed ineptitude, duplicity, and even illegality in U.S. involvement in Vietnam from the Truman administration through the Johnson administration.

113. A household made up of a father, mother, their children and their grandchildren, and the father's brother is called

(A) a nuclear family
(B) an extended family
(C) a nontraditional family
(D) a patriarchal society
(E) a matriarchal society

113. **(B)** is the correct answer. A nuclear family consists of a married man and woman and their natural and/or adoptive children. An extended family includes the nuclear family but can also include grandparents, uncles, aunts, and cousins. A nontraditional family might be a single-parent household, a gay couple, or any other family unit that is neither nuclear nor extended. A patriarchal society is one in which authority over the family belongs to the male household head. A matriarchal society is one in which authority over the family belongs to the female household head

114. The Buddha Gautama, founder of Buddhism, lived in

(A) India, during the sixth century B.C.
(B) Thailand, during the third century B.C.
(C) the Philippines, during the first century B.C.
(D) China, during the third century
(E) Japan, during the fifteenth century

114. **(A)** is the correct answer. The Buddha Gautama (born Prince Siddhartha and also sometimes referred to by the name Sakyamuni) lived in India. Early Buddhism flourished in India, spreading from the Indian subcontinent throughout Asia. The Muslim invasions of India, and the ensuing religious wars, pretty well wiped out Buddhism in India, so that today the religion is more closely associated with China, Japan, Thailand, and Tibet, among other countries in the region.

SECTION 4

QUESTIONS	EXPLANATIONS

115. One major difference between peasants and serfs during medieval times is that serfs

    (A) had more money and were therefore considered somewhat better off than peasants

    (B) were not free to move from the area in which they lived and worked

    (C) commonly received education, health care, and other amenities not available to peasants

    (D) were allowed by law to buy the land they worked

    (E) worked for the Church, whereas peasants worked for the king

115. **(B)** is the correct answer. The term peasant describes any member of the lowest rung of medieval society. Peasants served the vassals who in turn served their overlords and kings, and in return were allowed to eke out some measure of existence from the land. While serfs technically were peasants, they held the added distinction of being indentured to the land. They were, for all intents and purposes, slaves. Serfdom did not develop everywhere in the medieval world; like most medieval phenomena, it was local in nature.

116. Max Weber argued that Calvinist Protestantism was instrumental in the development of

    (A) liberation theology, because of its doctrines of compassion

    (B) capitalism, because it instilled a work ethic in its adherents

    (C) democracy, because of its emphasis on free will

    (D) charity, because of its emphasis on self-betterment through good deeds

    (E) communism, because it stressed the group over the individual

116. **(B)** is the correct answer. Max Weber is the father of modern sociology. His most famous work, *The Protestant Ethic and the Spirit of Capitalism*, argues that several features of Calvinist Protestantism facilitated the development of capitalism. The Calvinists believed in predestination (i.e., one's fate is determined before birth). They also believed that worldly success was an indicator of God's favor and a good omen of a favorable afterlife; thus, hard work and frugality, the necessary ingredients of a successful capitalist work force, were goals the Calvinists pursued fervently. Liberation theology is a development of the left wing of twentieth-century Catholicism and predominates in Latin America. Answer choice (C) must be wrong because the Calvinists did not believe in free will. Answer choice (D) contradicts the Calvinist notion of predestination (if one's fate is decided, self-betterment is impossible).

SECTION 4

117. The United States and Japan were able to establish friendly relations quickly after World War II primarily because

   (A) the strength of Japan's economy made Japan a desirable trading partner for the U.S.

   (B) their differences during the war had been only minor

   (C) the U.S. wished to take advantage of Japan's military strength in the region

   (D) the two shared a common enemy, the Soviet Union

   (E) the U.S., as a gesture of peace, restored the sovereignty of the emperor immediately after the war

117. **(D)** is the correct answer. This is a question that is most easily solved by a process of elimination. Answer choice (A) is wrong because Japan was decimated by the war; although it would later rise to economic power, it remained economically weak for a long time after the war. In fact, the phrase "Made in Japan" was, for a long time, synonymous with cheap merchandise and workmanship. Answer choice (B) is clearly wrong; Japan attacked the U.S. base in Pearl Harbor, many would say without provocation. The U.S. later dropped two atomic bombs on Japan. This is all evidence of some major differences. Answer choice (C) is wrong because one of the U.S.'s first acts after the war was to demilitarize Japan. Another was to strip the emperor of power (making answer choice (E) wrong). The East became one of the major theaters of the Cold War between the U.S. and the U.S.S.R., and the U.S. alliance with Japan was meant to deter the type of Communist takeovers that occurred in Korea, Vietnam, and elsewhere.

118. The Sugar Act, passed by the British Parliament in 1764, was intended to

   (A) increase the amount of sugar imported from Britain by its Asian colonies

   (B) shift the world production center of sugar from the Old World to the New World

   (C) raise revenue to offset the costs of the French and Indian War

   (D) provide the colonies with a greater measure of self-government

   (E) impose punitive measures on the American colonies to discourage their growing independence

118. **(C)** is the correct answer. The French and Indian Wars were fought between 1756 and 1763. It cast the British against an alliance of French and Indian troops, purportedly for the protection of the colonists but also for domination of the colonial territory east of the Mississippi. The British won in 1763, and the sentiment in Parliament was that the colonists were obliged to help offset the massive war debt incurred during the French and Indian Wars. The Sugar Act placed tariffs on those goods that the colonies imported in bulk, such as sugar, wine, and coffee. The colonists objected, the phrase "No taxation without representation" was coined, and a revolution was afoot.

119. The population of the United States is most heavily concentrated

   (A) along the coast of the Gulf of Mexico, from New Orleans to Tampa

   (B) on the northeast coast, from Boston to Washington, D.C.

   (C) along the entire length of the Pacific Coast, from San Diego to Seattle

   (D) in the western mountain region, from Denver to Salt Lake City

   (E) along the Mississippi River, from Memphis to St. Louis

119. **(B)** is the correct answer. Population density for the entire length of the Boston-D.C. stretch is over 260 people per square mile, a level reached elsewhere in the U.S. only in and immediately surrounding some major cities.

QUESTIONS	EXPLANATIONS

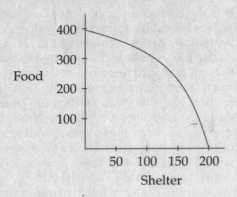

120. The production possibility curve for society X, illustrated above, indicates that

   (A) society X cannot produce adequate amounts of both food and shelter
   (B) society X would be best served by producing 150 units of shelter and 150 units of food
   (C) in order to produce 200 units of shelter, society X would have to forego the production of food
   (D) in order to produce 350 units of food, society X would have to forego the production of shelter
   (E) society X could simultaneously produce 400 units of food and 200 units of shelter

120. **(C)** is the correct answer. A production possibility curve demonstrates how a society may allocate resources in order to produce goods. Choose any point on the curve and you can find society X's maximum output of food and shelter. Move your finger along the curve to the left to see how much society X would have to give up in the production of shelter in order to increase its food production; to the right to see how much it would have to give up in the production of food to increase its production of shelter. A society could produce any combination of amounts on or within the curve, but not an amount outside of the curve.

121. "Until philosophers are kings, or the kings and princes of the world have the spirit and power of philosophy . . . cities will never have rest from their evils."

   The quotation above is from

   (A) Aristotle's *Ethics*
   (B) Ralph Waldo Emerson's *Politics*
   (C) Jonathan Swift's *A Modest Proposal*
   (D) John Locke's *Second Treatise of Government*
   (E) Plato's *Republic*

121. **(E)** is the correct answer. Plato's *Republic* concerns the Greek idealist philosopher's search for the perfect government. Plato's ideal state is ruled by philosopher-kings. Aristotle, a student of Plato and teacher of Alexander the Great, is often considered Plato's opposite, as Aristotle was a pragmatist. Emerson, an American transcendentalist, once wrote that "The less government we have, the better." Swift was a cynic and a satirist whose *A Modest Proposal* dryly and sarcastically suggests that the solution to poverty is to eat the children of the poor. Locke's writings provided the philosophical groundwork for the Federalist Papers and the American Declaration of Independence.

SECTION 4

QUESTIONS	EXPLANATIONS

122. The political party with which a citizen chooses to be affiliated is most powerfully influenced by that citizen's

   (A) religion
   (B) family
   (C) economic status
   (D) level of education
   (E) personal encounters with politicians

122. **(B)** is the correct answer. Numerous studies have demonstrated that the vast majority of citizens form their allegiance to a political party based primarily on their parents' party affiliation.

123. The process that causes people in a large crowd to lose some of their inhibitions is called

   (A) deindividuation
   (B) reciprocity
   (C) group polarization
   (D) guilt complex
   (E) aphasia

123. **(A)** is the correct answer. Deindividuation is the term used to describe the phenomenon that allows people to behave in crowds in ways they would not when alone: a violent mob is the most graphic example of such behavior. Reciprocity is the social norm that tells us that when someone does something nice for us we should return the favor. Group polarization is a process by which group opinions are formed; a majority view will tend to become more adamant in the face of opposition and, through this force, persuade others to join its side. A guilt complex is a condition in which an individual becomes obsessed with feelings of guilt and remorse. Aphasia is a pathology which causes the sufferer to lose partial or total understanding of language.

124. All of the following are Romance languages EXCEPT

   (A) Portuguese
   (B) German
   (C) Italian
   (D) French
   (E) Spanish

124. **(B)** is the correct answer. German is a Germanic language, as are English, Dutch, Danish, Norwegian, Swedish, and Icelandic. The family of Romance languages, so called because their roots are in Latin (which the Romans spoke—get it?), also includes Romanian.

125. In the U.S., the Radical Republicans of the nineteenth century campaigned most vigorously for

   (A) the dismantling of the federal government
   (B) a punitive Reconstruction
   (C) annexing Texas
   (D) the maintenance of slavery in Southern states
   (E) territorial expansion into Canada

125. **(B)** is the correct answer; Radical Republicans made up the extreme wing of Lincoln's party. While Lincoln favored a conciliatory plan to allow the South back into the Union—the requirement that 10 per cent of a Southern state's occupants take a loyalty oath was its main feature—the Radical Republicans favored a more protracted reunification, complete with reparation payments and, according to some plans, the redistribution of property ("forty acres and a mule").

PART ◆ VI

How to Crack the CLEP General Examination in Natural Sciences

19

Overview of the Natural Sciences Exam

WHAT'S ON THE TEST?

The CLEP General Examination in Natural Sciences is ninety minutes long, and is divided into two forty-five minute sections. The first half of the test covers biological science, and the second half covers physical science. Most of the questions will test your familiarity with basic facts, concepts, principles and definitions. There will also be questions where you will need to analyze graphs, diagrams, tables, and brief verbal passages.

During each forty-five minute section, you will be allowed to work only on that section. The two halves will total 120 questions. You'll receive a single score between 200 and 800 that will cover both sections.

SUBJECT	Approximate # OF QUESTIONS
Biological Science	60
Physical Science	60
Chemistry	25
Physics	15
Earth Science	12
Astronomy	8

Don't forget to bring a watch with you to the exam.

QUESTION FORMATS

There are two different question formats used on this test. The first fifteen questions on each section, give or take a few, will give a list of possible answers followed by between two and four questions. An answer can be right more than once for each group of questions.

Here's an example:

(A) Cell
(B) Molecule
(C) Element
(D) Gene
(E) Proton

1. This is a collection of atoms that are bonded together.

2. This is a positively charged subatomic particle.

Answers: 1. (B) 2. (E)

The rest of the questions in each section will be in the more standard multiple choice format:

3. Which of the following substances is more dense in its liquid phase than in its solid phase?

(A) Water
(B) Gold
(C) Nitrogen
(D) Carbon dioxide
(E) Sodium chloride

Answer: (A)

You'll also see a few sets of two to four multiple choice questions grouped together under a short verbal passage or diagram.

MAKING THE GRADE

No school requires a perfect score on the General Examination in Natural Sciences for those seeking college credit for the test. In fact, many require only that you score in the fiftieth percentile, which is the equivalent of a C grade. That means getting a score of about 500 on the test. So, roughly speaking, if you can get more than half of the questions on the test right, you are in pretty good shape. As far as most schools that accept the test are concerned, a 500 is exactly as valuable as an 800. For each, you will receive the exact same number of credits toward your degree.

Familiarize yourself thoroughly with all question formats BEFORE you take the exam. You want to spend your test time deciding which answer is correct, not reading directions.

A FAIR TEST

ETS writes a lot of "tricky" exams. The PSAT, SAT, GRE, and GMAT are all ETS exams on which the test writers often set out to confound the test taker. Oddly worded questions coupled with answer choices that appear correct at first glance (such answer choices touch on many of the same themes as the correct answer, but typically include an overgeneralization or an error on a tangential point) conspire to make the test taker's job much more difficult than it has to be. If you've ever taken one of these exams—and you almost certainly have—you might understandably have some anxiety about the CLEP Natural Sciences exam.

Well, rest easy. The good news is that the CLEP Natural Sciences test includes none of the tricks you've come to know and hate on other ETS exams. Questions on the CLEP are worded in a straightforward manner, usually in as few words as possible. Answer choices are straightforward: if you are familiar with the subject being tested, there will almost certainly be either an obvious correct answer or four obvious incorrect answers.

"The whole of science is nothing more than a refinement of everyday thinking."
—Albert Einstein

MAXIMIZE YOUR STRENGTHS AND MINIMIZE YOUR WEAKNESSES

Do NOT skip chapter 2. It is crammed full of important test-taking tips!

Tailor your test-taking approach to maximize your strengths and minimize your weaknesses. If you're a chemistry whiz, don't waste time agonizing over a physics question early in the test if it might keep you from getting to chemistry questions later on. Each question is worth the same number of points and your score won't reflect the fact that you did well in chemistry but not in physics. Save those questions in your areas of weakness for last; that way, if you never get to them, you will have minimized your losses.

The questions do not get more difficult as you proceed through the test. That's really important. Question 55 should not be any more difficult than question 2. That means if a question early in the test deals with a topic that you are unfamiliar with, don't worry about it, just take your best shot and move on. You're bound to find questions about topics you are familiar with later in the test.

Generally, when people run out of time on a test, it is not because they work too slowly overall. Rather, people run out of time because they become obsessed with two or three questions and waste a ton of time thinking about them.

TAILOR YOUR REVIEW TO THE TEST

The College Board publishes a book called *The Official Guide to the CLEP*. It is the only source for questions that have actually appeared on real CLEP tests. Buy it, or better still, look it over at the public library.

How should you study for this test? First, here's some good news. The Natural Sciences CLEP is not designed for science majors. This test is given mainly to non-science majors who wish to place out of a science distribution or general education requirement. The writers of the Natural Sciences CLEP do not expect you to have taken college level courses in physics, chemistry, biology, or earth science, so almost all of the questions will stick to the basics.

This means that you should not use course textbooks to study for the CLEP, because textbooks go into way too much depth. You probably know something about the material on this test already, or you wouldn't be planning on taking it, so what you'll need to do is review words, terms, and concepts—not learn them from scratch. Instead of textbooks, which are too expensive anyway, get yourself some review books geared towards high school students. Go to a local book store and leaf through the review books. When you find one that you can open and understand immediately, buy it.

The CLEP makers say that the test stresses basic principles and concepts of science rather than factual details. Don't believe it. Since they can't go into any great depth in their questions, most of the test will resemble a science trivia game, and many of the questions will depend on whether you know the meaning of a scientific vocabulary word. You'll do better on this test if you keep your studying shallow and wide, as opposed to narrow and deep. That is, you should know a little about a lot of science, rather than a lot about a little science.

Here's some more good news. There is almost no math on this test. The three or four math questions you will see should involve nothing more than simple arithmetic.

You should also think about how to concentrate your energies. If your study time is limited, you should put it to the best possible use. Let's say you've looked over the list of topics covered on the test, and the prospect of studying electricity and magnetism makes you want to crawl into a hole. This is understandable, as electricity and magnetism are particularly difficult topics. Fortunately, electricity and magnetism are minor topics on the CLEP; there should only be two or three electricity and magnetism questions. So, provided that you are comfortable with most of the other test topics, it's probably not worth your while to spend much time reviewing it.

On the other hand, genetics and heredity is also a difficult topic, but you may see ten or twelve genetics and heredity questions on the CLEP. In this case, there's no easy way out and you should put some time in studying genetics and heredity.

> Always take the path of least resistance on multiple-choice tests. Do not answer the questions that give you trouble until you have answered ALL the questions you can answer easily.

GENERAL OUTLINE OF WHAT YOU SHOULD KNOW

Here's a general outline of what you can expect to see on the CLEP General Exam in Natural Sciences:

BIOLOGICAL SCIENCE (SIXTY QUESTIONS)

Classification of organisms, origin and evolution of life (about twelve questions)

For the questions about the **classification of organisms**, you should be familiar with the standard classification system for living things: kingdom, phylum, class, order, family, genus, and species.

You should know the five different kingdoms: Monera, Protista, Fungi, Plants, and Animals. Viruses, which don't really fit into any of these five classifications, also come up on the test. You're expected to have an idea of the distinctions between the kingdoms and which organisms fit into the different categories. For instance, bacteria are monera and mushrooms are fungi.

For questions about the **origin of life**, you should be familiar with the slow evolutionary progression from simple single-celled organisms in water on up to extremely complex land animals.

For **evolution** questions, you should know some of the evidence that supports the theory of evolution, such as similarities among different species in anatomy and embryo development, universal similarities in cell respiration and genetic code, and results of domestic breeding experiments. You should also know the process by which evolution takes place. So you should be comfortable with such concepts as natural selection, mutation, and the gene pool.

> "I consider that a man's brain originally is like a little empty attic, and you have to stock it with such furniture as you choose."
> —Sir Arthur Conan Doyle

Cell organization and division, chemical nature of the gene, biosynthesis, and bioenergetics (about twelve questions):

You should know the different kinds of cells, eukaryotic versus prokaryotic, plant versus animal. **Cell organization** questions will expect you to have memorized the major parts of plant and animal cells and to know the basic functions of these parts. For instance, mitochondria are concerned with energy production and ribosomes are concerned with protein synthesis. There will also be questions about how cells move and how material is transported into and out of cells.

For questions about **cell division** and cell reproduction, you should know the difference between sexual and asexual reproduction and you should know the process by which each takes place. You should be familiar with the processes of mitosis and meiosis and know what the roles of the different cell parts are in each process.

Knowing the **chemical nature of the gene** means knowing about chromosomes and DNA. You'll be asked about the structure of the gene, the Watson-Crick model, the genetic code, and DNA replication.

There will also be questions about how DNA and RNA are used to transfer information and create proteins in **biosynthesis**.

All living things need energy to survive and reproduce. **Bioenergetics** questions will deal with the different ways in which living things generate this vital energy. You should be familiar with ATP—the main cellular fuel—and the ways in which it is used. There will be questions about photosynthesis, the process by which plants produce energy, and aerobic and anaerobic respiration, the processes by which animals and other organisms obtain energy.

Patterns of heredity; structure, function and development in organisms (about twenty-four questions):

For questions about **heredity**, you should be familiar with the work of Gregor Mendel. You should understand Mendel's laws of dominance, segregation, and independent assortment, and how they apply to the passing of traits from generation to generation. You should be able to use a Punnett square to solve genetics problems. The concepts of incomplete dominance, polygenetic inheritance, multiple alleles, and sex linkage are likely to come up.

Structure, function, and development in organisms cover a lot of ground. You should know the parts of different organisms, mainly plants and animals. You should know how plants grow, transport material, and respond to stimuli.

There will be many questions about the basics of human physiology. You should know something about digestion, nutrition, respiration, circulation, excretion, reproduction, the immune system, the endocrine system, the skeletal system, the brain, and the nervous system.

More specifically, you should know about human organs and their functions, where hormones are generated and how they affect the body, various diseases and their causes and effects, the process by which an embryo develops, and the various nutrients necessary for survival and where we get them.

"Aristotle could have avoided the mistake of thinking that women have fewer teeth than men, by the simple device of asking Mrs. Aristotle to keep her mouth open while he counted."
—Bertrand Russell

Concepts of population biology with emphasis on ecology (about twelve questions):

For **population biology and ecology** questions, you will be asked about the gradation from populations to communities to ecosystems to the biosphere. You should know about how evolution affects populations, and how communities interact with each other. You should know terms like competition, predation, symbiosis, the food chain, the food pyramid, producers, consumers, climax population, and growth curve.

Current events in ecology are important on this test. Many of the questions that you will see will deal with ecological issues that are currently in the news, such as global warming, ozone depletion, and conservation of natural resources.

PHYSICAL SCIENCE (SIXTY QUESTIONS)

Atomic structure and properties, elementary particles, nuclear reactions (about eight questions):

For questions about **atomic structure and properties**, you should know the Bohr model of the atom and be aware of the way that the elementary particles of an atom interact.

The **elementary particles** of an atom are electrons, protons, and neutrons.

For questions about **nuclear reactions**, you should know about nuclear decay and the concept of half-life. You will also be asked about the products of nuclear decay, such as alpha particles, beta particles, and gamma rays.

Chemical elements, chemical compounds, molecular structure, bonding, chemical reactions (about twelve questions):

The **chemical elements** are arranged on the periodic table. It's important to know why they're arranged the way they are. There might be questions about atomic weight, atomic number, ions, metals, nonmetals, and noble gases. You should know what a mole is.

Chemical compounds are formed when atoms bond together. For **bonding** questions, you should know how bonds are formed and know the distinctions between ionic and covalent bonds. Different arrangements of bonds will create compounds with different **molecular structures**. You should know the different kinds of bonds that make up molecules, liquids, and solids.

You'll be expected to know the basics about **chemical reactions**. You should be able to answer questions about acids and bases, oxidation and reduction, balancing, and solutions.

Heat, states of matter, and thermodynamics; classical mechanics; relativity (about fifteen questions):

For questions about **heat and states of matter**, you'll need to know the concepts of specific heat and heat capacity, as well as heats of fusion and vaporization. You should know what distinguishes a solid from a liquid from a gas and how phase changes occur. There may be questions about the properties of an ideal gas and how the ideal gas law works.

"Science may be described as the art of systematic over-simplification."
—Karl Popper

"I seem to have been only like a boy playing on the seashore, and diverting myself in now and then finding a smoother pebble or a prettier shell than ordinary, whilst the great ocean of truth lay all undiscovered before me."
—Sir Isaac Newton

After you've taken our practice exam, read the explanations for all the answers, including the ones for questions you answered correctly. The explanations describe the fastest, most efficient way to do the test problems.

Thermodynamics questions will deal with topics like enthalpy, entropy, and the effect of catalysts on reactions.

Classical mechanics is a broad topic. You should have some understanding of all these terms: vectors and scalars; displacement, velocity, and acceleration; force and Newton's laws; work and energy; conservation of energy; kinetic energy; potential energy; momentum; pressure; density; gravity; and torque.

You should know that Einstein came up with the theory of **relativity** and you should have a very basic idea of what it says.

Electricity and magnetism, waves, light, and sound (about five questions):

For **electricity and magnetism**, you should be familiar with the terms: charge, field, circuit, resistance, Coulomb's law, Ohm's law, and potential difference.

You should know that **light and sound** are both **waves**. You might be asked about the different properties of a wave: amplitude, frequency, period, velocity, and wavelength.

The universe: galaxies, stars, the solar system (about eight questions):

You should know the basics of astronomy. The **universe** has galaxies, **galaxies** have stars, the Sun is a star, the Sun has a **solar system**, there are nine planets in the solar system, and Earth is the third most distant planet from the Sun.

The Earth: atmosphere, hydrosphere, structure, properties, surface features, geological processes, history (about twelve questions):

In the same way as in the biological sciences section, questions about **Earth** will tend to have an ecological bent. That is, they will often deal with current issues in ecology and earth science.

You should know how the **atmosphere** changes as height above Earth increases and what the major gases are that make up the atmosphere (nitrogen and oxygen).

The **hydrosphere** is the oceans, seas, lakes, and rivers that cover Earth's surface.

For questions about Earth's **structure, properties, and surface features**, you should know something about the different kinds of rocks, weather, and Earth's interior.

Questions about **geological processes and history** will deal with topics such as glaciers, continental drift, earthquakes, erosion and deposition, and fossil dating.

20

The Princeton Review
Sample Natural Sciences Exam

PART I

Biological Science

Time—45 minutes

60 questions

Directions: Each group of questions below consists of five lettered choices followed by a list of numbered phrases or sentences. For each numbered phrase or sentence select the one choice that is most closely related to it. Each choice may be used once, more than once, or not at all in each group.

Questions 1 through 3

    (A) Adrenaline
    (B) Insulin
    (C) Testosterone
    (D) Gastrin
    (E) Histamine

1. This hormone, which regulates the amount of glucose in the blood, is produced in the pancreas.

2. This is released by damaged tissue and it acts to dilate blood vessels.

3. When the body is subjected to pain or anger, this hormone is produced.

Questions 4 and 5

    (A) Animals
    (B) Fungi
    (C) Monera
    (D) Plants
    (E) Protista

4. Members of this kingdom can be either vertebrates or invertebrates.

5. Bacteria are members of this kingdom.

Questions 6 through 8

    (A) Carbon dioxide
    (B) Helium
    (C) Nitrogen
    (D) Oxygen
    (E) Sulfur dioxide

6. This gas makes up most of Earth's atmosphere.

7. This gas is the main product of photosynthesis.

8. This gas combines with water in the atmosphere to form acid rain.

Questions 9 through 11

    (A) Artery
    (B) Atrium
    (C) Capillary
    (D) Vein
    (E) Ventricle

9. Material is exchanged between the blood and the body's interstitial fluid here.

10. The part of the circulatory system with the thickest, strongest muscle.

11. This carries deoxygenated blood from the limbs back to the heart.

GO ON TO THE NEXT PAGE.

Questions 12 and 13

The picture below represents the climatic conditions for some of Earth's biomes.

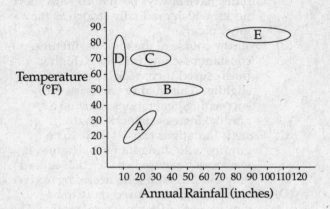

Temperature (°F)

Annual Rainfall (inches)

12. This region represents desert.

13. This region represents tropical forest.

Questions 14 and 15

(A) scurvy
(B) rickets
(C) measles
(D) tetanus
(E) ringworm

14. A condition caused by a diet poor in vitamin C.

15. A condition caused by a bacterial infection.

Directions: Each of the questions or incomplete statements below is followed by five suggested answers or completions. Select the one that is best in each case.

16. Which of the following is the most fundamental level in the organization of living things?

(A) Organism
(B) Tissue
(C) Organ system
(D) Organ
(E) Cell

17. The flippers of whales resemble the fins of fish in both form and function. What is the most likely explanation for this resemblance?

(A) Whales and fish evolved similar structures in response to similar environmental stresses.
(B) A whale is a kind of fish.
(C) Whales and fish have interbred, leading to certain physical similarities.
(D) Whales evolved flippers in imitation of fish.
(E) Both fins and flippers evolved from the legs of land creatures.

18. The largest part of the human brain and also the part of the brain most associated with intellectual capacity is called the

(A) cerebellum
(B) medulla
(C) thalamus
(D) hypothalamus
(E) cerebrum

19. A particle that is not considered a living thing, but reproduces by attaching itself to a living cell and injecting DNA or RNA into its host is called a

(A) fungus
(B) virus
(C) spore
(D) barnacle
(E) protozoa

GO ON TO THE NEXT PAGE.

20. Which of the following shows the progression of the food chain from producers to secondary consumers?

    (A) Carnivores, autotrophs, herbivores.
    (B) Autotrophs, carnivores, herbivores.
    (C) Autotrophs, herbivores, carnivores.
    (D) Herbivores, autotrophs, carnivores.
    (E) Herbivores, carnivores, autotrophs.

21. In order for the ecological balance in a certain pond to be maintained, the algae present in the pond must remain in dynamic equilibrium. This means that

    (A) no algae should be present in the pond
    (B) algae growth should be faster than algae depletion
    (C) algae growth should take place at the same rate as algae depletion
    (D) algae growth should take place more slowly than algae depletion
    (E) algae growth and depletion should not take place

22. A normal cell in a male human being contains 46 chromosomes. How many chromosomes are contained in a normal sperm cell?

    (A) 10
    (B) 23
    (C) 46
    (D) 92
    (E) 184

23. It is thought that modern-day giraffes evolved from ancestors with shorter necks. Which of the following explanations for this evolution is most in keeping with the modern theory of natural selection?

    (A) Giraffes have always been born with short necks, which gradually stretch as they grow older.
    (B) Over the course of the giraffes' lifetimes, constant reaching for foliage high in trees caused their necks to stretch slightly. This quality was passed to succeeding generations, causing a gradual increase in neck length.
    (C) Genetic mutations caused there to be giraffes with different neck lengths. It was purely random chance that caused only giraffes with long necks to survive.
    (D) Genetic mutations caused there to be giraffes with different neck lengths. The giraffes with long necks were better equipped to feed on the foliage high in trees. The long-necked giraffes were better able to reproduce and passed the mutation on to their offspring.
    (E) Giraffes with different neck lengths gravitated to different geographical regions. Natural disasters occurring in all of the regions except those occupied by long-necked giraffes caused all other giraffes to die out.

GO ON TO THE NEXT PAGE.

Questions 24 through 26

Blood type is a genetically inherited trait. There are three alleles for blood type: A, B, and O. The O allele is recessive to both the A allele and the B allele, so a person with an A allele and an O allele will be type A. Neither the A nor the B allele is dominant over the other, so a person with both the A and the B allele will be type AB.

24. Which of the following could NOT be the blood type of the offspring of two type AB parents?

 (A) A
 (B) B
 (C) AB
 (D) O
 (E) All blood types are possible.

25. Which of the following are possible gene combinations for a person with type B blood?

 (A) BO or AB
 (B) BB or AB
 (C) BB or BO
 (D) BO or AO
 (E) BB only

26. What is the probability that the offspring of a type AB parent and a type O parent will have blood that is type A?

 (A) 0 percent
 (B) 25 percent
 (C) 50 percent
 (D) 75 percent
 (E) 100 percent

27. Which of the following nitrogenous bases is contained in DNA but not in RNA?

 (A) Adenine
 (B) Cytosine
 (C) Guanine
 (D) Thymine
 (E) Uracil

28. The muscle cells of an animal require a great deal of energy. As a result of this need for energy, muscle cells would be expected to contain a relatively large number of

 (A) cilia
 (B) mitochondria
 (C) flagella
 (D) vacuoles
 (E) centrioles

29. It has been predicted that the destruction of the tropical rain forests will contribute to which of the following ecological effects?

 (A) Global warming
 (B) Glaciation
 (C) Volcanic activity
 (D) Shoreline erosion
 (E) Tidal waves

30. The process by which plants convert the energy in sunlight into chemical energy which can be stored and used by the plant is called

 (A) cellular respiration
 (B) mitosis
 (C) pinocytosis
 (D) fermentation
 (E) photosynthesis

31. In human reproduction, fertilization of the egg normally takes place in which part of the female's reproductive system?

 (A) Ovary
 (B) Uterus
 (C) Cervix
 (D) Fallopian tube
 (E) Labium major

GO ON TO THE NEXT PAGE.

32. Initially, a population of birds contains birds with beaks that vary randomly in length from long to short, with all gradations in between. Environmental factors change to provide better feeding opportunities for birds with very long beaks and for birds with very short beaks. Which of the following diagrams best shows the distribution of beak lengths among the birds after natural selection has taken place?

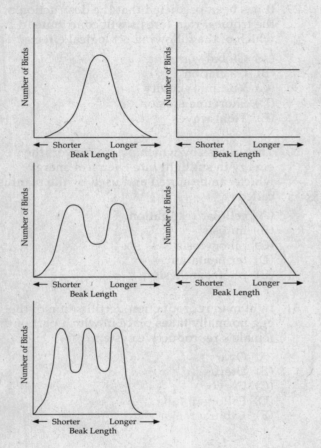

33. In the condition known as anemia, the body does not receive enough oxygen to maintain proper cell respiration. Anemia is caused by a deficiency in the body's supply of

(A) red blood cells
(B) white blood cells
(C) plasma
(D) platelets
(E) lymphocytes

34. In a certain flower, the trait for red color (R) is dominant over the trait for white color (w). In a breeding experiment, two parent plants of unknown genotype produce offspring. If approximately half of the offspring are white and half are red, what is the predicted genotype of the parent plants?

(A) Rw and Rw
(B) RR and Rw
(C) ww and Rw
(D) RR and RR
(E) ww and ww

35. Ribosomes, mitochondria, and lysosomes can be found in

(A) eukaryotic cells
(B) prokaryotic cells
(C) Golgi apparatus
(D) chloroplasts
(E) microfilaments

36. An example of bones in the human body that are connected by fused joints are the bones that comprise the

(A) hand
(B) foot
(C) arm
(D) leg
(E) skull

37. Flowers are important in the reproductive cycle of a plant because they

(A) prevent impurities from interfering with the parts of the plant involved in reproduction
(B) provide protection from wind and rain
(C) attract pollen-bearing insects
(D) are the major sites of photosynthesis in the plant
(E) provide shade for the parts of the plant involved in reproduction

GO ON TO THE NEXT PAGE.

38. A part of any standard medical examination is the measure of the patient's blood pressure. When a doctor measures a patient's blood pressure, the doctor measures

   (A) the number of heartbeats per minute
   (B) the volume of plasma in the body
   (C) the number of red blood cells in the body
   (D) the force per unit area exerted by the blood on the vessel walls
   (E) the ratio of red blood cells to white blood cells

39. Which of the following lists the types of species that make up the food pyramid in order of largest to smallest population?

   (A) Producers outnumber primary consumers, who outnumber secondary consumers.
   (B) Producers outnumber secondary consumers, who outnumber primary consumers.
   (C) Primary consumers outnumber secondary consumers, who outnumber producers.
   (D) Primary consumers outnumber producers, who outnumber secondary consumers.
   (E) Secondary consumers outnumber primary consumers, who outnumber producers.

40. Proteins are complex polymers made up of different combinations of smaller molecules that serve as building blocks. What are the building blocks that are combined to form proteins?

   (A) Polysaccharides
   (B) Phospholipids
   (C) Steroids
   (D) Amino acids
   (E) Fats

41. The most important substance that is used to provide energy for cellular functions is

   (A) ADP
   (B) ATP
   (C) DNA
   (D) rRNA
   (E) tRNA

42. Color-blindness is a recessive, sex-linked trait. The gene for color-blindness is found only on the X chromosome. If a color-blind female and a male with normal vision produce offspring, the probable result will be that

   (A) all of the males will be color-blind
   (B) half of the males will be color-blind
   (C) none of the males will be color-blind
   (D) all of the females will be color-blind
   (E) half of the females will be color-blind

GO ON TO THE NEXT PAGE.

Questions 43 and 44

The graph below represents the growth curve of a population. The graph shows the increasing density of the population over time.

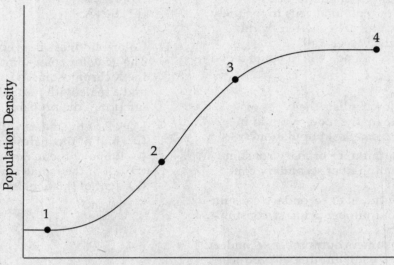

43. Which of the following is most likely true of the population at the time represented by point 4?
    (A) The population density is increasing very quickly.
    (B) Environmental conditions have changed, causing a sudden decrease in population density.
    (C) The population density is about the same as it was at the time represented by point 1.
    (D) The population density is at equilibrium at the carrying capacity of the environment.
    (E) The population density is undergoing random variation.

44. If a growth curve were assembled for a population that exists in an environment that is much less favorable to growth than that pictured above, how would the new curve be expected to differ from the curve above?
    (A) The slope from point 2 up to point 3 would be more steep and point 4 would be lower.
    (B) The slope from point 2 up to point 3 would be less steep and point 4 would be lower.
    (C) The slope from point 2 up to point 3 would be more steep and point 4 would be higher.
    (D) The slope from point 2 up to point 3 would be less steep and point 4 would be higher.
    (E) The slope from point 2 up to point 3 would be more steep and point 1 would be higher.

GO ON TO THE NEXT PAGE.

45. The green color of plants is due to the presence in plant cells of

(A) a cell wall
(B) chloroplasts
(C) cytoplasm
(D) lysosomes
(E) nuclei

46. The Hardy Weinberg law is a set of hypothetical conditions under which no genetic change will occur in a sexually reproducing population from generation to generation. Which of the following is NOT a condition necessary for a population to be in accordance with the Hardy Weinberg law of genetic equilibrium?

(A) The population must be large enough to eliminate chance as a factor in genetic change.
(B) The members of the population must have long life spans.
(C) Genetic mutations must not occur in the population.
(D) There must be no emigration from the population or immigration to it.
(E) Reproduction among the members of the population must be random.

47. The wolf belongs to the family Canidae, the order Carnivora, the species *lupus*, and the genus *Canis*. What is the Linnaean name for wolf?

(A) Canidae Carnivora
(B) Carnivora *Canis*
(C) *Canis* Canidae
(D) Carnivora *lupus*
(E) *Canis lupus*

48. Sensory information is passed throughout the body by nerve cells. Which of the following is the best description of the method by which sensory information is passed along the axon of a nerve cell?

(A) Sodium and potassium ions are passed through the nerve cell wall in a sequence along the axon.
(B) DNA makes its way through the cytoplasm from one end of the axon to the other.
(C) The nerve cell nucleus emits nitrogen, which is carried by vacuoles along the axon.
(D) Information is passed through the chemical stimulation of muscles along the axon.
(E) Oxygen gas is passed along the axon by the nerve cell cilia.

49. These cell structures are used when a cell moves through a fluid.

(A) Arteries
(B) Follicles
(C) Carrier molecules
(D) Enzymes
(E) Cilia

50. In order for sexual reproduction to occur, gametes must be produced during meiosis. How many gametes are produced from each parent cell over the entire course of meiosis?

(A) 1
(B) 2
(C) 4
(D) 8
(E) 16

GO ON TO THE NEXT PAGE.

51. Which of the following lists presents different kinds of animal life in the order in which they first appeared on the earth?
    (A) Amphibians, marine invertebrates, fish, mammals, reptiles.
    (B) Fish, amphibians, marine invertebrates, reptiles, mammals.
    (C) Reptiles, marine invertebrates, fish, amphibians, mammals.
    (D) Fish, marine invertebrates, amphibians, mammals, reptiles.
    (E) Marine invertebrates, fish, amphibians, reptiles, mammals.

52. Between the stages of zygote and embryo, a developing human develops three cell layers. Which of the following body parts develops from the ectoderm layer?
    (A) Stomach
    (B) Bones
    (C) Eyes
    (D) Lungs
    (E) Muscles

53. Materials move into and out of cells in many different ways. When material is moved across a cell membrane into a cell against a concentration gradient, which process is taking place?
    (A) Active transport
    (B) Osmosis
    (C) Passive diffusion
    (D) Facilitated diffusion
    (E) Endocytosis

Questions 54 and 55

Coral reefs provide the basis for one of the most lively ecosystems in the world. Coral reefs are underwater structures generated by the secretions of coral polyps. Coral polyps exist only in symbiosis with certain forms of green algae that engage in photosynthesis.

54. Which of the following could describe the symbiotic relationship between coral polyps and green algae?
    (A) There is no interaction between coral polyps and green algae.
    (B) The presence of coral polyps and green algae are mutually exclusive.
    (C) Coral polyps and green algae compete for the same energy sources.
    (D) The presence of green algae is required in order for coral polyps to thrive.
    (E) Coral polyps and green algae combine to form a third species.

55. Because of the symbiotic relationship between coral polyps and green algae, one would expect coral reefs to be found only in
    (A) the Southern Hemisphere
    (B) shallow water
    (C) fresh water
    (D) cold water
    (E) running water

56. Which of the following is NOT true of the ribosomes contained in cells?
    (A) Ribosomes are found on the surface of the endoplasmic reticulum.
    (B) The cytoplasm contains free ribosomes.
    (C) Ribosomes engage in protein synthesis.
    (D) Ribosomes are responsible for active diffusion.
    (E) Ribosomes contain RNA.

GO ON TO THE NEXT PAGE.

57. The heights of full-grown pine trees in a Canadian forest are found to vary from 40 feet to 65 feet. If natural selection acts to stabilize the height of the forest, the greatest number of trees would be expected to fall into which height category?

(A) 40-45 feet
(B) 45-50 feet
(C) 50-55 feet
(D) 55-60 feet
(E) 60-65 feet

58. Which of the following lists of biological classifications starts with the most general category and becomes more specific as it proceeds?

(A) Kingdom, order, class, species, genus.
(B) Kingdom, class, order, genus, species.
(C) Order, kingdom, genus, species, class.
(D) Order, class, kingdom, species, genus.
(E) Class, kingdom, order, genus, species.

59. The part of the human digestive system where water used in digestion is reabsorbed into the body is called the

(A) stomach
(B) esophagus
(C) large intestine
(D) small intestine
(E) oral cavity

60. A plant whose stem bends toward sunlight and whose roots grow toward a water source is said to be exhibiting which of the following tendencies?

(A) Phototropism and positive geotropism
(B) Phototropism and negative geotropism
(C) Phototropism and hydrotropism
(D) Hydrotropism and positive geotropism
(A) Hydrotropism and negative geotropism

STOP

IF YOU FINISH BEFORE TIME IS CALLED, YOU MAY CHECK YOUR WORK ON THIS SECTION ONLY.
DO NOT WORK ON ANY OTHER SECTION IN THE TEST.

Part II

Physical Science

Time—45 minutes

60 questions

Directions: Each group of questions below consists of five lettered choices followed by a list of numbered phrases or sentences. For each numbered phrase or sentence select the one choice that is most closely related to it. Each choice may be used once, more than once, or not at all in each group.

Questions 1 and 2

    (A) Atomic bond
    (B) Metallic bond
    (C) Ionic bond
    (D) Network bond
    (E) Molecular bond

1. A solid exhibiting which bond structure will be the best conductor of heat and electricity?

2. Diamond, one of the hardest materials known, is held together by these bonds.

Questions 3 and 4

    (A) Current
    (B) Capacitance
    (C) Power
    (D) Resistance
    (E) Voltage

3. This is the flow of positive charge.

4. This is the same as potential difference.

Questions 5 through 8

    (A) Acceleration
    (B) Force
    (C) Momentum
    (D) Velocity
    (E) Energy

5. This is not a vector quantity.

6. This is a measure of the inertia of an object.

7. This is the change in the displacement of an object over time.

8. This is the capacity to do work.

Questions 9 through 11

    (A) Jupiter
    (B) Mercury
    (C) Pluto
    (D) Saturn
    (E) Venus

9. This planet has the shortest orbit time of all the planets in the solar system.

10. This is the largest planet in the solar system.

11. This was the last planet in the solar system to be discovered.

GO ON TO THE NEXT PAGE.

Questions 12 and 13

(A) $Ni^{2+} + 2e^- \rightarrow Ni^0$
(B) $HNO_3 \rightarrow H^+ + NO_3^-$
(C) $Ag^0 \rightarrow Ag^+ + e^-$
(D) $NaCl \rightarrow Na^+ + Cl^-$
(E) $Mg(OH)_2 \rightarrow Mg^{2+} + 2\,OH^-$

12. This reaction shows the dissociation of an acid.

13. This is an oxidation reaction.

Questions 14 and 15

(A) Alpha particle
(B) Beta particle
(C) Electron
(D) Neutron
(E) Proton

14. This is an uncharged subatomic particle.

15. Of the particles listed, this one has the greatest mass.

Directions: Each of the questions or incomplete statements below is followed by five suggested answers or completions. Select the one that is best in each case.

16. A rock that results from a change to another rock brought about by such factors as temperature, pressure, or chemical reaction is called a(n)

(A) sedimentary rock
(B) igneous rock
(C) extrusive rock
(D) intrusive rock
(E) metamorphic rock

17. During a thunderstorm, an observer notices that a flash of lightning is seen a few seconds before a clap of thunder is heard. What is the best explanation for this phenomenon?

(A) The event that causes thunder occurs before the event that causes lightning.
(B) The event that causes lightning occurs before the event that causes thunder.
(C) Sound waves travel faster than light waves.
(D) Light waves travel faster than sound waves.
(E) The delay is an illusion caused by the movement of the storm.

18. Which of the molecules listed below is a polar molecule?

(A) H_2
(B) N_2
(C) CO_2
(D) Cl_2
(E) H_2O

19. During a solar eclipse

(A) Earth passes directly between the Moon and the Sun
(B) the Moon passes directly between Earth and the Sun
(C) the Sun passes directly between Earth and the Moon
(D) Earth, the Sun, and the Moon form a right angle with Earth as the vertex
(E) Earth, the Sun, and the Moon form a right angle with the Moon as the vertex

GO ON TO THE NEXT PAGE.

20. When a substance changes phase, energy must be absorbed or released, depending on the process which is occurring. When molten iron solidifies, the energy released during the phase change is the

(A) heat of vaporization
(B) heat of fusion
(C) specific heat
(D) heat capacity
(E) freezing point

21. The figure below shows a small section of the periodic table of the elements.

8 O 16	9 F 19	10 Ne 20
16 S 32	17 Cl 35	18 Ar 40

The chemical behavior of which of the following elements will be most similar to that of chlorine?

(A) Sulfur
(B) Oxygen
(C) Fluorine
(D) Neon
(E) Argon

22. An object that is set in motion in the absence of any external force will

(A) eventually slow down and stop
(B) continue to move at the same speed in a straight line
(C) accelerate until it reaches the speed of light
(D) continue to move at the same speed in a circular path
(E) move in an inward spiral until it stops

23. For which of the following states of matter is entropy the greatest?

(A) Solid
(B) Liquid
(C) Gas
(D) Solution
(E) Colloid

24. Which of the following descriptions of Earth's location in space goes from the most specific to the most general?

(A) Universe, solar system, Milky Way galaxy.
(B) Milky Way galaxy, solar system, universe.
(C) Milky Way galaxy, universe, solar system.
(D) Solar system, Milky Way galaxy, universe.
(E) Solar system, universe, Milky Way galaxy.

25. If a 0.01 molar solution of hydrochloric acid reacts with a 0.01 molar solution of sodium hydroxide, the resulting solution will contain

(A) hydrochloric acid and water
(B) sodium hydroxide and water
(C) ammonia and water
(D) sodium chloride and water
(E) only water

26. The tidal ebb and flow of Earth's water systems is caused mainly by

(A) variations in rainfall over different parts of Earth
(B) the melting and refreezing of the polar ice caps
(C) the interaction of fresh water and salt water in coastal areas
(D) the effects of underwater seismic activity
(E) the gravitational pull of the Moon

GO ON TO THE NEXT PAGE.

Questions 27 through 30

Carbon-14 undergoes beta decay into an isotope of nitrogen as shown in the table below. The amount of carbon-14 present in an organic object can be used to tell how old the object is because the decay rate of carbon-14 is constant and the amount of carbon-14 begins to decrease when the organism dies. Carbon dating is done by comparing the amount of carbon-14 present in an object to the amount that would be expected to be found in a living organism.

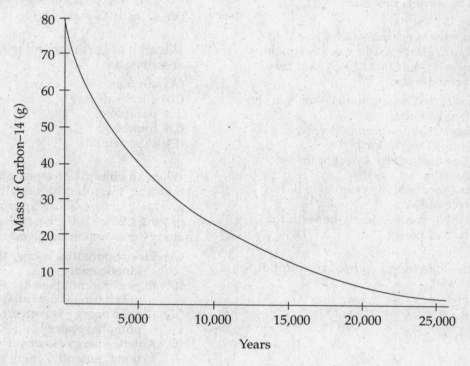

27. What is the half-life of carbon-14?
    (A) 1,000 years
    (B) 2,300 years
    (C) 5,700 years
    (D) 11,400 years
    (E) 22,800 years

28. Carbon-14 dating can be used to fix the date of a book. The date found by carbon-14 dating will be the date when
    (A) the book was written
    (B) the book was published
    (C) the tree that produced the pages for the book was planted
    (D) the tree that produced the pages for the book was cut down
    (E) the ink was applied to the pages

29. Which isotope of nitrogen is produced as a result of the decay of carbon-14?
    (A) Nitrogen-12
    (B) Nitrogen-13
    (C) Nitrogen-14
    (D) Nitrogen-15
    (E) Nitrogen-16

30. Approximately what percent of the carbon-14 in an object will remain when 17,000 years have passed?
    (A) 13 percent
    (B) 25 percent
    (C) 50 percent
    (D) 75 percent
    (E) 88 percent

GO ON TO THE NEXT PAGE.

31. Which of the following will be true of a substance that has a specific gravity of 0.5?

   (A) It will float in water.
   (B) It will sink in water.
   (C) It will absorb water.
   (D) It will repel water.
   (E) It will be soluble in water.

32. An igneous rock is examined and found to have a smooth, glassy texture and no distinct crystal structure. It is most likely that this rock was formed from

   (A) sediments that accumulated slowly at the surface of Earth
   (B) sediments that accumulated very quickly at the surface of Earth
   (C) glacial activity which brought many kinds of rocks together
   (D) magma that cooled very quickly at the surface of Earth
   (E) magma that cooled slowly beneath the surface of Earth

33. Which of the following is the longest unit of geological time?

   (A) Eon
   (B) Epoch
   (C) Era
   (D) Period
   (E) Year

34. The atomic number of boron is five. This means that a boron atom must always contain five

   (A) protons
   (B) neutrons
   (C) ions
   (D) nucleons
   (E) electrons

35. In the Northern Hemisphere, daylight hours are longest in the month of June and the weather is warmest around this time. This is because during the month of June

   (A) Earth is closer to the sun than it is at any other time during the year
   (B) Earth is farther away from the Sun than it is at any other time during the year
   (C) Earth is the same distance from the Sun as it is during the rest of the year
   (D) the Northern Hemisphere is tilted toward the Sun
   (E) the Northern Hemisphere is tilted away from the Sun

36. What is the definition of density?

   (A) Density is the same as mass.
   (B) Density is the same as weight.
   (C) Density is mass multiplied by acceleration due to gravity.
   (D) Density is mass divided by acceleration due to gravity.
   (E) Density is mass divided by volume.

37. The orbit of Earth around the Sun can best be described as

   (A) circular
   (B) elliptical
   (C) parabolic
   (D) hyperbolic
   (E) exponential

38. When an object is dropped off the roof of a building, the speed of the falling object will gradually increase as it approaches the ground. What is the best description of the energy conversion involved in this process?

   (A) Elastic potential energy is converted to kinetic energy.
   (B) Elastic potential energy is converted to gravitational potential energy.
   (C) Kinetic energy is converted to elastic potential energy.
   (D) Kinetic energy is converted to gravitational potential energy.
   (E) Gravitational potential energy is converted to kinetic energy.

39. The vapor pressure of a liquid is gradually increased until it becomes equal to the surrounding atmospheric pressure. What will happen to a liquid under these conditions?

   (A) It will boil.
   (B) It will freeze.
   (C) Its color will become darker.
   (D) Its color will become lighter.
   (E) It will become more dense.

GO ON TO THE NEXT PAGE.

Questions 40 and 41

A simple balance scale is set up as shown below:

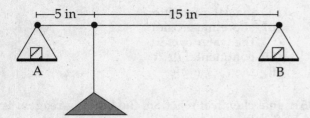

An object of unknown weight is hung from side A. Blocks of known weight are then hung from side B until the scale is found to be in rotational equilibrium. The weight of the object hanging from side A can then be calculated by using the known weight hanging from side B.

40. The balance reaches rotational equilibrium when a 6-pound weight is hung from side B. What is the weight of the object hanging from side A?

(A) 2 pounds
(B) 3 pounds
(C) 6 pounds
(D) 12 pounds
(E) 18 pounds

41. What is the name given to a force applied to a lever arm in such a way as to cause a rotation about an axis?

(A) Pressure
(B) Torque
(C) Vector
(D) Inertia
(E) Power

42. Which of the following metals has the weakest intermolecular bonds?

(A) Iron
(B) Copper
(C) Mercury
(D) Silver
(E) Gold

43. When a catalyst is added to a chemical reaction, the rate of the reaction is increased. The rate of reaction increases because the catalyst

(A) increases the activation energy of the reaction
(B) decreases the activation energy of the reaction
(C) increases the enthalpy change of the reaction
(D) decreases the enthalpy change of the reaction
(E) increases the free energy change of the reaction

44. A phenomenon known as *red shift* is often cited as proof that the universe is expanding. When observers on Earth look at a distant star, the light they see is redder than the light actually emitted by the star. This occurs because the star is moving away from the observer. What is the difference between the light wave seen by the observer on Earth and the wave emitted by the star?

(A) The observer will see a light wave with a lower frequency.
(B) The observer will see a light wave with a higher frequency.
(C) The observer will see a light wave with a lower velocity.
(D) The observer will see a light wave with a higher velocity.
(E) The light wave seen by the observer will be identical to the light wave emitted at the source.

45. What is the layer of the atmosphere that lies closest to the surface of Earth?

(A) Troposphere
(B) Hydrosphere
(C) Thermosphere
(D) Lithosphere
(E) Stratosphere

GO ON TO THE NEXT PAGE.

46. In an experiment, two objects, A and B, travel towards each other and meet in a head-on collision. The two objects then stick together and continue to move. If, after the collision, the two objects move in the same direction that object A was traveling in before the collision, the experimenters can conclude that object A had greater

    (A) energy
    (B) momentum
    (C) velocity
    (D) acceleration
    (E) mass

47. Elemental potassium contains only one electron in its valence shell. Which of the following can be predicted about potassium based on this fact?

    (A) Potassium is rarely found in its uncombined, elemental form.
    (B) Potassium has a low freezing point.
    (C) Potassium is a gas at room temperature.
    (D) Potassium is a noble gas.
    (E) Potassium does not form bonds easily.

48. The planets in our solar system are maintained in their orbits around the Sun by

    (A) electrostatic force
    (B) nuclear force
    (C) magnetic force
    (D) gravitational force
    (E) frictional force

49. Which of the following energy sources produces no harmful waste products and depletes no natural resources?

    (A) Natural gas energy
    (B) Nuclear energy
    (C) Solar energy
    (D) Oil energy
    (E) Coal energy

50. The theory that all of Earth's continents were once part of the same land mass and have gradually moved apart to their present positions is known as

    (A) glacial deposition
    (B) shoreline erosion
    (C) the water cycle
    (D) continental drift
    (E) the rock cycle

51. In a chemical reaction, the limiting reagent is the reactant that is

    (A) present in the greatest molar quantity
    (B) present in the smallest molar quantity
    (C) present in the greatest quantity by mass
    (D) present in the smallest quantity by mass
    (E) the first to be used up over the course of the reaction

52. Three sets of fossils are found buried in an area consisting of many layers of sedimentary rock. Fossils A and B are found buried at about the same depth. Fossil C is found after digging deeper. Which of following judgments can be made about the ages of the fossils?

    (A) Fossil A is older than fossils B and C.
    (B) Fossil B is older than fossils A and C.
    (C) Fossil C is older than fossils A and B.
    (D) Fossil A is older than fossil B, which is older than fossil C.
    (E) All of the fossils are the same age.

GO ON TO THE NEXT PAGE.

Questions 53 and 54

A sealed chamber of fixed volume contains several different kinds of gas. The chamber contains one mole of oxygen gas (molecular weight = 32 amu), one mole of carbon dioxide gas (molecular weight = 44 amu), and two moles of nitrogen gas (molecular weight = 28 amu). It can be assumed that the ideal gas laws apply to the gases in the chamber.

53. What percent of the pressure in the chamber is due to the oxygen gas?

(A) 25 percent
(B) 33 percent
(C) 50 percent
(D) 67 percent
(E) 75 percent

54. If the temperature inside the chamber is gradually increased, what will be the most likely result?

(A) The pressure in the chamber will increase.
(B) The pressure in the chamber will decrease.
(C) The number of moles of gas in the chamber will increase.
(D) The number of moles of gas in the chamber will decrease.
(E) The volume of the chamber will decrease.

55. A region in space that contains so much mass that even light can not escape from its gravitational pull is called a

(A) red giant
(B) black hole
(C) quasar
(D) white dwarf
(E) sunspot

56. Given the reaction for the formation of ammonia from hydrogen and nitrogen gases:

$$3\,H_2(g) \;+\; N_2(g) \;\rightarrow\; 2\,NH_3(g)$$

If one mole of hydrogen gas is consumed over the course of the reaction, how many moles of ammonia are produced?

(A) $\frac{1}{3}$ mole

(B) $\frac{2}{3}$ mole

(C) 1 mole

(D) 2 moles

(E) 3 moles

57. What is the approximate percentage of Earth's surface that is covered with water?

(A) 10 percent
(B) 30 percent
(C) 50 percent
(D) 70 percent
(E) 90 percent

58. The number of times that a wave cycle repeats itself over the course of one second is called the wave's

(A) wavelength
(B) period
(C) amplitude
(D) phase
(E) frequency

GO ON TO THE NEXT PAGE.

59. A compass point held near the surface of Earth will swing around to indicate North. This is because

    (A) Earth's gravity is strongest near the North Pole
    (B) Earth's gravity is weakest near the North Pole
    (C) a magnetic field runs along the surface of Earth
    (D) the North Pole is always pointed toward the Moon
    (E) the North Pole is always pointed away from the Moon

60. An experiment was conducted to test the effects of different acid solutions on the weathering of solid calcium carbonate. The experiment was conducted by pouring various solutions of acetic acid, hydrochloric acid, nitric acid, and pure water over limestone rocks in separate trials and observing the results. Which of the following trials would serve as the control for the experiment?

    (A) Pouring nitric acid on a rock
    (B) Pouring acetic acid on a rock
    (C) Pouring hydrochloric acid on a rock
    (D) Pouring pure water on a rock
    (E) Pouring a mixture of all four liquids on a rock

STOP

IF YOU FINISH BEFORE TIME IS CALLED, YOU MAY CHECK YOUR WORK ON THIS SECTION ONLY.
DO NOT WORK ON ANY OTHER SECTION IN THE TEST.

NO TEST MATERIAL ON THIS PAGE.

SCORING YOUR TEST

This test is a facsimile of the ETS-written CLEP general exam in Natural Sciences. Care has been taken to make sure that this test closely resembles the actual exam both in content and format. In other words, when you take the real CLEP, it should look a lot like the test you've just taken.

ETS has never released its scoring methods for the CLEP. ETS states in its literature that, if you get half the raw score points available to you on the test, you should score the national medium—usually between 480 and 500—on a given test.

Your raw score is determined by subtracting 1/4 the number of questions you answer incorrectly from the number of questions you answer correctly. Questions you leave blank are worth 0 points.

Typically, you need about 2/3 of the raw score points available on a test to score in the mid-600s on an ETS test, but, again, this is only speculation regarding the CLEP.

21

Answers and Explanations to the Natural Sciences Exam

SECTION 5

Read this entire section, even the explanations for the questions you answered correctly. The material covered in these explanations add up to a pretty thorough review of the material tested on the CLEP. Plus, many explanations contain helpful test-taking tips.

Questions 1 to 3

    (A) Adrenaline
    (B) Insulin
    (C) Testosterone
    (D) Gastrin
    (E) Histamine

1. This hormone, which regulates the amount of glucose in the blood, is produced in the pancreas.

2. This is released by damaged tissue and it acts to dilate blood vessels.

3. When the body is subjected to pain or anger, this hormone is produced.

1. **(B)** is the correct answer. Insulin regulates the amount of glucose in the blood and is produced in the islets of Langerhans, in the pancreas. A deficiency of insulin in the body results in the condition known as diabetes.

2. **(E)** is the correct answer. Histamine causes the muscles in blood vessels to relax, making it easier for infection-fighting agents to get to the damaged area.

3. **(A)** is the correct answer. Adrenaline is released by the adrenal glands when the body is subjected to stress, causing the fight-or-flight response.

(D) Gastrin is produced by the stomach and intestine to aid in digestion.

(E) Testosterone, which is produced in the testes, regulates the male sex organs.

SECTION 5

<u>Questions 4 and 5</u>

    (A) Animals
    (B) Fungi
    (C) Monera
    (D) Plants
    (E) Protista

4. Members of this kingdom can be either vertebrates or invertebrates.

4. (A) is the correct answer. Animals are classified as vertebrates (animals with backbones) and invertebrates (animals without backbones).

5. Bacteria are members of this kingdom.

5. (B) is the correct answer. Bacteria are part of the kingdom Monera.

The answer choices (A)-(E) are the five kingdoms into which all living things are generally divided. Here are some rough definitions:

Monera: simple single-celled organisms (bacteria).

Protista: more complex single celled organisms (protozoa, single-celled algae).

Fungi: relatively simple multicelled organisms that can't produce their own food (mold, yeast, mushrooms)

Plants: multicelled organisms that produce their own food through photosynthesis.

Animals: complex multicelled organisms that can't produce their own food.

<u>Questions 6 to 8</u>

    (A) Carbon dioxide
    (B) Helium
    (C) Nitrogen
    (D) Oxygen
    (E) Sulfur dioxide

6. This gas makes up most of Earth's atmosphere.

6. (C) is the correct answer. Nitrogen is far and away the most common gas in the Earth's atmosphere, making up 78 percent of the air. Oxygen is next, at 21 percent.

7. This gas is the main product of photosynthesis.

7. (D) is the correct answer. Photosynthesis consumes carbon dioxide and produces oxygen.

8. This gas combines with water in the atmosphere to form acid rain.

8. (E) is the correct answer. Sulfur dioxide, a common industrial waste product, combines with water to form acid rain.

(A) Carbon dioxide is produced by respiration and consumed by photosynthesis.

(B) Helium is a noble gas. It is present in the atmosphere in trace amounts.

SECTION 5

Questions 9 to 11

    (A) Artery
    (B) Atrium
    (C) Capillary
    (D) Vein
    (E) Ventricle

9. Material is exchanged between the blood and the body's interstitial fluid here.

10. The part of the circulatory system with the thickest, strongest muscle.

11. This carries deoxygenated blood from the limbs back to the heart.

9. **(C)** is the correct answer. Capillaries are extremely thin blood vessels that allow material to be passed back and forth between the blood and the tissues through which it passes.

10. **(E)** is the correct answer. The ventricles are the parts of the heart responsible for pumping the blood into the body, so they must have the strongest muscles in the circulatory system.

11. **(D)** is the correct answer. Oxygenated blood is carried away from the heart and toward the limbs in arteries. In the limbs, the blood passes through capillaries, where oxygen is passed to the body's tissues. The deoxygenated blood then returns to the heart in veins.

(A) Arteries carry blood away from the heart.

(B) Blood returning to the heart enters the atrium first, then passes to the ventricle.

SECTION 5

Questions 12 and 13

The picture below represents the climatic conditions for some of Earth's biomes.

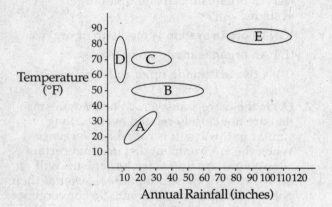

12. This region represents desert.

13. This region represents tropical forest.

Questions 14 and 15

    (A) Scurvy
    (B) Rickets
    (C) Measles
    (D) Tetanus
    (E) Ringworm

14. A condition caused by a diet poor in vitamin C.

15. A condition caused by a bacterial infection.

12. **(D)** is the correct answer. Deserts have relatively high temperatures and very little rainfall.

13. **(E)** is the correct answer. Tropical forests have very high temperatures and an extremely large amount of rainfall.

14. **(A)** is the correct answer. Scurvy, a disease which produces anemia, slow healing, bleeding gums, and swollen joints, is caused by a vitamin C deficiency.

15. **(D)** is the correct answer. Tetanus, also called lockjaw, is caused by a bacterial infection.

    (B) Rickets, in which the bones become soft, is caused by a vitamin D deficiency.

    (C) Measles is caused by a viral infection.

    (E) Ringworm is caused by a fungal infection.

SECTION 5

QUESTIONS	EXPLANATIONS

16. Which of the following is the most fundamental level in the organization of living things?

 (A) Organism
 (B) Tissue
 (C) Organ system
 (D) Organ
 (E) Cell

16. **(E)** is the correct answer. Each of the other four items listed is made up of cells. The hierarchy of the other four answers goes like this:

 (A) An organism is made up of organ systems.

 (C) An organ system is made up of organs.

 (D) An organ is made up of tissues.

 (B) A tissue is made up of cells.

17. The flippers of whales resemble the fins of fish in both form and function. What is the most likely explanation for this resemblance?

 (A) Whales and fish evolved similar structures in response to similar environmental stresses.
 (B) A whale is a kind of fish.
 (C) Whales and fish have interbred, leading to certain physical similarities.
 (D) Whales evolved flippers in imitation of fish.
 (E) Both fins and flippers evolved from the legs of land creatures.

17. **(A)** is the correct answer. When organisms that are not closely related evolve along similar pathways, it is called convergence. When the environment dictates that certain adaptations are necessary, organisms will evolve toward these adaptations, even if their points of origin are different. So convergence occurs when two different organisms evolve toward the same adaptations independently because that is what the environment requires.

18. The largest part of the human brain and also the part of the brain most associated with intellectual capacity is called the

 (A) cerebellum
 (B) medulla
 (C) thalamus
 (D) hypothalamus
 (E) cerebrum

18. **(E)** is the correct answer. In humans, the cerebrum occupies about 80 percent of the total brain volume. It is the site of the brain's actual thinking processes.

 Here are some rough descriptions of the functions of the other parts of the brain listed as answer choices:

 (A) The cerebellum is concerned with balance and coordination.

 (B) The medulla is concerned with visceral functions such as breathing and heartbeat.

 (C) The thalamus is involved with the integration of sensory input.

 (D) The hypothalamus synthesizes hormones.

19. A particle that is not considered a living thing, but reproduces by attaching itself to a living cell and injecting DNA or RNA into its host is called a

 (A) fungus
 (B) virus
 (C) spore
 (D) barnacle
 (E) protozoa

19. **(B)** is the correct answer. Viruses are not considered to be living things, but they use living things to propagate themselves. All of the other choices are living things.

SECTION 5

QUESTIONS	EXPLANATIONS

20. Which of the following shows the progression of the food chain from producers to secondary consumers?

    (A) Carnivores, autotrophs, herbivores.
    (B) Autotrophs, carnivores, herbivores.
    (C) Autotrophs, herbivores, carnivores.
    (D) Herbivores, autotrophs, carnivores.
    (E) Herbivores, carnivores, autotrophs.

20. **(C)** is the correct answer. Autotrophs, such as plants, use light energy to produce the chemical energy they need, so they are producers. Herbivores (plant-eating animals) consume autotrophs to get the energy they need, so they are primary consumers. Carnivores must consume animals to get the energy they need, so they are secondary consumers.

21. In order for the ecological balance in a certain pond to be maintained, the algae present in the pond must remain in dynamic equilibrium. This means that

    (A) no algae should be present in the pond
    (B) algae growth should be faster than algae depletion
    (C) algae growth should take place at the same rate as algae depletion
    (D) algae growth should take place more slowly than algae depletion
    (E) algae growth and depletion should not take place

21. **(C)** is the correct answer. Dynamic equilibrium means that all processes are taking place at the same rate, so no overall change can be seen.

Here's why the other answers are wrong:

(A) If no algae is present, there is no dynamic equilibrium.

(B) If algae growth is faster than depletion, the amount of algae increases, thus destroying the equilibrium.

(C) If algae growth is slower than depletion, the amount of algae decreases, thus destroying the equilibrium.

(E) This might be an equilibrium situation (nothing is changing), but it would be a *static* equilibrium.

22. A normal cell in a male human being contains 46 chromosomes. How many chromosomes are contained in a normal sperm cell?

    (A) 10
    (B) 23
    (C) 46
    (D) 92
    (E) 184

22. **(B)** is the correct answer. A human sperm cell is a haploid cell, with half as many chromosomes as the normal diploid cell. The sperm cell, with 23 chromosomes, unites with an egg cell, also with 23 chromosomes, to form a cell with 46 chromosomes.

SECTION 5

QUESTIONS	EXPLANATIONS

23. It is thought that modern-day giraffes evolved from ancestors with shorter necks. Which of the following explanations for this evolution is most in keeping with the modern theory of natural selection?

(A) Giraffes have always been born with short necks, which gradually stretch as they grow older.

(B) Over the course of the giraffes' lifetimes, constant reaching for foliage high in trees caused their necks to stretch slightly. This quality was passed to succeeding generations, causing a gradual increase in neck length.

(C) Genetic mutations caused there to be giraffes with different neck lengths. It was purely random chance that caused only giraffes with long necks to survive.

(D) Genetic mutations caused there to be giraffes with different neck lengths. The giraffes with long necks were better equipped to feed on the foliage high in trees. The long-necked giraffes were better able to reproduce and passed the mutation on to their offspring.

(E) Giraffes with different neck lengths gravitated to different geographical regions. Natural disasters occurring in all of the regions except those occupied by long-necked giraffes caused all other giraffes to die out.

23. **(D)** is the correct answer. According to the modern theory of natural selection, mutations occur at random. If a particular mutation, such as a long neck in a giraffe, provides an advantage over other mutations, then the possessor of that mutation stands a better chance of surviving and passing that mutation on to its offspring. Long-necked giraffes had better access to food, so every time a mutation occurred that lengthened a giraffes neck, the favorable environment for that mutation caused it to be passed on to succeeding generations. None of the other answers is in keeping with the modern theory of natural selection.

SECTION 5

QUESTIONS	EXPLANATIONS

<u>Questions 24 to 26</u>

Blood type is a genetically inherited trait. There are three alleles for blood type: A, B, and O. The O allele is recessive to both the A allele and the B allele, so a person with an A allele and an O allele will by type A. Neither the A nor the B allele is dominant over the other, so a person with both the A and the B allele will be type AB.

24. Which of the following could NOT be the blood type of the offspring of two type AB parents?

 (A) A
 (B) B
 (C) AB
 (D) O
 (E) All blood types are possible.

24. **(D)** is the correct answer. The offspring of two type AB parents will all have A or B alleles. Since A and B alleles dominate over O alleles, none of the offspring can be type O.

25. Which of the following are possible gene combinations for a person with type B blood?

 (A) BO or AB
 (B) BB or AB
 (C) BB or BO
 (D) BO or AO
 (E) BB only

25. **(C)** is the correct answer. In order for a person to be type B, he or she must have the B allele and must not have the A allele. So both BB and BO will produce type B blood.

26. What is the probability that the offspring of a type AB parent and a type O parent will have blood that is type A?

 (A)   0 percent
 (B) 25 percent
 (C) 50 percent
 (D) 75 percent
 (E) 100 percent

26. **(C)** is the correct answer. Use the Punnett square:

	A	B
O	AO	BO
O	AO	BO

The chances are 50 percent that the offspring will be type A and 50 percent that the offspring will be type B.

SECTION 5

27. Which of the following nitrogenous bases is contained in DNA but not in RNA?

    (A) Adenine
    (B) Cytosine
    (C) Guanine
    (D) Thymine
    (E) Uracil

27. **(D)** is the correct answer. DNA and RNA each contain combinations of four nitrogenous bases. They have three bases in common and they differ on the fourth. Thymine is contained only in DNA.

    (A), (B) and (C) are three nitrogenous bases are contained in both DNA and RNA. (E) Uracil is contained in RNA, but not in DNA.

28. The muscle cells of an animal require a great deal of energy. As a result of this need for energy, muscle cells would be expected to contain a relatively large number of

    (A) cilia
    (B) mitochondria
    (C) flagella
    (D) vacuoles
    (E) centrioles

28. **(B)** is the correct answer. Mitochondria supply the cell with chemical energy, so they can be found in greatest numbers in cells with high energy requirements.

    Here are some rough descriptions of the functions of the other cell parts listed as answer choices:

    (A) Cilia and (C) flagella play a part in cell locomotion.

    (D) Vacuoles are used by cells for storage.

    (E) Centrioles play a part in cell reproduction.

29. It has been predicted that the destruction of the tropical rain forests will contribute to which of the following ecological effects?

    (A) Global warming
    (B) Glaciation
    (C) Volcanic activity
    (D) Shoreline erosion
    (E) Tidal waves

29. **(A)** is the correct answer. Carbon dioxide, which is consumed by the rain forests, plays a large part in producing the greenhouse effect, which warms the surface of the Earth. Scientists fear that if the destruction of the rain forests continues, the concentration of carbon dioxide in the atmosphere will increase, resulting in global warming.

30. The process by which plants convert the energy in sunlight into chemical energy which can be stored and used by the plant is called

    (A) cellular respiration
    (B) mitosis
    (C) pinocytosis
    (D) fermentation
    (E) photosynthesis

30. **(E)** is the correct answer. In photosynthesis, plants convert the energy in sunlight into energy stored in chemical bonds.

    Here are some brief descriptions of the other answer choices:

    (A) Cellular respiration is the process by which animals convert the energy stored in plants into energy that they can use.

    (B) Mitosis is part of the process of cell reproduction.

    (C) Pinocytosis is one method by which matter is transported into a cell from the outside.

    (D) Fermentation is a process in which energy is released in the absence of oxygen.

SECTION 5

QUESTIONS	EXPLANATIONS

31. In human reproduction, fertilization of the egg normally takes place in which part of the female's reproductive system?

    (A) Ovary
    (B) Uterus
    (C) Cervix
    (D) Fallopian tube
    (E) Labium major

32. Initially, a population of birds contains birds with beaks that vary randomly in length from long to short, with all gradations in between. Environmental factors change to provide better feeding opportunities for birds with very long beaks and for birds with very short beaks. Which of the following diagrams best shows the distribution of beak lengths among the birds after natural selection has taken place?

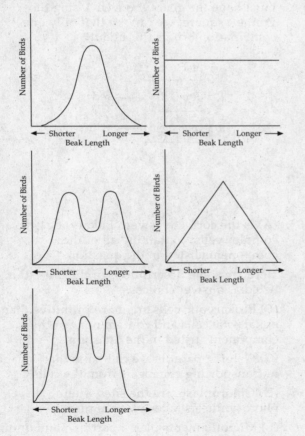

31. **(D)** is the correct answer. The egg is produced in the ovary. It gradually passes down the fallopian tube. Fertilization can occur if sperm comes in contact with the egg as it passes through the fallopian tube. The fertilized egg then passes into the uterus, where the embryo develops. The cervix and labium major are located in the outer areas of the female reproductive system.

32. **(C)** is the correct answer. The graph shows that the greatest number of birds will have short beaks or long beaks. There will be a dip in the middle of the curve, because medium beaks are not favored by the environment.

SECTION 5

QUESTIONS	EXPLANATIONS

33. In the condition known as anemia, the body does not receive enough oxygen to maintain proper cell respiration. Anemia is caused by a deficiency in the body's supply of

    (A) red blood cells
    (B) white blood cells
    (C) plasma
    (D) platelets
    (E) lymphocytes

33. **(A)** is the correct answer. Red blood cells contain hemoglobin, the protein responsible for oxygen transport. Since red blood cells are directly responsible for oxygen transport, a shortage of red blood cells will cause a shortage of oxygen.

Here are some descriptions of the other blood parts listed as answer choices:

(B) White blood cells act to fight foreign matter introduced into the body.

(C) Plasma is the liquid part of the blood.

(D) Platelets play a part in the clotting of blood.

(E) A lymphocyte is a kind of white blood cell, so its job is to fight infection.

34. In a certain flower, the trait for red color (R) is dominant over the trait for white color (w). In a breeding experiment, two parent plants of unknown genotype produce offspring. If approximately half of the offspring are white and half are red, what is the predicted genotype of the parent plants?

    (A) Rw and Rw
    (B) RR and Rw
    (C) ww and Rw
    (D) RR and RR
    (E) ww and ww

34. **(C)** is the correct answer. In order for half of the offspring to be white, half of the offspring must have the genotype ww. Using the Punnett square, we can see that only one combination brings this about.

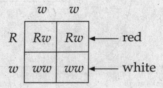

35. Ribosomes, mitochondria, and lysosomes can be found in

    (A) eukaryotic cells
    (B) prokaryotic cells
    (C) Golgi apparatus
    (D) chloroplasts
    (E) microfilaments

35. **(A)** is the correct answer. Eukaryotic cells are complex cells, containing all of the components listed in the question.

Here are some descriptions of the other things listed as answer choices:

(B) Prokaryotic cells are more primitive than eukaryotic cells and contain none of the components listed in the question.

(C) Golgi apparatus are cell parts that engage in transporting chemicals from the cells.

(D) Chloroplasts are the sites where photosynthesis takes place in plants.

(E) Microfilaments play a part in maintaining the structure of the cell.

SECTION 5

QUESTIONS	EXPLANATIONS

36. An example of bones in the human body that are connected by fused joints are the bones that comprise the

(A) hand
(B) foot
(C) arm
(D) leg
(E) skull

36. **(E)** is the correct answer. The bones that make up the skull are held together by fused joints, which make them immovable. The joints of the bones in the limbs are held together by ligaments, so that they are moveable.

37. Flowers are important in the reproductive cycle of a plant because they

(A) prevent impurities from interfering with the parts of the plant involved in reproduction
(B) provide protection from wind and rain
(C) attract pollen-bearing insects
(D) are the major sites of photosynthesis in the plant
(E) provide shade for the parts of the plant involved in reproduction

37. **(C)** is the correct answer. Flowers, with their bright colors and scents, attract insects. Insects bring pollen from flower to flower, allowing fertilization to take place.

38. A part of any standard medical examination is the measure of the patient's blood pressure. When a doctor measures a patient's blood pressure, the doctor measures

(A) the number of heartbeats per minute
(B) the volume of plasma in the body
(C) the number of red blood cells in the body
(D) the force per unit area exerted by the blood on the vessel walls
(E) the ratio of red blood cells to white blood cells

38. **(D)** is the correct answer. Blood pressure is the pressure exerted by the blood on the walls of the blood vessels. It is recorded with two different numbers. The systolic pressure is the larger number, which represents the pressure exerted when the heart's ventricles are contracting. The diastolic pressure is the smaller number, representing the pressure when the ventricles are relaxed.

39. Which of the following lists the types of species that make up the food pyramid in order of largest to smallest population?

(A) Producers outnumber primary consumers, who outnumber secondary consumers.
(B) Producers outnumber secondary consumers, who outnumber primary consumers.
(C) Primary consumers outnumber secondary consumers, who outnumber producers.
(D) Primary consumers outnumber producers, who outnumber secondary consumers.
(E) Secondary consumers outnumber primary consumers, who outnumber producers.

39. **(A)** is the correct answer. In order for the food chain to be maintained, prey must outnumber predators. So living things at the bottom of the chain must outnumber those at the top of the chain, creating a food pyramid, with lots of producers on the bottom and a few secondary consumers at the top.

SECTION 5

QUESTIONS	EXPLANATIONS

40. Proteins are complex polymers made up of different combinations of smaller molecules that serve as building blocks. What are the building blocks that are combined to form proteins?

    (A) Polysaccharides
    (B) Phospholipids
    (C) Steroids
    (D) Amino acids
    (E) Fats

40. **(D)** is the correct answer. Proteins are long chains of amino acids that are connected by peptide bonds.

    The other answers:

    (A) Polysaccharides are types of carbohydrates.

    (B) (C) and (E) are types of lipids.

41. The most important substance that is used to provide energy for cellular functions is

    (A) ADP
    (B) ATP
    (C) DNA
    (D) rRNA
    (E) tRNA

41. **(B)** is the correct answer. ATP (adenosine triphosphate) is consumed by cells in order to provide energy.

    The other answer choices are acronyms you should be familiar with:

    (A) ADP (adenosine diphosphate) is used to form ATP and is created when ATP is consumed.

    (C) DNA (deoxyribonucleic acid) is the basis for genetics.

    (D) rRNA (ribosomal ribonucleic acid) and (E) tRNA (transfer ribonucleic acid) play a part in protein synthesis.

42. Color-blindness is a recessive, sex-linked trait. The gene for color-blindness is found only on the X chromosome. If a color-blind female and a male with normal vision produce offspring, the probable result will be that

    (A) all of the males will be color-blind
    (B) half of the males will be color-blind
    (C) none of the males will be color-blind
    (D) all of the females will be color-blind
    (E) half of the females will be color-blind

42. **(A)** is the correct answer. Males have the chromosome combination XY. Females have the chromosome combination XX. All of the males will get their X chromosome from the color-blind female, both of whose X chromosomes must have the gene for color-blindness. So all of the male offspring must be color-blind. All female offspring must get one X chromosome from the male parent. His non–color-blind X chromosome will dominate, so none of the female offsping will be color-blind.

SECTION 5

QUESTIONS

Questions 43 and 44

The graph below represents the growth curve of a population. The graph shows the increasing density of the population over time.

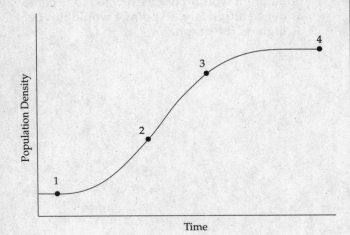

43. Which of the following is most likely true of the population at the time represented by point 4?
    (A) The population density is increasing very quickly.
    (B) Environmental conditions have changed, causing a sudden decrease in population density.
    (C) The population density is about the same as it was at the time represented by point 1.
    (D) The population density is at equilibrium at the carrying capacity of the environment.
    (E) The population density is undergoing random variation.

EXPLANATIONS

43. **(D)** is the correct answer. Population increase generally follows the S shaped curve shown in the diagram. At the top of the curve (point 4) the population has reached the maximum density that the environment can handle. Another way of saying this is to say that the population has reached the carrying capacity of the environment. Unless the environment changes radically, the population will stabilize at this density.

QUESTIONS	EXPLANATIONS

44. If a growth curve were assembled for a population that exists in an environment that is much less favorable to growth than that pictured above, how would the new curve be expected to differ from the curve above?

   (A) The slope from point 2 up to point 3 would be more steep and point 4 would be lower.

   (B) The slope from point 2 up to point 3 would be less steep and point 4 would be lower.

   (C) The slope from point 2 up to point 3 would be more steep and point 4 would be higher.

   (D) The slope from point 2 up to point 3 would be less steep and point 4 would be higher.

   (E) The slope from point 2 up to point 3 would be more steep and point 1 would be higher.

44. **(B)** is the correct answer. Under less favorable conditions, the population would grow more slowly, so the upward slope from point 2 to point 3 would be less steep. Also, under less favorable conditions, the population would not be expected to become as dense ultimately, so point 4 would not be as high on the graph.

45. The green color of plants is due to the presence in plant cells of

   (A) a cell wall
   (B) chloroplasts
   (C) cytoplasm
   (D) lysosomes
   (E) nuclei

45. **(B)** is the correct answer. Chloroplasts contain chlorophyll, which gives plants their green color.

   None of the other cell parts listed has anything to do with cell color. (A) Cell walls are thick outer membranes composed of cellulose present in plant cells. (C) Cytoplasm is the gel that all of the other cell components float around in. (D) Lysosomes are sacs containing enzymes in the cytoplasm. (E) The nucleus is the "brain" of the cell; it contains DNA.

SECTION 5

| QUESTIONS | EXPLANATIONS |

46. The Hardy Weinberg law is a set of hypothetical conditions under which no genetic change will occur in a sexually reproducing population from generation to generation. Which of the following is NOT a condition necessary for a population to be in accordance with the Hardy Weinberg law of genetic equilibrium?

(A) The population must be large enough to eliminate chance as a factor in genetic change.
(B) The members of the population must have long life spans.
(C) Genetic mutations must not occur in the population.
(D) There must be no emigration from the population or immigration to it.
(E) Reproduction among the members of the population must be random.

46. **(B)** is the correct answer. The genetic makeup of a population depends on the reproductive choices available; the life span of the members of a population has no bearing on its genetic makeup.

The other answers are all necessary to keep genetic change from occurring. (A) This condition is necessary because, in a small population, random genetic factors may be exaggerated by chance, causing genetic drift. (C) Mutations bring about random change in genetic makeup, so they must be ruled out if genetic makeup is to remain constant. (D) Emigration and immigration must be ruled out because they alter the genetic pool. (E) Random reproduction insures that certain genotypes won't come to dominate the gene pool.

47. The wolf belongs to the family Canidae, the order Carnivora, the species *lupus*, and the genus *Canis*. What is the Linnaean name for wolf?

(A) Canidae Carnivora
(B) Carnivora *Canis*
(C) *Canis* Canidae
(D) Carnivora *lupus*
(E) *Canis lupus*

47. **(E)** is the correct answer. The modern method of naming species dates from the Swedish naturalist Linnaeus, who lived in the eighteenth century. Linnaeus named species with the genus name first, followed by the species name. So if a wolf is of the genus *canis* and the species *lupus*, its Linnaean name is *Canis lupus*.

48. Sensory information is passed throughout the body by nerve cells. Which of the following is the best description of the method by which sensory information is passed along the axon of a nerve cell?

(A) Sodium and potassium ions are passed through the nerve cell wall in a sequence along the axon.
(B) DNA makes its way through the cytoplasm from one end of the axon to the other.
(C) The nerve cell nucleus emits nitrogen, which is carried by vacuoles along the axon.
(D) Information is passed through the chemical stimulation of muscles along the axon.
(E) Oxygen gas is passed along the axon by the nerve cell cilia.

48. **(A)** is the correct answer. The axon is a long, thin section that stretches out from a nerve cell. Basically, when the nerve cell is at rest, sodium ions are outside the axon and potassium ions are inside the axon. Information is passed along the axon when sodium and potassium ions cross the cell membrane in a sequence that moves from one end of the axon to the other. The other answers are just distractions, and they have nothing to do with nerve cells.

SECTION 5

QUESTIONS	EXPLANATIONS

49. These cell structures are used when a cell moves through a fluid.

    (A) Arteries
    (B) Follicles
    (C) Carrier molecules
    (D) Enzymes
    (E) Cilia

49. **(E)** is the correct answer. Cilia are long, thin organelles at the surface of a cell. They move back an forth, propelling the cell.

    The other answers:

    (A) Arteries carry blood in animals.

    (B) The follicle is the part of the ovary that produces the egg.

    (C) Carrier molecules move substances into and out of the cell.

    (D) Enzymes act as catalysts for biological reactions.

50. In order for sexual reproduction to occur, gametes must be produced during meiosis. How many gametes are produced from each parent cell over the entire course of meiosis?

    (A) 1
    (B) 2
    (C) 4
    (D) 8
    (E) 16

50. **(C)** is the correct answer. During meiosis, the parent cell splits into two daughter cells, each of which has the same number of chromosomes as the parent cell. Each of the daughter cells then splits into two gametes, which have half as many chromosomes as the parent cell. Thus, each parent cell produces four gametes.

51. Which of the following lists presents different kinds of animal life in the order in which they first appeared on the earth?

    (A) Amphibians, marine invertebrates, fish, mammals, reptiles.
    (B) Fish, amphibians, marine invertebrates, reptiles, mammals.
    (C) Reptiles, marine invertebrates, fish, amphibians, mammals.
    (D) Fish, marine invertebrates, amphibians, mammals, reptiles.
    (E) Marine invertebrates, fish, amphibians, reptiles, mammals.

51. **(E)** is the correct answer. Marine invertebrates appeared on the Earth first. Mammals appeared most recently.

52. Between the stages of zygote and embryo, the developing human embryo develops three cell layers.

Which of the following body parts develops from the ectoderm layer?

    (A) Stomach
    (B) Bones
    (C) Eyes
    (D) Lungs
    (E) Muscles

52. **(C)** is the correct answer. The eyes are formed from the ectoderm, which also forms the epidermis (outer skin) and the nervous system.

The other answer choices listed are formed from the other two cell layers, the endoderm and mesoderm. The inner parts of the digestive and respiratory organs, choices (A) and (D), are formed from the endoderm. The outer parts of these organs are formed from the mesoderm. Bones and muscles, choices (B) and (E), are formed from the mesoderm.

SECTION 5

QUESTIONS	EXPLANATIONS

53. Materials move into and out of cells in many different ways. When material is moved across a cell membrane into a cell against a concentration gradient, which process is taking place?

(A) Active transport
(B) Osmosis
(C) Passive diffusion
(D) Facilitated diffusion
(E) Endocytosis

53. **(A)** is the correct answer. In active transport, the cell expends energy in moving material against a concentration gradient (from a region of low concentration to a region of high concentration).

The other answer choices are other processes by which material is moved into and out of cells. In (B) osmosis, water moves across a membrane in an attempt to equalize the concentrations on both sides of the membrane. In (C) passive diffusion, material moves along a concentration gradient (from a region of high concentration to a region of low concentration) without any assistance from the cell. In (D) facilitated diffusion, the cell expends energy in moving material along a concentration gradient (from a region of high concentration to a region of low concentration). In (E) endocytosis, the cell membrane engulfs material and brings it into the cell.

Questions 54 and 55

Coral reefs provide the basis for one of the most lively ecosystems in the world. Coral reefs are underwater structures generated by the secretions of coral polyps. Coral polyps exist only in symbiosis with certain forms of green algae that engage in photosynthesis.

54. Which of the following could describe the symbiotic relationship between coral polyps and green algae?

(A) There is no interaction between coral polyps and green algae.
(B) The presence of coral polyps and green algae are mutually exclusive.
(C) Coral polyps and green algae compete for the same energy sources.
(D) The presence of green algae is required in order for coral polyps to thrive.
(E) Coral polyps and green algae combine to form a third species.

54. **(D)** is the correct answer. In symbiosis, two species have a long-term relationship that acts to benefit one or both of the species. If coral polyps exist only in symbiosis with green algae, then green algae is required for coral polyps to thrive.

55. Because of the symbiotic relationship between coral polyps and green algae, one would expect coral reefs to be found only in

(A) the Southern Hemisphere
(B) shallow water
(C) fresh water
(D) cold water
(E) running water

55. **(B)** is the correct answer. Because the green algae must engage in photosynthesis, the reefs must be located where light can reach them easily. So the reefs must be in shallow water.

SECTION 5

56. Which of the following is NOT true of the ribosomes contained in cells?

   (A) Ribosomes are found on the surface of the endoplasmic reticulum.
   (B) The cytoplasm contains free ribosomes.
   (C) Ribosomes engage in protein synthesis.
   (D) Ribosomes are responsible for active diffusion.
   (E) Ribosomes contain RNA.

56. **(E)** is the correct answer. Ribosomes contain RNA, which is used in protein synthesis. They can be found on the endoplasmic reticulum and in the cytoplasm. Ribosomes are not responsible for active diffusion.

57. The heights of full-grown pine trees in a Canadian forest are found to vary from 40 feet to 65 feet. If natural selection acts to stabilize the height of the forest, the greatest number of trees would be expected to fall into which height category?

   (A) 40-45 feet
   (B) 45-50 feet
   (C) 50-55 feet
   (D) 55-60 feet
   (E) 60-65 feet

57. **(C)** is the correct answer. If natural selection has a stabilizing effect on the height of the trees, then the forest will have very few trees at the extremes of the height spectrum. Most of the trees will be in the center of the height spectrum, as shown below.

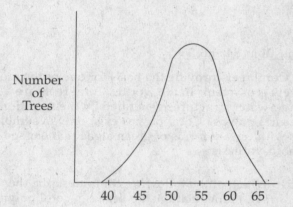

58. Which of the following lists of biological classifications starts with the most general category and becomes more specific as it proceeds?

   (A) Kingdom, order, class, species, genus.
   (B) Kingdom, class, order, genus, species.
   (C) Order, kingdom, genus, species, class.
   (D) Order, class, kingdom, species, genus.
   (E) Class, kingdom, order, genus, species.

58. **(B)** is the correct answer. Kingdom is the most general classification and species is the most specific classification. This is the only answer choice that has these two in their proper places.

SECTION 5

QUESTIONS	EXPLANATIONS

59. The part of the human digestive system where water used in digestion is reabsorbed into the body is called the

    (A) stomach
    (B) esophagus
    (C) large intestine
    (D) small intestine
    (E) oral cavity

59. **(C)** is the correct answer. The main function of the large intestine is to reabsorb water into the body. If the large intestine did not reabsorb water at this point, the body would quickly become dehydrated.

Here are brief descriptions of the other parts of the digestive system listed as answer choices:

(A) The stomach stores food and breaks it down into a digestible state.

(B) Food passes from the mouth to the stomach through the esophagus.

(D) Most digestion and absorption of nutrients takes place in the small intestine.

(E) Digestion begins in the oral cavity, or mouth.

60. A plant whose stem bends toward sunlight and whose roots grow toward a water source is said to be exhibiting which of the following tendencies?

    (A) Phototropism and positive geotropism.
    (B) Phototropism and negative geotropism.
    (C) Phototropism and hydrotropism.
    (D) Hydrotropism and positive geotropism.
    (E) Hydrotropism and negative geotropism.

60. **(C)** is the correct answer. Plant stem growth towards sunlight is called phototropism. Plant root growth towards water is called hydrotropism.

These are the other terms used in the answer choices:

Negative geotropism is the growth of the stem upward, away from the earth.

Positive geotropism is the growth of the root downward, towards the earth.

SECTION 5

QUESTIONS	EXPLANATIONS

Part II

Physical Science

Questions 1 and 2

    (A) Atomic bond
    (B) Metallic bond
    (C) Ionic bond
    (D) Network bond
    (E) Molecular bond

1. A solid exhibiting which bond structure will be the best conductor of heat and electricity?

2. Diamond, one of the hardest materials known, is held together by these bonds.

1. **(B)** is the correct answer. In a metallic solid, nuclei share a large "sea" of mobile electrons. Because the electrons are free to move from nucleus to nucleus, heat and electricity are easily transferred across the solid.

2. **(D)** is the correct answer. Diamond is composed of carbon atoms held together by network bonds. In the network bonding of a diamond, the carbon atoms are held together in a three-dimensional lattice structure with no easy breaking points.

The other answer choices list other kinds of intermolecular bonds. (A) Atomic and (E) molecular bonds are weak bonds formed among atoms and molecules that are normally gases at room temperature. (C) Ionic bonds are formed by the electrostatic attractions between ions.

SECTION 5

Questions 3 and 4

    (A) Current
    (B) Capacitance
    (C) Power
    (D) Resistance
    (E) Voltage

3. This is the flow of positive charge.

3. **(A)** is the correct answer. Current is defined as the flow of positive charge. Since current in a metal wire is actually the flow of electrons, which are negatively charged, we have the strange situation in which electrons are flowing in one direction and we say that current is flowing in the opposite direction.

4. This is the same as potential difference.

4. **(E)** is the correct answer. Voltage is the same as potential difference. The potential difference between two points is a measure of how likely charge is to flow from one point to another. The larger the potential difference, the more likely charge is to flow.

(B) Capacitance is a measure of how much charge can be stored in a particular place (called a capacitor). A capacitor stores charge in the same way that a reservoir stores water.

(C) Power is a measure of how much energy can be delivered per unit of time. Electrical power is defined as current multiplied by voltage ($P = IV$).

(D) Resistance is a measure of how strongly a given material will resist the flow of electrical current.

SECTION 5

QUESTIONS	EXPLANATIONS

<u>Questions 5 through 8</u>

    (A) Acceleration
    (B) Force
    (C) Momentum
    (D) Velocity
    (E) Energy

5. This is not a vector quantity.

5. **(E)** is the correct answer. A vector quantity is a quantity that has both a magnitude and a direction associated with it (For instance, a car's velocity has a magnitude, 55 miles per hour, and a direction, east). Energy has a magnitude, but no direction. That makes it a scalar quantity instead of a vector quantity.

6. This is a measure of the inertia of an object.

6. **(C)** is the correct answer. Inertia is a measure of the likelihood that an object will keep doing whatever it is doing (moving or standing still). Momentum (mass multiplied by velocity) is a direct measure of inertia.

7. This is the change in the displacement of an object over time.

7. **(D)** is the correct answer. Velocity tells us how fast an object is moving as time changes. In physical terms, this is the change in displacement divided by the change in time.

8. This is the capacity to do work.

8. **(E)** is the correct answer. Energy is defined as the capacity to do work. The more energy an object has, the more work it can do.

(A) Acceleration is the change in velocity of an object. Acceleration is a vector quantity.

(B) When force is applied to an object, it will accelerate according to Newton's second law of motion: (force) = (mass)(acceleration). Force is a vector quantity.

SECTION 5

QUESTIONS	EXPLANATIONS

Questions 9 through 11

   (A) Jupiter
   (B) Mercury
   (C) Pluto
   (D) Saturn
   (E) Venus

9. This planet has the shortest orbit time of all the planets in the solar system.

9. **(B)** is the correct answer. Mercury is the planet closest to the Sun, so it has the shortest orbit time. Mercury completes one revolution around the Sun every 88 days.

10. This is the largest planet in the solar system.

10. **(A)** is the correct answer. Jupiter is the largest planet in the solar system, with a diameter of 88,700 miles. Jupiter's diameter is roughly 11 times Earth's.

11. This was the last planet in the solar system to be discovered.

11. **(C)** is the correct answer. Pluto is the farthest of the nine major planets from the Sun. It was discovered in 1930 by C.W. Tombaugh.

(D) Saturn is the sixth planet from the Sun. Saturn is surrounded by a system of rings.

(E) Venus is the second planet from the Sun.

Questions 12 and 13

   (A) $Ni^{2+} + 2\,e^- \rightarrow Ni^0$
   (B) $HNO_3 \rightarrow H^+ + NO_3^-$
   (C) $Ag^0 \rightarrow Ag^+ + e^-$
   (D) $NaCl \rightarrow Na^+ + Cl^-$
   (E) $Mg(OH)_2 \rightarrow Mg^{2+} + 2\,OH^-$

12. This reaction shows the dissociation of an acid.

12. **(B)** is the correct answer. An acid dissociates by giving up a hydrogen ion. In this case, nitric acid (HNO_3) gives up a hydrogen ion (H^+), leaving a nitrate ion (NO_3^-).

13. This is an oxidation reaction.

13. **(C)** is the correct answer. In an oxidation reaction, an atom or ion gives up electrons. In this case, a neutral silver atom gives up an electron and becomes a positively charged ion.

(A) This is a reduction reaction. In a reduction reaction, an atom or ion gains electrons.

(D) This reaction shows the dissociation of a salt.

(E) This reaction shows the dissociation of a base.

SECTION 5

QUESTIONS	EXPLANATIONS

Questions 14 and 15

    (A) Alpha particle
    (B) Beta particle
    (C) Electron
    (D) Neutron
    (E) Proton

14. This is an uncharged subatomic particle.

15. Of the particles listed, this one has the greatest mass.

14. **(D)** is the correct answer. A neutron has neither positive nor negative charge. It has a mass of 1 amu.

15. **(A)** is the correct answer. An alpha particle contains two neutrons and two protons. It is positively charged and has the same mass as a helium nucleus (4 amu).

(B) A beta particle is just like an electron, so it is negatively charged and is has negligible mass.

(C) An electron is negatively charged and has negligible mass.

(E) A proton is positively charged and it has a mass of 1 amu.

16. A rock that results from a change to another rock brought about by such factors as temperature, pressure, or chemical reaction is called a(n)
    (A) sedimentary rock
    (B) igneous rock
    (C) extrusive rock
    (D) intrusive rock
    (E) metamorphic rock

16. **(E)** is the correct answer. Metamorphic rocks are formed by changes to other rocks.

Here are brief descriptions of the other kinds of rocks listed as answer choices:

(A) Sedimentary rocks are formed by the hardening of sediments.

(B) Igneous rocks are formed by the cooling of magma or lava.

(C) Extrusive rocks are igneous rocks formed by the cooling of lava (molten rock outside the Earth's surface).

(D) Intrusive rocks are igneous rocks formed by the cooling of magma (molten rock inside the Earth's surface).

SECTION 5

QUESTIONS	EXPLANATIONS

17. During a thunderstorm, an observer notices that a flash of lightning is seen a few seconds before a clap of thunder is heard. What is the best explanation for this phenomenon?

   (A) The event that causes thunder occurs before the event that causes lightning.

   (B) The event that causes lightning occurs before the event that causes thunder.

   (C) Sound waves travel faster than light waves.

   (D) Light waves travel faster than sound waves.

   (E) The delay is an illusion caused by the movement of the storm.

17. **(D)** is the correct answer. Thunder and lightning are caused by the same event, a sudden rush of charge between a cloud and a point on the Earth's surface. Lightning is seen before thunder is heard because light travels about a million times faster than sound.

18. Which of the molecules listed below is a polar molecule?

   (A) H_2

   (B) N_2

   (C) CO_2

   (D) Cl_2

   (E) H_2O

18. **(E)** is the correct answer. Molecules become polar when electrons are more strongly attracted to one side of the molecule than to the other side. The side with more electrons will be negatively charged and the side with fewer electrons will be positively charged.

Electrons are more strongly attracted to the oxygen in the water molecule than to the hydrogen. Because of the bent structure of the water molecule, one side of the molecule ends up positively charged (the hydrogen side), and one side ends up negatively charged (the oxygen side).

The other answers:

(A), (B), and (D) These are all diatomic molecules, with electrons attracted equally to both sides of the molecule, so neither side becomes positively or negatively charged.

(C) In the carbon dioxide molecule, electrons are drawn away from the carbon atom in the center toward the oxygen atoms.

$$(-)\,O = C = O\,(-)$$

Because the carbon dioxide molecule is arranged in a straight line, both sides of the molecule are negatively charged. In order for a molecule to be polar, it must have a positive and a negative pole. Carbon dioxide's poles are both negative, so CO_2 is not a polar molecule.

QUESTIONS	EXPLANATIONS

19. During a solar eclipse

(A) Earth passes directly between the Moon and the Sun
(B) the Moon passes directly between Earth and the Sun
(C) the Sun passes directly between Earth and the Moon
(D) Earth, the Sun, and the Moon form a right angle with Earth as the vertex
(E) Earth, the Sun, and the Moon form a right angle with the Moon as the vertex

19. **(B)** is the correct answer. During a solar eclipse, the Moon passes between Earth and the Sun, blocking out the light from the Sun to Earth.

Sun   Moon Earth

Choice (A) describes a lunar eclipse, where Earth passes between the Sun and the Moon, blocking the Sun's light to the Moon, and making the Moon invisible in the night sky.

Sun   Earth Moon

20. When a substance changes phase, energy must be absorbed or released, depending on the process which is occurring. When molten iron solidifies, the energy released during the phase change is the

(A) heat of vaporization
(B) heat of fusion
(C) specific heat
(D) heat capacity
(E) freezing point

20. **(B)** is the correct answer. The heat of fusion is the energy released when a substance freezes and absorbed when a substance melts.

The other answer choices all pertain to temperature and phase change. (A) The heat of vaporization is the energy released when a substance condenses and absorbed when a substance evaporates. (C) and (D) are constants that tell you how much the temperature of a substance in a given phase will increase when heat is added. Choice (E), the freezing point, is the temperature at which a substance will freeze or melt.

SECTION 5

QUESTIONS	EXPLANATIONS

21. The figure below shows a small section of the periodic table of the elements.

8 O 16	9 F 19	10 Ne 20
16 S 32	17 Cl 35	18 Ar 40

The chemical behavior of which of the following elements will be most similar to that of chlorine?

(A) Sulfur
(B) Oxygen
(C) Fluorine
(D) Neon
(E) Argon

21. **(C)** is the correct answer. The periodic table is organized so that elements that are similar chemically are grouped vertically. The chemical behavior of an element is determined mainly by the number of electrons present in the outer shell (valence electrons) of the neutral atom.

22. An object that is set in motion in the absence of any external force will

(A) eventually slow down and stop
(B) continue to move at the same speed in a straight line
(C) accelerate until it reaches the speed of light
(D) continue to move at the same speed in a circular path
(E) move in an inward spiral until it stops

22. **(B)** is the correct answer. According to Newton's first law of motion, an object will continue to move at a constant speed in a straight line unless some force is applied to it.

23. For which of the following states of matter is entropy the greatest?

(A) Solid
(B) Liquid
(C) Gas
(D) Solution
(E) Colloid

23. **(C)** is the correct answer. Entropy is a measure of randomness. Gas is the most random state of matter because gas particles are held to each other by very few bonds.

The other answers:

(A) Solids are highly bonded and highly organized.

(B) Liquids are more random than solids, but less random than gases.

(D) Solutions have molecules and atoms suspended in a liquid. Solutions are less random than gases.

(E) Colloids have particles that are larger than molecules suspended in a liquid. Colloids are less random than gases.

SECTION 5

QUESTIONS	EXPLANATIONS

24. Which of the following descriptions of Earth's location in space goes from the most specific to the most general?

    (A) Universe, solar system, Milky Way galaxy.
    (B) Milky Way galaxy, solar system, universe.
    (C) Milky Way galaxy, universe, solar system.
    (D) Solar system, Milky Way galaxy, universe.
    (E) Solar system, universe, Milky Way galaxy.

24. **(D)** is the correct answer. Earth is one of nine planets orbiting the Sun in the solar system. The Sun is one of billions of stars contained in the Milky Way galaxy. The Milky Way galaxy is one of billions of galaxies in the universe.

25. If a 0.01 molar solution of hydrochloric acid reacts with a 0.01 molar solution of sodium hydroxide, the resulting solution will contain

    (A) hydrochloric acid and water
    (B) sodium hydroxide and water
    (C) ammonia and water
    (D) sodium chloride and water
    (E) only water

25. **(D)** is the correct answer. When strong acid reacts with a strong base, it's called a neutralization reaction. In a neutralization reaction, the products are water and a salt. In this case the reaction is:

    $$HCl + NaOH \rightarrow H_2O + NaCl$$

    Since the concentrations of the acid and the base are the same, the products will be only water and sodium hydroxide (table salt).

26. The tidal ebb and flow of Earth's water systems is caused mainly by

    (A) variations in rainfall over different parts of Earth
    (B) the melting and refreezing of the polar ice caps
    (C) the interaction of fresh water and salt water in coastal areas
    (D) the effects of underwater seismic activity
    (E) the gravitational pull of the Moon

26. **(E)** is the correct answer. Tides are caused by the gravitational pull of the Moon, and to a lesser extent, the gravitational pull of the Sun.

SECTION 5

Questions 27 through 30

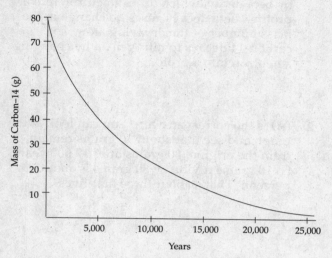

Carbon-14 undergoes beta decay into an isotope of nitrogen as shown in the table above. The amount of carbon-14 present in an organic object can be used to tell how old the object is because the decay rate of carbon-14 is constant and the amount of carbon-14 begins to decrease when the organism dies. Carbon dating is done by comparing the amount of carbon-14 present in an object to the amount that would be expected to be found in a living organism.

27. What is the half-life of carbon-14?

  (A) 1,000 years
  (B) 2,300 years
  (C) 5,700 years
  (D) 11,400 years
  (E) 22,800 years

27. **(C)** is the correct answer. From the graph, we can see that the mass of carbon-14 present goes from 80 grams to 40 grams in approximately 5,700 years. It takes the same amount of time to go from 40 grams to 20 grams.

28. Carbon-14 dating can be used to fix the date of a book. The date found by carbon-14 dating will be the date when

  (A) the book was written
  (B) the book was published
  (C) the tree that produced the pages for the book was planted
  (D) the tree that produced the pages for the book was cut down
  (E) the ink was applied to the pages of the book

28. **(D)** is the correct answer. Carbon-14 dating dates organic matter from the time that it dies. So carbon-14 dating tells nothing about the authorship or printing of the book, only about when the organic matter in the book died.

QUESTIONS	EXPLANATIONS

29. Which isotope of nitrogen is produced as a result of the decay of carbon-14?

   (A) Nitrogen-12
   (B) Nitrogen-13
   (C) Nitrogen-14
   (D) Nitrogen-15
   (E) Nitrogen-16

29. **(C)** is the correct answer. Carbon-14 decays by beta decay, which turns a neutron into a proton. Beta decay causes no change in the mass number of the decaying atom, so carbon-14 decays to nitrogen-14 by changing a neutron into a proton.

30. Approximately what percent of the carbon-14 in an object will remain when 17,000 years have passed?

   (A) 13 percent
   (B) 25 percent
   (C) 50 percent
   (D) 75 percent
   (E) 88 percent

30. **(A)** is the correct answer. You can look at the graph and see that about 10 grams remain from the original 80 grams after 17,000 years. So 10 grams divide by 80 grams is about 13 percent. That's about three half-lives.

31. Which of the following will be true of a substance that has a specific gravity of 0.5?

   (A) It will float in water.
   (B) It will sink in water.
   (C) It will absorb water.
   (D) It will repel water.
   (E) It will be soluble in water.

31. **(A)** is the correct answer. Specific gravity is the ratio of the density of a substance to the density of water. If a substance has a specific gravity of less than one, then the substance is less dense than water. If a substance is less dense than water, then it will float in water.

32. An igneous rock is examined and found to have a smooth, glassy texture and no distinct crystal structure. It is most likely that this rock was formed from

   (A) sediments that accumulated slowly at the surface of the Earth
   (B) sediments that accumulated very quickly at the surface of the Earth
   (C) glacial activity which brought many kinds of rocks together
   (D) magma that cooled very quickly at the surface of the Earth
   (E) magma that cooled slowly beneath the surface of the Earth

32. **(D)** is the correct answer. Igneous rocks are formed by cooling magma. If the magma cools very quickly, as is likely to happen at the surface of the Earth, there will be no time for a crystal structure to form and the rock will be smooth and glassy.

   (A), (B), and (C) None of these processes will form an igneous rock.

   (E) If magma cools slowly, crystals will form and the rock will not be smooth.

33. Which of the following is the longest unit of geological time?

   (A) Eon
   (B) Epoch
   (C) Era
   (D) Period
   (E) Year

33. **(A)** is the correct answer. Eons are the longest units of geological time.

   The other answers are all subdivisions of geological time. Eons are divided into (C) eras. Eras are divided into (D) periods. Periods are divided into (B) epochs. (E) Years are pretty short in terms of geological time.

SECTION 5

QUESTIONS	EXPLANATIONS

34. The atomic number of boron is five. This means that a boron atom must always contain five

   (A) protons
   (B) neutrons
   (C) ions
   (D) nucleons
   (E) electrons

34. **(A)** is the correct answer. The atomic number of an element is determined by the number of protons contained in the element's nucleus. If the number of protons changes, then the identity of the element changes. All of the other items listed in the answer choices can vary for an element.

(B) Boron can exist with different numbers of neutrons. Atoms of the same element with different numbers of neutrons are called isotopes.

(C) Ions are atoms that have gained or lost electrons to become negatively or positively charged.

(D) Nucleon is a name given to both protons and neutrons.

(E) Boron can exist with different numbers of electrons. If it has more than nine electrons, it becomes a negatively charged ion. If it has fewer than nine electrons, it becomes a positively charged ion. If it has exactly nine electrons, it is a neutral atom.

35. In the Northern Hemisphere, daylight hours are longest in the month of June and the weather is warmest around this time. This is because during the month of June

   (A) Earth is closer to the sun than it is at any other time during the year
   (B) Earth is farther away from the Sun than it is at any other time during the year
   (C) Earth is the same distance from the Sun as it is during the rest of the year
   (D) the Northern Hemisphere is tilted toward the Sun
   (E) the Northern Hemisphere is tilted away from the Sun

35. **(D)** is the correct answer. The Northern Hemisphere experiences summer in June because the Northern Hemisphere is tilted toward the Sun. At the same time, the Southern Hemisphere experiences winter. The distance between Earth and the Sun is not constant, but the distance between them has less effect on the seasons than does the tilt of the Earth. In fact, during summer in the Northern Hemisphere, Earth is at its greatest distance from the sun.

36. What is the definition of density?

   (A) Density is the same as mass.
   (B) Density is the same as weight.
   (C) Density is mass multiplied by acceleration due to gravity.
   (D) Density is mass divided by acceleration due to gravity.
   (E) Density is mass divided by volume.

36. **(E)** is the correct answer. Density is defined as mass per unit volume.

SECTION 5

QUESTIONS	EXPLANATIONS

37. The orbit of Earth around the Sun can best be described as

    (A) circular
    (B) elliptical
    (C) parabolic
    (D) hyperbolic
    (E) exponential

37. **(B)** is the correct answer. Earth travels in an elliptical path around the Sun, with the Sun resting at one of the ellipse's foci.

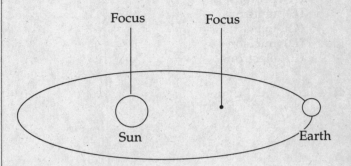

38. When an object is dropped off the roof of a building, the speed of the falling object will gradually increase as it approaches the ground. What is the best description of the energy conversion involved in this process?

    (A) Elastic potential energy is converted to kinetic energy.
    (B) Elastic potential energy is converted to gravitational potential energy.
    (C) Kinetic energy is converted to elastic potential energy.
    (D) Kinetic energy is converted to gravitational potential energy.
    (E) Gravitational potential energy is converted to kinetic energy.

38. **(E)** is the correct answer. When an object is lifted off the ground, it has gravitational potential energy. The higher off the ground it is lifted, the more gravitational potential energy it has. When an object is moving, it has kinetic energy. The faster it is moving, the more kinetic energy it has. As the object falls towards the ground and picks up speed, gravitational potential energy is gradually being exchanged for kinetic energy.

39. The vapor pressure of a liquid is gradually increased until it becomes equal to the surrounding atmospheric pressure. What will happen to a liquid under these conditions?

    (A) It will boil.
    (B) It will freeze.
    (C) Its color will become darker.
    (D) Its color will become lighter.
    (E) It will become more dense.

39. **(A)** is the correct answer. When the vapor pressure of a liquid is equal to the surrounding atmospheric pressure, the molecules in the liquid can escape very easily into the surrounding air. This escape of great numbers of liquid molecules is what we call boiling.

SECTION 5

| QUESTIONS | EXPLANATIONS |

<u>Questions 40 and 41</u>

A simple balance scale is set up as shown below:

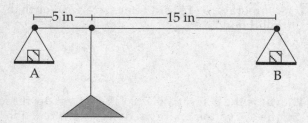

An object of unknown weight is hung from side A. Blocks of known weight are then hung from side B until the scale is found to be in rotational equilibrium. The weight of the object hanging from side A can then be calculated by using the known weight hanging from side B.

40. The balance reaches rotational equilibrium when a 6-pound. weight is hung from side B. What is the weight of the object hanging from side A?

(A) 2 pounds
(B) 3 pounds
(C) 6 pounds
(D) 12 pounds
(E) 18 pounds

40. **(E)** is the correct answer. Use torques. Remember, (torque) = (force)(lever arm). At equilibrium, the downward torque exerted on side A must be balanced by the downward torque exerted by side B. The equation looks like this:

(weight A)(lever arm A) = (weight B)(lever arm B)

(weight A)(5 in.) = (6 lb.)(15 in.)

(weight A) = 18 lb.

41. What is the name given to a force applied to a lever arm in such a way as to cause a rotation about an axis?

(A) Pressure
(B) Torque
(C) Vector
(D) Inertia
(E) Power

41. **(B)** is the correct answer. When a force is applied to a lever arm in such a way as to cause a rotation around an axis, as happens when we put a weight on one side of the balance scale pictured, it's called torque.

The other answers are terms used in mechanics:

(A) *Pressure* is force applied per unit area.

(C) A *vector* is a quantity that has both magnitude and direction.

(D) *Inertia* is a property that describes how likely it is that an object will keep standing still or moving in a straight line.

(E) *Power* is energy per unit of time.

SECTION 5

| QUESTIONS | EXPLANATIONS |

42. Which of the following metals has the weakest intermolecular bonds?

   (A) Iron
   (B) Copper
   (C) Mercury
   (D) Silver
   (E) Gold

42. **(C)** is the correct answer. Of the five metals listed, mercury is the only one that is liquid at room temperature. In fact, mercury is the only metal that is a liquid at room temperature. Liquid bonds are weaker than solid bonds.

43. When a catalyst is added to a chemical reaction, the rate of the reaction is increased. The rate of reaction increases because the catalyst

   (A) increases the activation energy of the reaction
   (B) decreases the activation energy of the reaction
   (C) increases the enthalpy change of the reaction
   (D) decreases the enthalpy change of the reaction
   (E) increases the free energy change of the reaction

43. **(B)** is the correct answer. A catalyst decreases the activation energy required for a reaction to proceed, making it easier for the reaction to occur. The enthalpy change and free energy change depend only on the change in energy from the beginning to the end of a reaction. A catalyst affects only the energy of the activation energy, which is an intermediate step in a reaction, so a catalyst has no effect on the enthalpy change or free energy change of a reaction.

44. A phenomenon known as *red shift* is often cited as proof that the universe is expanding. When observers on Earth look at a distant star, the light they see is redder than the light actually emitted by the star. This occurs because the star is moving away from the observer. What is the difference between the light wave seen by the observer on Earth and the wave emitted by the star?

   (A) The observer will see a light wave with a lower frequency.
   (B) The observer will see a light wave with a higher frequency.
   (C) The observer will see a light wave with a lower velocity.
   (D) The observer will see a light wave with a higher velocity.
   (E) The light wave seen by the observer will be identical to the light wave emitted at the source.

44. **(A)** is the correct answer. Because of the Doppler effect, when a wave is emitted by a moving source, the frequency noticed by an observer will be greater than the original frequency if the source is approaching the observer and lower if the source is moving away from the observer. We've all noticed this when we've watched a train or a fire truck approach us and then pass us by. The pitch of the sound increases until the train or truck reaches us and then it decreases as its source moves away. It works the same way for light from the stars. If the stars were coming toward us, their light would be shifted toward the higher end of the spectrum, and they would appear blue.

SECTION 5

| QUESTIONS | EXPLANATIONS |

45. What is the layer of the atmosphere that lies closest to the surface of the Earth?

    (A) Troposphere
    (B) Hydrosphere
    (C) Thermosphere
    (D) Lithosphere
    (E) Stratosphere

45. **(A)** is the correct answer. The troposphere is the layer of the atmosphere that lies closest to Earth's surface. About 75 percent of the mass that makes up the atmosphere is contained in the troposphere.

    What about the other "spheres" listed as answer choices?

    (A) and (E) In order of increasing distance from Earth's surface, the atmospheric layers are: troposphere, stratosphere, mesosphere, thermosphere, and exosphere.

    (B) Hydrosphere is the name give to the layer of water that surrounds the surface of the Earth, making up the oceans.

    (D) Lithosphere is the name given to the solid part of the Earth.

46. In an experiment, two objects, A and B, travel towards each other and meet in a head-on collision. The two objects then stick together and continue to move. If, after the collision, the two objects move in the same direction that object A was traveling in before the collision, the experimenters can conclude that object A had greater

    (A) energy
    (B) momentum
    (C) velocity
    (D) acceleration
    (E) mass

46. **(B)** is the correct answer. Momentum is a measure of the inertia of an object; that is, it is a measure of how likely it is that an object will keep doing whatever it is doing. So if two objects collide, the object with the greater momentum will have the most effect on the outcome of the collision. All of the other choices can play a part in a collision, but object B could have had greater energy, velocity, acceleration, or mass, and still have been moved backward after the collision, so long as object A's momentum was greater.

47. Elemental potassium contains only one electron in its valence shell. Which of the following can be predicted about potassium based on this fact?

    (A) Potassium is rarely found in its uncombined, elemental form.
    (B) Potassium has a low freezing point.
    (C) Potassium is a gas at room temperature.
    (D) Potassium is a noble gas.
    (E) Potassium does not form bonds easily.

47. **(A)** is the correct answer. An element with only one valence electron will be extremely reactive because it wants to get rid of the single electron and thus have a complete outer shell. Therefore, potassium will almost never be found in uncombined, non-reactive form.

48. The planets in our solar system are maintained in their orbits around the Sun by

    (A) electrostatic force
    (B) nuclear force
    (C) magnetic force
    (D) gravitational force
    (E) frictional force

48. **(D)** is the correct answer. All objects with mass are attracted to each other by gravitational force.

SECTION 5

QUESTIONS	EXPLANATIONS

49. Which of the following energy sources produces no harmful waste products and depletes no natural resources?

   (A) Natural gas energy
   (B) Nuclear energy
   (C) Solar energy
   (D) Oil energy
   (E) Coal energy

49. **(C)** is the correct answer. Solar energy harnesses the heat and light provided by the Sun, so it doesn't burn any of Earth's resources and doesn't produce any harmful wastes. The main drawback to solar energy is that it is still prohibitively expensive to harness. All of the other energy sources listed consume Earth's natural resources and produce harmful wastes, but they are more economically feasible than solar energy.

50. The theory that all of Earth's continents were once part of the same land mass and have gradually moved apart to their present positions is known as

   (A) glacial deposition
   (B) shoreline erosion
   (C) the water cycle
   (D) continental drift
   (E) the rock cycle

50. **(D)** is the correct answer. Continental drift describes the slow movement of the continents. It is part of a larger theory about the Earth's surface called plate tectonics.

The other answers:

(A) Glacial deposition refers to the movement of material by a glacier.

(B) In shoreline erosion, sediment is carried into the sea by the breaking action of waves.

(C) The water cycle describes the movement of water back and forth between Earth and the atmosphere.

(E) The rock cycle describes how rocks are formed, broken down, and re-formed.

51. In a chemical reaction, the limiting reagent is the reactant that is

   (A) present in the greatest molar quantity
   (B) present in the smallest molar quantity
   (C) present in the greatest quantity by mass
   (D) present in the smallest quantity by mass
   (E) the first to be used up over the course of the reaction

51. **(E)** is the correct answer. The limiting reagent is the first reactant to be used up. However, it isn't necessarily the reactant that you have the least of.

52. Three sets of fossils are found buried in an area consisting of many layers of sedimentary rock. Fossils A and B are found buried at about the same depth. Fossil C is found after digging deeper. Which of following judgments can be made about the ages of the fossils?

   (A) Fossil A is older than fossils B and C.
   (B) Fossil B is older than fossils A and C.
   (C) Fossil C is older than fossils A and B.
   (D) Fossil A is older than fossil B, which is older than fossil C.
   (E) All of the fossils are the same age.

52. **(C)** is the correct answer. According to the principle of superposition, when there are several layers of rock, the deepest layer is the oldest layer and the shallowest layer is the most recent layer. So the fossils found in the deepest layer would be the oldest. No judgments can be made about the ages of the fossils found at the same depth.

SECTION 5

QUESTIONS	EXPLANATIONS

<u>Questions 53 and 54</u>

A sealed chamber of fixed volume contains several different kinds of gas. The chamber contains one mole of oxygen gas (molecular weight = 32 amu), one mole of carbon dioxide gas (molecular weight = 44 amu), and two moles of nitrogen gas (molecular weight = 28 amu). It can be assumed that the ideal gas laws apply to the gases in the chamber.

53. What percent of the pressure in the chamber is due to the oxygen gas?

   (A) 25 percent
   (B) 33 percent
   (C) 50 percent
   (D) 67 percent
   (E) 75 percent

53. **(A)** is the correct answer. There is one mole of oxygen gas present, out of a total of four moles of gas. So the pressure exerted by the oxygen gas will be one-fourth of the total pressure. As long as the ideal gas laws apply, the molecular weight of the gases makes no difference.

54. If the temperature inside the chamber is gradually increased, what will be the most likely result?

   (A) The pressure in the chamber will increase.
   (B) The pressure in the chamber will decrease.
   (C) The number of moles of gas in the chamber will increase.
   (D) The number of moles of gas in the chamber will decrease.
   (E) The volume of the chamber will decrease.

54. **(A)** is the correct answer. The ideal gas equation applies:

   (pressure)(volume) = (number of moles)(R)(temperature)

   The volume of the container and the number of moles of gas in it don't change, and R is a constant, so when the temperature increases, the pressure has to increase.

55. A region in space that contains so much mass that even light cannot escape from its gravitational pull is called a

   (A) red giant
   (B) black hole
   (C) quasar
   (D) white dwarf
   (E) sunspot

55. **(B)** is the correct answer. Black holes are collapsed stars that are extremely massive. They are so massive that even light can not escape their gravitational pull.

   The other answer choices all refer to astronomical phenomena. (A) Red giant and (D) white dwarf are both earlier stages in the development of a star. (C) Quasars are faint celestial bodies that emit radio signals. (E) Sunspots are relatively dark and cool areas on the surface of the sun.

SECTION 5

QUESTIONS	EXPLANATIONS

56. Given the reaction for the formation of ammonia from hydrogen and nitrogen gases:

$$3 H_2(g) + N_2(g) \rightarrow 2 NH_3(g)$$

If one mole of hydrogen gas is consumed over the course of the reaction, how many moles of ammonia are produced?

(A) 1/3 mole
(B) 2/3 mole
(C) 1 mole
(D) 2 moles
(E) 3 moles

56. **(B)** is the correct answer. According to the balanced equation, 3 moles of hydrogen gas produce 2 moles of ammonia. If only 1 mole of hydrogen gas reacts (instead of 3), then only 1/3 of the expected 2 moles of ammonia will be produced. So 1/3 of 2 is 2/3.

57. What is the approximate percentage of Earth's surface that is covered with water?

(A) 10 percent
(B) 30 percent
(C) 50 percent
(D) 70 percent
(E) 90 percent

57. **(D)** is the correct answer. About 70 percent of Earth's surface is covered with water.

58. The number of times that a wave cycle repeats itself over the course of one second is called the wave's

(A) wavelength
(B) period
(C) amplitude
(D) phase
(E) frequency

58. **(E)** is the correct answer. Frequency is measured in cycles per second, or hertz. The higher the frequency of a wave, the more often it repeats its cycle.

All of the answer choices refer to different properties of waves.

(A) Wavelength is the length of a wave in distance, as opposed to time. (B) A wave's period is the length of time that the wave takes to complete one cycle. (C) Amplitude is the height, or the amount of displacement, achieved by the wave. (D) Phase refers to differences between two different waves.

SECTION 5

QUESTIONS	EXPLANATIONS

59. A compass point held near the surface of the Earth will swing around to indicate North. This is because

   (A) Earth's gravity is strongest near the North Pole
   (B) Earth's gravity is weakest near the North Pole
   (C) a magnetic field runs along the surface of the Earth
   (D) the North Pole is always pointed toward the Moon
   (E) the North Pole is always pointed away from the Moon

59. **(C)** is the correct answer. A magnetic field runs along the surface of the Earth between the North and South Poles. A compass needle is a magnet, so it will always orient itself in the same way in a magnetic field.

   The wrong answers:

   (A) and (B) Compasses have nothing to do with gravity, which is about the same at the two poles.

   (D) and (E) Compasses have nothing to do with the Moon, and the North Pole is not always pointed toward or away from the Moon.

60. An experiment was conducted to test the effects of different acid solutions on the weathering of solid calcium carbonate. The experiment was conducted by pouring various solutions of acetic acid, hydrochloric acid, nitric acid, and pure water over limestone rocks in separate trials and observing the results. Which of the following trials would serve as the control for the experiment?

   (A) Pouring nitric acid on a rock
   (B) Pouring acetic acid on a rock
   (C) Pouring hydrochloric acid on a rock
   (D) Pouring pure water on a rock
   (E) Pouring a mixture of all four liquids on a rock

60. **(D)** is the correct answer. The control in an experiment is the trial in which nothing is changed. The results of the other trials can then be compared to the control to examine the effects of various changes. In this case, the experimenters wish to determine the effect of acid on the weathering of rocks, so pouring water, which is neutral, will not show any of the effects of acid on the rock. By the way, pouring water on the rock is better than doing nothing because pouring water shows whatever weathering action will take place due to the pouring action of fluid, without the effects of acid.

PART ◆ VII

CLEP Subject Examinations

22

Overview of the CLEP Subject Exams

WHAT ARE THE CLEP SUBJECT EXAMS?

In addition to the five CLEP General Examinations, the College Board offers twenty-nine Subject Examinations, in five subject areas: Composition and Literature, Foreign Languages, History and Social Sciences, Science and Mathematics, and Business. Whereas the General Examinations are designed to correspond to those survey courses generally required of freshmen, the Subject Examinations are designed to correspond to the more advanced, more subject-specific courses taken by upperclassmen and -women.

Sample questions from each exam can be found in the College Board book *The Official Handbook for the CLEP Examinations* (The College Board). A copy of this book can usually be found in your local public library, or you can buy one at one of the big book chains for around $16.

Below is a list of those exams, along with a brief description of each:

COMPOSITION AND LITERATURE

American Literature (100 questions)

The format of this exam is very much like that of the Humanities General Exam. About half the questions cover "trivial pursuit" information (identifying plots, authors, settings, etc.); another third of the questions involve interpreting prose and poetry. Ten percent of the questions concern the historical setting in which works were created; for example, a question about *Huckleberry Finn* might require you to know about race relations at the time Twain wrote the book. Five percent of the questions require knowledge of the literary theories and devices of famous American authors.

English Literature (approx. 105 questions)

The English Literature exam covers all literature written in the English language (not just literature originating in England). Approximately half the questions fall under the category of "trivial pursuit" (identifying plots, authors, settings, metrical patterns in poetry, etc.). The other half test your ability to interpret literary images and symbols, identify elements of style, and recognize the tone and mood.

Analyzing and Interpreting Religion (90 questions)

The Analysis and Interpretation of Literature exam differs from the English and American Literature exams in that it does not contain any identifications (e.g., who is the author of. . .?). About two-fifths of the exam involves analysis of poetry; another two-fifths, the analysis of prose; and the final fifth, the analysis of dramatic passages. Between one-half and two-thirds of the passages will be of British origin; one-third to two-fifths will be American; the remainder will be works in translation. All major historical periods are covered, with about half the works originating in the nineteenth and twentieth centuries. Passages are followed by a relatively large number of questions (between three and ten) that test your comprehension of vocabulary, syntax, literary style, author's intent, metaphor, symbology, and other literary devices. Some questions test your familiarity with basic literary terminology.

Freshman College Composition (approx. 100 questions):

This test is a lot like the English Composition General Exam. The two tests share the following question types: identifying sentence errors, improving sentences, revising a work in progress, analyzing writing, and an optional essay section. It also has two question types not found on the general exam: one is called "recognizing and applying writing skills", the other "analyzing and evaluating writers' choices." The former presents questions about the proper format for footnotes and bibliographies, research methods, etc. The latter presents either a single sentence or a short passage, followed by one or two questions about choices in vocabulary, syntax, grammar, and tone.

FOREIGN LANGUAGES

College French (145 questions):

College German (135 questions):

College Spanish (140 questions):

The foreign language subject exams are offered at two levels of difficulty. Many schools award two semesters credit for successful completion of the level 1 exam and four semesters credit for the successful completion of the level 2 exam. The level 2 exam, needless to say, is much more difficult.

All CLEP foreign language exams are divided in two parts: the first is a reading section, the second a listening section. Although there are more questions in the reading section than in the listening section (except on the Spanish exam, which has an equal number of both question types), scores for the two sections are weighted so that each has equal value on your final score.

The reading section tests vocabulary, grammar, and comprehension. Many of the questions involve choosing the correct word to fill in a blank in an incomplete sentence. Others involve replacing an underlined word in a sentence with another. Others still involve reading a passage and answering questions designed to test comprehension.

The listening section tests ability to understand the language as spoken by native speakers and also requires a solid grasp of vocabulary and grammar. Some spoken segments describe an action; you must then choose the drawing that depicts that action. Many of these drawings are (unintentionally) quite comical. Other segments provide a snippet of dialogue about which you are asked one or more questions. All questions on both sections are in the foreign language; directions are in English.

Before you take a foreign language exam, find out about your potential college's CLEP policy. Some will give you credit for the test, others only advanced placement, and others don't accept the tests at all.

HISTORY AND SOCIAL SCIENCES

American Government (approx. 100 questions):

The American Government exam covers basic principles of U.S. government and politics. A few more than half the questions involve simple factual recall. About ten percent involve reading a graph and interpreting data. The rest require you to identify trends and patterns in American politics and the political behavior of Americans. Approximately half the questions focus on the three branches of government (executive, judicial, legislative). About one-fifth cover political parties and advocacy groups. Another 10 to 15 percent ask about political beliefs and behavior, and the remaining 15 to 20 percent cover the Constitution, with particular emphasis on the amendments. Some of these questions deal with the framers of the Constitution and those events and beliefs that led them to write it as they did.

American History I: Early Colonizations to 1877 (approx. 120 questions):

American History II: 1865 to the Present (approx. 120 questions):

Overall, both exams are very similar to the American History questions on the Social Science General Examination; however, they do require a greater knowledge of detail. About half the questions on the American History exams involve factual recall: who did what to whom, the causes of events, etc. One-fifth concern the explanation and evaluation of historical events and phenomena: for example, you might be asked about the effects of America's Vietnam policy on post-Vietnam War politics in the U.S. Other questions ask you to compare and contrast historical events or to characterize them (as emblematic of a certain political movement or sentiment, for example). Both tests pretty much confine themselves to the "greatest hits" of history: almost all the information you need to do well could be found in a "pop" history book such as *Don't Know Much About History* (Avon).

Western Civilization I: Ancient Near East to 1648 (approx. 120 questions):

Western Civilization II: 1648 to the Present (approx. 120 questions):

The Western Civilization exams closely resemble the Western Civilization questions on the Social Science General Examination; however, they do require a greater knowledge of detail.

Subjects covered on the Western Civilization I exam consist of a pretty even spread of questions about ancient Greece, ancient Rome, the Middle Ages, the Renaissance, and the beginning of modern Europe. The Western Civilization II exam covers a wide range of wars, economic developments, cultural and scientific advances, and historical and political movements and events. Anything from the English Revolution to post-Cold War Europe is fair game.

Approximately one-third of the questions involve factual recall (dates, names, events, etc.). About one-quarter of the test requires you to understand textual (e.g., descriptions of nations, excerpts from famous history texts) and graphic material (e.g., political cartoons). About 20 percent of the questions test your ability "to distinguish the relevant from the irrelevant." Other questions ask you to draw conclusions based on historical facts and to identify the causes of major historical events. Questions about the arts and sciences are included.

"What is government itself but the greatest of all reflections on human nature? If men were angels, no government would be necessary. If angels were to govern men, neither external nor internal controls on government would be necessary."
—James Madison, *The Federalist Papers*

Principles of Macroeconomics (approx. 80 questions):

If you don't know the difference between macroeconomics and microeconomics, you probably shouldn't take either of the economics exams. For the record, macroeconomics is the study of economic phenomena as they apply to an entire economic system. This test requires you to know the definitions of important terms and to understand certain concepts (such as the accelerator, the multiplier, and aggregate demand); to be able to interpret and evaluate economic graphs, charts, and data; and to apply simple economic models (in order to predict interest rates, monetary flow, etc.) Most of the questions concern national economics, particularly as it relates to income and the determination of prices. Fiscal policy, banking policy, and market dynamics are all covered on this test, as are the standard measurements of national economic performance (e.g. GNP, unemployment rate, consumer confidence index, etc.).

Principles of Microeconomics (approx. 80 questions):

Microeconomics is the study of economic principles as they apply to groups, organizations, businesses, and individuals within the larger national economy. This test requires you to know the definitions of important terms and to understand certain concepts (such as the scarcity, supply and demand, marginal product, and diminishing returns); to be able to interpret and evaluate economic graphs, charts, and data; and to apply simple economic models (in order to predict consumer demand and profitability, for example). Most questions concern the nature of the product market and cover the above-mentioned topics as well as maximizing profit, competition and monopolies, and antitrust laws.

"The mention of Greece fills the mind with the most exalted sentiments and arouses in our bosoms the best feelings of which our nature is capable."
—James Monroe, U.S. president

Introductory Psychology (approx. 100 questions):

The Introductory Psychology exam covers the history and basic principles of psychology. Knowledge of the theories of the major figures in psychology—Freud, Jung, Piaget, Skinner—is required, as is an understanding of experimental methodology. All fields of psychology are touched on, which means that none are covered in any particular depth. Common sense and a familiarity with the basic vocabulary of psychology go a long way on this exam.

Introduction to Educational Psychology (approx. 100 questions):

The Educational Psychology exam tests knowledge of theories of learning and cognition, teaching methods and management of the classroom, child development, and methods of evaluating a child's level of learning. You must be familiar with the behaviorist and cognitive theories of learning, good research techniques, and issues of motivation. Common sense and a familiarity with the basic vocabulary of psychology go a long way on this exam.

Human Growth and Development (approx. 90 questions):

The Human Growth and Development exam tests material that would be covered in a one-semester course on child development, child psychology, or developmental psychology. The test covers infancy through adolescence. It requires a familiarity with the major theories of physical, cognitive, social, emotional, and personality development, and the ability to apply them in very simple case studies. As on the Psychology exam, common sense and a familiarity with the basic vocabulary of psychology go a long way.

Introductory Sociology (approx. 100 questions):

The Sociology exam covers a wide swath of sociological history, theory, and practice. Questions ask you to recall major facts and names, identify major concepts and whether they can be related to one another, apply those major concepts to hypothetical scenarios, and interpret charts and tables of data. Because the test covers all of sociology, it touches on no single topic in any great detail. Common sense and a familiarity with the basic vocabulary of sociology go a long way on this exam.

SCIENCE AND MATHEMATICS

General Biology (approx. 120 questions):

The Biology exam gives equal weight to the areas of molecular/cellular biology, organism biology, and population biology. The test gives perfunctory treatment to a very wide array of subjects within these three fields. *The Official Handbook for the CLEP* contains twenty-five sample questions from the test; if you can get over half of those questions right, you probably have enough wide-ranging knowledge of biology to pass this exam.

The College Board publication *The Official Guide to the CLEP* contains sample questions from every subject exam. A copy of this book should be available at the local library.

General Chemistry (approximately 80 questions):

The Chemistry exam includes questions about the structure of matter and its different states, types of chemical reactions, stoichiometry, equilibrium, kinetics, thermodynamics, experimental chemistry, and descriptive chemistry. Some questions ask that you simply recall facts, others that you apply concepts and solve equations, and others still that you interpret data from charts and graphs. You may use a calculator on this exam; however, its memory must be cleared of all programs and data prior to the start of the exam. The test booklet contains a copy of the periodic table of the elements.

College Algebra (approx. 70 questions):

The College Algebra exam contains questions about basic algebraic operations, the graphs of equations and inequalities, functions (algebraic, exponential, and logarithmic), sets, real numbers, complex numbers, sequences, and series. About half the test involves solving routine equations; the other half involves non-routine equations designed to test your ability to apply basic principles of college algebra. You may use a non-graphing, non-programmable calculator on this exam.

Trigonometry (approx. 80 questions):

The Trigonometry exam includes questions about trigonometric functions and their cofunctional, reciprocal, and Pythagorean relationships; trig equations and inequalities; graphs of functions; trigonometry of the triangle (SOHCAHTOA); and inverse functions. A little over half the test involves solving routine equations; the rest involves non-routine equations designed to test your ability to apply basic principles of trigonometry.

College Algebra-Trigonometry (approx. 80 questions):
The College Algebra-Trigonometry exam, as its name implies, combines the College Algebra and Trigonometry exams into one. It covers the subjects mentioned in the descriptions of those two tests above, but in less detail. The use of a calculator is not permitted on this exam.

Calculus with Elementary Functions (45 questions):
   The Calculus exam contains questions about the properties of algebraic, trigonometric, exponential, and logarithmic functions; limits and the number of derivatives and antiderivatives, and their applications; and the definite integral. The current version of the Calculus exam allows the use of a scientific, non-graphing calculator. Unlike its predecessor, this version of the exam does not offer an optional 'free-response' (i.e. non-multiple choice) section.

BUSINESS

Information Systems and Computer Applications (approx. 100 questions):

The Information Systems exam is divided roughly in half between questions that ask you to recall basic definitions and information and questions that ask you to apply basic principles of the field. Subjects tested include: computer hardware and software; system development life cycle methodologies; programming; data management; telecommunications; information processing; user support systems; and social and ethical issues. If you've ever worked in an office, you will know the answer to some of these questions, but not enough to pass the exam, unless you became a serious computer person in the process.

Principles of Management (approx. 100 questions):

The Management exam covers the following subjects: organization and human resources; operational aspects of management, such as scheduling, planning, and productivity; functional aspects of management, such as exercising authority, decision making, leadership, and budgeting; and such miscellaneous subjects as the history of management and management theory, ethics, international management and competition, and the social responsibilities of business. A solid grasp of management terminology and basic concepts is a must for this exam.

Introductory Accounting (approx. 80 questions):

The Accounting exam focuses primarily on financial accounting; about one-third of the exam tests issues relating to managerial accounting. Subjects tested include capital; profits; the accounting cycle; general-purpose financial statements; the valuation of accounts, notes receivable, and inventories; debt; cash control; budgeting; standard costs and variances; process and job-order cost systems; funds flow analysis; and direct and absorption costing. *The Official Handbook for the CLEP* contains twenty-five sample questions from the test; if you can get over half of those questions right, you probably have enough wide-enough knowledge of accounting to pass this exam.

"Every formula which expresses a law of nature is a hymn of praise to God."
—Maria Mitchell, U.S. astronomer

Introductory Business Law (approx. 100 questions):

Over half the Business Law exam concerns contracts, their terms, obligations, and those situations under which contracts are breached and/or voided. Other questions cover torts, property, liability, the American legal system, and the history and background of American law. About one-third of the questions present hypothetical situations, about which you are asked to predict a court's decision. The rest involve factual recall and the application of basic concepts and principles.

Principles of Marketing (approx. 100 questions):

Nearly one-half the marketing exam covers "the marketing mix," including product planning, pricing, advertising, sales promotion, and management. Consumer and industrial markets are the subject of about one-fifth of the questions on the test; such questions typically ask about methods of predicting and measuring demand, demographics, marketing segmentation, targeting, and positioning. Other questions ask about the role of marketing in society; the role of marketing within a firm and within the political/social/cultural world; the institutions of marketing, including the structure of wholesale and retail markets; and international marketing.

"Nobody before the Pythagoreans had thought that mathematical relations held the secret of the universe. Twenty-five centuries later, Europe is still blessed and cursed with their heritage. To non-European civilizations, the idea that numbers are the key to both wisdom and power, seems never to have occurred."
—Arthur Koestler, author, *Darkness at Noon*

VIII

Answers to
Grammar Review Drills

ANSWERS TO GRAMMAR REVIEW DRILLS

MISPLACED MODIFIERS

1. Correct as written.

2. Injected into cattle to increase milk output, bovine growth hormone worries many consumers.
   or
   Many consumers worry about the safety of bovine growth hormone, which is injected into cattle to increase milk output.

3. Correct as written.

4. Pete preferred watching the movie, which had the benefit of taking much less time to accomplish, to reading the 500-page book.

PRONOUN ERRORS

1. A teacher may try to win a class over with friendliness, but he (or she) must be careful not to be too friendly, or he (or she) will lose his (or her) authority.

2. The publishing company decided to postpone its October releases until November, when it could take advantage of Christmas shopping.

3. Correct as written ('her' can be substituted for 'his').

4. When a ship is moored at a wooden dock for too long a time, the ship may rot.

SUBJECT-VERB AGREEMENT

1. Among the largest casinos of Atlantic City sits one of the oldest churches in the United States.

2. The union negotiator, fearful that a hard-line approach would result in the closing of the factory and the firing of all employees, is offering to accept some layoffs.

3. The United States is still idealized by many outsiders because it has a functional democracy and a constitutional commitment to fundamental individual rights.

4. The ability of athletes to recuperate from long-term injuries is determined primarily by their physical condition before their injuries were sustained.

"The most sensible people to be met with in society are men of business and of the world, who argue from what they see and know, instead of spinning cobweb distinctions of what things ought to be."
—William Hazlitt, English essayist

Good luck on your CLEP exams!

Verb Tense

1. Guidance counselors suggest that students consider as many potential colleges as possible because doing so increases their chances of finding the perfect school for them.

2. Correct as written.

3. After the two nations signed the treaty, they disarmed the weapons amassed at each others borders.

4. We arrived home to find that Marvin had eaten the bean dip.

Parallel Construction

1. Working longer hours is one way to earn more money, and getting a raise is another.

2. Correct as written.

3. All but the most masochistic athletes prefer the thrill of victory to the agony of defeat.

4. The general was convinced that he had secured the armory by massing his defensive forces at the only vulnerable spots, arming those forces, and barricading the entryway so that only a few enemy forces could get through at a time. (Delete the word "by" before "barricading.")

Faulty Comparison

1. Cecily enjoys watching tennis more than she enjoys watching opera.

2. Joe prefers solid-body guitars which, unlike hollow-body electric guitars, have increased sustain.
   or
   Unlike hollow-body electric guitars, solid body guitars have the increased sustain that Joe prefers.

3. Correct as written.

4. The cooks of western China use many more hot spices than do other cooks.

Redundancy

1. Bill prefers his sports car to his RV.

2. A surprise party is possible.

3. I am running for office not because I am seeking any personal gain, but because I wish to serve the public interest.

4. The doctor recommends that I get plenty of bed rest.

ABOUT THE AUTHORS

Tom Meltzer has taught for The Princeton Review for over 10 years. He is one of several authors of *The Best 311 Colleges* and has written numerous tests, manuals, and other materials for Princeton Review courses.

Paul Foglino has also taught for The Princeton Review for more than a decade and has authored tests and materials for many of its courses, most recently for the MCAT.

Paul and Tom are also musicians; they perform together in a band called Five Chinese Brothers. Their CDs, "Singer Songwriter Beggarman Thief," "Stone Soup," and "Let's Kill Saturday Night," are available in fine record stores everywhere.

NOTES

NOTES

NOTES

THE PRINCETON REVIEW

Completely darken bubbles with a No. 2 pencil. If you make a mistake, be sure to erase mark completely. Erase all stray marks.

1

YOUR NAME: _____
(Print)
Last   First   M.I.

SIGNATURE: _____ DATE: ___ / ___ / ___

HOME ADDRESS: _____
(Print)
Number and Street

_____
City   State   Zip Code

PHONE NO.: _____
(Print)

IMPORTANT: Please fill in these boxes exactly as shown on the back cover of your test book.

2. TEST FORM

3. TEST CODE

4. REGISTRATION NUMBER

5. YOUR NAME

First 4 letters of last name | FIRST INIT | MID INIT

6. DATE OF BIRTH

Month	Day	Year
JAN		
FEB		
MAR	0 0	0 0
APR	1 1	1 1
MAY	2 2	2 2
JUN	3 3	3 3
JUL	4 4	4
AUG	5 5	5
SEP	7 7	7
OCT	8 8	8
NOV	9 9	9
DEC		

7. SEX

MALE
FEMALE

THE PRINCETON REVIEW
© 1996 Princeton Review L.L.C.
FORM NO. 00001-PR

Section 1

Start with number 1 for each new section.
If a section has fewer questions than answer spaces, leave the extra answer spaces blank.

1. A B C D E
2. A B C D E
3. A B C D E
4. A B C D E
5. A B C D E
6. A B C D E
7. A B C D E
8. A B C D E
9. A B C D E
10. A B C D E
11. A B C D E
12. A B C D E
13. A B C D E
14. A B C D E
15. A B C D E
16. A B C D E
17. A B C D E
18. A B C D E
19. A B C D E
20. A B C D E
21. A B C D E
22. A B C D E
23. A B C D E
24. A B C D E
25. A B C D E
26. A B C D E
27. A B C D E
28. A B C D E
29. A B C D E
30. A B C D E

31. A B C D E
32. A B C D E
33. A B C D E
34. A B C D E
35. A B C D E
36. A B C D E
37. A B C D E
38. A B C D E
39. A B C D E
40. A B C D E
41. A B C D E
42. A B C D E
43. A B C D E
44. A B C D E
45. A B C D E
46. A B C D E
47. A B C D E
48. A B C D E
49. A B C D E
50. A B C D E
51. A B C D E
52. A B C D E
53. A B C D E
54. A B C D E
55. A B C D E
56. A B C D E
57. A B C D E
58. A B C D E
59. A B C D E
60. A B C D E

61. A B C D E
62. A B C D E
63. A B C D E
64. A B C D E
65. A B C D E
66. A B C D E
67. A B C D E
68. A B C D E
69. A B C D E
70. A B C D E
71. A B C D E
72. A B C D E
73. A B C D E
74. A B C D E
75. A B C D E
76. A B C D E
77. A B C D E
78. A B C D E
79. A B C D E
80. A B C D E
81. A B C D E
82. A B C D E
83. A B C D E
84. A B C D E
85. A B C D E
86. A B C D E
87. A B C D E
88. A B C D E
89. A B C D E
90. A B C D E

91. A B C D E
92. A B C D E
93. A B C D E
94. A B C D E
95. A B C D E
96. A B C D E
97. A B C D E
98. A B C D E
99. A B C D E
100. A B C D E
101. A B C D E
102. A B C D E
103. A B C D E
104. A B C D E
105. A B C D E
106. A B C D E
107. A B C D E
108. A B C D E
109. A B C D E
110. A B C D E
111. A B C D E
112. A B C D E
113. A B C D E
114. A B C D E
115. A B C D E
116. A B C D E
117. A B C D E
118. A B C D E
119. A B C D E
120. A B C D E

121. A B C D E
122. A B C D E
123. A B C D E
124. A B C D E
125. A B C D E
126. A B C D E
127. A B C D E
128. A B C D E
129. A B C D E
130. A B C D E
131. A B C D E
132. A B C D E
133. A B C D E
134. A B C D E
135. A B C D E
136. A B C D E
137. A B C D E
138. A B C D E
139. A B C D E
140. A B C D E
141. A B C D E
142. A B C D E
143. A B C D E
144. A B C D E
145. A B C D E
146. A B C D E
147. A B C D E
148. A B C D E
149. A B C D E
150. A B C D E

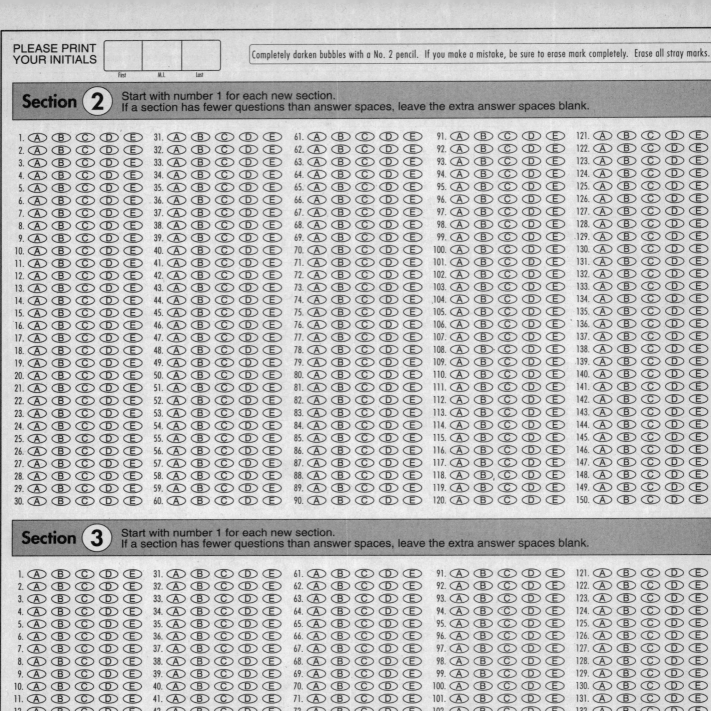

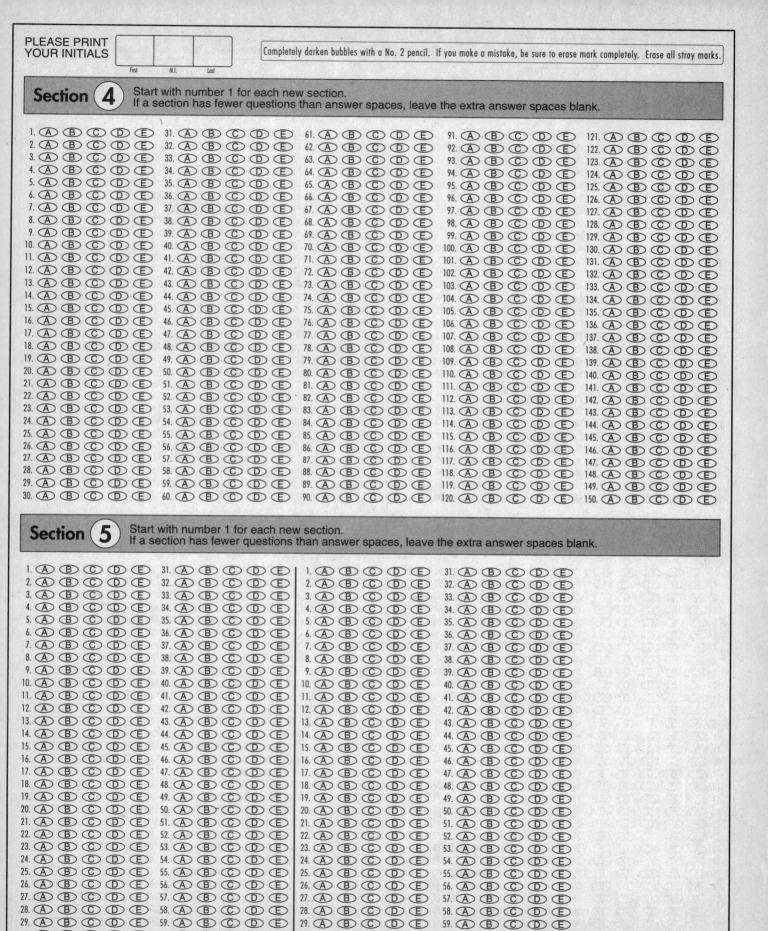

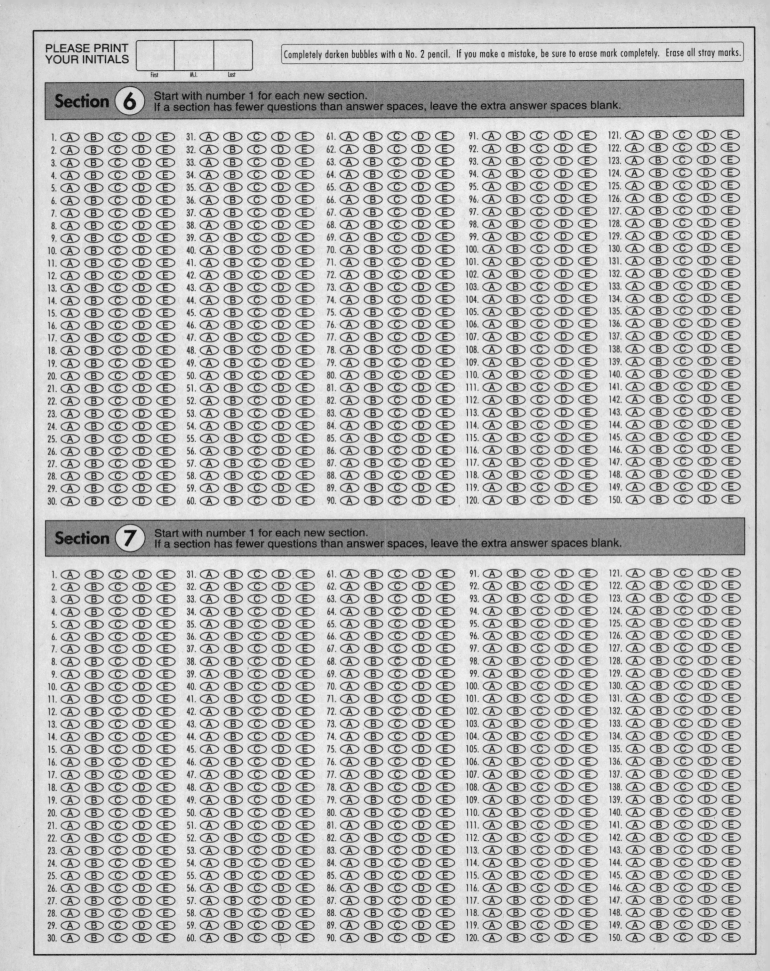

FIND US...

International

Hong Kong
4/F Sun Hung Kai Centre
30 Harbour Road, Wan Chai,
Hong Kong
Tel: (011)85-2-517-3016

Japan
Fuji Building 40, 15-14
Sakuragaokacho, Shibuya Ku,
Tokyo 150, Japan
Tel: (011)81-3-3463-1343

Korea
Tae Young Bldg, 944-24,
Daechi- Dong, Kangnam-Ku
The Princeton Review- ANC
Seoul, Korea 135-280,
South Korea
Tel: (011)82-2-554-7763

Mexico City
PR Mex S De RL De Cv
Guanajuato 228 Col. Roma
06700 Mexico D.F., Mexico
Tel: 525-564-9468

Montreal
666 Sherbrooke St.
West, Suite 202
Montreal, QC H3A 1E7 Canada
Tel: (514) 499-0870

Pakistan
1 Bawa Park - 90 Upper Mall
Lahore, Pakistan
Tel: (011)92-42-571-2315

Spain
Pza. Castilla, 3 - 5° A, 28046
Madrid, Spain
Tel: (011)341-323-4212

Taiwan
155 Chung Hsiao East Road
Section 4 - 4th Floor,
Taipei R.O.C., Taiwan
Tel: (011)886-2-751-1243

Thailand
Building One, 99 Wireless Road
Bangkok, Thailand 10330
Tel: (662) 256-7080

Toronto
1240 Bay Street, Suite 300
Toronto M5R 2A7 Canada
Tel: (800) 495-7737
Tel: (716) 839-4391

Vancouver
4212 University Way NE,
Suite 204
Seattle, WA 98105
Tel: (206) 548-1100

National (U.S.)
We have over 60 offices around the U.S. and
run courses in over 400 sites. For courses and locations
within the U.S. call 1 (800) 2/Review and you will be
routed to the nearest office.

Expert Advice

www.review.com

Talk About It

www.review.com

Pop Surveys

Paying for it

www.review.com

THE
PRINCETON
REVIEW

www.review.com

Getting in

Word du Jour

www.review.com

Find-O-Rama School & Career Search

www.review.com

Best Schools

Finding it

www.review.com